THE JEWISH LAW ANNUAL

The Institute of Jewish Law
Boston University School of Law
765 Commonwealth Avenue
Boston, MA 02215
Publication No. 8

THE JEWISH LAW ANNUAL

VOLUME SEVEN

THE INSTITUTE OF JEWISH LAW
BOSTON UNIVERSITY SCHOOL OF LAW

hodp harwood academic publishers
chur london paris new york melbourne

Published by Harwood Academic Publishers

Post Office Box 197
London WC2E 9PX
England

58, rue Lhomond
75005 Paris
France

Post Office Box 786
Cooper Station
New York, New York 10276
United States of America

Private Bag 8
Camberwell, Victoria 3124
Australia

Library of Congress Catalogue Card No. 79-648405

We express our appreciation to Edward M. Abramson
through whose generosity this volume has been
published in memory of David Hecht

This book is part of a series. The publisher will accept continuation orders which may be cancelled at any time and which provide for automatic billing and shipping of each title in the series upon publication. Please write for details.

CONTENTS

PART ONE

THE PHILOSOPHY OF JEWISH LAW (II)

PART TWO

FROM THE EDITOR

This volume concludes the symposium on the Philosophy of Jewish Law which commenced in volume VI. It concludes with a response by the late Julius Stone to most of the preceding articles. The seriousness with which Professor Stone approached his task indicates the maturity which modern research into the philosophy of Jewish law has attained. The Jewish Law Annual is privileged to publish this major posthumous essay, and my thanks are due to Zena Sachs for her assistance in seeing the text through the press.

Due to pressure of space, the normal "Chronicle" section has been held over to the next issue.

The next two issues will carry symposia on criminal law and on medico-legal problems. As from volume VIII, most issues will also include an open section, not confined to the particular symposium topic. Intending authors are invited to contact me in advance of sending a typescript; style-sheets and advice on the possibility of submitting material on disc are available by writing to me at Keynes College, The University, Canterbury, Kent CT2 7NP, England.

PART ONE

THE PHILOSOPHY OF JEWISH LAW (II)

JUDAISM AND NATURAL LAW

by

J. DAVID BLEICH[*]

During the seventeenth and eighteenth centuries a number of Christian scholars, including the prominent Dutch scholar Hugo Grotius, sought to demonstrate that a concept of natural law might be traced to the Pentateuch. If so, the doctrine of natural law might be regarded as part of the Jewish contribution to Western thought. The Cambridge Hebraist, John Selden, developed a much more elaborate and sophisticated argument in a work entitled *De Jure Naturalis et Gentium Juxta Disciplinam Ebraeorum*, in which he advances the thesis that the Seven Noachide Commandments constitute, in effect, a highly developed doctrine of natural law. The Noachide Code, he argued, is regarded by Judaism both as predating the Sinaitic revelation and as binding upon gentile nations which did not participate in the Sinaitic experience. Accordingly, he maintained, the content of the Noachide Code must be regarded as universally binding on the basis of reason alone.[1]

On the surface, this thesis presents many features auguring in favour of acceptance. The basic proscriptions of the Noachide Code, homicide, theft, sexual licentiousness, etc., involve acts universally viewed with opprobrium.[2] Judaism teaches that all gentiles are bound by the provisions of the Noachide Code and are to be punished

---

[*] Rosh Yeshiva, Rabbi Isaac Elchanan Theological Seminary; Professor of Law, Benjamin N. Cardozo School of Law, Yeshiva University.

[1] This position is also espoused by R. Chaim Hirschensohn, "Sevarah", *Otsar Yisrael*, ed. J.D. Eisenstein (New York: Hebrew Publishing Co., 1906), VII, 136; *idem, Malki ba ḳode sh* (St. Louis, 5679), I, 21; and *idem, Eleh Divre habrit* (Jerusalem, 5686), I, 5f. Cf., however, R. Eleazar Meir Preil, *Hama'or* (Jerusalem, 5689), no. 80.

[2] The Roman legal system similarly contained a corpus of law, the *ius gentium*, which governed cases in which one of the litigants was not a Roman citizen or in which both litigants were resident aliens. Gaius apparently took the *ius gentium* as the model of a law practiced by all mankind and dictated to all men by natural reason as distinct from the *ius civile* or system of law which each nation gives itself. Selden apparently perceived a similar division in Jewish law.

for infractions thereof. Since the nations of the world were denied
the benefit of direct divine revelation, the binding nature of these
commandments can only be rooted in reason.

This thesis is, however, difficult to substantiate in terms of the
legal traditions of Judaism. Nowhere in the vast corpus of rabbinic,
legal or philosophical literature is there to be found a fully-devel-
oped doctrine of natural law; nor, as Marvin Fox has pointed out,[3] is
the term natural law used by any Jewish philosopher or legal
scholar prior to Joseph Albo in the fifteenth century. Of course, as
Norman Lamm and Aaron Kirschenbaum have argued, "Ideas may be
implicit in a text or body of literature, and receive their formulation
in sophisticated terminology much later"[4] and undoubtedly
"concepts, like people, have an existence independent of their
names."[5] Nevertheless, it is remarkable that a philosophical doctrine which may be traced back as far as Cicero and which played a
major role in the Latin tradition should not receive explicit reference, not to speak of detailed analysis, in Jewish philosophical or
legal writings. Any *argumentum ad silencium* is weak at best, yet in
the present instance silence[6] with regard to so significant a doctrine
does constitute *prima facie* evidence that the notion of natural law

3 M. Fox, "Maimonides and Aquinas on Natural Law", *Diné Israel* V
   (1972), xi. The term is also used by a later fifteenth-century scholar, R.
   Shem Tov ben Shem Tov, *Derashot hatorah* (Venice: 5307), 25a, as a
   synonym for *mitsvot sikhliyot;* see below, note 34.

4 N. Lamm and A. Kirschenbaum, "Freedom and Constraint in the Jewish
   Judicial Process", *Cardozo Law Review* I/1 (Spring, 1979), 110, note 40.

5 *Ibid.*, at 112.

6 There is, to my knowledge, only one latter-day rabbinic scholar who
   recognizes normatively binding halakhic prescriptions based upon
   considerations other than revelation. R. Moses Samuel Glazner, in his
   commentary on *Ḥullin, Dor Revi'i* (Jerusalem, 5738), *Pet iḥah Kelalit,*
   sec.2 and in his comments on *Ḥullin* 89b, regards, for example, public
   nudity, despite the absence of a direct biblical prohibition, as
   constituting a transgression even more severe in nature than violation of a
   negative commandment. Consumption of human flesh and of rancid
   carrion are categorized by this scholar in a similar manner. The concept
   invoked by *Dor Revi'i* is not, strictly speaking, that of a natural law
   theory but of *a priori* moral repugnance. He does, however, posit a notion
   closely akin to that of *obligationes naturales* of Roman law in affirming
   an obligation to support one's infant children that is not predicated upon
   biblical command or rabbinic legislation.

was not taken seriously by Judaism. It was ignored because it played no significant role in the development of Jewish philosophy or legal theory.

More devastating to Selden's contention that the Noachide Code is a reflection of a natural law position are the comments of Maimonides in his *Mishneh Torah, Hilkhot Melakhim* 8:11:

> Any person [i.e., gentile] who accepts the Seven Commandments and is meticulous in observing them is one of the pious of the nations of the world and he possesses a share in the world to come. But this is [only] if he accepts them and performs them because God commanded them in the Torah and made known to us through Moses, our teacher, that the children of Noah were previously commanded with regard to them.[7] However, if he performs them because of the determination of reason *[hekhra hada'at]* this [person] is not a *ger toshav* [resident-alien] and he is not of the pious of the nations nor of their wise men.[8]

This passage clearly expresses Maimonides' opinion[9] that non-Jews are required to accept the Noachide Code on the basis of revelation, not on the basis of reason.[10] Revelation - and not reason - is endowed with binding force. Furthermore, the perfectly moral Noachide can claim no special merit in the world to come save on the basis of prior acceptance of the Noachide Code as the revealed mandate of the Deity.[11] Moreover, when this statement is read in conjunction with Maimonides' statement in *Hilkhot Iṣure Bi'ah* 14:7, in which Maimonides equates and identifies *ḥaṣide umot ha'olam* with those who acquire the status of a *ger toshav*, it is evident that yet another condition must be satisfied in order for a gentile to achieve the status

7   See extended endnote A.

8   See extended endnote B.

9   Although, as discussed in endnote B, Maimonides' source is obscure, the only authority who explicitly postulates an opposing view is *Toṣafot Re'em*, commentary on *Sefer Yer'eim* 233:2.

10 Cf., Maimonides, *Hilkhot Avodat Kokhavim* 10:6 and Rabad, *ad loc.*, cf., also *Minḥat Ḥinnukh* , no. 94, and *Ḥazon Ish, Hilkhot Avodat Kokhavim* 65:3 and *Shevi'it* 24:3.

11 A similar assertion is made by Maimonides with regard to the reward of Noachides for the fulfillment of other commandments whose performance is not obligatory for non-Jews. See *Teshuvot harambam*, ed. Afred Freimann (Jerusalem: Mekize Nirdamim, 1934), no.124 and *Teshuvot harambam*, ed. Yehoshua Blau (Jerusalem, Mekize Nirdamim, 1957), I, no.148.

of "one of the pious of the nations." In *Hilkhot Avodah Zarah* 10:6 Maimonides declares that status as a *ger toshav* is conferred only upon formal acceptance before a *Bet Din*. Indeed, this condition is recorded in *Hilkhot Melakhim* 8:11 through incorporation of the phrase "who accepts" *(shek ibel alav)*. [12] It is therefore evident that not only is observance of the Noachide Code on the basis of revelation a necessary condition for achieving a share in the world to come, but that such observance must be preceded by formal acknowledgment in the presence of a qualified *Bet Din* of the obligations inherent in the Seven Commandments. [13]

The demand that in order to merit eternal reward non-Jews accept the Noachide Code on the basis of revelation does not, of course, preclude acceptance of a natural law doctrine. This possibility is, however, barred by Maimonides' apparently gratuitous concluding phrase *"velo meh akhamehem* nor of their wise men." Numerous scholars have argued that our reading is the result of a scribal or printing error and that the correct version of the passage is *"ela meh akhamehem* - but of their scholars", which, of course has exactly the reverse import. The discrepancy involves the change of a single Hebrew letter and could have occurred quite readily. The principal support for this emendation is the reading found in the Bodleian manuscript of the *Mishneh Torah*. [14] However, most

---

12 See Steven S. Schwarzschild, "Do Noachites Have to Believe in Revelation?", *Jewish Quarterly Review* 53/1 (1962), 36 n.35, who questions whether the term *ger toshav* in *Hilkhot Melakhim* is used in precisely the same way as in *Hilkhot Is ure Bi'ah*. See, however, *Hiddushe Maran Riz halevi*, p. 164, who states explicitly that formal *kabbalah* or acceptance of the Seven Commandments in the presence of a *Bet Din* is required and that in the absence of formal *kabbalah* the Noachide is not deemed to be in the category of "the pious of the nations of the world". The identical point was earlier made by R. Raphael hakohen of Hamburg, *Teshuvot veshev hakohen*, no. 38. The latter authority also endeavors to identify the talmudic source from which Maimonides' statement is derived.

13 The novel interpretation of Maimonides' statement offered somewhat tentatively by R. Abraham I. Kook, *Iggerot Re'iyah* (Jerusalem: Mosad Harav Kook, 5722), I no. 89, yields a diametrically opposite position but is contra the plain meaning of the text and the manner in which Maimonides has been understood by all previous rabbinic and philosophic scholars.

14 For early citations of the *"ela"* reading see *Encyclopedia Talmudit* VI

manuscripts and virtually all printed editions including the *editio princeps* published in Rome in 1480 contain the reading *"velo -* nor"[15] It should be noted that acceptance of the *"ela"* reading does not at all signify that in calling such persons wise men Maimonides necessarily accepted a theory of natural law. A person may be termed wise not solely because of his knowledge of transcendental truth but also, for example, by virtue of his acceptance of pragmatic[16] princi-

----

(Jerusalem, 1954), 290, n.11.

15 For a discussion of the textual problem see J. Katz, *Exclusiveness and Tolerance* (New York: Schocken Books, 1962), 175ff; Steven S. Schwarzschild, "Do Noachites Have to Believe in Revelation?" *Jewish Quarterly Review* 52/4 (1962), 301-303; Fox, *supra* n. 2, at xiv; and J. Faur, *Iyunim bemishneh Torah: Şefer hamadda* (Jerusalem: Mosad Harav Kook, 1978), 151 note 43. Among rabbinic scholars the reading *ela* is found twice in the citation of this passage in the responsa of the 16th-century authority R. Moses al-Ashkar, *Teshuvot Maharam alashkar*, no. 117 (on pp. 302 and 320 of the Jerusalem, 5719 edition), and more recently by R. Abraham I. Kook, *Iggerot Re'iyah, supra* n. 9, at I, 89. The text cited in R. Yosef ben Shem Tob, *Kevod Elokim* (Fürth, 1556), 29a, reads *aval* which is a synonym for *ela*. Textual considerations aside, there is one cogent reason for assuming the published text to be accurate and the Bodleian manuscript to be corrupt. It is virtually an axiom of halakhic hermeneutics that early authorities in general, and Maimonides in particular, did not employ unnecessary verbiage. The phrase *velo meḥakhamehem* serves to negate natural law doctrines and hence Maimonides would have had reason for its inclusion. The phrase *ela meḥakhamehem* has neither halakhic nor philosophical import and would constitute an irrelevant interpolation.

16 Cf., Lamm and Kirschenbaum, *supra* n. 3, at 117, who write, "it is reasonable to assume, if this reading is correct, that this indicates a natural law theory by Maimonides. The single letter in Maimonides' Code is thus of the greatest moment in deciding the question of whether Jewry's greatest jurist and most eminent philosopher advocated or rejected natural law." Quite to the contrary, Maimonides' dismissal of "some of our later sages" who speak of rational laws as suffering from the disease of the Mutakallimun (see *Eight Chapters*, VI, and *Guide*, III, 17) would appear to constitute a denial of natural law. See Munk's note to his translation of this passage in the *Guide*, III, 127 n. 1; L. Strauss, *Persecution and the Art of Writing* (Westport: Greenwood Press, 1977), 97; and R. Lerner, "Moses Maimonides", *History of Political Philosophy*, 2nd edition, eds. L. Strauss and J. Cropsey (Chicago: Rand McNally,1972), 218-219.

ples. Aristotle, after all, wrote extensively concerning *praktikos* or practical wisdom yet is not generally regarded as a natural law theorist. Although the *"ela"* reading does not conclusively establish Maimonides' position as an advocate of natural law, the *"velo"* reading does indicate rejection of a doctrine of natural law. Regardless of which version is accepted as being correct, I do not believe that Maimonides did, in fact, accept a theory of natural law in the usual sense of the notion.[17] This conclusion is based upon a statement found in his *Treatise on Logic,* as will be shown later.

Despite Maimonides' apparent rejection of any possible natural law theory in the phrase *"velo meḥakhamehem"* (assuming for the purposes of our discussion that this is the correct version) some talmudic evidence may be adduced for the existence of at least a germinal theory of natural law in rabbinic thought. It is evident that the Talmud recognized the binding legal authority not only of revelation but of ṣevarah or reason as well. A sharp distinction must be made between ṣevarah in the sense of "legal logic," i.e., the derivation of legal principles and even laws from already dogmatically accepted principles, and ṣevarah in the sense of a direct and independent source of law.[18] The former can hardly be assimilated to a notion of natural law; its operation is effected by application of the formal rules of logic or of common sense while ultimate authority for incorporation into law of the resultant conclusions rests upon prior acceptance, on completely different grounds, of the corpus of law upon which intellect is allowed to operate. On the other hand, ṣevarah as an antonomous source of law is *sui generis* in the sense that reason need not look beyond itself for authoritative validation.

Although the Talmud abounds in examples of the former applications of ṣevarah, at times explicitly employing the term,[19] but more often implicitly accepting the methodology of ṣevarah with-

---

17 In this I concur with Marvin Fox, *supra* n. 2, at xiv, but on entirely different grounds.

18 Cf., M. Elon, *Hamishpat Ha'ivri* (Jerusalem: Magnes Press, 1973), II, 805-828 and "Severah", *Encyclopedia Judaica* (Jerusalem: Keter, 1971), XIV, 195-1198. Cf., also, R. Eleazar Meir Preil, *Hama'or*, no. 80, who does not recognize the latter category of *severah* and fails to discuss, or even mention, the example found in *Sanhedrin* 74a.

19 E.g., *Gittin* 6b; *Shabbat* 63a; *Sukkah* 29a. See also examples cited by R. Reuben Margulies, *Margaliyot Hayam* (Jerusalem: Mosad Harav Kook, 5718), *Sanhedrin* 15a, sec.4.

out explicitly applying the label,[20] examples of the latter are rare. Instances of the latter type of *s̩evarah* appear to be, in total, no more than three in number,[21] of which two do not really bear upon a doctrine of natural law.

The Gemara, *Baba Kamma* 46b, establishes as a principle of law the rule that the burden of proof is on the claimant. Citation of a biblical verse (*Ex.* 24:14) to substantiate this principle is dismissed as superfluous and the verse in question is interpreted as establishing an entirely different rule, viz., that the plaintiff must be heard first. In declaring scriptural support to be unnecessary, the Gemara exclaims, "What need have I for a verse? - *Sevarah hu!* A person who is in pain goes to the house of a doctor," i.e., it is the patient who seeks the ministrations of the physician and not the physician who pursues potential patients to determine who is ill. Similarly, the person who has a claim against another must bring proof to substantiate his claim and the defendant need not first prove that he is liable. The appeal to *s̩evarah* in this instance does not establish the authority of reason as a source of law for several reasons. First, the matter is one of judicial procedure rather than of substantive law; no normative obligation is born of this application of *s̩evarah*. Secondly, given a dogmatic system of jurisprudence and statutory provisions for judicial adjudication, a procedural rule for the burden of proof must be established. Failure to do so would result in a legal impasse and effectively eliminate any possible judicial remedy. This would reduce the system of jurisprudence set forth in Scripture to a mere theoretical construct. Hence common sense, as reflected in the therapeutic model adduced by the Gemara, dictates that the burden of proof be upon the plaintiff. Reason is here brought to bear in developing a detail of law; it hardly functions as a forum of original jurisdiction.

The second example is somewhat less clear but upon analysis appears to be of the same genre as well. The Mishnah, *Ketubot* 22a,

20 See Rabbi Z. H. Chajes, *The Student's Guide Through the Talmud*, trans. by Jacob Schachter (New York: Feldheim Publishing Co., 1960), 29-31.

21 *Berakhot* 35a also posits *severah* as the source of the obligation to recite a blessing prior to partaking of food. However, the *severah* cited in that instance cannot be understood as compelling in an absolute sense since the obligation is rabbinic rather than biblical. For a discussion of *severah* as establishing a rabbinic obligation see R. Hayyim Medini, *Sede Hemed, Kuntres hakelalim, ma'arekhet hasemakh*, sec.63.

discusses the credence to be given certain types of self-serving statements. The issue in point is the liberty of a woman whose marital
status is unknown to contract a marriage. In the absence of knowledge
of prior marriage a woman is presumed to be free to marry. If the existence of a prior marriage has been established, the woman's own
statement that the marriage has been terminated by divorce is not
acceptable in the absence of corroborating evidence. However, if
knowledge of prior marriage is established only on the basis of the
woman's own statement, her testimony with regard to subsequent divorce is acceptable. Thus, in the absence of witnesses as to the existence of a prior marriage, the woman's statement that she was married and became divorced is accepted. The rule which is formulated
is "The mouth which has rendered prohibited is the mouth which
has rendered permissible." In this instance as well, the Gemara
seeks scriptural justification only to reject the cited verse (*Deut.*
22:16) with the statement "What need have I for verse? *Sevarah
hu!*" The selfsame testimony which is the source of any possible restriction simultaneously establishes permission to remarry. Here we
are confronted not with a rule of procedure, but with a rule of evidence which effectively determines whether or not marriage shall
be permitted. Nevertheless, here too, we are not confronted with a
matter involving a substantive normative *halakhah* but with a
question of juridical determination. *Sevarah* is here not employed to
determine an actual law of marriage or adultery but merely to
establish the basis of juridical determination that a state of marriage does or does not exist. Here, again, reason does not operate *sui
generis* as the authority to prescribe or to proscribe but enjoys only a
certain narrow latitude in determining a question of objective fact - a
matter which is a far cry from endowing the intellect with legislative authority.

The third example is a matter of an entirely different nature. In
general, a person confronted with a choice between transgression of a
biblical prohibition or death should transgress in order to preserve
life. Martyrdom is required only in face of coercion with regard to
idolatry, certain forms of sexual licentiousness, including incest and
adultery, and murder. Insofar as idolatry and sexual licentiousness
are concerned, this principle is established on the basis of biblical
exegesis. However, with regard to murder the rule is derived by the
Gemara, *Sanhedrin* 74a, solely on the basis of reason: "It is a
sevarah..., How do you know that your blood is sweeter? Perhaps

the blood of the other person is sweeter!" Clearly, the matter at hand involves a substantive issue and establishes a prohibition against homicide which is universal in nature and admits of no exception. In effect, then, the prohibition against homicide is legislated by reason and, at least in this area, the prohibition is identical in nature to a natural law prohibition.[22] The effect of the ṣevarah adduced in this instance has the full force and authority of law and stands on par with dogmatic scriptural prohibitions. This becomes dramatically apparent upon examining the exegesis which yields the same rule with regard to sexual licentiousness. That exegesis is based upon the juxtaposition of homicide and adultery in the same verse (Deut. 22:26). The hermeneutical principle involved is that of heḳesh, i.e., the juxtaposition of two words or phrases. In this case Scripture explicitly compares murder and adultery: "... for as when a man rises against his neighbor and slays him, even so is this matter." As a result of the heḳesh between murder and adultery the already established rule with regard to murder is transposed and applied to adultery, with regard to which there exists no otherwise delineated rule. In this case the rule with regard to murder, which is derived on the basis of ṣevarah alone, is transposed as if it were explicit in Scripture and, accordingly, is transposed and applied to adultery. Here we find a legal prohibition derived from ṣevarah which is clearly regarded as having the selfsame binding authority as a divinely revealed biblical law.

The sole Jewish philosopher who explicitly assigns any role to natural law is Joseph Albo. In a short, almost cryptic passage in his Ṣefer ha'iḳarim, Book I, chapter 7, Albo states, "The purpose of natural law is to repress wrong and to promote right in order that

22 It would appear that, as a natural law principle, the obligation to suffer martyrdom rather than commit murder is incumbent upon non-Jews as well. This is explicitly stated by R. Judah Rosanes, Mishneh lemelekh, Hilkhot Melakhim 10:2 and idem, Perashat Derakhim, Derush 2, as well as by R. Joseph Babad, Minḥat Ḥinnukh , no. 296, and in a note appended by the grandson of R. Isaac Schorr to the latter's Teshuvot Koaḥ Shor, no. 20, p.35a. See also Ṭevat Gom'e, cited by Pit ḥe Teshuvah, Yoreh De'ah 154:4. An opposing view is adopted by R. Shmuel Jaffe-Ashkenazi, in his commentary on Bereshit Rabbah, Yefeh To'ar, (Fürth, 5452), Gen. 44:5; R. Shlomoh Algazi, Shama Shlomoh (Amsterdam, 5470), p. 15b; Shenot Ḥayyim , p. 36b; R. Barzilai Baruch Ya'avets, Leshon Arumim (Izmir, 5516), 7; and R. Abraham Samuel Meyuchas, Sede ha'arets I, 55. See also Faur, supra n. 10, at 161.

people be kept away from theft, robbery and murder, that society may be able to exist among men and every one be safe from the wrongdoer and oppressor." Albo cites theft, robbery and murder as the sole instances in which natural law is operative. The infractions enumerated are not merely examples taken from a larger body of natural law; they are the sole areas in which Albo deemed natural law to be operative. We may presume that Albo found talmudic evidence for the authority of natural law in these areas of proscribed conduct but not in others.

The talmudic locus of a natural law prohibition against murder has been cited. A source for theft and robbery as infractions of an authoritative natural law prohibition is much less clear. I believe that Albo's source for a natural law prohibition against theft and robbery may be found in *Baba Metsia* 61b. The Gemara questions the need for a prohibition against theft, "You shall not steal" (*Lev.* 19:11) and responds with the statement that the prohibition is required in order to ban (1) theft designed for purposes of annoyance and (2) theft designed for the purpose of benefitting the victim by incurring a legal obligation to pay him the fine which is levied upon the thief. Ordinary theft, however, requires no scriptural prohibition. Rashi, undoubtedly troubled by the problem that in the absence of a formal admonition Jewish law would lack a ban against theft, explains that assumed in the Gemara's query is the presumption that a formal prohibition might be derived exegetically on the basis of *meh hatsad*, i.e., a derivation predicated upon a factor common to two other proscribed activities and present in theft as well. Since both proscribed activities share a common factor it may be assumed that the presence of that consideration constitutes the essence of the prohibition and hence any activity in which that factor is present must be considered to be banned as well. In this instance Rashi states that a prohibition against theft might be deduced from the fact that usury and fraud are both explicitly forbidden by the Torah. Both usury and fraud involve diminution of the material wealth of another (or what in contemporary legal parlance would be termed "unjust enrichment"). Since theft is the example par excellence of diminution of the material wealth of another (*meh aṣer mammon*) it would follow that theft is also forbidden by virtue of the fact that it is a form of *meh aṣer mammon*.

No part of this argumentation is, however, explicit in the words of the Gemara. Albo may well have understood the query of the

Gemara in a simple and literal way. Theft requires no scriptural admonition, not because a prohibition may be derived on the basis of hermeneutics, but because theft is known to be forbidden by virtue of natural law. If so, a scriptural admonition is required only in order to encompass within the scope of the prohibition actions which reason alone does not incontrovertibly proscribe.[23] Thus, for Albo, natural law proscribes not only murder but theft and robbery as well.

Other examples of the operation of natural law in the Jewish legal system are more obscure and their talmudic sources uncertain. Albo states that the purpose of natural law is "that society may be able to exist among men and every one be safe from the wrongdoer and oppressor." This formulation is advanced by Albo simply as a final cause or explanation of why it is that reason legislates against theft, robbery and murder. There is no evidence that preservation of society *per se* is regarded by Albo as directly mandated by natural law[24] or that any other action, whether positive or negative, is commanded or proscribed by natural law as a means of preserving society. Yet other measures designed to preserve the social structure are posited as a matter of law by other early authorities and appear to be rooted solely in natural law concepts.

Maimonides, *Hilkhot Melakhim* 10:11, following his codification of the laws pertaining to non-Jews, declares:

> [The] *Bet Din* of Israel is obligated to establish judges for these resident-aliens to judge them on the basis of these laws so that the world will not become corrupt. If [the] *Bet Din* determines to appoint judges from among them they may [so] appoint; and if they determine to appoint [judges] from among Israel they may [so] appoint.

It is, to be sure , Maimonides' position, *Hilkhot Melakhim* 9:14, that the last of the enumerated Seven Noachide Commandments, *dinin*, constitutes an obligation making it incumbent upon Noachides to sit

23 The same question may, of course, be raised with regard to the need for a scriptural prohibition against murder, which the Gemara explicitly states can be known on the basis of *sevarah*. It would appear to me that a formal prohibition is required for the one type of homicide in which reason does not unequivocally serve to establish a prohibition, viz., euthanasia. See R. Jacob Zevi Mecklenburg, *Haketav vehak̲abbalah*, *Gen.* 9:5. Moreover, absent a scriptural prohibition, capital punishment could not be imposed. See *Sanhedrin* 56b.

24 See extended endnote C.

in judgment and to mete out punishment for infractions of the other six commandments of the Noachide Code. The *mitsvah* of *dinin* is, however, binding only upon non-Jews. It is also the case that Maimonides, *Hilkhot Melakhim* 8:10, states that Moses was commanded by God to force all inhabitants of the world to accept the *mitsvot* which were commanded to the sons of Noah and put to death any who refuse to accept them.[25] However, that penalty, which is to be imposed by Jews, seems to be mandated only in the event of total rejection as manifest in refusal formally to accept the Seven Commandments. Indeed, mere refusal formally to accept the Seven Commandments even though no actual violation has occurred warrants the penalty described in 8:10. Punishment for actual infractions subsequent to acceptance of the Seven Commandments does not seem to be encompassed in this provision.[26] Indeed, it is presumably for precisely this reason that Maimonides found it necessary to add the explanatory phrase "lest the world become corrupt" in 10:11 but does not provide any such explanation in the codification of the earlier regulation in 8:10 which is presented simply as a divine fiat.

Incorporation of the phrase "lest the world become corrupt" would tend to indicate that while the *halakhah* recorded in 8:10 is a dogmatic obligation based on revelation, the principle reflected in 10:11 is derived by means of reason alone. 8:10 cannot be predicated upon a similar rationale since a person who does not violate any of the provisions of the Noachide Code does not endanger the social order and hence there is no readily apparent reason for punishing him simply for refusing to make a formal declaration of acceptance. Punishment of evildoers, however, is mandated, even in the absence of a revealed *mitsvah*, by reason alone; were evildoers not to be punished, the very fabric of society would be destroyed. Thus, this provision is a reflection of a natural law consideration.

Punishment for infractions of the Seven Commandments may be

---

25   Formal acceptance is required only by virtue of the Sinaitic revelation but was not part of the Noachide obligation prior to Sinai. This requirement was established at Sinai because observance of the Noachide Code had largely lapsed among non-Jews. See *Ḥiddushe Maran Riz halevi, loc. cit.*

26   Cf., Nahmanides, *Commentary on the Bible, Deut.* 23:18, who declares that Jews bear no responsibility vis-à-vis infractions committed by Noachides other than being obliged to prevent Noachides from engaging in idol worship.

dictated by natural law even though the content of the Noachide Code is not itself the product of natural law, i.e., the provisions of the Noachide Code cannot be viewed as binding obligations on the basis of reason alone. Yet obedience to a law whose authority is established on other grounds *is* compelled by reason alone: otherwise law would be devoid of meaning. Law can be successful in achieving its legitimate goals only if transgressors are punished; otherwise law would be honored solely in the breach with the result that the world would "become corrupt".

The same concept seems to appear in a different guise in Rashi, *Gittin* 9b. The Mishnah there cited declares that all bills and deeds executed in non-Jewish courts are valid, with the exception of bills of divorce and manumission, even if they bear the signature of gentile witnesses. The exclusion of bills of divorce and manumission is readily explainable. *Gentiles* are not *bene kritut*. The institutions of divorce and manumission are constructs of Jewish law from which non-Jews are excluded and therefore gentiles cannot execute efficacious documents of this nature. However, the validity of other documents witnessed by gentiles is problematic. It would appear that all bills and deeds of any nature should be invalid when signed by gentiles because non-Jews are not qualified to serve as witnesses in Jewish courts. Non-Jews are precluded from serving not only as testifying witnesses but also from serving as attesting witnesses. Nevertheless, the rule formulated in the Mishnah states that legal documents witnessed by non-Jews are valid for transactions between Jewish parties. The Gemara, *Gittin* 10b, questions how it is possible for such documents to effect transfer of title. In the absence of any other ḳinyan, or formal mode of transfer, title does not pass by deed unless the deed is properly witnessed. This problem is resolved by the Gemara in two alternative ways. The first response is that such documents are deemed valid by virtue of the principle *dina demalkhuta dina*, i.e. "the law of the land is the law." The second response is that bills which are performative rather than evidentiary are indeed invalid and are subsumed in the Mishnah under the category of bills of divorce which are ruled to be nugatory.

The first resolution is somewhat problematic. Early authorities sought to justify the principle of *dina demalkhuta dina* on a variety of grounds. Yet, it is not at all clear why the principle of *dina demalkhuta dina* should apply to jurisprudential matters between Jews in which the government has no active interest. It was obviously this difficulty which prompted Rashi, *Gittin* 9b, to comment, "... but non-Jews were commanded concerning *dinin.*" Although he fails to cite explicitly the explanation advanced by the Gemara, *Gittin* 10b, Rashi is obviously advancing his own formulation of the rationale underlying the principle of *dina demalkhuta* with a view toward providing an explanation for its extension to the rule formulated by the Mishnah.

Quite obviously, Rashi rejects the analysis of *dinin* formulated by Maimonides, *Hilkhot Melakhim* 9:14, viz., that *dinin* constitutes an obligation to enforce the other provisions of the Noachide Code. Instead, he accepts a view closely paralleling that advanced by Nahmanides in his *Commentary on the Bible, Genesis* 34:13, viz., that *dinin* constitutes a commandment to Noachides to establish a comprehensive system of law to govern the manifold facets of commercial and interpersonal relationships. *Dina demalkhuta* is then no more than the actualization and implementation of such a system of law.[27] Thus the legitimacy of *dina demalkhuta* is rooted in the *mitsvah* of *dinin.*

However, the basic problem remains. The *mitsvah* of *dinin* is ostensibly solely addressed to, and binding upon, non-Jews. By what authority, then, is *dina demalkhuta* binding upon Jews? The matter is resolved if it is understood that the *mitsvah* of *dinin* is, in essence, a *mitsvah* enjoining preservation of the social order. It can be regarded as binding upon Jews only if its authority may be derived from natural law.[28] For Rashi, as well as for Maimonides, preserva-

---

27 If this is indeed the correct analysis of Rashi's position, Rashi then maintains that non-Jews need not necessarily comport themselves in such matters in accordance with the details of Jewish law but are free to enact any equitable system of law. This is contrary to the manner in which Nahmanides' position is understood by R. Moshe Isserles, *Teshuvot Rema,* no. 10, and R. Moshe Ṣofer, *Teshuvot Ḥatam Ṣofer, likuṭim,* no. 14. These authorities interpret Nahmanides as asserting that all of Jewish law pertaining to such matters is incorporated in the Noachide Code via the *mitsvah* of *dinin.* The analysis of Rashi's position here presented is, however, consistent with R. Naphtali Zevi Yehudah Berlin's understanding of Nahmanides as presented in R. Berlin's *Ha'amek She'alah, She'ilta* 2:3. Cf., R. Iser Zalman Meltzer, *Even he'azel, Hilkhot Malveh veloveh* 27:1.

28 A similar position, albeit not predicated upon the notion of *dinin,* is espoused by R. Shlomo Luria, *Yam shel Shlomoh, Baba Kamma* 6:14. *Yam shel Shlomoh* declares, "It appears that [the king] can promulgate

tion of an ordered society is mandated by reason.[29]

It is evident that, as found in these sources, the scope of natural law is limited to say the least. In a sense it would be easier to understand a total exclusion of natural law from Jewish legal theory. Total exclusion would lead to the conclusion that reason is not legislatively autonomous and that divine sanction accompanies revealed law but not law mandated by reason. Once the authority of reason is accepted in a limited area the problem to be addressed is why Jewish thought does not accept a fully developed system of *lex naturalis*.

A solution to this vexing problem may be found in Maimonides, *Hilkhot Melakhim* 9:1. Chapter eight of *Hilkhot Melakhim* concludes with the statement that the Seven Commandments must be accepted on the basis of Sinaitic revelation and the corollary that acceptance on the basis of determination of reason does not engender the status either of one of the "pious of the nations of the world" or of one of "their wise men". The very next chapter, 9:1, begins with the statement, "Adam was commanded with regard to six matters ... even though all of them are a tradition in our hands from our teacher Moses and reason inclines toward them it may be seen from the context of the words of the Torah that he was commanded with regard to these." At first glance, Maimonides seems to have contradicted himself. In 8:11 he declares that one who accepts the Noachide Code on the basis of *hekhra hada'at* is not a wise man, whereas in 9:1 he states that indeed *hada'at noteh lahen*. The difficulty, however, dissipates if the terminology is examined carefully. "*Hada'at noteh*" means literally that reason inclines in a certain direction; *hekhra hada'at* is a final, conclusive determination of the intellect. Herein lies not only a resolution of the apparent contradiction but also an explanation of why Judaism cannot admit a

---

laws and practices in his land and punish one who violates his edict... for, if not,.the world would not exist and will be destroyed."
29 Consistent with this position, Rashi, *Niddah*, 61a, s.v. *mehash leh miba'i*, may be understood as applying the identical concept in legitimization of penal sanctions for violation of criminal codes promulgated by virtue of *dina demalkhuta*. See also *Yam shel Shlomoh*, *supra* n.28. For a fuller discussion of Rashi's comment in *Niddah*, see this writer's "*Haşgarat Posh'ea shebaraḥ le'erets yisra'el*", *Or Ham iz ra ḥ*, Nisan-Tammuz (5747), 247-269.

fully developed system of natural law. Reason is by no means infallible. There are many matters which appear to be true by virtue of reason but which cannot be known with certainty. The propositions of logic are the best examples of *a priori* truths which are known with certainty. Those propositions commend themselves to the intellect with compelling rational force; they cannot be rejected by any rational person. Moral propositions may be commended to the intellect by reason but their binding validity cannot, in most cases,[30] be known with compelling certainty. Reason certainly "inclines" toward their acceptance but rational inclination falls short of final determination. Thus the intellect of a wise man will incline strongly toward acceptance, but the same wise man will recognize that, epistemologically, even strong inclination cannot be equated with *hekhra hada'at* or absolute certainty of determination. One who mistakenly confuses rational inclination, no matter how strong, with certainty fails to perceive a crucial epistemological distinction. Such confusion reflects ignorance of a fundamental nature; hence such an individual assuredly does not merit the encomium "wise man"

Certainly, not all propositions postulated by various natural law theorists commend themselves with equal moral force. Undoubtedly, the most compelling of such moral propositions is the admonition "thou shalt not kill." At the other extreme of the spectrum, the natural law argument against onanism, for example, is so weak that objective moralists would probably be disinclined to view it as a legitimate application of *lex naturalis*. The very fact that law theorists frequently dispute whether or not natural law is applicable with regard to a particular act or activity surely demonstrates the absence of rational compulsion of a nature similar to that which is evident in the propositions of logic.[31] Thus in Jewish legal theory the prohibition against murder is accepted by all as interdicted by *s̩evarah* or *lex naturalis*. This is because in a system of moral judgments the admonition "Thou shalt not kill" is the epistemological equivalent of the propositions of logic. With regard to proscription of theft, the force of reason is less clear, while preservation of the social order as a natural law imperative is perhaps even more debatable. The crucial question is that of determining at which point along the epistemological spectrum "inclination" is so

30   See extended endnote D.
31   *Cf.*, Thomas Aquinas, *Summa theologica* II, 2, 57.

strong that it becomes endowed with legal authority. If homicide alone is to be accepted as a legitimate application of *lex naturalis* then only the certainty which accompanies the moral equivalent of the propositions of logic and mathematics is acceptable. If other propositions are to be admitted as well, then something less than absolute certainly must be accepted as sufficient for purposes of establishing legal prohibitions. Be that as it may, failure to recognize the precise point on the spectrum which establishes legal certainty, or mistaken identification of a less compelling inclination with a more compelling inclination sufficient to establish legal certainty, reflects ignorance which is not the hallmark of a wise man.[32]

This analysis entails the acceptance of at least the prohibition against murder on the basis of natural law and, arguably, a limited number of other moral principles as well. Other moral rules may not be established with certainty but are indeed rational in the sense that it is reason which inclines toward their acceptance.

Marvin Fox argues that Maimonides consistently maintains that moral rules are not capable of demonstration.[33] Moral judgments, like aesthetic perceptions, are not subject to logical demonstration; either they are perceived or they are not. Moreover, he argues, moral rules, for Maimonides, are mere conventions. The most crucial passage in establishing this thesis occurs in Maimonides' well-known discussion of the punishment of Adam and Eve in the *Guide of the Perplexed,* Book I, chapter 2: "Through the intellect one distinguishes between truth and falsehood, and that was found in Adam in its perfection and integrity. Beautiful and ugly, on the other hand, belong to the things generally accepted as known [i.e., conventions] not to those cognized by the intellect."[34] This statement does not, however, serve to establish that moral judgments are devoid of objective validity.

The crucial point which Maimonides is intent upon establishing is a resolution of the problem of how "knowledge" can be described as punishment rather than perfection. To this he responds that when Adam was yet in a state of innocence there was no reason to judge nudity to be unbecoming to man. "After Adam's disobedience ... he began to give way to desires which had their source in the imagination and in the gratification of his bodily appetites..." With his

---

32 See extended endnote E.
33 *Supra* n. 2, at xv-xviii.
34 See Fox, *supra* n. 2, at xviii, note 27.

disobedience Adam became a sensual creature to whom avoidance of nakedness became a meaningful concept. Adam's punishment was metamorphosis into a sensual being. Aversion to nakedness is a meaningful judgment only when made by a sensual creature. This passage does not, therefore, serve to demonstrate that all moral judgements are subjective or matters of convention or even that aversion to nakedness is a matter of convention.

Moreover, the statement that moral rules are not capable of demonstration does not entail the conclusion that all moral judgments are mere conventions and that particular moral decisions are subjective in the sense that there exists not even a theoretical norm against which such decisions can be measured. Such a standard or norm may well exist, yet not be available to the human intellect. Nevertheless, since such norms are not perceived by means of the rational faculty, moral judgments are made on other grounds. Accordingly, Adam cannot be deemed to have been granted greater rational perceptions subsequent to his disobedience.

A statement which appears in the opening section of the eighth chapter of Maimonides' *Treatise on Logic* provides much stronger support for Fox's contention. "The propositions which are known[35] and require no proof for their truthfulness are of four kinds ... first ideas as when we know that the whole is greater than the part, that two is an even number, and things equal to the very same thing are equal to each other; conventions, as when we know that uncovering the privy parts is ugly, that compensating a benefactor generously is beautiful..." The first example of a convention is identical with Maimonides' later statement in the *Guide* and may be understood in the same way. The second example, namely that compensating a benefactor is beautiful, is another matter entirely. Maimonides here declares that the propriety of compensating a benefactor is a matter of convention and explicitly distinguishes this proposition from those which he categorizes as first ideas, i.e., those ideas immediately perceived by the intellect.

---

35 Fox is correct in rejecting Efros' insertion of the phrase "to be true" for two reasons: (1) The phrase is absent in the ibn Tibbon text which reads, *hamishpaṭim asher yevade'u velo yitstarekh ra'ayah al amitatam;* (2) Maimonides, in the *Guide*, explicitly rejects the adjective "true" as a categorization of aversion to nakedness. These proportions requires "no proof for their truth" because, although they are "known", they are neither true nor false. See Fox, *supra* n. 2, at xv, note 22.

Yet, one should not extrapolate from this example and universalize the statement as applying to all moral judgments. There may well be other moral perceptions which *are* in the category of first ideas, e.g., the prohibition against homicide. Hence, even for Maimonides, there remains room for a limited theory of natural law.

Marvin Fox states:

> One of the marks of a well trained mind, according to Aristotle, is that it knows how to distinguish between various types of subject-matters, and that it never expects more precision than a subject is capable of yielding.[36] Maimonides knew his Aristotle well and had great regard for the Philosopher. As a follower of the Aristotelian teaching, he quite properly would refuse to recognize a man as wise who could be so confused that he would treat matters of convention or taste as if they were capable of rational demonstration. There is, in addition, a danger to society in such an error, since it rejects authority for pseudo-reason, an error which cannot long be suppressed. Once it is clear that moral distinctions are not rational, and they are no longer accepted on the authority of sovereign or God, there is no longer any ground whatsoever for restraint in human behavior.[37]

I would recast the statement somewhat by stating that when reason "inclines" toward acceptance of a moral proposition, but is not compelling, the proposition cannot be regarded as a first principle; acceptance is therefore in the category of convention. One who confuses a convention with a first principle is hardly a wise man.

II

Two talmudic citations are frequently cited as proof texts demonstrating that Judaism accepts a much broader doctrine of natural law than has been here outlined. *Erubin* 100b teaches,"If the Torah had not been given we could have learned modesty from the cat, aversion to robbery from the ant, chastity from the dove and sexual mores from the rooster." Assumed in this passage, it has been argued, is the existence of a natural morality which, upon reflection, is apparent to the properly attuned mind. Yet, as one contemporary scholar has queried, "But what does this passage really prove?

---

36 Aristotle, *Nicomachean Ethics*, I, iii, 1094b, 12-28.
37 *Supra* n. 2, at xix.

How many Jews (or gentiles, for that matter) have learned modesty
from the cat? And if one could learn modesty from a cat, why not
promiscuity from a dog?"[38] The last question is certainly cogent. If
nature is the model for a moral conduct why is chastity valued and
promiscuity disparaged? Why should respect for the property of
others be emulated and theft eschewed? The latter are certainly
much more common than the former. Indeed, in nature, as in the human jungle, the practice of what are regarded as virtues is the
exception rather than the rule. Most certainly, we cannot discern a
uniform message simply by observing the conduct of members of the
animal kingdom.

Properly understood, the passage does not at all establish the
binding, prescriptive power of reason.[39] It does, however, eloquently
demonstrate a certain "inclination" of reason. Confronted with different, diverse and conflicting models in nature some persons commit
themselves to be guided by moral principles and some do not. Were
reason totally autonomous it would look solely to itself, not to the
cat, the ant, the dove or the rooster. The faculty of moral reason is,
however, attracted by certain forms of behavior and repulsed by
others. It is precisely because morality is so infrequently encountered
in nature that man must seek out models of moral behavior for emu-
lation. In the absence of a revealed corpus of law man could "learn"

38   S.Z. Leiman, "Critique of Louis Jacobs", in *Contemporary Jewish Ethics*,
     ed. M. Kellner (New York: Hebrew Publishing Co.,1978), 59. Similarly,
     M. Fox, *The Philosophical Foundations of Jewish Ethics: Some Initial
     Reflections* (Louis Feinberg Memorial Lecture, University of Cincinnati,
     1979), 14, queries, "Might we not have decided just as readily to imitate
     the ferocity of the lion, the murderousness of an aroused pack of wolves,
     or the sexual behavior of a rabbit?" See also R Wollheim, "Natural
     Law", *Encyclopedia of Philosophy* (New York: MacMillan Publishing
     Co. and The Free Press, 1967), V, 451, who, without reference to *Erub.*
     100b, asks, "Are we ... to model ourselves upon the peaceful habits of
     sheep or upon the internecine conflicts of ants? Is the equalitarianism of
     the beaver or the hierarchical life of the bee the proper example for
     human society? Should we imitate the widespread polygamy of the
     animal kingdom, or is there some higher regularity of which this is no
     more than a misleading instance?"

39   Fox, *supra* n. 2, at viii-ix, is quite right in rejecting a natural law
     interpretation of the passage. However, I do not see a reflection of
     pragmatism in this statement as does Fox. Cf. Aharon Lichtenstein,
     "Does Jewish Tradition Recognize an Ethic Independent of Halakha?",
     in *Contemporary Jewish Ethics, supra* n.31, at 104.

moral principles from nature in the sense that when confronted by antithetical models man would make choices on the basis of intuitive responses. Man might emulate certain models of behavior found in the animal kingdom and adopt them as the paradigms for his own conduct but could legislate them as binding law on the basis of reason alone. The product of such an endeavor would not be a system of law but an emotivist ethic. Reason could not be so certain of itself as to proclaim a universally binding law. In the absence of epistemological certainty moral decisions are essentially aesthetic judgments. Under such circumstances reason can but exclaim in the manner of C.L. Stevenson, "I do like this; do so as well." The result is a subjective morality which one recommends to others.

Yoma 67b seems at first glance to provide stronger support for a theory of natural law, but upon further examination is even less compelling. " 'You shall keep My statutes' (*Lev.* 18:5). This refers to those commandments which had they not been written [in Scripture] should properly have been written. These include the prohibitions against idolatry, adultery, bloodshed, robbery and blasphemy." The crucial phrase is *"re'uyim hayu lekotevan"* meaning "it would have been proper" or "it would have been fitting" for them to be written.[40] "Proper" or "fitting" means simply that such laws serve a necessary function. This statement implies only that in the absence of divine legislation society would find it useful to enact such laws. Indeed such legislation is found in countless societies which deny the authority of divine law. Here, then, we find not an exposition of natural law but a recognition of the need for what Albo refers to as conventional law. In context, the Gemara then proceeds to distinguish such laws from commandments which are entirely ritual in nature and which, therefore, can derive sanction only from divine law.

Saadia's distinction between *mitsvot sikhliyot* and *mitsvot shimiyot* should be understood in precisely the same manner. There are laws which *hasekhel meh ayev*, i.e., which reason mandates, not in the sense that reason serves as a sufficient and authoritative source of law, but which reason commends to us for enactment. Those are known as "rational laws" as distinct from laws which are ac-

---

40   The Soncino translation, "they should by right have been written" is stylistically felicitous but conveys a wrong connotation; cf. Fox, *supra* n. 2, at viii, note 8.

cepted solely on the basis of tradition, i.e., revelation.[41] In dismissing this distinction, and in asserting that all of the divine law is ultimately rational, Maimonides certainly does not imply that reason could endow all such rules with the authority of law; he means simply that were human reason capable of fathoming the purpose and benefit of every divine law it would recommend such modes of behavior in order that man might achieve the desired ends.

III

There is, however, another sense in which Jewish thought may be said to reflect natural law theory. Various forms of natural law theory have been advanced over the centuries by a host of thinkers from Zeno to John Locke. The simplest and oldest developed theory is found in the writings of the Stoics who observed that the entire universe is governed by laws which exhibit rationality. Inanimate objects adhere to such laws because they are inherent in nature itself. The laws of physics and chemistry exhibit rationality in establishing regularity and predictability. The conduct of animals is regulated by a rational pattern of behavior which we call instinct. Since the universe is a unitary whole governed by rational principles it follows that similar rational, natural laws should exist for the ordering of human conduct. Such rules or laws are readily discoverable by application of the rational faculty with which man has been endowed. Thomas Aquinas, in part as an aid in discovering the rational principles which govern the universe and hence which should be adopted by man in ordering his conduct, invoked the Aristotelian concept of nature as a teleological system. The essence of every created entity stipulates an end. Reason, and hence natural law, requires the fulfillment of those ends and militates against any form of behavior which will serve to thwart such fulfillment. Common to all formulations of natural law theory is the notion that man should seek to identify the rational principles inherent in the natural order and seek to guide himself by "the light of reason".

It is the demand that human conduct be modeled upon the rationality of the natural order which poses a formidable problem. Law, as the term is used by jurists and legal scholars, is a rule which is authoritative and binding and which, when violated, may result in

41   See extended endnote F.

imposition of sanctions against the violator. Law, as the term is used by scientists, is merely a manifestation of regularity and rationality in nature. The former is prescriptive; the latter descriptive. Reducing laws prescribed by the intellect to the rational principles manifest in the universe fails to answer the one crucial metaethical question which must be asked of any moral system: Why be moral? Granted that the universe exhibits rationality and that human conduct is part of a unitary rational mosaic of cosmic proportions, the question remains: Why must man endeavor to manifest such patterns of rationality in his moral behavior? Or as the question is put in its classic formulation: how can prescriptive laws be derived from descriptive laws?

This, in turn, is but a variant of the most crucial of all metaethical problems, viz., the bifurcation of "is" and "ought". Granted that we have successfully accomplished the task of defining and identifying the good and the moral, the question remains, "Why be moral?" The religionist who posits a theistic system of morality has a relatively simple solution to this question, viz., divine authority. One must be moral because such is the will and command of God. Any natural law theory is subject to challenge on the following grounds. Granted that the universe exhibits unitary reason, granted that such rationality was instilled in the universe by the Creator, and granted that man can govern himself by the same rationality only if he obeys the injunction "Follow nature", there is as yet no moral imperative which demands of man that he identify with the rationality of the universe and regulate his conduct accordingly.[42]

The question may be resolved only by an appeal to an antecedent metaphysical principle, viz., man ought to obey the will of the Deity insofar as he is capable of discerning His will. Since it was created by God, and since it exhibits a ubiquitous rationality, the universe testifies to God's desire that all of creation guide itself by the principles of reason. Therefore, in regulating his personal con-

---

42 See *Shab.* 133b which records Abba Sha'ul's exegetical interpretation of the phrase *"ve'anvehu"* which occurs in *Ex.* 15:2. Interpreting this phrase as a contraction of the words *"ani vehu"* Abba Sha'ul understands this passage as declaring "Be similar to Him. Just as He is merciful and gracious so also you be merciful and gracious." See also *Sot.* 14a and *Midrash Rabbah, Shemot* 26:2. In his codification of this *halakhah,* Maimonides, *Hilkhot De'ot* 1:6, explicitly incorporates other divine attributes as well.

duct, man is bound to pursue the dictates of natural law as discerned by reason. Recasting this explanation in the Jewish version of the doctrine of *imitatio Dei*, it is as if God were to address His creatures and to say to them, "Even as I am rational (as evidenced by the rationality of the universe which I have created), be you also rational!"[43] Only by invoking a notion such as this can prescriptive law be made to flow from its descriptive counterpart. It should be remembered that the admonition upon which the principle of *imitatio Dei* is based is regarded as a formal commandment included in the enumeration of the 613 binding precepts. The scriptural authority for regarding the doctrine of *imitatio Dei* as a formal *mitsvah* is the verse "... and you shall walk in His ways" *(Deut.* 28:9).[44]

Thus, if Judaism does attribute even limited legislative authority to the intellect, this, too, is so only because such authority is vested in reason by virtue of a direct divine command.

Of course, in a certain fundamental sense casting even a limited natural law theory in a "mitsvahitic" guise only pushes the question back one step. The question which then must be pondered is: "Why must man obey the will of God?" Fear of retribution, while it may constitute a compelling motive for many, is not a complete answer. Conceivably, a person may be willing to accept the punishment entailed in disobeying the will of God, yet no religionist would agree that morally man has a right to do so. One may park overtime at a

---

43   Aristotle, *supra* n.29, at   VII, iii, 1146b24-1147b17, argues that the conclusion of a moral syllogism is as compelling as that of a logical syllogism. No rational person can accept the premises, "All men are mortal" and "Socrates is a man", and deny the conclusion, "Socrates is mortal." Aristotle argues that the moral syllogism, when the premises are properly perceived, compels conduct in a manner analogous to the manner in which a logical syllogism compels the assent of reason. The natural law moralist goes beyond this position in arguing, not that man is compelled in the intuitive sense, but that man is morally bound to act in conformity with the principles of reason. This leaves us with precisely the original question: Granted that the moral is to be identified with the demand of reason, by what authority is man bound to accept rational principles in regulating his conduct?

44   See Maimonides, *Şefer hamitsvot, mitsvot aseh*, no. 8; *Ba'al Halakhot Gedolot, mitsvot aseh; Şefer Yere'im*, no. 4; *Şefer Mitsvot Ķatser*, no. 46; *Şefer Mitsvot Gadol, mitsvot aseh*, no. 7;*Şefer ha hhinnukh*, no. 611. See also *Sifre* on *Deut.* 13:5: "'After the Lord your God shall you walk' - this is a positive commandment."

JUDAISM AND NATURAL LAW

meter and pay the fine because the infraction does not involve moral turpitude, but no legal moralist would sanction a felony on the plea that the perpetrator is quite willing to pay the penalty exacted by society. Moreover, religious teaching demands that the moral agent strive to act out of a sense of love rather than out of a sense of fear.

The question thus formulated is a challenge not only to the acceptance of moral maxims predicated upon a natural law theory but to the entire corpus of *mitsvot*. It should be remembered that *Ba'al Halakhot Gedolot*, the earliest authority to compose a detailed enumeration of the 613 precepts of Judaism, failed to include belief in God as one of the 613 commandments. The problem for *Ba'al Halakhot Gedolot* is not only that belief cannot be commanded but that the notion of a commandment presupposes a commander. As Bertrand Russell stated in formulating his Theory of Types, a statement about a class cannot itself be a member of that class. God, the commander, stands outside the system of commandments and constitutes the authority by which commandments must be accepted. Commandments are binding because they are decreed by God. But logically prior to a system of commandment is the principle that God's decrees must be obeyed. A commandment to that effect is not self-validating. By what authority is the commandment to accept God's authority mandated?

At this point there must perforce be an appeal to some *a priori* concept. Saadia declares, "reason calls for gratitude to God for His kindness."[45] Filial devotion is common to all members of the human species. The child reacts with love and devotion to parents who have bestowed the gift of love upon him and who have showered him with concern and affection. This reaction is instinctive and intuitive; it is an *a priori* response rooted in reason. It follows, *a fortiori*, that man should respond in the same manner to his heavenly Father, the author of life itself, Who continuously exercises providential guardianship over His creatures. Such a reaction need not be commanded; it is demanded by reason. It follows, then, that obedience to the will of God is a dictate of reason and is the *a priori* assumption underlying the binding nature of the entire corpus of divine commandments.

45 *Book of Beliefs and Opinions*, Treatise III, chap. 3.

IV

The crucial notion that reason demands that man obey the will
of God - even that he seek to discover the propositions mandated by
divine will - is a concept for which explicit talmudic support may be
found.[46] Jewish law prescribes that Noachides are to be held accountable even for transgressions committed in ignorance of the law.
The Noachide is culpable, declares the Gemara, *Makkot* 9b,
"because he should have learned but did not learn." This is probably
the earliest formulation of the legal maxim "Ignorance of the law is
no excuse," although in Jewish law this principle is restricted to
violations of the Noachide Code. This dictum, which is ostensibly
merely the formulation of a punitive principle, implies much more
than appears on the surface. The Noachide Code applies to all gentiles, whether or not they are or were exposed to information
regarding the historical phenomenon of revelation at Sinai and
whether or not the Noachide tradition was transmitted to their
progenitors. Judaism recognizes no doctrine of invincible ignorance.
The problem of theodicy is self-apparent. How can a just God hold
disadvantaged creatures who have not been the privileged recipi-
ents of revelation accountable for obedience to a law of which they
have no knowledge? The answer, "He should have learned," is a
cogent answer only if an underlying prior assumption is accepted,
namely, that there exists an *obligation* on the part of Noachides to
seek such information. By what authority is a person obliged to seek
such knowledge? Indeed, in the absence of revelation, how is the
uninitiated to be held responsible for (a) the discovery of the exis-

46   Of interest with regard to this point is the citation by the Gemara, *Baba
Kamma* 85a, of *Ex.* 21:19 and the declaration, "From here [it is derived]
that the physician is granted permission to cure." The obvious
implication is that in the absence of scriptural dispensation such
activity would be forbidden. Rashi comments that a biblical verse is
required to teach us that we are not to say "How is it that God smites and
man heals?" In much the same vein *Tosafot* and R. Solomon ben Abraham
Adret state that without such sanction, "he who heals might appear as
if he invalidated a divine decree." The implications of the Gemara's
statement are: (1) Reason itself perceives that intervention in
physiological processes in the absence of specific divine permission to do
so is an attempt to thwart the will of God; and (2) man, even in the
absence of a formal prohibition, ought not to act in a manner which is
contrary to the will of God.

tence of God, and (b) an awareness that God has revealed a corpus of law which is binding upon all mankind? Clearly, only if both premises are known and accepted can one address the question of obligation to discover and learn the contents of that corpus of law.

It should, however, be recognized that Judaism posits that the existence of God is readily discernible to the human mind, either on the basis of an immediate *a priori* awareness or on the basis of a simple formulation of one of the classic proofs for the existence of God. Judaism must also posit that a rational mind necessarily perceives that God may well make certain demands of man and, furthermore, if He does so, God must have made His will known to mankind. Reason demands that man obey the will of God; therefore, reason demands both that man make an effort to discover God's will as expressed in revelation to man and that man obey the revealed will of God.[47] All of this must be accepted by man, not on the basis of divine command, because at this point in his intellectual inquiry man has not become aware of the content of divine commandments, but on the basis of reason alone. In this sense one may indeed speak of the presence of a natural law theory in Jewish thought, albeit the natural law here described is of a very particular and limited kind.

Extended Notes

A. Maimonides requires not merely that non-Jews accept the Noachide Code on the basis of revelation but specifically on the basis of Sinaitic revelation. Maimonides here extends to non-Jews the principle earlier formulated by him with regard to Jews. The Mishnah, Ḥullin 7:6, declares that the prohibition concerning the sciatic sinew does not extend to the sciatic sinew of non-kosher animals. R. Judah, in objecting to the ruling, argues that the prohibition was directed to the children of Jacob at a time when all animals were permitted. Responding to the objection, the Sages declare, "[The prohibition] was stated at Sinai but written in its proper place." Rashi, Ḥullin 100b, amplifies this statement and interprets it in a literal manner as meaning that the passage prohibiting the sciatic sinew, *Gen.* 32:33, was transmitted for the first time at Sinai

---

47 See R. Elchanan Wasserman, "*Dugma lebi'ure Aggadot al Derekh hapeshat*", no. 1; Ḳovets He'arot (New York, 5712); reprinted in *idem*, "Maamar al Emunah", Sefer Ḳovets Ma'amarim (Jerusalem, 5723), 11-16.

but "until Sinai they were not admonished." The verse in question "was written in its place after it was declared at Sinai; and Moses, [when] he wrote and arranged the Torah recorded this verse in association with the event...". According to Rashi, the prohibition was promulgated at Sinai for the first time but was recorded in the Torah in conjunction with the narrative concerning Jacob's strife with the angel since that incident is the reason underlying the subsequent prohibition.

Maimonides, in his *Commentary on the Mishnah,* explains the statement of the Mishnah in a quite different manner:

> Give heart to this great principle which is included in the Mishnah, viz., ... all that we disdain or perform today we do so solely by virtue of the command of the Holy One, blessed be He, through our teacher Moses, may he rest in peace, not because the Holy One, blessed be He, stated this to the prophets who preceded him. For example, we do not eat a limb torn from a live animal because God forbade [it] to Noah, but because Moses forbade to us a limb torn from a live animal by virtue of what he was commanded at Sinai to the effect that the prohibition against [eating] a limb torn from a living animal remains in effect; similarly, we do not circumcise because our father Abraham, may he rest in peace, circumcised himself and the members of his household but because the Holy One, blessed be He, commanded us through our teacher Moses, may he rest in peace, that we circumcise just as our father Abraham, may he rest in peace, circumcised; and, similarly [with regard to] the sciatic sinew, we do not follow the prohibition of our father Jacob, but the command of our teacher Moses, may he rest in peace...

[Cf., however, *Tos.afot, Sanhedrin* 56b, s.v. *eser mitsvot;* R. Reuben Margulies, *Margaliyot hayam* (Jerusalem: Mosad Harav Kook, 5718), *ad locum;* and R. Shimon Moshe Diskin, *Ohel Yehoshu'a* (Jerusalem: 5738), 56ff.] Maimonides, thus, accepts the notion of binding prohibitions before Sinai, other than those of the Noachide Code, but maintains that the original command of such prohibitions lacks binding authority subsequent to Sinai. In the cited passage in the *Mishneh Torah,* Maimonides extends this principle to the Noachide Code as well. The original revelation to Adam and Noah was binding only until Sinai; the Noachide Code continues to be binding only because it was renewed at Sinai. Gentiles must accept the Noachide Code, not on the basis of the original revelation, but on the basis of Sinaitic revelation. Thus, in addition to moral conduct, a faith commitment in the form of acceptance of the validity of the Sinaitic revelation is required of all non-Jews and such acceptance is a precondition of eternal heavenly reward. See this writer's *With Perfect Faith: The Foundations of Jewish Belief* (New York: Ktav Publishing House, 1983), 15-18. *Cf.*, however, R. Yom Tov Lipman Heilprin, *Teshuvot Oneg Yom Tov* (Vilna, 5640), no.19.

B. A similar dictum occurs in a letter to R. Hasdai halevi; see *Teshuvot harambam ve'iggerotav* (Leipzig: Mekize Nirdamim, 1859), Part 2, 23b. R. Joseph Karo in his commentary on the *Mishneh Torah, K̤eṣef Mishneh, loc. cit.*, states that this is Maimonides' own opinion and lacks earlier textual support, but is correct nonetheless. A number of later scholars have attempted to demonstrate that Maimonides' statement is based upon earlier authority.

R. Ezekiel Feivel, *S̤efer Toldot Adam* (Dyhrenfurth, 1801), chapter 6, 35a, reports that an anonymous scholar from the Orient visited Vilna and, marveling at the encyclopedic knowledge of R. Zalman of Volozhin (a brother of the famed R. Chaim of Volozhin), asked him to elucidate a number of difficult passages in Maimonides' writings. When questioned with regard to the source of Maimonides' statement concerning Noachides and their obligation to accept the Seven Commandments on the basis of Sinaitic revelation, R. Zalman produced an unidentified Midrash which states:

> Rabbi Y. said, "I have heard that the pious of the nations of the world have a share in the world to come. We have, however, not been taught this with regard to the wise men of the nations of the world. Who is a pious man from among the nations of the world? He who accepts the Seven Commandments because they are written in the Torah. A wise man from among the nations of the world is one who fulfills them on the basis of the determination of his reason."

It is interesting to note that this Midrash refers to one who accepts the Seven Commandments on the basis of reason as "a wise man". See Steven S. Schwarzschild, "Do Noachites Have to Believe in Revelation?" *Jewish Quarterly Review* 52/4 (1962), 305-306.

One midrashic collection, *The Mishnah of R. Eliezer (The Midrash of Thirty-two Hermeneutic Rules)*, ed. H.G. Enelow (New York: Bloch Publishing Co., 1933), 121, contains a most interesting statement with regard to the definition of "the pious of the nations of the world". Such an appellation may be ascribed, declares the Midrash, "only when they perform [the Seven Commandments] and say 'we perform [them] because our father Noah commanded us [regarding them] by the mouth of God.' ... But if they fulfill the Seven Commandments and say, 'We have heard them from so and so' or [if they perform them] of their own accord for so does reason determine ... they receive their reward only in this world." Maimonides' central point, viz., that the Noachide Code must be accepted on the basis of revelation is certainly substantiated by this midrashic passage. Yet this Midrash could not have been Maimonides' source since Maimonides differs from the Midrash with regard to one important point. The Midrash states that Noachides may accept the Seven Commandments because they were revealed to Noah. Maimonides insists (as will be further clarified in the text) that Noachides must accept the Seven Commandments on the basis of revelation at Sinai rather than on the basis of revelation to Adam or Noah. For Maimonides, Noachides may aspire to reward in the world to come only upon acceptance of the veracity and validity of the Sinaitic revelation; see R. Abraham I. Karelitz, Ḥazon Ish, Shevi'it 24:2 and Hilkhot Avodat Kokhavim 65:2. Moreover, while the Mishnah of R. Eliezer speaks of "reward only in this world", Teshuvot harambam, ed. Alfred Freimann (Jerusalem: Mekize Nirdamim, 1934), no.124 and Teshuvot harambam, ed. Yehoshua Blau (Jerusalem: Mekize Nirdamim, 1957), I, no.148, appears to exclude any type of reward unless observance is predicated upon revelation. Nevertheless, the Midrash, precisely because it could not have been Maimonides' source, constitutes strong corroborative evidence for his contention that the Noachide Code must be accepted by non-Jews on the basis of revelation. Since the Midrash could not have been Maimonides' source it must reflect the existence of a well-established tradition with regard to this point. Cf. Schwarzschild, supra n. B, at 306. Although Maimonides, in his earlier noted Teshuvot harambam cites a work bearing the title Beraita shel R. Eli'ezer as a source for this position that work, because of the reasons indicated, does not seem to be identical with the extant text of the Mishnah of R. Eli'ezer. Cf., however, Encyclopedia Talmudit, VI (Jerusalem, 1954), 290, n.11.

In a letter addressed to Moses Mendelssohn and published in Mendelssohn's Gesammelte Schriften, XVI (Berlin: Akademie-Verlag, 1929), R. Jacob Emden states that Maimonides' position is based upon Sanh. 105a. R. Joshua, who maintains that non-Jews may share in the world to come, interprets the verse "The wicked shall return to the nether-world, even all the nations that forget God" (Ps.

9:18) as follows: "'The wicked shall return to the nether-world' ... Who are they? [They are] 'all the nations who forget God.'" Maimonides, avers R. Emden, understands 'the nations who forget God' as including those who observe the Noachide Code but 'forget' that it was commanded by God.

In a posthumously published article, R. Malkiel Zvi Tennenbaum (author of *Teshuvot Divre Malki'el*), *Torah shebe'al Peh*, XV (5733), 164), suggests that Maimonides' position is deduced from *Baba Kamma* 38a. The Gemara cites the verse "He standeth and shaketh the earth. He beholdeth and maketh the nations to tremble" (*Hab.* 3:6), and comments, "What did He see? He saw the Seven Commandments which the sons of Noah accepted but did not observe [therefore] 'He arose and He permitted them [to the sons of Noah]." The Gemara, for exegetical purposes, renders the word *"vayater"* as "permitted" rather than "maketh to tremble". The Gemara, in the ensuing discussion, modifies this interpretation by stating that the prohibitions of the Noachide Code were not actually rescinded, but were reduced in status so that a non-Jew who observes them is rewarded "as one who is not commanded but observes", i.e., receives lesser compensation than "one who is commanded and observes". R. Tennenbaum avers that acceptance of the Noachide Code on the basis of Sinaitic revelation carries with it reward as "one who is commanded and observes". Such compensation is only just since gentiles are indeed bound by the Noachide Code as revealed at Sinai. A new revelation of the Noachide Code at Sinai became necessary because of widespread non-adherence to its provisions by gentiles. Accordingly, the original mandate was revoked at Sinai to be replaced by a new obligation. In speaking of one who observes the Noachide Code as being rewarded as "one who is not commanded", the Gemara, declares Rabbi Tennenbaum, refers solely to the non-Jew who does not accept the Seven Commandments on the basis of Sinaitic revelation but accepts them on the basis of an earlier revelation or because of some extraneous consideration. [This analysis of *Baba Kamma* 38a is also independently advanced by R. Meir Simhah hakohen of Dvinsk, *Or Sameah*, *Hilkhot Isure Bi'ah* 14:7, and by R. Yitshak Ze'ev Soloveitchik, *Hiddushe Maran Riz halevi* (Jerusalem, 5723), 164. This position is also explicitly formulated by an early authority, Ritva, in his commentary to *Makkot* 9a.] R. Tennenbaum adds that Maimonides inferred that only the gentile who observes the Noachide Code as "one who is commanded and performs" receives a share in the world to come. See also R. Yitshak Ze'ev Soloveitchik, *H̤iddushe hagriz al hatorah (mipi hashemu'ah)* (undated), no. 152, who finds Maimonides' position reflected in the words of *II Kings* 5:8. See also R. Shlomoh ben Shimon Duran, *Teshuvot harashbash*, no. 543, who finds a source for Rambam's position in *Sanh*. 59a and R. Zevi Hirsch Chajes, *Torat hanevi'im*, chap. 11, who finds a source in *H̤ullin* 92a; see also *idem*, in R. Abraham Naphtali Jener, *Zekhuta de'avraham* (Lemberg, 1868), no. 21.

See also R. Chaim Hirschensohn, *Eleh Divre habrit*, I, 6, who advances a deductive argument in explanation of Maimonides' position predicated upon his view that prior to the Sinaitic revelation the Noachide commandments were binding solely by virtue of *sevarah*; see *infra* note 1.

The foregoing is merely an attempt to uncover a talmudic or midrashic source for Maimonides' view regarding Noachides and the world to come but does not address the question of why belief in Sinaitic revelation should be a necessary condition for eternal reward; see above, note A.

C   Earlier, in Book One, chapter 5, Albo does state:

> It is because association and aggregation are necessary for the existence and support of the human species that the wise men have said that man is political by nature. They mean by this that it is almost necessary for a man by his nature to live in a city (state) with a large group of men that he may be able to obtain what he needs for his life and support. It is clear therefore that the whole group residing in a city, or a district, or a region, or all the human beings in the world should have some order which they follow in their conduct, maintaining justice in general and suppressing wrong, so as to keep men from quarreling in their transactions and business relations with one another. Such order would include protection against murder, theft, robbery and the like, and in general all those measures which are calculated to maintain the political group and enable the people to live in welfare. This order the wise men call natural law, meaning by natural that it is necessary for man by his nature, whether the order emanates from a wise man or a prophet.

"Association and aggregation" are "almost necessary" but not absolutely necessary. Society, to exist, requires "some order" and it is this order which "the wise men" call natural law. Such order which includes "protection against murder, theft, robbery and the like" is necessary for man by his nature. It is because such order is natural to man by virtue of his nature that Albo asserts that men can coexist within a society without difficulty. Albo does not argue that preservation of society is mandated by natural law but, rather, that natural law is logically prior to formation of society, and makes possible the existence of society.

On the other hand, it would be an error to suppose that, for Albo, natural law is manifest only in an organized society. Ralph Lerner has stated, "Albo suggests that this natural law is not absolutely necessary for man because it is not absolutely necessary for man to live in political society; moreover, he suggests that the validity of this natural law depends upon its establishment by some human individual. By pointing to the possibility of life outside the city, Albo casts some doubt on the obligatory character of natural law. By further distinguishing the purpose of this natural law from the perfection that is proper to man, Albo in effect denies that natural law is, strictly speaking, natural." See "Moses Maimonides", *History of Political Philosophy, supra* n. 11, at 221. Elsewhere, the same author writes, "We may say more generally, then, that natural law's injunctions are needed for human perfection as such, but only insofar as man is part of a city or of some kind of association." See "Natural Law in Albo's *Book of Roots*", in *Ancients and Moderns*, ed. Joseph Cropsey (New York, London: Basic Books, 1964), 141ff. However, in chapter 7, Albo does not at all present natural law as a function of political philosophy and even in chapter 5, as has been stated, natural law is cited as a logically prior concept which has the salutary effect of making society possible. The validity of natural law certainly does not "depend upon its establishment by some human individual." Albo does speak of an order which "emanates from a wise man or a prophet" but the function of such individuals is pedagogic rather than legislative. The order to which reference is made "is necessary for man by his nature" even though society itself is only "almost necessary" in contradistinction to being absolutely necessary.

D   The principle "How do you know that your blood is sweeter than the blood of your fellow" which is postulated by the Gemara on the basis of ṣevarah is one proposition which is declared to be known with certainty on the basis of reason. Nevertheless, Maimonides, *Hilkhot Yeṣode hatorah* 5:7, speaks of this principle as "*davar shehada'at noṭeh lo*", although even stronger terminology would be in order.

It is conceivable that Maimonides used the weaker expression in order to indicate that the obligation to suffer martyrdom rather than commit an act of murder encompasses situations in which this ṣevarah is not applicable. In the same chapter, *Hilkhot Yeṣode hatorah* 5:5, Maimonides rules that the principle "be killed and do not transgress" applies even in a situation in which a victim is singled out and the entire group warned that, if the specific individual is not delivered, all will perish. The ṣevarah "How do you know that your blood is sweeter" certainly does not apply in this instance. *Keṣef Mishneh, ad loc.*, states that the Sages were in possession of a tradition extending this principle even to cases in which this ṣevarah docs not apply. R. Chaim Ozer Grodzinsky, *Teshuvot Ahiezer*, II no. 16, sec. 5, presents a formal hermeneutic derivation substantiating the extension of the rule to encompass situations in which this ṣevarah is not applicable. Similarly, it may cogently be argued that, according to Maimonides, the principle "be killed but do not transgress" applies even to the taking of fetal life despite the fact that fetal life is "less sweet" as evidenced by the fact that feticide does not constitute a capital crime. See J. David Bleich, "Abortion in Halakhic Literature", *Jewish Bioethics,* ed. Fred Rosner and J. David Bleich (New York: Hebrew Publishing Co., 1979), 141-142 and 173 note 71.

Maimonides' statement, *Hilkhot Yeṣode hatorah* 5:2, describing as a *mitsvah* the obligation to accept martyrdom rather than commit an act of homicide, should not be misunderstood. Maimonides means thereby only that once established as an obligation on the basis of ṣevarah actual fulfillment constitutes an act of sanctification of the Divine Name; in the absence of the ṣevarah such an obligation would not be subsumed under the *mitsvah* of sanctification of the Divine Name. Faur, *supra* n. 10, at 121, apparently misses this point.

E   This analysis of Maimonides' position is at variance with the position set forth by Strauss, *Persecution, supra* n. 10, at 97, note 4. Strauss declares, "The Noahidic commandments cannot be identified with the natural law, at least not according to Maimonides. For - to say nothing of *ever min haḥai* - the prohibition against incest or unchastity which occupies the central place in his enumeration of the Noahidic commandments ... is considered by him to belong to the revealed laws as distinguished from the so-called rational laws (*Eight Chapters*, vi)... This is not contradicted by Maimonides' statement that the *da'at* inclines man toward six of the seven Noahidic commandments ... for *da'at* does not necessarily mean 'reason' or 'intelligence.'" [Strauss infers from Maimonides' statement, *Hilkhot Melakhim* 9:1, "Adam was commanded with regard to six matters ... and reason inclines toward them ... He added to Noah [the prohibition against] the limb of a living animal ..." that reason inclines only toward the first six. To be sure, the phrase "and reason inclines toward them" was used by Maimonides in association with the six commandments revealed to Adam, but there is no reason to assume that Maimonides intends to exclude the seventh from this categorization. Certainly, the *ela* reading in 8:11 which refers to all seven Noachide commandments encompasses *ever min haḥai* as well.]

It is my contention that *da'at* does indeed mean "reason" or "intelligence". Reason would indeed be inclined to abjure *ever min haḥai* as involving wanton and needless cruelty to animals.

The problem which Strauss raises with regard to *arayot* (and which was noted earlier by R. Isaiah Pik in a marginal gloss to *Yoma* 67b) does, however, require resolution. This problem may be resolved upon careful analysis of Maimonides' source. *Yoma* 67b declares:

> Our Rabbis taught: "Mine ordinances shall ye do," i.e., such commandments which, if they were not written [in Scripture], they should by right have been written and these are they: [the laws concerning] idolatry, immorality and bloodshed, robbery and blasphemy. "And My statutes shall ye keep," i.e., such commandments to which Satan objects, they are [those relating to] the putting on of *sha'atnez*, *halitsah* [performed] by a sister-in-law, the purification of the leper, and the he-goat-to-be-sent-away. And perhaps you might think these are vain things, therefore Scripture says: "I am the Lord," i.e., I, the Lord have made it a statute and you have no right to criticize it.

The Gemara clearly lists *giluy arayot* among the *mishpaṭim* rather than among the *ḥukim* or "revealed laws". The Gemara then proceeds to enumerate five examples of *ḥukim*. Maimonides initially gives only three examples in the passage cited but shortly thereafter adds additional ones:

Rather they cite matters all of which are based on tradition; partaking of meat and milk together, wearing clothes made of wool and linen and forbidden sexual relationships *(arayot)*. These and similar commandments are what God called "My statutes *(hukkotai)* which as they [the Sages] said, are statutes which I have enacted for you, which you have no permission to question, which the nations of the world attack and which Satan denounces, such as the red heifer, the scapegoat and so forth.

If one compares the five examples listed by Maimonides with the five enumerated by the Gemara it is readily evident that the second and fifth are identical in both listings. The first example of the Gemara, *akhilat ḥazir* is replaced by *basar beḥalav* in Maimonides' enumeration; the fourth, *ṭaharat metsora*, is replaced with *parah adumah*. In both cases the substitute is of a like for a like: one dietary prohibition for another dietary prohibition and one purification ritual for another. The third in the Gemara's series, *ḥalitsat yevamot*, i.e., the rite of removing the shoe which releases the childless widow from the obligation of levirate marriage, is replaced by the term *arayot*. It is, of course, possible that the text of the Eight Chapters is corrupt. This would, however, not really resolve the problem completely for reasons which will be indicated shortly. More likely, Maimonides' reference is not to consanguineous or blood relatives but to a specific type of *ervah*, namely, to the prohibition against marrying a sister-in-law who has borne a child - and perhaps to the prohibition against marriage between the childless widow and any person save her deceased husband's brother. Such marriage is certainly not negated by reason. [See R. Abraham ibn Ezra, *Yeṣod Mora*, chap. 5, who declares that the prohibition against simultaneous marriage to two sisters could not have been prior to Sinai on the basis of *"shiḳul hada'at"* but that *arayot* are *nit'av betoladah*.] Indeed, were there a natural abhorrence militating against marrying a brother's wife, the distinction between the childless widow and a widow with children would not be readily discernible. Maimonides' reference to *arayot* is thus a reference to the laws of levirate obligation which is a paraphrase of the Gemara's *ḥalitsat yevamah* and certainly falls within the category of *ḥuḳim*. Reason, however, does incline against conjugal relationships with blood relatives. Prohibitions in the category of *giluy arayot* in the Noachide Code are solely of the latter nature: a widowed sister-in-law is never proscribed to Noachides.

Indeed, this distinction must be made even in the absence of

Maimonides' statement classifying *arayot* among the *ḥuḳim*. *Ṣifra* on *Lev.* 20:26 states:

> R. Elazar b. Azariyah said: From whence [is it known] that men should not say "I do not wish to eat the flesh of the swine; I do not wish to co-habit with an *ervah*" rather [he should say] "I wish, but what shall I do for my Father in heaven has decreed upon me thus."

Assuming, as does Maimonides, that a worthy person has no desire for that which is forbidden by the *mishpaṭim* but that the opposite is true with regard to *ḥuḳim*, *Ṣifra* appears to contradict *Yoma* 67b. *Arayot* are among the rational laws, declares *Yoma*, yet *Ṣifra* states that one should eschew an *ervah* only because "my Father in heaven decreed upon me." The contradiction is resolved if it is understood that *Yoma* refers to blood relatives only, whereas *Ṣifra* refers solely to other types of *ervah*. Cf., D. Rosen, *Die Ethik des Maimonides* (Breslau: 1879), 94, note 4. It should be noted that both R. Isaiah Pik, in his gloss to *Yoma* 67b, and R. David Kapah in annotations to his translation of *Maimonides' Commentary on the Mishnah, Nashim-Neziḳin* (Jerusalem: Mosad Harav Kook, 5724), 268 note 14, suggest that the phrase *giluy arayot* did not appear in Maimonides' text of *Yoma* 67b. See also *Ḥiddushe Maharasha, Yoma* 67b.

F. Fox's analysis of this point, *supra* n. 2, at x-xi, is correct, although I believe he overemphasizes the concept of "useful" as the criterion of the rational. I cannot agree with Lamm and Kirschenbaum, *supra* n.3, at 111-113, who ascribe a natural law position to Saadia. Saadia's *mitsvot sikhliyot* are quite distinct from the concept of natural law. The former, since they include many laws which are not binding upon Noachides are not at all universal in nature and hence lack the crucial determinant criterion of natural law. Cf. also, Lerner, "Natural Law", *Ancients and Moderns, supra* n. 11, at 143f. Similarly, Grotius, citing Maimonides, *Guide,* III, 26, identifies *mishpaṭim* with natural law: see I. Husik, "The Law of Nature, Hugo Grotius, and the Bible", *Hebrew Union College Annual* II (1925), 399.

Some support for identification of the term *mitsvot sikhliyot* with the concept of natural law may be found in the following passage of R. Shem Tov ben Shem Tov's *Derashot hatorah* 25:

> It should be known that of the laws and ordinances some are called nat-

ural, some are called conventional, and some are called divine. The rational are those which nature mandates and consist of all the laws and ordinances which are identical in the entire world, such as "Thou shalt not kill" and the like. In sum, all matters which reason (sekhel) mandates are called in our Torah rational commandments.

Nevertheless, in context it appears that R. Shem Tov presents no more than the standard definition of sikhliyot and merely introduces the term teva as a synonym for sekhel. It cannot be deduced from this statement that reason constitutes binding authority for natural law.

NATURAL LAW, *HALAKHAH* AND THE COVENANT

by

DAVID NOVAK[*]

1. *Introduction*

Philosophers of law, certainly in modern times, can be divided into two main groups: legal positivists and natural law theorists. In essence, the difference between the two groups can be seen in their understanding of the relation of authority and right within a legal system. For legal positivists, authority is prior to right, that is, a legal system is grounded in the power of *an* authority to make laws which then determine what is right and what is wrong. For natural law theorists, right is prior to authority, that is, *an* authority is ordained to make laws because such power is conceived to be right. For both schools of thought, legal authority is a manifestation of political power. For both, "right" means "that which is to be done" and "wrong" means "that which is not to be done." The point of difference, then, is whether there is a transpolitical validation for political power manifest as legal authority. Legal positivists would say that society itself (either collectively or in the person of its sovereign) is the *terminus a quo* of its own authority. Natural law theorists would say that the political power qua legal authority of a society is derivative from something else - traditionally called "nature."[1]

One can see into which school of thought a modern philosopher of law fits by looking at his or her answer to the challenge made by an outstanding contemporary colleague, Professor Ronald Dworkin, that one constitute rights as "the one feature that distinguishes law from ordered brutality."[2] A legal positivist would say that this

---

[*] Rabbi of Congregation Darchay Noam, Far Rockaway, New York, U.S.A.; Adjunct Associate Professor of Philosophy, The City University of New York, Baruch College.
1 See extended end-note.
2 *Taking Rights Seriously* (Cambridge, MA: Harvard University Press, 1978), 205.

distinction lies in *how* a legal system is ordered. If a legal system's commands are norms, that is, clearly defined rules consistent with an overall normative structure, then there is a sufficient distinction between these prescriptions and the arbitrary, erratic, commands associated with "ordered brutality."[3] Natural law theorists would say that this distinction lies in the purpose, the *why*, of a legal system. If a legal system's prescriptions are rational norms, that is, ordered towards objective human goods qua ends, which themselves transcend the system, then there is a sufficient distinction between these prescriptions and the commands associated with "ordered brutality", commands which serve no end other than the exercise of political power as an end in itself.[4]

In times such as these, when rival political claims are so pronounced and have such staggering global consequences, it is easy to see why philosophy of law is of such current intellectual interest. Aside from the fact that Jewish theologians have always been interested in perennial philosophical problems (and, indeed, the philosophical problem of legal positivism versus natural law theory can be traced back to Socrates), and aside from the fact that Jews are part of the current international scene, there are two more particular historical factors that make this issue the point of the considerable contemporary Jewish discussion that Dr. Jackson has so thoroughly shown it to be in his introduction to this two-volume symposium in *The Jewish Law Annual*. These two factors are the most overriding events of modern Jewish history: the Holocaust and the establishment of the State of Israel. Both of these events call for discussion by Jews of the differences between legal positivism and natural law theory as a pressing practical need and not just as *pilpula b'alma*. In the Holocaust Jews were the most cruelly decimated victims of the most ordered brutality in history. They were not just as victims of random acts of violence, but they were victims of a system legally structured and aimed at their annihilation. The immediate Jewish reaction of "never again!" leads either consciously or unconsciously, I believe, to a concern with defining for all

3   See Hans Kelsen, *The Pure Theory of Law*, trans. M. Knight (Berkeley, CA: University of California Press, 1970), 44ff.
4   See Thomas Aquinas, *Summa Theologiae*, II-I, q.90, aa.1-2. For the teleological thrust of Aquinas' philosophy of law, see my teacher, Germain G. Grisez, "The First Principle of Practical Reason", *Natural Law Forum* 10 (1965), 168-201.

humanity the difference between law, which Judaism has always affirmed as being international in scope, and ordered brutality as an aberational imitation of legal order.   However, if Jews are interested in law on an international level, they cannot avoid asking the same philosophical questions about their own system of law, *Halakhah*. One cannot speak to the conscience of humanity without simultaneously speaking to his or her own conscience.[5] These philosophical questions, as we have just seen, concern the relation of right and authority.   Now the establishment of the State of Israel has given the Jewish people for the first time in over 2,000 years sovereign political power. The political issues which concern the State of Israel, and along with it the overwhelming number of Jews throughout the world who have accepted Zionism as integral to their Judaism, practically involve the philosophical question of the relation of right and authority. Thus, for example, how *Halakhah* is used to determine a legal approach to non-Jews living under Israeli rule, will probably be decided differently depending on whether the particular halakhist is an advocate of legal positivism or natural law theory.

One can see an antinomy between legal positivism and natural law theory and the Jewish theologian must bear it in mind in his or her attempt to define the essential character of *Halakhah*. The antinomy is as follows:

Natural law is a body of norms, rationally apprehended, universally applicable, independent of the promulgation of any authority.	*Positive law is a body of norms, given, for application in a particular society (and whomever they control), dependent on promulgation by a particular authority.*

Now it is clear that the natural law theorist can resolve this antinomy, that is, incorporate the two extremes into one coherent position, whereas the legal positivist cannot. Traditionally, natural law theorists have resolved the antinomy by positing that positive law is the historical specification of the general principles of natu-

---

5   For the necessary personal involvement in all moral questions, see R.M. Hare, *Freedom and Reason* (New York: Oxford University Press, 1963), 73.

ral law, that is, whereas right is in principle eternal, authority is the temporal application of right by *an* authority conscious of both the general principles of natural law and the particular circumstances of an historical society.[6] Legal positivists, on the other hand, regard the natural law position as little more than an illusion, not required by the cogent operation of any system of positive law.[7]

It would seem that this position of legal positivism is the one that Jewish theologians would adopt in their essential characterization of *Halakhah*. For one can easily translate the positivist position into the following proposition:

> *Halakhah is a body of norms, given for application among the Jewish people (and whomever they control), promulgated by God and subsequently by the rabbis authorized by God in the revealed sources: the Written Torah and the Oral Torah.*[8]

It would seem that the adoption of a natural law position would require the authority of God's will as the prime authority of the halakhic system to be subordinated to a higher order of right. This seems to go against the transcendent theocentricity of Judaism so directly and, hence, it is not difficult to see why many Jewish theologians have willingly included themselves in the positivist school and have rejected the claim that *Halakhah* can be essentially characterized using natural law theory.

In this paper, I propose that natural law theory is necessary for an adequate essential characterization of *Halakhah*. I will specifically argue against the claims of two contemporary Jewish theologians, Marvin Fox and José Faur, who have rejected natural law theory in their discussions of the character of *Halakhah*. In developing my proposal, I will present the idea of covenant as one which correlates natural law and positive aspects of *Halakhah* in such a way as to avoid the attempt of positivists to deny natural law claims altogether, and the attempt of some natural law theorists to assume that an acceptance of natural law necessarily requires that all positive laws, in our case the *mitsvot*, be subordinated to it.

6   See Aquinas, *op. cit.*, q.91, a.3.
7   See Kelsen, *op. cit.*, 217ff.
8   See M. Elon, *The Principles of Jewish Law* (Jerusalem: Keter, 1975), 10.

2. Marvin Fox: Law as Commandment

One of the most consistent advocates of legal positivism in contemporary Jewish thought is the American Orthodox theologian, Professor Marvin Fox. In several papers devoted to the legal philosophy of Maimonides, he has argued against other Jewish thinkers (one gets the impression that he is arguing against Jewish neo-Kantians who follow Hermann Cohen) who have maintained that Maimonides is a natural law theorist. In presenting what he considers Maimonides' true position, Fox has generalized that Judaism itself is antithetical to any natural law position. "In Judaism there is no natural law doctrine, and, in principle there cannot be ... "[9] Commenting on the famous passage on *Yoma* 67b that if the laws prohibiting idolatry, sexual immorality, murder, robbery and blasphemy had not been written in the Torah "reason would have required that they be written *(din hu sheyikatevu)*," Fox writes, "what is asserted is only that, having been commanded to avoid these prohibited acts, we can now see after the fact, that these prohibitions are useful and desirable."[10] He goes on to say, "Seen this way, we can say of them that though they are not rational, in the sense of being demonstrable, they are reasonable in the sense that we can give good reasons for them."[11] Finally, he notes, "Just as the commandments are reasonable without being rationally demonstrable, so are they in accord with man's nature without being

9   "Maimonides and Aquinas on Natural Law", *Diné Israel* 3 (1972), v. Also, see Fox's prolegomenon to A. Cohen, *The Teachings of Maimonides* (New York: KTAV, 1968), xii-xlii, and his "On the Rational Commandments in Saadia's Philosophy: A Reexamination" in *Modern Jewish Ethics*, ed. M. Fox (Columbus, OH: Ohio State University Press, 1975), 174ff. For a critique of Fox re Maimonides, see D. Hartman, *Maimonides: Torah and Philosophic Quest* (Philadelphia: Jewish Publication Society of America, 1976), 260-261 n. 38. For another Orthodox rejection of natural law in Judaism, see Y. Leibowitz, *Yahadut, Am Yehudi Umedinat Yisra'el* (Jerusalem: Schocken, 1976), 26-27.

10   Fox, *op. cit.*, viii. See the parallel to *Yom.* 67b in *Sifra, a hare-Mot*, ed. Weiss, 86a. For a view similar to Fox's, see E. E. Urbach, *Hazal : Emunot Vede'ot* (Jerusalem: Magnes Press, 1971), 283ff.

11   *Ibid.*, xxvi.

natural."[12]

Elsewhere I have criticized the positivist interpretation of Maimonides advocated by Fox and others.[13] It would take us too far afield to repeat those criticisms here. Let me, therefore, confine myself to Fox's rejection of a natural law position within Judaism *per se.* I would suggest that Fox's position is untenable on three grounds: (1) the theological sources he ignores; (2) the classical sources he interprets; (3) the philosophical questions he does not discuss.

In denying a place for a natural law theory in Judaism, Fox has ignored evidence to the contrary in Saadyah, R. Judah Halevi, Nahmanides and R. Joseph Albo.[14] Even Maimonides, whom Fox goes to such great length to show rejected natural law theory in the area of morality, nevertheless speaks of laws which "reason persuades" *(hekhr'e hada'at)* and to which "reason inclines" *(hada'at noṭeh),* even though he denies such prudential reasoning alone transcendent validity.[15] Now one certainly has the option of arguing against the position of the five theologians cited above (let alone the position of someone as unorthodox as Hermann Cohen).[16] However, unless one is prepared to eliminate their thought from Judaism, one cannot, therefore, say, "In Judaism there is no natural law doctrine."

In the much quoted rabbinic source Fox explicates, one could well contend that what is rational before the fact can indeed be logically separated from what is only perceived as useful and desirable after the fact. One could say, taking an example of what the rabbis clearly considered a nonrational commandment, that having been commanded to refrain from eating pork, I can subsequently consider this act to be "useful" (it reduced the amount of saturated fat in my

---

12 *Ibid.,* xxvii.

13 *The Image of the Non-Jew in Judaism: An Historical and Constructive Study of the Noahide Laws* (New York and Toronto: The Edwin Mellen Press, 1983), chap. 10.

14 See Saadyah, *Emunot Vede'ot,* 9.2; *Halevi, Kuzari,* 1.48; Nahmanides, *Torah Commentary* on Gen. 6:2, 34:13; *Deut.* 6:20; Albo, *Iḳarim,* 1.5.

15 See Maimonides, *Mishneh Torah: Melakhim,* 8, end and 9, beg.; also, *Yesode Hatorah,* 5.7; *Gezelah,* 4.16; *Shemonah Peraḳim,* chap. 6 and *Commentary on the Mishnah, Peah,* beg.

16 See, e.g., *Religion of Reason Out of the Sources of Judaism,* trans. S. Kaplan (New York: Frederick Ungar, 1972), 123ff.

diet, thus lessening the build-up of cholesterol in my blood vessels)[17] and "desirable" (it helps me curb my gluttony).[18] These subsequent explanations are not rational in the sense that I could not have invented the exact prohibition by being aware of its "uses" and "benefits" before my actual obedience of the commandment, "and the pig ... from its flesh you shall not eat" (*Lev.* 11:7-8). However, this is the case because the needs fulfilled by ordinary eating do not lead one directly to the conclusion that eating pork will contradict them. Refraining from pork, then, introduces one to a leval of cultural experience that is not universal. Thus the meaning of this experience can only be inferred *ex post facto*, that is, after the commandment has already been fulfilled. Nevertheless, this type of explanation will not suffice when dealing with the first category of commandments with which the celebrated rabbinic source deals. First of all, they are all prohibitions dealing with what the rabbis considered ordinary, universal experience. Let us take the most indisputable of these prohibitions, the prohibition of murder (*shefikhut damim*). Does not our experience of society and our need for it indicate to us *in advance* of any promulgated prohibition that murder is the most fundamentally antisocial act, that the permission of murder will destroy ordinary social intercourse? In other words, this commandment does not introduce us to a new experience whose meaning is only subsequently inferred; rather, it itself is inferred from an experience the rabbis considered to be universal. Thus Maimonides, Fox's prime example of an antinatural law Jewish theologian, writes about the prohibition of murder, "Even though there are transgressions more serious than murder, none of them involves the destruction of society (*yishuvo shel olam*) as does murder."[19] The difference, then, between these two types of commandments, which the rabbis so clearly separated, is that in the nonrational commandments the phenomenological sequence is: (1) the commandment, (2) the experience, (3) the inference of secondary meaning. In the rational commandments, on the other hand, the phenomenological sequence is: (1)

---

17 See Maimonides, *Moreh Nevukhim*, 3.48; *Mishneh Torah: De'ot*, 3.3 re *Ab.* 2.2; *Ma'akhalot Aṣurot*, 17. 29-31. Cf. *Ṣifra, Ḳedoshim*, 93b and D. Novak, *Law and Theology in Judaism* II (New York: KTAV, 1976), 38ff.

18 Cf. Nahmanides, *Torah Commentary* on *Lev.* 19:2.

19 *Mishneh Torah: Retsiḥah*, 4.9. See *Taan.* 23a. Cf. Aristotle, *Nic. Eth.*, 1155a1ff.; *Pol.*, 1263a1ff.

the experience, (2) the inference of primary meaning, (3) the commandment, whose reason is the continued duration of that which the experience showed to be good. In our example of the prohibition of murder the phenomenological sequence is as follows: (1) the experience of human society; (2) the inference from this experience that human society is a good that is required for satisfactory human life; (3) that acts which will counteract this good and prevent its duration in any situation are wrong and thus not to be done. The fact that a prohibition like that of murder is also a Divine commandment indicates that it has covenantal meaning *over and above* its ordinary human meaning.[20] The nonrational commandments, on the other hand, only have covenantal meaning, at least for us in this world.

It is clear, then, that explanations after the fact only apply to nonrational commandments. To give an explanation after the fact when dealing with a rational commandment such as the prohibition of murder, when there is perfectly obvious reason/primary meaning for it, is to give a *rationalisation*. A rationalisation is the substitution of a secondary meaning/effect when a primary meaning/clause is available.[21] This is theoretically intolerable because it is a distortion of what we know to be true. In the case of the nonrational commandments, on the other hand, such as the prohibition of eating pork, we admit that the primary meaning/reason/cause is unknown to us. Hence any secondary meaning we infer subsequent to our acceptance and observance of the prohibition is clearly only secondary and does not in any way masquerade as the primary meaning. Thus Fox's attempt to see the category of commandments universally practiced as only having meaning after the fact is untenable precisely because it ignores the clear distinction between the two types of commandments made by the rabbis. Because some of the commandments only have secondary meanings known to us does not necessitate our looking at all the other commandments this way. By making a serious confusion between "reasons" for these other commandments and "rationalisations" for them, he has misinterpreted the famous rabbinic passage whose main point is that at least some of the commandments have reasons clearly evident even *before* the actual promulgation of the law. By not recognizing this distinction, I think,

---

20 See E. Fackenheim, *Quest for Past and Future* (Bloomington, IN: Indiana University Press, 1968), 208ff.
21 See Plato, *Euth.*, 10A-E.

Fox has seriously underestimated this aspect of the *ṭa'ame hamitsvot* tradition in Judaism.

Fox's characterisation of *Halakhah* as only positive law does not answer two basic philosophical questions: (1) Why did God command the people of Israel?; (2) why did the people of Israel accept God's commandments? Now the first question can be considered unanswerable in the sense of "My thoughts are not your thoughts" (*Is.* 55:8), although the Kabbalists, especially, devoted considerable effort to formulating an answer to it.[22] Nevertheless, this question is more one for metaphysics than philosophy of law. Therefore, let us deal with the second question. It is especially pertinent in our day when the majority of the Jewish people do not seem to consider themselves obligated by Divine commandments.

It would seem that there are three possible answers as to why the people of Israel accepted God's commandments: (1) fear of immediate consequences, (2) total caprice, (3) faith in Divine goodness and wisdom. These three alternatives are treated in several important aggadic sources. Indeed such questions cannot be the subject of halakhic answers since they deal with the presuppositions of the whole halakhic system itself.

Concerning acceptance of the Torah because of fear of immediate consequences we read the following,

> 'And they stood at the foot (*b et aḥtit*) of the mountain' (*Ex.* 19:17). R. Avdimi bar Hama bar Hasa said that this teaches us that the Holy-One-blessed-be-He turned the mountain over them like a tank and said to them that if you accept the Torah, it is well and good (*mutav*); if not, this will be your grave. R. Aha bar Jacob said that this is a great protest (*moda'a raba*) against the Torah.[23]

According to Rashi this means that such acceptance of the Torah out of fear of immediate death implies compulsion (*sheḳ ibluha b'oneṣ*).[24] Rabbenu Tam says that such Divine compulsion implies lack of sufficient human response (*keb'al korḥ am*). [25] Both commentators, no doubt, had in mind the halakhic rule that "one is

---

22 See Gershom Scholem, *Kabbalah and Its Symbolism*, trans. R. Manheim (New York: Schocken, 1969), 115-117.
23 *Shab.* 88a. See *Pes.* 68b re *Jer.* 33:25 and *A.Zar.* 3a re *Gen.* 1:31.
24 S.v. "*moda'a raba.*"
25 S.v. "*moda'a raba*". See also, *Yeb.* 48a, *Tos.*, s.v. "*ela*" (end).

not liable for acts done under compulsion" (ones̩ Raḥamana patrayh). [26] Indeed the term moda'a ("protest") is a halakhic term used to denote the nullification of a legal agreement because of coercion.[27]

Concerning acceptance of the Torah capriciously, the continuation of the Talmudic discussion above notes that a certain non-believer accused the Jews of being an impetuous people (ama peziza) because they accepted the Torah without first inquiring about its contents and judging whether or not to accept them.[28] The Amora, Rava, answered him that this is a sign of Jewish perfection. About this Rashi notes, "according to the way of love (me'ahavah) we relied on Him that He would not burden us with anything we could not stand."[29] This answer states that there is a fundamental difference between a capricious and a loving response.

A loving response to God's revelation provides an adequate reason for the acceptance of the Torah by the people of Israel. This is brought out by the following midrash.

> 'I am the Lord your God who brought you out of the land of Egypt ... ' (Ex. 20:2) ... So did the All-Present-One (Hama k̄om) bring Israel out of Egypt, split the sea for them ... He said to them, 'may I rule over you?' They said, 'yes, yes.'[30]

Later this same midrashic text continues,

> He said to them, 'Am I He whose kingship you accepted yourself in Egypt?' They said to Him, 'yes'. 'As you have accepted My kingship upon yourself so also accept My decrees (gezerotay).'[31]

In the Talmudic text we examined earlier, the same Amora, Rava, who answered the non-believer's accusation of Jewish impetuousness with the retort that the Jewish response to revelation was one of love, answered that in the days of Ahashuerus the Jews willingly

---

26   B.K. 28b re Deut. 22:26.

27   See B.B. 39b-40a and Rashbam, s.v. "vekhen" and Tos., s.v. "meha'ah."

28   The Talmudic text interprets Ex. 24:7 to mean that they agreed to do the commandments before understanding their specific meanings.

29   Shab. 88b, s.v. "desaginan".

30   Mekhilta, Yitro, ed. Horovitz-Rabin, 219.

31   Ibid., 222. See M.Ber. 2.2.

upheld what had been forced upon them at Sinai.[32] As Rabbenu Tam interpreted this answer, "they accepted willingly *(meda'atam)* because of the love of the miracle," namely, the deliverance from the extermination plot of Haman recorded in the book of *Esther.* [33]

It is the understanding of this reason for Jewish acceptance of the Torah, a motif having considerable development in the *Aggadah* and later theological writing, that enables one to see how the inclusion of a natural law position into Jewish reflection on the giving and the acceptance of the Torah is so helpful for our insight. The point underlying this whole discussion is that the Jews experienced God as good and thus judged it right to respond to His commandments. Before they responded to His specific commandments they responded to His presence in Egypt. In accepting God's offer of liberation, they judged freedom to be good and, therefore, rejected Pharoah's enslavement of them as wrong.[34] In other words, their response to God's presence presupposed that they had general criteria of good and evil thus judging what acts were right and what acts were wrong. This is what made their response rational and not capricious. Their response to God's presence involved their admission that God's knowledge of their needs was greater than Pharoah's and even greater than their own, and they were willing to accept the commandments of such a loving and knowing God even before understanding their meaning in specific detail. "And God saw the Israelites and God knew" *(Ex. 2:25).*

Finally, the famous *aggadah* which describes God's offering the Torah to all the nations of the world, and its acceptance by Israel alone, implies prior standards of right and wrong which enable the Jewish people to accept the Torah rationally. The interesting thing about this *aggadah,* in all its versions, is that the nations of the world reject the Torah because they cannot accept the prohibitions of

---

32 *Shab.* 88a re *Est.* 9:27. Re rabbinic debate over whether or not future generations, who accepted the Torah voluntarily, were not more meritorious than the "generation of the wilderness", upon whom it was forced, see *M.Sanh.* 10:3, *T.Sanh.* 13:10-11; *Y.Sanh.* 10:4 (29c); *Sanh.* 110b re *Ps.* 50:5; also, *Y.Sheb.* 6:1 (36a) re *Neh.* 10:1. Cf. *A.Zar.* 3a and parallels.

33 *Tos.,* s.v. *"moda'a raba."*

34 Later on some of them had a change of heart. See *Num.* 11:4-5. For the notion that they were rejecting moral responsibility here, see *Yom.* 75a and *Rashi,* s.v. *"hanakh".*

murder, sexual immorality and robbery.[35] Why are they not told about the Sabbath or the dietary and clothing restrictions, which are themselves unique to the Mosaic Torah? The *aggadah* answers that these are some of the Noahide laws incumbent upon all humanity, laws which the nations of the world have already thrown off.[36] If, then, they cannot uphold these seven laws, how can they uphold the 613 commandments of the Mosaic Torah? Now it should be recalled that these three prohibitions are most of the about which the Talmudic text from *Yoma* 67b, brought by Fox, stated "had they not been written, reason would have required that they be written." Therefore, one can see how the rabbis regarded these prohibitions as the necessary rational preconditions required for the acceptance of the Torah. The point made by Fox and other Jewish positivists is that all standards of right and wrong are subsequent to the promulgation of the specific commandments of the Torah. These aggadic passages which we have been examining seem to assume otherwise.

3. José Faur: Covenantal Law

The contemporary Sephardi theologian, Professor José Faur,[37]

---

35 *Şifre, Vezot Haberakhah*, no. 343, ed. Finkelstein, 395-397 and *A.Zar.* 2b re *Deut.* 33:2.

36 See *T.A.Zar.* 8:4 and *Sanh.* 56a-b. The entire topic is presented in Novak, *The Image of the Non-Jew in Judaism*.

37 "Understanding the Covenant", *Tradition* 9:4 (Spring, 1968), 41. Faur also writes, "It is pertinent to add that the term and notion 'nature' are absent in the entire Biblical and rabbinical literature, and they are introduced into Jewish thought and vocabulary in the Arabic period" (*ibid.*). Leo Strauss also noted (for opposite reasons, I believe) that "the Old Testament, whose basic premise may be said to be the implicit rejection of philosophy, does not know 'nature'; the Hebrew term for 'nature' is unknown in the Hebrew Bible. It goes without saying that 'heaven and earth', for example, is not the same thing as 'nature'" (*Natural Right and History*, 81). Nevertheless, both Faur and Strauss fail to take into serious consideration the Biblical notion of *created order* (see, e.g., *Jer.* 8:7; *Amos* 3:3ff.; *Job* 28:23-28 and 38:1ff.). For the rabbiss, this notion of created order was expressed in such terms as *nivra ha'olam* and *beriyato shel olam* (*M.Gitt.* 4.4; *Yeb.* 61b). Although this order is the form of being, personal relationship with God is the substance of being, that for which this formal structure is the background not the ground, as

like Fox rejects the notion of natural law as "totally foreign to Jewish thought." However, unlike Fox he does see a necessary precondition for the acceptance of the commandments of the Torah. This precondition is the covenant, which Faur contrasts with the classical philosophical idea of nature, as the foundation of law.

> The effect of this conception of religion is the establishment of a bilateral pact, a *berit*, between God and man which both parties freely agree to maintain a relationship between themselves. Thus conceived, religion for Judaism is a relationship between God and man, the sole ground of which is the free and mutual election of God and man.[38]

In dealing with Faur's theory I propose three questions: (1) Are covenant and natural law in truth mutually exclusive ideas?; (2) Is the *berit* in truth a "bilateral pact"?; (3) Is man's choice of God the same as God's choice of man?

I would certainly agree with Faur that the authority of the Torah's law *(Halakhah)* should be understood covenantally. Nevertheless, natural law need only be excluded from one's understanding of the covenant if he accepts the definition of natural law proposed by Cicero (which both Faur and Fox seem to assume is the only definition of natural law ever proposed), a definition consistent with Stoic philosophy and having its roots in Plato.[39] In this

---

it is for Platonic-Stoic metaphysics. For Faur's sustained critique of Jewish natural theory, see his *Iyunim Bemishneh Torah Leharambam: Sefer Hamada* (Jerusalem: Mosad Harav Kook, 1978), 61ff. Cf my late revered teacher, Boaz Cohen, *Jewish and Roman Law* I (New York: Jewish Theological Seminary of America, 1966), 28 n. 97; also, Moshe Silberg, *Ba'in K'ehad* (Jerusalem: Magnes Press, 1981), 166.

38 "Understanding the Covenant", 42. See Otto Gierke, *Natural Law and the Theory of Society*, Trans. E. Barker (Boston: Beacon Press, 1957), 108-109; also, S. Federbush, *Mishpat Hamelukhah Beyisra'el*, 2nd. rev. ed.(Jerusalem: Mosad Harav Kook, 1973), 33.

39 Thus Cicero writes, "Therefore, since there is nothing better than reason, and since it exists both in man and God, the first common possession of man and God is reason *(prima homini cum deo rationis societas)*. But those who have reason in common must also have right reason in common. And since right reason is Law, we must believe that men have Law in common with the gods ... Hence we must now conceive of this whole universe as one commonwealth *(una civitas communis)* of which both gods and men are members" - *De Legibus*, 3.23, trans. C.W. Keynes

definition of natural law, both God and man are included in a whole called *nature*, a whole which subsumes them and governs them. However, if one adopts a more modest and limited definition of natural law, understanding it as the body of elementary norms without which a society of interpersonal communion would not be possible, then he can see these norms being presupposed by the covenant as the supreme example of such interpersonal communion. Thus the twentieth century Italian, neo-Kantian, philosopher of law, Giorgio Del Vecchio, wrote,

> Moreover, even when we distinguish ... the various types of equality, there remains always the consideration that they have nothing to do with justice except in so far as they refer to subjects or persons; an equality or proportion of things ... is not, properly speaking, either just or unjust. Only by beginning with the value of the person, and considering in some way its identity in different individuals, can one arrive at the basis of the concept of justice, which ... is essentially a coordination and inter-subjective relation.[40]

Del Vecchio clearly and persuasively puts forth a theory of natural law which does not subsume the norms of interpersonal relationship under some prior cosmic whole. Rather, he presents these norms as formal requirements of any genuine field of interpersonal relationships. In this formalism he is indebted to Kant. I think by seeing the relevance of this formalism for our understanding of the covenant, we can successfully avoid the type of natural law theory that Faur rightly sees as being incompatible with the covenant.

In Kantian formalism, the data of experience, its "matter", manifest themselves particularly. The structure of experience, its

---

(Cambridge, MA: Harvard University Press, Loeb Classical Library, 1928), 320-323. For Plato's notion that the gods are subject to higher law/forms, see *Tim.*, 29A-C; also D. Novak, *Suicide and Morality* (New York: Scholars Studies Press, 1975), 33-35. Cf. Aristotle, *Meta.*, 1015a15.

40 *Justice: An Historical and Philosophical Essay*, trans. Lady Guthrie (Edinburgh: University of Edinburgh Press, 1952), 87 n.3 See Aristotle, *Pol.*, 1282b5ff. Even such a supposed legal positivist as H.L.A. Hart acknowledges a certain minimal natural law, in content not too different from what I am advocating here in a theological context. See *The Concept of Law* (New York: Oxford University Press, 1961), 188-189; also D. Novak, *The Image of the Non-Jew in Judaism*, 345-346.

"form", manifests itself conceptually, that is, as general categories.[41] However, because conceptual form structures perceptual matter, this does not mean that form has any substantial priority over matter. It is simply an intellectual precondition for matter's intelligibility; it is only a *conditio sine qua non* not a *conditio per quam*. This is why Kant (as opposed to many later idealists) insisted on positing the *Ding an sich*, that is, that the particularities which experience intends themselves ontologically transcend our general categories of understanding.[42] What neo-Kantians like Del Vecchio have done is to apply Kant's formalism to the area of our social experience and its law, whereas Kant himself seemed to have limited his theory of experience to experience of sense data. (In his moral theory autonomous man qua *homo noumenon* seems to create his own social experience).[43] In other words, the Kantian formalism of someone like Del Vecchio saves the social meaning of natural law theory from being reduced to Platonic-Stoic metaphysics, which is so incompatible with the Jewish ideas of creation and covenant. Faur, it would seem, has too quickly eliminated natural law theory from covenantal theology.

Indeed, it would seem that Faur's covenantal theology requires natural law theory even more evidently than Fox's positivism. For Faur is basically taking the philosophical idea of the social contract and placing it in a theological context. Now historically speaking, social contract theorists have themselves been proponents of natural law theory, some in a wider and some in a narrower sense, in that all of them posit some "state of nature" as the background of the social contract. One can see this in the theories of Hobbes, Locke, Rousseau, and most recently, John Rawls (whose theory is admittedly indebted to Kantian formalism).[44] Furthermore, two perennial philosophical questions must be dealt with in any cogent social contract theory: (1) why do the parties choose to enter the social contract?; (2) what enables the contract to endure?

---

41 *Kritik der reinen Vernunft*, B34.

42 *Ibid.*, B164, A249.

43 *Ibid.*, B575ff.

44 See C.J. Friedrich, *The Philosophy of Law in Historical Perspective*, 2nd rev. ed. (Chicago: University of Chicago Press, 1963), 88-91, 101-103, 127. For Rawls' Kantianism, see his *A Theory of Justice* (Cambridge, MA: Harvard University Press, 1971), 179ff., 251-257.

In the context of the covenant the first question breaks up into two subquestions: (1a) why does God choose to covenant with man?; (1b) why does man choose to covenant with God? As we saw before, the first subquestion might well be unanswerable (see *Deut.* 7:7-9), although the Kabbalists did speculate about it. The second subquestion, however, must be answered because if it is not, then the ancient charge of Jewish capriciousness in accepting the covenant is true. If this is the case, then how can people who stood at Sinai be considered to be bound by a totally irrational, blind choice - much less their descendants? Rational choice presupposes intelligent judgment *(nihil volitum nisi praecognitum)*. Therefore, it seems to me that the best reason for the choice of the Jewish people to covenant with God, as we saw before, was their judgment that God's knowledge of their needs and His concern for them was sufficient reason for them to choose to accept His authority, to accept His decrees as continually binding laws. For the keeping of these laws themselves is man's active participation in this same Divine concern first manifest in Egypt. "And it will be right *(tsedaḳah)* for us when we observe and do all this commandment before the Lord our God as He has commanded us" *(Deut.* 6:25).[45] In order for the people to know that God's commandments are right for them they obviously have to possess some knowledge of what is right in general. This precondition is simply unavoidable.

The second question, namely, what enables the contract to endure, also involves natural law theory. For a contract presupposes the norm that promises are to be kept *(pacta sunt servanda)*. Without this presupposition, a contract would have no duration and would be, therefore, meaningless. This natural law precondition seems to be an integral part of the covenantal theory in Scripture. Israel is frequently accused by the prophets of being unfaithful to the covenant, that is, of not keeping their word. "Instead you have broken faith *(begadatem)* with Me, as a woman breaks faith with a paramour, O' house of Israel ..." *(Jer.* 3:20). And this unfaithfulness is the same as breaking a covenant between two persons. "Thus says the Lord, for three sins of Tyre, for four I will not forgive ... for they did not remember the covenant *(berit)* of brothers" *(Amos* 1:9). If the

---

45 For *tseda ḳah* as "right" rather than "merit", see *Gen.* 18:19 and *Yom.* 38b; also, *Gen.* 15:6 and Nahmanides thereon (contra LXX; *I Macc.* 2:52; *Targumim* and *Rom.* 4:3).

covenant is the foundation of the Law, as Faur rightly maintains, then covenantal faithfulness cannot be commanded by the Law inasmuch as it is already presupposed by the Law itself.[46]

Before we can analyze the covenant as that which cogently correlates natural law and positive aspects of *Halakhah*, I must seriously question Faur's definition of the covenant between God and Israel as a "bilateral pact". It is bilateral in the sense that both God and Israel are bound by it. However, it is not bilateral in terms of its initiation or its enduring authority. In a bilateral pact, a social contract, both parties enter the agreement as legal equals. The contract is initiated for mutually agreed upon goals and the requirements of the contract are based on *their* mutual authority. In the *berit*, on the other hand, God initiates the covenant as Sovereign, the goals of the covenant are set down by God, and the authority of the covenantal requirements is the will of God.[47] This does not mean that men cannot freely accept or reject the covenant. The covenant and its commandments make no sense without this presupposition, as Maimonides most persuasively argued.[48] In constituting what is involved in this freedom to accept or reject the covenant and its norms, we have seen natural law theory cannot be avoided. However, there is an essential difference between freedom of response and freedom of initiation. This is a crucial point overlooked by Faur.

46 For the notion that the Torah itself presupposes obligation, see, e.g., *Kidd.* 13b and *Rashi*, s.v. *"delav"* and *Tos.*, s.v, *"malveh"*. In the same logical sense, belief in the existence of God cannot be commanded by Divine law because such a belief is itself presupposed by the acceptance of that very law. See D. Novak, *Law and Theology in Judaism* I (New York: KTAV, 1974), 138ff.

47 Thus, the Hebrew word *berit* is rendered by LXX (e.g. *Ex.* 24:7) *diatheke* in the sense of the Latin *testamentum* rather than *syntheke* in the sense of the Latin *pactio*. See Arndt and Gingrich, *A Greek-English Lexicon of the New Testament* (Chicago: University of Chicago Press, 1957), 182. This is also the sense of *diatheke* in rabbinic nomenclature. See, e.g., M.B.B. 8:6; *Bamidbar Rabbah* 2:7; *Y.Sanh.* 2:6 (20c). See, also, Philo, *De Mut.*, 5.52-53; my late revered teacher, Abraham J. Heschel, *The Prophets* (Philadelphia: Jewish Publication Society of America, 1962), 229-230; Novak, *Law and Theology in Judaism* II, 18ff.

48 *Mishneh Torah: Teshuvah*, 5.1-4. For the difference between freedom of choice (*liberum arbitrio*) and freedom of will (*Willensfreiheit*), see Hannah Arendt, *The Life of the Mind: Willing* (New York: Harcourt, Bruce and Jovanovich, 1978), 28-29.

This leads us into our last question about Faur's position, namely, is human choice of God the same as God's choice of man? It would seem, viewed from the Scriptural and rabbinic sources of Jewish theology, that God's choice is fundamentally different from man's choice. Covenantal theory must be seen in the context of creation theory. Creation theory always emphasizes the absolute freedom of God. There are no causes for his creative acts and, therefore, there is no necessity for them. "For He spoke and it came to be" (Ps. 33.9). Just as nothing required that God create the world, nothing required that He covenant with Israel. His was always the option not to initiate the covenant. "To Me O' Israelites you are just like the Ethiopians" (Amos 9:7). Thus from God's perspective the covenant is like a contract in that *a party cannot be bound unless he chooses to be bound by binding himself.* [49] However, man's choice seems to be much more limited in that it is only his freedom to respond or not. The obligation for man already exists; man in no way creates it or even co-creates it. It is this point that makes the *berit* for man unlike a contract. In a contract, one in essence obligates himself in general *beforehand,* and then participates in the creation of mutual obligations with the contractual partner *thereafter.* In the *berit,* on the other hand, man is called by God to respond to a relationship which God has already initiated and structured.[50] In a contract, written or tacit, there is always the assumption that the agreement is initiated in mutual freedom and maintained in mutual freedom. Thus it is always assumed that the contractual partners have other good options both before the initiation of the contract and after its expiration.[51] In the *berit,* these free options are only God's; for man the

---

49 Re God's binding Himself to covenantal norms, not just the enforcement of covenantal sanctions, see Y.R.H. 1:3 /57a-b re *Lev.* 22.9; *Ber.* 6a re *I Chron.* 17-21.

50 Re the Biblical *berit* see D.R. Hillers, *Covenant: The History of a Biblical Idea* (Baltimore: John Hopkins University Press, 1969), 49.

51 Thus Socrates, who conceives of man's relation to an historical community as founded on tacit agreement (*homologia*) and contract (*syntheke*), presents the policy of Athens declaring to him, "anyone who is not pleased with us may take his property and go wherever he pleases. And none of us prevents or prohibits any of you to take his property and go away whenever he wants ..." (*Crito*, 51D). This rejection of a real possibility to do otherwise with impunity rather than remain an Athenian citizen convinces Socrates that he is morally bound to obey the laws of Athens (52D-E). See Strauss, *Natural Right and History,*

covenant is co-temporous with his life. He can accept it or reject it, but he cannot escape it because the covenant is the most immediately normative aspect of God's everlasting presence. "The corrupt one (*naval*) says in his heart "there is no God' (*ayn Elohim*) ... God looks down from heaven on all mankind ..." (*Ps.* 54:2-3). "Where can I go away from Your spirit, and where can I flee from Your presence?" (*Ps.* 139:7). Even God, although having the absolute freedom to initiate the covenant or not, seems to have bound Himself to it forever." ... This is My covenant with them, says the Lord ... from this time forth and forever" (*Is.* 59:21). Israel has no identity outside the covenant. "If these statutes pass away from before Me, says the Lord, so also will the seed of Israel cease to be a nation before Me all the days" (*Jer.* 31:35).

In this sense, then, the covenant is like natural law in that it is unavoidable. In other words, just as the fact of human sociality makes such norms as the prohibition of murder unavoidable, so does the fact of the covenant make such norms as the prohibition of idolatry unavoidable. Without this inescapable element, an element due to God's everlasting presence, the covenantal obligation could not be understood to be valid transgenerationally. Hence, if for argument's sake we accept Faur's definition of the *berit* as a contract, then why are the descendants of the Israelites who stood at Sinai and on the plains of Moab morally bound by a covenant accepted by their ancestors? It seems to be a rational norm, one certainly expressed in the *Halakhah*, that personal obligation involves consent (*ayn havin l'adam shelo bifanav*). [52] Faur states that "the nation of Israel of the future participates in the pact by their solidarity with

---

119. The *berit*, on the other hand, does not allow any such "checkout" clause.

52 See R. Isaac Abrabanel, *Commentary on the Torah, Nitsavim*, no. 1 re *M.Erub.* 7.11; *Ket.* 11a. Abrabanel argues that the acceptance of the covenant by ancestors bound their descendants into perpetual slavery (*medin ha'avdut*). Aside from the irrelevance of this explanation today, when slavery is regarded as morally repugnant by *consensus gentium*, even children's involvement in parental obligation/responsibility is seen as contingent on their own choice. See, e.g., *Ber.* 7a re *Ex.* 20:5. For the noncontractual character of the *berit*, see R. Isaiah Halevi Horowitz, *Shene L uḥot Haberit*, ed. Amsterdam (1648), *Ma'amar* II:31b-32a.

Israel of Sinai-Moab."[53] That is well and good if the future Jews
themselves choose this solidarity. However, what if they do not?
(In an age of such widespread Jewish secularity this is more than just
an academic question.) Does that mean that they are not, therefore,
bound by the covenant? Although such people might very well believe just that and act accordingly, the *Halakhah* itself refuses to
accept this in that it rules that "even when he sins a Jew is still a
Jew."[54] This even applies to one who becomes an apostate *(mumar)*.
Thus the only way to explain why the covenant is binding on all
generations of Jews is because God never stops offering it to them.[55] It
is Divine offering, not human acceptance, that creates the obligation. This seems to be the meaning of the well-known rabbinic doctrine that all Jews were present at Sinai-Moab for the giving of the
Torah.[56] In this context human agreement is confirmation after the
fact. This seems to be especially appropriate for traditionalists to
emphasize in an age when they are clearly a minority in Jewry,
when the majority of Jews do not seem to regard themselves bound by
the covenant and its Law in any consistent way.

4. The Human Side of the Covenant

We have heretofore seen that the covenant presupposes natural
law and human freedom of choice, that is, human freedom to respond
or not respond to God's covenant, based on rational judgment. It does
not, however, presuppose human freedom of will, that is, the free-

53 "Understanding the Covenant", 42. For the notion of the original power
    of a community to perpetually bind individuals, even trans-
    generationally, see R. Solomon ibn Adret, *Responsa Rashba Attributed to
    Nahmanides* (Warsaw, 1883), nos. 280 and 285 (end).

54 See *Sanh.* 44a re *Josh.* 7:11; *T.Demai* 2:4; *Bekh.* 30b; *Tur, Yoreh De'ah*, 266
    (end) and Karo, *Bet Yosef* thereon. See, also, *Shab.* 87a and *Tos.* s.v.
    "*umah*"; *Yeb.* 62a and *Tos.* s.v. "*hatorah*"; cf. *Mekhilta, Bo*, 53 and *Zeb.*
    22b re *Ex.* 12:43.

55 See *Sheb.* 29a-b and *Tos.*, s.v. "*ki*"; *Hiddushe Haramban* thereon, ed.
    Lichtenstein (Jerusalem: Makhon Hatalmud Hayisraeli Hashalem,
    1976), 132-133; Maimonides, *Mishneh Torah: Shebuot*, 6:8-9. See further
    end notes.

56 *Tanhuma, Nitsavim*, end, ed. Buber, 25b and *Y. Ned.* 1:3 (37d) re *Deut.*
    29:14. See *Sifre, Vée hanan*, no. 33, p. 59 re *Deut.* 6:6; *Responsa Ribash*
    (Constantinople, 1507), no. 511.

dom to either initiate the covenant itself or to terminate it. Both those decisions are God's alone. Indeed both of these decisions are based on grace. "For the mountains will depart and the hills will be moved, but My kindness will not depart from you and My covenant of peace will not be moved, says the Lord who loves you" (*Is.* 54:10).

Nevertheless, the *Halakhah* and its development seem to manifest a role for human freedom over and above the choice to respond or not to what God has commanded In this sense, the covenant seems to call forth not only a human response but, moreover, human initiative. This greater human freedom within the covenant is best seen in the role assigned to human implementation of the covenant. The Torah states, "According to the instruction (*torah*) which they will instruct you and the judgment (*mishpat*) which they will say to you shall you act; you shall not depart (*lo tas̄ ur*) from the matter which they will declare to you ..." (*Deut.* 17:11). Now according to the *prima facie* meaning (*peshat*) of the text here, this verse is authorizing judicial application of the norms of the Written Torah by the duly constituted authorities of the Jewish people. Surely the Law itself requires judicial authority to be operative. However, this verse was used by the rabbis to justify rabbinic innovation, that is, the rabbinic creation of positive law.[57] The Law itself, strictly speaking, does not require any such innovations, and this was the ancient Sadducee position. Nevertheless, the covenant does require these innovations lest new areas of Jewish experience (for example, Ḥanukah as a response to the Hasmonean restoration of the Temple) be constituted outside its context and ultimately compete with it.[58] This freedom of innovation is broader than the freedom of choice presupposed by the covenant and its revealed law.

This power of human innovation entails the limitation of revelation to make room for this essentially human contribution to the covenant. Thus the rabbinic doctrine that although the Torah is "from Heaven" (*min hashamayim*) it is no longer "in Heaven" (*lo bashamayim hi*) performs this function of limitation.[59] The Written Torah as the repository of the direct Divine revelation is now limited to the five books of the Mosaic Torah to which no new norma-

---

57 *Ber.* 20b; *Shab.* 23a.
58 See Novak, *Law and Theology in Judaism* II, 129-132.
59 *M.Sanh.* 10:1, *B.M.* 59b re *Deut.* 30:12. See *Tem.* 16a.

tive revelation can be added.[60] Indeed, even the prophetic books and the hagiographa only function as either illustrations of the norms of the Mosaic Torah or as admonitions to be faithful to them. In themselves these latter two thirds of Scripture are not normative *(divray Torah medivray Kabalah la yalfinin)*. [61] Rabbinic law, although seen as being authorized by Scriptural law *(d'Oraita)* is, however, essentially different in that human beings now have the power of initiation of law and repeal of law. In rabbinic law, the humanly appointed authorities can make either positive enactments *(takanot)* or restrictions *(gezerot)*, and they have the power to repeal this legislation *(bitul)* - at least in principle.[62]

In considering the covenant in its aspect of Divine revelation, we saw how natural law and positive factors are correlated. The so-called nonrational commandments of the Torah are indeed *jus divinum positivum*. However, natural law conditions must be assumed or else human assent to this law will be nothing more than caprice, itself having no binding moral force. Furthermore, if the hallmark of natural law is that its norms are part of an intelligible order, then the assumption that the Divine positive law too has its reasons *(ta'ame hamitsvot)* is the point these two orders have in common.[63] Both are aspects of the Torah qua *lex aeterna*. Their point of specific difference is that the norms of natural law, because of their very generality, are easily known *(ratio quod nos)*, whereas the norms of *jus divinum positivum*, because of their greater specificity and because they seem to rely more immediately on the mysterious will of God, are assumed to be intelligible *(ratio per se)* even if that intelligibility is only partially perceived by us in this world.

In considering the covenant in its aspect of human institutions

---

60 The commandments, "you shall not add *(lo tosifu)* unto the word *(davar)* which I command you" *(Deut.* 4:2) was interpreted by the rabbis using *davar* in its specific rather than general sense (cf. *Isa.* 40:8), viz., new details cannot be introduced into commandments accepted as *d'oraita.* See *Sifre, Ve'ethanan*, no. 82, p.148. However, by freeing the general sense of *davar* from this restriction, rabbinic exegesis justified all the rabbinic additions to the corpus of the Law as a whole.

61 *B.K.* 2b See C. Tchernowitz, *Toldot Hahalakhah* I, 2nd rev. ed. (New York: Jubilee Committee, 1945), 19.

62 *M.Eduy.* 1:5; Maimonides, *Mishneh Torah: Mamrim*, 2:2-7.

63 See I. Heinemann, *Ta'ame Hamitsvot Besifrut Yisra'el I* (Jerusalem: Jewish Agency, 1959), 29; Novak, *Law and theology in Judaism* I, 136-138.

(derabanan) we can see how natural law and positive factors are again correlated. For the interpretation of the Divine law and, even more so, the legislation of the rabbis, requires natural law factors in order to be rationally convincing. Thus a number of important rabbinic institutions were justified on the basis of their being "for the benefit of society" *(mipnay tiḳun haolam).* [64] Here we see the natural law principle of the common good, namely that which enhances the life of the human community.[65] The covenantal element in this type of legislation is that the relationship with God is considered to be the highest human good. Therefore, the composition of liturgy is seen as a positive human contribution to the covenant[66] On the other hand, negatively speaking, any compromise with idolatry, even if in the interest of human good will, is to be rejected as countercovenantal.[67] Along these lines, the natural law principle that society is maintained to enhance inherent human dignity *(kevod haberiyot)* finds important applications in rabbinic interpretations of Scriptural law, and even more so, in independent rabbinic legislation.[68] Thus positive rabbinic law, precisely because it is humanly ordained, involves natural law factors in its very initiation. In Divinely revealed positive law natural law factors are only immediately present in the conditions for human response to the commandments of God. However, even here, we assume that the reasons for the Divine decrees are far better than those we see more readily in humanly instituted law precisely because of the greater wisdom of God. Indeed part of the messianic hope is that we will fully understand God's law so that it will immediately persuade us and require no external coercion. At this time we will fully and immediately understand the law of God in all its manifestations. "It will not be like the covenant which I made with their fathers on the day I forced them *(heḥ eziḳ i beyadam)* to leave Egypt ... For this is

---

64   *M.Gitt.* 4:2ff.

65   See Aristotle, *Nic. Eth.,* 1129b15; *Pol.,* 1252al; Thomas Aquinas, *Summa Theologiae,* II-I, q.90, a.2.

66   *Ber.* 28b-29a; Maimonides, *Mishneh Torah: Tefilah,* 2:1-1.

67   See *M.Gitt.* 5:8; *Y.Demai* 4:3 (24a); *Y.Gitt.* 5:9 (47c); *Y.A.Zar.* 1:3 (39c). Cf. *A.Zar.* 8a re *Ex.* 34:15.

68   See *Ber.* 19b; *Y.Kil.* 9:1 (32a). For the idea of *imago Dei* as a more sufficient ground for human dignity than either rationality or political freedom, see D. Novak, "Judaism and Contemporary Bio-Ethics", *The Journal of Medicine and Philosophy* 4:4 (Dec., 1979), 361-366.

the covenant which I will make with the house of Israel after these days, says the lord: I will place My Torah in their innermost parts and I will write it upon their hearts, I will be for them God and they will be for me a people " (Jer. 31:31-32).

Extended Notes

1   This discussion comes out as early as Plato's contraposition of the views of Thrasymachus and Socrates. Thus when Thrasymachus states, "the right (dikaion) for subjects (tois archomenois) is that which is to the rulers' advantage (ksympheron) and whoever deviates from it they call a lawbreaker and unjust" (Rep., 338E), Socrates asks, "Do you not hold that it is right to obey those in authority(mentoi tois archousi)?" (339C). In other words, Socrates argues that political authority can only function because those following it have judged it (however inadequately) to be right. (See Theat., 177D; Gorg., 483C). This distinction comes out in modern times in Leo Strauss' polemic against Hans Kelsen. Whereas Kelsen wrote, "Vollends sinnlos ist die Behauptung, dass in der Despoten herrsche ... stellt doch auch der despotisch regierte Staat irgendeine Ordnung menschlichen Verhalten dar ... Diese Ordnung ist eben die Rechtsordnung" (Algemeine Staatslehre, Berlin, 1925, 335, quoted in L. Strauss, Natural Right and History, Chicago: University Press, 1953, 4 n.2), Strauss wrote contrarily, "To reject natural right is tantamount to saying that all right is positive right, and this means that what is right is determined exclusively by the legislators and the courts of various countries. Now it is obviously meaningful, and sometimes even necessary, to speak of 'unjust' laws or 'unjust' decisions. In passing such judgments we imply that there is a standard of right and wrong independent of positive right and higher than positive right ..." (ibid., 2).

55   Many statements about the obligation to obey Divine law seem to imply that the acceptance of this law creates the obligation to obey it (see, e.g., Shab. 88a; A.Zar. 2b). However, we have seen that such is not the case. (Re the primordial character of the covenant, see Nidd. 30b and R. Hanokh Zundel, Ets Yosef thereon in Ayn Ya'aḳov; cf. Plato, Meno, 81Cff.) Perhaps such statements, that imply acceptance as a ground of the Law rather than a subjective condition

for its observance, can be illuminated by Maimonides' solution of the conflict between the law that a man can only divorce his wife of his own free choice (*M.Yeb.* 14:1) and the law enables the Jewish court and even its agents to force him to do so against his will in certain cases *M.Gitt.* 9:8; *M.Arak.* 5:6). Is such a case not acting under coercion (*me'ones*) ? Maimonides writes, "We do not say that one is coerced unless he is forced and pressured to do something for which he is not commanded by the Torah ... but he is overcome by passion (*shetaḳ fo yitsro hara*) ... his own bad character (*beda'ato haraah*) coerced him ... he really wants to do all the commandments and to separate himself from sin, but his passions overcame him" - *Mishneh Torah: Gerushin*, 2.10. In other words, we assume that if one were fully rational, he would have so internalized the Divine law *as if it were his own free will.* See *Ab.* 2:4; also, *Bamidbar Rabbah* 2.16 re *Ezek.* 20:32-33, *Kidd.* 50a.

THE COVENANT: THE TRANSCENDENT
THRUST IN JEWISH LAW

by

ELLIOT N. DORFF*

Jewish Law presents an intriguing set of issues for legal philosophers. In some respects it resembles secular legal systems very closely: it prescribes rules which range across the whole gamut of human concerns, and it uses familiar legal mechanisms to apply and change the law and to adjudicate disputes under it. On the other hand, there are elements within Jewish law which make it a distinctly religious legal system. These include its claims that God acts as its ultimate author, executor, and judge as well as more subtle religious influences on the scope of its content and the motivations for obeying it.[1]

To explain the secular and religious features of Jewish law, writers have invoked several models from non-Jewish legal theories. Professor Jackson has described them in his introductory essay to this symposium. There are philosophical and educational reasons for such analogies. Since Jewish law functions in large measure as other legal systems do, one would expect that a legal theory worth its salt would be applicable to Jewish law as well. If the theory is philosophically correct, the areas where it fails to fit Jewish law should be directly attributable to the special religious character of Jewish law. The attempt to apply a general legal theory to Jewish law is therefore potentially enlightening about both the legal theory and Jewish law: the application should test the validity of the legal theory on a somewhat unusual legal system, and it should reveal the extent to which Jewish law is indeed unusual as a legal system - and, perhaps, why. This philosophic goal coalesces with an educational one: a common

* Provost and Professor of Philosophy, University of Judaism; Lecturer, School of Law, University of California at Los Angeles and University of Southern California Law Center.

1 I have explored the ways in which Jewish law is both a legal system in the secular sense of the term and also a distinctly religious phenomenon in "Judaism as a Religious Legal System", *The Hastings Law Journal* 29 (1978), 1331-1360.

educational technique is to compare an unknown quantity with something known, and so explication of Jewish law through analogy with other legal systems is a natural method to gain better understanding of the nature and functioning of Jewish law.

In three previous articles[2] I have suggested that conceiving Jewish law as a covenant can help to illuminate its nature and operation. In those articles I did not address the underlying jurisprudential difficulties involved in using that concept, and Professor Jackson's criticism of it have challenged me to do so. I welcome this opportunity to take up that challenge because I remain convinced that the covenant analogy, while not perfect, is the best available: it is genuinely helpful in understanding the phenomena of Jewish law, and to the extent that it is misleading, it is not seriously so.

A. What the Covenant Theory Explains

Since any analogy must ultimately be evaluated in terms of its strengths and weaknesses as an explanation, it is important that we first delineate the reasons why anyone would be tempted to use the covenant analogy in the first place.

The most obvious rationale for its use is that the Jewish tradition itself describes Jewish law in covenantal terms. "Covenant" is not a word or concept that is imported from the outside to explain Jewish law: it comes from the very roots of the Jewish tradition. It is the original and natural language in which the tradition expressed and understood itself.

Self-perceptions may be mistaken, however, and so it is important to spell out the ways in which the covenantal terminology reports the facts about Jewish law. To do that we must first clarify what understanding of "covenant" we mean to apply to Jewish law, for even in the Bible the word "covenant" is used for a wide variety of relationships. When it denotes a bond among human beings, it sometimes describes ties of friendship, with no legal

2   Specifically, the essay listed in note 1; "The Meaning of Covenant: A Contemporary Understanding", in *Issues in the Jewish-Christian Dialogue: Jewish Perspectives on Covenant, Mission, and Witness*, ed. Helga Croner and Leon Klenicki (New York: Paulist Press, 1979), 38-61; and "The Covenant: How Jews Understand Themselves and Others", *Anglican Theological Review* 64:4 (1982), 481-501.

dimensions whatsoever (e.g., *I Sam.* 18:3, 20:8, 23:18), or the deeper bond of marriage (*Mal.* 2:14, *Prov.* 2:17). It is more commonly used, however, to designate a legal tie, and then, while it can refer to a contract between two individuals (e.g., *Gen.* 14:13, 21:22ff., 31:44ff.), it is used more often to describe a pact between nations (e.g., *Exod.* 23:32; 34:12,15; *Deut.* 7:2; *Josh.* 9:6,7, etc.; *I Sam.* 11:1; *I Kings* 5:26; *Ezek.* 17:13-19; *Ps.* 83:6). The political connotations of the term are also evident in its use as a constitution between a monarch and his subject (*II Sam.* 5:3 = *I Chron.* 11:3; *Jer.* 34:8-18), similar to ancient Near Eastern suzerainty treaties between kings and their vassals.[3] Such agreements are probably the model for the Biblical covenants that God contracts with Noah (*Gen.* 9:9-17, *Isa.* 54:10, *Jer.* 33:20,25), the Patriarchs (*Gen.* 15:18, 17:2-21, *Exod.* 2:24, 6:4,5, etc.), Joshua and the people (*Josh.* 24:25), David (*Ps.* 89:4, 29, 34, 39; 132:12; *Jer.* 33:21), Jehoiada and the people (*II Kings* 11:17 = *II Chron.* 23:3), Hezekiah and the people (*II Chron.* 29:10), Josiah and the people (*II Kings* 23:3), Ezra and the people (*Ezra* 10:3), and, especially, Moses and the people at Sinai (*Exod.* 19:5; 24:7,8; 34:10, 27, 28; etc.). In a number of these cases the "covenant" is not strictly a contract in the common law sense of the term since God only promises something without a clear specification of the consideration that He is to receive from human beings in compensation, but whatever is missing in one context is unambiguously supplied in others: God demands obedience for the protections and blessings that He will bestow, and failure to obey will result in punishment (e.g., *Lev.* 26; *Deut.* 28, 29). It is this

---

3   For examples of such documents, cf. James B. Pritchard, ed., *Ancient Near Eastern Texts Relating to the Old Testament* (Princeton: Princeton University Press, 1950), 159-161 (Lipit-Ishtar Lawcode) and at 163ff. (The Code of Hammurabi - cf. esp. the Prologue on pp. 164-5 and Epilogue on pp. 177-180). Good secondary reading on this includes D.J. McCarthy, *Old Testament Covenant: A Survey of Current Opinions* (Oxford: Basil Blackwell, 1973) and Delbert R. Hillers, *Covenant: The History of a Biblical Idea* (Baltimore: Johns Hopkins Press, 1969).

Moshe Weinfeld has noted ("Covenant", *Encyclopedia Judaica*, Vol. 5, p. 1021) that the idea of a covenant between a god and a people is unknown in other religions and cultures; it was a special feature of the religions of Israel. That makes sense when we remember that it was only the religion of Israel that demanded exclusive loyalty to its deity, and hence it was only in Israel that the covenant model was appropriate, for suzerainty covenants also demanded exclusive loyalty to the sovereign.

suzerainty treaty, or Covenant,[4] between God and the People of Israel at Sinai that is the foundation of Jewish law, and it is that Covenant on which we will concentrate in this study.

The Covenant theme pinpoints and clarifies at least these facts about the nature and practice of Jewish law:

1. *God as Legislator and Judge*

The Covenant is between God and the Jewish people and therefore it clearly expresses the Jewish belief in the divine authorship of Jewish law. Jewish philosophers interpret the process by which God commands Jewish law in a variety of ways,[5] but most are at pains to retain God's legislative role, even if they must explain it in untraditional ways. Jewish law must be construed as God-given not only because the Torah portrays it as such; as Professor Simon Greenberg has pointed out,[6] several phenomena of the ongoing practice of Jewish law can only be adequately understood if we presume divine authorship. The Jews' "sense of overwhelming awe when they contemplated the grandeur and majesty of the Law"[7] is certainly part of the religious feeling motivating those who observe it. Another element in the Jews' commitment to Jewish law is their conviction that through it they perform a cosmic role in helping God complete creation. The strength of these perceptions of God's role in creating Jewish law is especially evident in the numerous sacrifices which Jews have made to uphold it; only their belief that law expresses the will of God can explain their persistence. They also, of course, were motivated by their faith in divine reward for those who obey Jewish law and divine punishment

---

4   From here on I shall adopt the convention of using "Covenant" (with a capital "C") to denote God's Covenant with Israel at Sinai and a small letter "c" for all other covenants.

5   For a summary of the range of modern interpretations of God's legislative role, *cf.* my *Conservative Judaism: Our Ancestors to Our Descendants* (New York: United Synagogue Youth, 1977), Chapter 3, Section D.

6   Simon Greenberg, "A Revealed Law", *Conservative Judaism* 19 (1946), 36-50; reprinted in Seymour Siegel, ed., *Conservative Judaism and Jewish Law* [hereinafter cited as Siegel] (New York: Rabbinical Assembly, 1977), 175-194, and discussed in E. Dorff, "Judaism as a Religious Legal System", *supra* note 1, at 1348-1349.

7   *Ibid.*, at 41 (in Siegel, ed., at 182).

for those who disobey it. That tenet is so central to Judaism that the
Rabbis defined a heretic as one who claims that "there is no justice
and no Judge."[8] God is legislator, judge, and enforcer, and any
adequate philosophy of Jewish law must articulate that pivotal
doctrine clearly. The Covenant does just that: God announces His
Covenant amidst thunder and lightning at Sinai (*Exod.* 19-24), and
He will avenge breaches of the Covenant with vigor (*Lev.* 26, *Deut.*
28).

2. *Love of God as a Motivation for Obedience*

The Covenant theme not only declares God's authorship and
enforcement of Jewish law; it also articulates the relationships
which underlie the law. Although we commonly think of elaborate
governmental agencies when we think about law, those institutions
really only account for a small percentage of the operations of a
legal system. A legal system works only when the vast majority of
those bound by it abide by its rules automatically. Then legal
authorities can handle the conflicts that arise and the small
minority of the society that seriously disobeys the law. To procure
consistent and largely voluntary obedience, societies must create
feelings of pride, respect, and even love for their community and its
laws. That is hard because government and law are abstract and
inanimate. It is much easier to relate to people. Therefore secular
societies typically teach the history of the group, its songs, stories,
and exemplary personalities in order to instill strong commitments to
social institutions, and they reinforce those commitments through
recurring rituals.

Jews do that too: Jewish education usually includes a study of the
same subjects, and Jewish ritual patterns provide ample opportunity
to renew national ties. But there is a difference. Jewish law is
obeyed not only out of a sense of kinship and loyalty to other Jews,
but to God Himself. God is the King and Judge, but He is also the
covenanted partner, and that provides the context for covenantal
obligations.

The Bible develops the personal implications of the Covenant
fully. It speaks of God having chosen the People of Israel as His
special people out of an act of love, and Jews should observe the

8   *Gen. Rabb.* 26:6.

commandments because of that love and not spurn their Divine lover through disobedience (*Deut.* 7:6-11):

> For you are a people consecrated to the LORD your GOD: of all the peoples on earth the LORD your GOD chose you to be His treasured people. It is not because you are the most numerous of peoples that the LORD set His heart on you and chose you - indeed, you are the smallest of peoples; but it was because the LORD loved you and kept the oath He made to your fathers that the LORD freed you with a mighty hand and rescued you from the house of bondage, from the power of Pharaoh king of Egypt.
>   Know, therefore, that only the Lord your GOD is GOD, the steadfast GOD who keeps His gracious covenant to the thousandth generation of those who love Him and keep His commandments, but who instantly requites with destruction those who reject Him - never slow with those who reject Him, but requiting them instantly. Therefore, observe faithfully the Instruction, the laws, and the norms, with which I charge you today.

Conversely, just as God loves Israel, so should Israel love God. God will reward those who obey Him and punish those who do not, but that should not be the exclusive motivation for obedience. Beyond pragmatics, Israel should obey God as an act of love; "Love the Lord your God, and always keep His charge, His laws, His norms, and His commandments" (*Deut.* 11:1). The Prophets picture God and Israel as husband and wife, joined in a covenant of marriage (e.g., *Jer.* 2:2, 3:20; *Ezek.* 16:8; *Hos.* 2). Obedience out of love of God is thus deeply rooted in the Jewish tradition. While that may seem natural to Jews, it should be remembered that most legal systems do not describe themselves as the fruit of a relationship between the lawgiver and the people, and so most legal theories do not speak to this important element in Jewish law. The covenant model does.[9]

9   William Moran has argued in "Ancient Near Eastern Background of the Love of God in Deuteronomy", *Catholic Biblical Quarterly* XXV (1963), 77-87, that the root "*ahv*" is a technical, political term in the Bible denoting obedience and loyalty rather than love. Even if he is right, later generations of Jews understood it to designate the full gamut of emotions that we call "love". Thus the Rabbis accepted Rabbi Akiva's interpretations of Song of Songs as love poetry between God and Israel (*M.Yad.* 3:5; *cf. M. Eduy.* 5:3 and *Tos. Sanh.* 12:10, *Yad.* 2:14), and Rabbi Akiva said: "Beloved is Israel, for they are called the children of God, and it was a special token of love that they became conscious of it" (*M. Avot* 3:18).

3. *Promise-keeping as the Source of Obligation*

There is another aspect of the personal relationship between God and Israel that affects Jewish law significantly. Legal systems commonly hold native-born citizens liable for obeying the law (once they achieve the age of majority) without ever asking them for their consent. Enjoying the benefits of a society is generally taken to be sufficient justification for imposing its obligations on the grounds of fairness and also on the basis of the "tacit consent" that is implied by continuing to live within it. Judaism goes much further. It claims that Jews at all times and places *explicitly* promised to obey the law because they all stood at Sinai. The Bible expresses this with regard to the generation after the Exodus:

> It was not with our fathers that the Lord made this covenant, but with us, the living, every one of us who is here today. Face to face the Lord spoke to you on the mountain out of the fire. (*Deut.* 5:3-4)

> I make this covenant, with its sanctions, not with you alone, but both with those who are standing here with us this day before the LORD our GOD and with those who are not with us here this day. (*Deut.* 29:13-14).

And the Rabbis expand the theme to cover all subsequent generations, as this famous passage from the Haggadah of Passover declares:

> In every generation one must look upon himself as if he personally had come out of Egypt, as the Bible says: "And you shall explain to your child on that day, 'It is because of what the Lord did for *me* when *I* went free from Egypt'" (*Exod.* 13:8). For it was not alone our forefathers whom the Holy One, praised be He, redeemed, but He redeemed us together with them, as it is said: "He freed *us* from there to bring us to, and give us, the land that He promised on oath to our forefathers" (*Deut.* 6:23).

Moreover, the people promised God to obey the law not out of fear alone but for ample consideration: God made His will known to the People of Israel, redeemed them, and gave them the land of Israel, and therefore the promise that they made is clearly valid (*Exod.* 19:2-8, *cf. Deut.* 4:32-40):

> Israel encamped there in front of the mountain, and Moses went up to God.

The LORD called to him from the mountain, saying, "Thus shall you say to the house of Jacob and declare to the children of Israel: 'You have seen what I did to the Egyptians, how I bore you on eagles' wings and brought you to Me. Now then, if you will obey Me faithfully and keep My covenant, you shall be My treasured possession among all the peoples. Indeed, all the earth is Mine, but you shall be to Me a kingdom of priests and a holy nation.' These are the words that you shall speak to the children of Israel."

Moses came and summoned the elders of the people and put before them all the words that the LORD had commanded him. All the people answered as one, saying, "All that the LORD has spoken we will do!" And Moses brought back the people's words to the LORD.

This justification of obligation through the explicit promise of the people is a major element of Jewish legal theory, and it is best explicated through the concept of two contracting parties, each of whom promises something to the other to form the agreement.

4. *The National Domain of Jewish Law*

The Covenant is specifically between God and the Jewish people; its terms do not apply to others. The Rabbis make this explicit by claiming that non-Jews are subject to only the Seven Commandments of the Children of Noah,[10] but the Bible is also quite clear in restricting the jurisdiction of its commandments to Israelites.[11] While positivist theories could account for this, theories which base Jewish law on universal phenomena like natural law or reason would be hard-pressed. The Covenant clearly expresses the national character of Jewish law since it is specifically a Covenant between God and the People Israel.

During the nineteenth and the first third of the twentieth centuries, some Jews tried to minimize the national character of Jewish law because of the danger of producing a narrow, chauvinistic

10 *Cf. Sanh.* 56-60, *A.Zar.* 64b, *Gen. Rabb.* 34:4. The Bible (*Gen.* 9:8-17) speaks about a covenant between God and all living beings; but the Rabbis do not connect their doctrine of the Seven Noahide Laws to that covenant. They derive it instead from *Gen.* 2:16 (R. Yohanan on *Sanh.* 56b) or seven separate verses from *Gen.* 6 and 9 (The School of Menashe on *Sanh.* 56b-57a). The *Book of Jubilees* (Chapter 7), which has a slightly different list, derives it from *Gen.* 9 on the death of Noah.

11 For example, *cf. Exod.* 19:5-6, 34:10; *Lev.* 20:22-26; 25:39-46; *Deut.* 7:1-11; 10:12-22; 33:4; *Jer.* 11:1-13.

outlook, thus undermining the universal, messianic goals of Judaism. Those who have taken that view have found the Covenant problematic precisely because of its nationalism. Hermann Cohen, for example, bitterly attacked the cliquish consequences of a national Covenant and stressed that its restriction to Israel was to be temporary in the messianic sweep of Biblical historiography;[12] Franz Rosenzweig was more comfortable with Israel's special Covenant with God but claimed that Christians had one too (albeit an inferior one) in his famous "dual-covenant" theory.[13] In the last forty years the value of ethnic roots has been recognized even by those who would deny that the Jewish People are specially chosen, and so the Covenant has been reinterpreted but reasserted. Probably the best example of this is Mordecai Kaplan, who conscientiously denies that God chose the Jewish People for both theological and moral reasons but who affirms the Covenant equally strongly because it is only through national affiliation that one can contribute creatively to mankind. Jews are not chosen to serve God over and above any other nation of the world according to Kaplan, but they do have a unique calling to serve God in their own specific circumstances

12 Hermann Cohen, *Religion of Reason out of the Sources of Judaism,* trld. Simon Kaplan (New York: Frederick Ungar, 1972), Chapter 13, paras. 35, 38, 40, at 252-254; Chapter 14, para. 4, 271; Chapter 16, 353; *Religion and Hope: Selections from the Jewish Writings of Hermann Cohen,* ed. and trans. Eva Jospe (New York: W.W. Norton, 1971), 46-50, 168ff., and Chapter 6; *cf.* also my discussion of his doctrine of Covenant in the second article cited in note 2, *supra, at* 46-50.

13 Franz Rosenzweig, *The Star of Redemption,* trld. William W. Hallo (New York: Holt, Rinehard and Winston, 1970, 1971), Part III, Books I and II. The Bible is *a* revelation of God but not the only one since revelation is to the *individual; cf.* Part II, Book I, 309 and Book II, esp. 167-188. Consequently, other claims to revelation might well be true: "Did God wait for Mount Sinai or, perhaps, Golgotha? No paths that lead from Sinai and Golgotha are guaranteed to lead to Him, but neither can He possibly have failed to come to one who sought Him on the trails skirting Olympus. There is no temple built so close to Him as to give man reassurance in its closeness, and none is so far from Him as to make it too difficult for man's hand to reach. There is no direction from which it would not be possible for Him to come, and none from which He must come; no block of wood in which He may not take up His dwelling, and no psalm of David that will always reach His ear" (from Nahum N. Glatzer, *Franz Rosenzweig: His Life and Thought* [New York: Schocken Books, 1953, 1961], 29).

and their own unique way:

> If we regard God as the Life of the universe, the Power that evokes personality in men and nations, then the sense of the nation's responsibility for contributing creatively to human welfare and progress in the light of its own best experience becomes the modern equivalent of the covenant idea. In it is implied that reciprocity between God and the nation that the term covenant denotes.[14]

The ability of the Covenant theme to express the national character of Jewish law is thus increasingly being recognized as an advantage for both historical and philosophical reasons.

5. *The Relationship of Jewish Law to Nature*

While Jewish law is specifically the law of the Jewish People, it is not only that: the classical Jewish texts picture it as rooted in nature. *Psalm* 19, for example, describes God's ordering of nature and then easily shifts to God's ordering of human life through the Torah in order to make the point that the two acts of God are parallel. Similarly, the Prophets complain that animals know and follow the rules that God has set for them, but Israel does not know or obey the Torah, which should be equally as obvious to them (e.g., *Isa.* 1:3; *Jer.* 8:7). Moses invokes heaven and earth as witnesses to the Covenant (*Deut.* 4:26; 32:1), and Jeremiah proclaims that the heavens are astounded when Israel flagrantly breaks the Covenant (*Jer.* 2:12; *cf.* 4:22-8, 6:19). Nature itself, in fact, takes vengeance on Israel when it breaks some provisions of the Covenant (e.g., *Lev.* 18:26-30). Israel's Covenant is thus rooted in nature in ways that no other legal system is, and that is part of the reason why Israel is warned not to follow other nations' laws (*Lev.* 20:22-26; *Jer.* 10:1-5). The Rabbis, in fact, claimed that the very existence of the world is dependent upon Israel's acceptance of the Torah (*Shabbat* 88a):

> What is the meaning of the words, "The earth feared and was still" (*Ps.*

---

14 Mordecai M. Kaplan, *The Meaning of God in Modern Jewish Religion* (New York: The Jewish Reconstructionist Foundation, Inc., 1947), 102; *cf.* also his *Judaism as a Civilization* (New York: The Reconstructionist Press, 1934, 1957), 258f *Cf.* also my discussion of Kaplan's doctrine of Covenant in the second article cited in note 2, *supra*, and, in general, the third article cited there.

76:9)? .... Before Israel accepted the Torah, the earth was afraid; after they accepted the Torah, it was still.. For the Holy One, blessed be He, stipulated a condition with the earth: If Israel accepts the Torah, you may exist, but if not, I will return you to the state of being unformed and void.

In direct contrast to the previous section, natural law theories (and perhaps other absolutist approaches) can account for this element of Jewish law, while positivist views cannot. The Covenant expresses both the particular, national character of Jewish law and also its universal, natural roots: God, who created the world, enters into a covenantal relationship with Israel so that the law of at least one human society may reflect Divine purpose just as natural law does.

6. *The Scope and Specifics of the Law*

Because God gave the law, it can speak to every area of life, including many that fall outside of the jurisdiction of other legal systems. Jewish law sets an order not only for society but also for the private lives of an individual and a family, and it assumes competence to regulate even the speech patterns and thoughts of Jews. So, for example, it includes rules which determine even the shoe that you are to tie first when getting dressed and the position in which you are to sleep, and it specifies with remarkable particularity the duties incumbent upon spouses to each other, including even the number of times that a man must offer to have sex with his wife.[15] The Talmud forbids oppressing one's neighbor in speech and gives a number of examples of that, and it also commands that one who intends to give a gift to a needy person should consider himself bound by that thought even if he never promised verbally or in writing.[16] These are all areas which legal systems do not dare to touch, let alone regulate, but Jewish law exercises jurisdiction on these subjects because its author is God (however that authorship is

15 On shoes *cf. Shul han Arukh, Or ah Hayyim* 2:4,5; on sleeping positions *cf. M.T., Hilkhot De'ot* 4:5; on the duties incumbent on spouses to each other *cf. M.Ket.* 5:5-7,9 and *Mishneh TOr ah, Laws of Marriage* 12:10,11,14,15; 13:3-6; on sexual obligations *cf. M.Ket.* 5:6.

16 On oppression through speech *cf. Mishnah B.M.* 4:10 and *B.M.* 58b-59b; on carrying through with an intended gift *cf. Kitsur Shulh an Arukh* 62:17.

understood), and God has the power, the right, and perhaps even the obligation to address these crucial areas of life.

Since human beings are all a part of nature, natural law theories could presumably have an equally expansive scope and detail. In practice, however, they vary widely when it comes to specifying exactly what natural law demands, ranging from a few general rules to Maritain's rather specific list.[17] Positivist theories would probably find it easier to account for the specificity of Jewish law, but they would have to be substantially modified to explain its scope through providing for a divine legislator and enforcer; human positive law is severely limited in these areas. The Covenant model nicely describes both the wide range of concerns treated by Jewish law and the specificity of its rules: a covenant has specific clauses, and when God is the author, they can cover the whole gamut of human experience.

7. The Legal Techniques Used in Jewish Law

The Biblical picture of God giving the law amidst thunder and lightning at Sinai (*Exod.* 19:20) misleads many into thinking that Jewish law does not operate as other legal systems do. The Bible not only implies but explicitly states that its rules are never to be amended (*Deut.* 4:2; 13:1), and human legal systems do not include such prohibitions, even in regard to their constitutions. The Rabbis, however, interpreted their Biblical mandate to judge very broadly, with the result that Jewish law in fact has changed over the centuries through differentiation of cases and other normal legal techniques. That is a surprising development for a God-given law. After all, God's rules *should* be constant, and if they are to be changed at all, it should be by new revelations from God Himself, as the Protestants claim. The Covenant model, however, provides the basis for Jewish legal development, for God not only commands but enters into a legal relationship through the Covenant. Therefore such legal techniques as interpretation, usage, and recourse to course of dealings became appropriate legal techniques to give meaning to the parties' original relationship. That would not be true if Jewish law were God's commands or natural laws outside the framework of

---

17 Jacques Maritain, *The Rights of Man and Natural Law* (New York: Charles Scribner's Sons, 1949), 111-114.

a covenant - at least not as clearly so - for then God's rules would not be explicitly legal in character and would not be part of an ongoing development in time. The Covenant makes them law and thereby makes them amenable to human legal reasoning.

8. *The Messianic Goal of Jewish Law*

Preambles to constitutions commonly spell out noble purposes for the law, but they do not aspire to transform both human and animal nature. The Covenant does, at least as it was developed by the Prophets and Rabbis. The ultimate aim is that all people worship God (e.g., *Isa.* 2:2-4, *Zeph.* 2:11, 3:8) with the result that there will be universal peace among people and in nature to the extent that the lion will lie down with the lamb (e.g., *Isa.* 2:2-4; 11-12). Toward that end Israel is to be "a light unto the nations" (*Isa.* 49:1-6, 51:4). Jeremiah experienced the failure of Israel to perform its role of moral leadership and the consequent destruction wrought by God, but he promises that God will not destroy Israel completely (5:18, 30:11, 46:28) and looks forward to a time when the law will be abrogated because there will be no need for it: it will be written in the heart and thus totally internalized (*Jer.* 31:31-34; *cf.* 3:14-18):

> See, a time is coming - declares the Lord - when I will make a new covenant with the House of Israel and the House of Judah. It will not be like the covenant I made with their fathers, when I took them by the hand to lead them out of the land of Egypt, a covenant which they broke, so that I rejected them - declares the Lord. But such is the covenant I will make with the House of Israel after these days - declares the Lord: I will put My Teaching into their inmost being and inscribe it upon their hearts. Then I will be their God, and they shall be My people. No longer will they need to teach one another and say to one another, "Heed the Lord": for all of them, from the least of them to the greatest, shall heed Me - declares the Lord.

The Bible and most Rabbinic opinion assumes that the Torah is immutable and eternal and that in Messianic times it will be better understood and better fulfilled than ever before, but some Rabbinic sources envisage a world so changed that the Law itself will be radically altered.[18] The following *Midrash* clearly illustrates this

18 *Cf.* Joseph Klausner, *The Messianic Idea in Israel* (London: George Allen and Unwin, Ltd., 1956), 444-450; Raphael Patai, *The Messaiah Texts*

dispute (*Midrash Psalms* 146, par. 4):

"The Lord permits forbidden things" (*Psalms* 146:7, usually rendered, "The Lord sets the bound loose"): what does "permits forbidden things" mean? Some say: Every beast declared forbidden in this world the Holy One, blessed be He, will one day allow... And why has He forbidden them? In order to see who would accept His words and who would not. In the time to come, however, He will allow everything which He has forbidden. But others say, He will not permit forbidden animals in the hereafter.

In later Jewish history the doctrine of a radically new Torah was popular in those times and places where the Messiah seemed to be coming soon or already here; the more conservative notion of a more complete observance of the present Torah held sway when the Messianic idea was a distant abstraction.

The Covenant theme accommodates both the anticipated changes in animal and human nature and the possible revision of the Law: since God is Creator of our present world, He can presumably change the nature of creation; and since Jewish law is based on a contract with God, it can be amended or even totally rewritten in a new age - although it would not necessarily have to be. In contrast, a realist approach that would interpret Jewish law as simply the policies practiced in Jewish courts and society now would ignore the Messianic orientation of Jewish law, its hope not only to regulate what is but to produce what ought to be. And it is not only the psychological context of Jewish law which realism distorts, but its very operation, for the long-term goals embedded in Jewish law affect it in concrete ways. Traditional Jewish jurists sometimes override present desires and practices in an effort to realize Judaism's long-term goals, and that goal-directedness is absent in realist accounts. On the other hand, Jewish law is not to be identified with the law of nature along the lines of natural law theories. God has established law for mankind as He has established law for nature, and the one fits the other to the extent

---

(Detroit: Wayne State University Press, 1979), 247-257 (a convenient selection of primary texts in translation); W.D. Davies, *Torah in the Messianic Age* (Philadelphia: Society of Biblical Literature, 1952); G. Scholem, *The Messianic Idea in Judaism* (New York: Schocken Books, 1971), 49-77.

that nature even enforces some Jewish laws according to the Bible, as we have seen; but God can change both the laws of nature and the laws of mankind. Natural law theory is rooted in nature as it now is; the Covenant provides for the present tie of Jewish law to nature as we know it as well as the possibility of a future in which both natural law and Jewish law would be significantly changed. The Covenant theory therefore has the advantage of accommodating the future, Messianic thrust of Jewish law in ways that competing theories do not.

B. The Problems with the Covenant Theory

An analogy by its very nature must compare two different things: if the objects of comparison were the same, we would have not an analogy but an equivalence. Analogies are useful for the philosophical and educational purposes described at the beginning of this essay, but they inevitably involve the danger of drawing false comparisons on the basis of the analogy. The only way to prevent that is constantly to keep in mind that the analogy is just that - a comparison that may illuminate certain features of an object or phenomenon but may be downright misleading in regard to others.

Both the advantages and the problems with using analogies are heightened when speaking about God. On the one hand, the only language available to us is derived from human experience, and so to talk about God it would seem that we must use symbols and analogies. On the other hand, if such metaphors can never be translated without remainder to words used literally, how can we ever be sure what the symbols and analogies mean - let alone whether they make true claims. Those philosophical problems have been discussed by a number of medieval and modern philosophers,[19] and theologians constantly warn us that any speech

---

19 E.g., Maimonides, *Guide of the Perplexed*, Part I, Chapters 51-61; David Hume, *Dialogues Concerning Natural Religion*, Part II; Paul Tillich, *Dynamics of Faith* (New York: Harper and Row, 1957), 41-54; Paul Edwards, "Being-Itself and Irreducible Metaphors", *Mind* 74 (1965), 197-206; Eric L. Mascall, *Existence and Analogy* (London: Langmans, Green, and Co., Ltd., 1949; Anchor Books, 1967), 97-121. The last three articles are reprinted in Ronald E. Santoni, ed., *Religious Language and the Problem of Religious Knowledge* (Bloomington and London: Indiana University Press, 1968), Chapters 7-9.

about God is inevitably limited by the constraints of our human abilities.

With that general background in mind, we should not be surprised that the problems with analogical thinking in general and the extra problems in using analogies with reference to God are all very much in evidence when we try to talk about a set of laws given by God. No analogy to human legal practice is going to be totally satisfying, and yet we must find some way to capture the idea of God's legislative activity if we are ever going to make sense of the fundamental assumptions of Jewish law, and we must also find a way to explain how this God-given law can be interpreted and applied openly and aggressively by human beings if we are ever to capture the methodology that has actually been used in the development of Jewish law. The real question, then, is the extent to which a given theory illuminates the axioms and methods of Jewish law and the extent to which it is misleading. My contention is that the covenant analogy is the least misleading of the available theories and that, in fact, it is not very misleading at all because the places where the Covenant deviates from human covenants are rather obvious. To demonstrate the latter part of this claim, I shall consider nine arguments against describing Jewish law in covenantal terms. The first three raise questions about whether the sense of "covenant" is at all preserved in God's Covenant with Israel; the remaining six are theological objections to the model based upon what the model says about God and man.

1. *How can God's authority be independent of, and antecedent to, the contract?*

Social contracts are usually understood to be agreements among the inhabitants of a region to abide by certain rules. Authority to define and enforce those rules is created through the contract: before the contract is concluded people live in a "state of nature" in which nobody has moral or legal authority over anyone else, except as the laws of nature provide (however that is interpreted). In Judaism, however, God's authority precedes the Covenant and is independent of it. That is why, despite all of the talk of a "covenant" in the Bible, God ultimately *commands* the law unilaterally rather than negotiating its terms with His covenanted partner, Israel. In what sense, then, is this a covenant?

The question assumes that the model for the Biblical Covenant is the social contract that we know from the world of philosophy, but it is not: it is rather the suzerainty agreements of the ancient Near East. Monarchs concluded covenants with their subjects in which they spelled out the history of their relationship to the nation, the commands of the monarch, and the blessings and curses that would accrue to those who obeyed and disobeyed respectively. As in the Biblical Covenant, the suzerainty compacts did not create the sovereign power; that existed antecedently.

The importance of remembering the historical origins of the Biblical idea of Covenant is underscored by the fact that the Rabbis use that common Biblical theme very little. By their time it was not the practice of kings to write covenants with their subjects; they simply insisted that those whom they ruled accept the yoke of their reign. Consequently, the Rabbis expressed the Covenant idea in language appropriate to their times, i.e., as "giving the Torah" (*Mattan Torah*) and "accepting the yoke of the Kingdom of Heaven" (*Kabalat ol Malkhut Shamayim*), parallel to, but also in contrast with, accepting the Roman yoke.[20] The idea, however, remained the same: Jewish law was to be seen as the product of God's command and Israel's acceptance, acts which created a special relationship between them, but God existed and held sway over the world before He entered into that special relationship.

2. *If the Covenant is not a social contract in the modern sense, how does it provide an explicatory model for us at all?*

As indicated above, there are at least two goals in suggesting a philosophical model for a legal system, one philosophical and one educational. This question casts doubt on the effectiveness of the Covenant as an educational tool. After all, the didactic purpose of suggesting an analogy is to enhance understanding of Jewish law by reference to other, better known phenomena, but if the Covenant model is based on ancient suzerainty treaties and not modern social contracts, how does it help to communicate the essence of Jewish law? The point could be taken even further: is not the term

---

20 I am indebted to Mr. Seymour Rosenberg, an M.A. student at the University of Judaism and a member of its Board of Directors, for pointing this out to me.

"covenant" downright misleading to modern people since they would most likely understand it as a social contract similar to other "covenants" which establish legal systems?

Theories are always subject to misunderstanding, of course, but the question is whether the Covenant promotes that. If people not expert in Judaica were asked to think about Jewish law, their first associations might well be the scene at Sinai. That would prevent them from making the mistake in Question (1) above since God's commanding authority is certainly in evidence at Sinai. The very assertion that the Covenant is with God should alert people to the fact that the Covenant is not a social contract. If anything, it is the opposite error that is more likely: people may conclude from the Sinai event that Jewish law is not a legal system in any normal sense at all, that it is entirely composed of immutable, apodictic commands spoken in awesome circumstances. That is a real danger, but any further study of the subject will quickly dispel the misconception. The chapters immediately following the description of Sinai in *Exod.* 19 and 20 already speak in a very different tone and beg for normal legal analysis. Consequently, while the Covenant theme may be somewhat misleading, it is not seriously so.

There may be no absolute monarchs who engage in formal covenants with their nations any more, but it is not difficult to imagine how one could. The scene, in fact, would probably be not so different from Sinai, with due allowance, of course, for the different degrees of awe inspired by human kings and God. The model, therefore, can be educationally availing. Indeed, if Section (A) is right, it should be pedagogically quite productive.

3. *Did Jewish Law ever operate like a suzerainty treaty?*

This question probes the philosophical status of the Covenant theory: Is it a description of how Jewish law operated historically, either consciously or unconsciously? Is it a justification for observing Jewish law? Is it an analysis of some of the fundamental assumptions of Jewish law? Is it an explanatory analogy to elucidate some features of Jewish law?

It is certainly an educational device, as we have developed in the previous section. It may also serve as a way of justifying obedience to the law by reminding us that God legislated it, enforces it, and judges under it, that we owe obedience to Him as an expression of our love for Him, and that we made a covenantal promise to obey.[21] Its success in that role would clearly vary from listener to listener, but the very assertion of a close bond between the individual Jew, the Jewish people, and God through the Covenant can be a powerful motivation for new and continuing adherence to its terms.

The Covenant model may even serve as a description of the historical functioning of Jewish law if we understand that Jewish tradition modified the role of the receiver of the Covenant considerably. Specifically, it is the case that Jews have continually seen themselves bound to God through Jewish law; that even God is understood to be bound by His promises (hence the liturgical and literary complaints to God that are produced in times of distress); and that, for the Jewish tradition, God sets the rules. These are all features of a relationship based on the Covenant: complaints to God in particular are hard to reconcile with either natural law theory or positivism. It is also the case that the Jewish tradition created ways to repeatedly celebrate the Covenant. The talmudic Rabbis, for example, connected the festival of Shavuot with the Sinai revelation (*Pes.* 68b), and medieval Jewish tradition initiated the festival of Simhat Torah and utilized all of the symbolism of a couple (in this case Israel and God) entering into a marital relationship. The verses from Hosea that are prescribed for putting on *tefillin* each morning (*Hos.* 2:21-22) are explicitly reaffirmations of the Covenant, as the context indicates (*cf. Hos.* 2:20). It is therefore probable that Jews not only acted, but consciously thought in Covenantal terms throughout Jewish history. The operation of Jewish law, however, did not follow the model of ancient suzerainty treaties (at least as far as we know them), for Jewish law provided for ample room for the rabbis of each generation to interpret and apply Jewish law in new ways, and in some periods it even recognized the customs of the laity to be legally authoritative under specific conditions. That active role for the receivers of the treaty seems to be absent in the monarchical covenants of yore, but other features of those covenants do in fact fit the historical functioning of Jewish law.

For our purposes, however, the most important contribution of the Covenantal model is strictly philosophic: it reveals some of the

21 *Cf.* sections A-1, A-2, and A-3 above.

fundamental assumptions of Jewish law, specifically, all of those mentioned in Section (A) of this essay. Consequently, while it may be useful in the educational, motivational, and historical contexts that we have discussed, it is the philosophical strengths and weaknesses of the model that most concern us here. Aside from the assertion of a relationship between God and Israel, Covenantal legal theory has a number of implications for the nature of God and mankind, some of which are quite problematic. It is to those that we now turn.

4.   *How can the Covenant bind God?*

Even if the Covenant does not create sovereignty, it does establish obligations upon God as well as man. It must do that if it is to be a "covenant" - even on the model of the monarchical compacts of the ancient Near East - but how can that be? How can any obligations of God's be enforced? And if they cannot be enforced, in what sense are they obligations?

God does, of course, take upon Himself a number of specific obligations in the Bible, including the duties to give the People Israel posterity and the land of Israel and the responsibility to reward those who obey the commandments and punish those who do not. God's justice extends to other nations as well as Israel (e.g., *Amos* chs. 1-3; *Isa.* 2:4; *Jer.* chs. 46-51), and both Abraham (*Gen.* 18:25) and Job assume that small groups and even individuals should be rewarded and punished by God according to their merits. That sets the stage for raising Question (4) in the piercing way that Job does:

9.1 Then Job answered and said,
2   I surely know that it is so,
       when you say, "How can a man be just before God?"
3   If one wished to contend with Him,
       He would not answer once in a thousand times.
4   However wise and stouthearted a man might be,
       has he ever argued with God and emerged
       unscathed?

10 Yes, He does great things beyond understanding,
       and wonders without number.

11 Lo, He passes by me, and I do not see Him,
        He moves on, and I do not perceive Him.
12 Behold, when He robs, who can make Him return it?
        Who can say to Him, "What are you doing?"
13 God will not restrain His wrath,
        before which Rahab's helpers were brought low.
14 How then can I answer Him,
        choosing my words with Him?
15 For even if I am right, I cannot respond,
        but must make supplication to my opponent.
16 If I called Him, would He answer me?
        I cannot believe that He would hear my voice.
17 For He crushes me for a trifle,
        and increases my wounds without cause.
18 He does not let me catch my breath,
        but fills me with bitterness.
19 If it be a matter of power, here He is!
        But if of justice who will arraign Him?
20 Though I am in the right, my mouth would condemn me;
        though I am blameless, it would prove me perverse.

32 For God is not a man like me, whom I could answer
        when we came to trial together.
33 If only there were an arbiter between us
        who would lay his hand upon us both,
34 who would remove God's rod from me
        so that my dread of Him would not terrify me.
35 Then I would speak, and not fear Him,
        for He is far from just to me.[22]

Job dares to speak for several reasons. There may not be a third
party who can adjudicate disputes between God and Israel or enforce
the rules against God, but God's personality is such that He keeps
His promises. Nobody can force Him to do so, of course, but there is
no need for that: God does so automatically. Even after an enraging
incident like the Golden Calf God foregoes His desire to destroy the

22 *Job* 9:1-4, 10-20, 32-35, as translated by R. Gordis, *The Book of God and
    Man: A Study of Job* (London and Chicago: University of Chicago Press,
    1965), 248-249.

People Israel when Moses reminds Him that He promised the Patriarchs not to do so (*Exod.* 32:13-14). Moreover God has chosen Israel in love and therefore will not deceive or disappoint Israel in carrying out His part of the bargain (*Exod.* 20:6, 34:6-7; *Deut.* 7:1-16; etc.). Proof of His good intentions are His past acts of loyalty to the Covenant and love of Israel (e.g., *Deut.* 4:1-14, 32-40). Consequently, while God cannot be coerced into abiding by the Covenant, He can be trusted to do so.

Once again, the situation is similar to a covenant with an absolute monarch: there can be no suits against him to force him to carry out his responsibilities, but he is generally trusted to do so, at least as long as his reign lasts. It is also similar to a child-parent relationship in that the child assumes that he has no recourse against his parent if the parent fails to fulfill his duties, but the child nevertheless expects the parents to act responsibly and honorably. And indeed, two of the most common appellations of God in the tradition are King and Father.

5. *Does the Covenant limit God?*

Even if the Covenant cannot be enforced by a third party, it does impose obligations on God. Does that not limit God?

The truth is that it does, but the Jewish tradition has generally not found such limitations theologically opprobrious because they were voluntarily assumed by God and because they are ultimately unenforceable.

6. *Can God revoke the Covenant unilaterally?*

Just as human beings would be left without recourse if God failed to fulfill His responsibilities under the Covenant, so there is no way to prevent God from abrogating the Covenant entirely if He so chooses. But God's nature is such that He can be generally trusted not to renege on His commitments under the Covenant, and He similarly is to be trusted not to rescind the Covenant completely.

The Covenant is thus crucially dependent upon man's faith in God. As we have seen, trust also plays a key role in human king-subject and parent-child relationships, and so we should not be surprised about this feature of the Covenantal relationship with God. These human analogues will also be helpful in understanding man's rights under the Covenant, to which we now turn.

7. Was man's acquiescence necessary to validate the Covenant?

The Biblical and Rabbinic traditions were both ambivalent on
this. The Bible clearly records Israel's agreement to the Covenant
both at Sinai (*Exod.*19:8, 24:3,7), and during the reaffirmation in
Ezra's time (*Neh.* ch.10), and it asserts that the Covenant was made
with the People Israel of all generations (*Deut.* 5:3; 29:13-14, 28),
who presumably agreed to it. The Bible also speaks, however, of
God "commanding" the clauses of the Torah amidst thunder and
lightning, it describes the people's fear at the time (e.g., *Deut.*
5:19ff), it expresses God's wish that the people fear Him enough to
obey the commandments (e.g., *Deut.* 5:26), and it confirms the
Covenant in a ceremony that is designed to inspire awe in the people
(*Deut.* 11:26-32, 27:11-26). All of that certainly does not sound like
voluntary acceptance of the Covenant! The Rabbis continue this: one
popular Midrash describes God's fruitless search for a people to
accept the Torah until He asked the People Israel, who said, "We
shall do and we shall hear" (*Exod.* 24:7) (*Ṣifre Deut* par.343;
Num.R. 14:10), while another equally popular Midrash pictures God
overturning Mount Sinai over the people and telling them that He
will bury them with the mountain unless they accept the Torah
(*Shab.* 88a, *A.Zar.* 2b, etc.).

The situation is not as strange as it sounds. In both king-subject
relationships and parent-child relationships there is an element of
voluntary acceptance, and both the king and parent would like to
maximize that for both practical and moral reasons: practically, it
is simply easier to gain adherence to the rules if there is willing
obedience; morally, it is easier to justify the authority of the rules if
they are accepted voluntarily. Free acceptance is not only a nice
adornment for a legal system: it is absolutely crucial to its viability
because enforcement procedures can never be totally effective. Thus
the Bible contemplates the possibility of disobedience even to God,
the perfect Enforcer. But neither Jewish law nor any other legal
system is totally dependent upon uncompelled obedience: there must
be means of enforcement. Moreover, there are situations in life in
which there are no choices about accepting a set of rules in the first
place. Subjects of an absolute monarchy are one good example of this,
and children's duty to obey their parents' rules are another. The

Jewish tradition depicts Israel's special status and even her existence as being dependent upon her obedience of the Torah because that was the mission God assigned her. Israel's acceptance of the Torah was therefore good and proper, but the authority of its laws is not dependent upon that: God, even more than a human king or father, can dictate the rules.

8. Can man change the terms of the Covenant?

The immediate answer to that question is "no", and the Torah says as much: "You shall not add anything to what I command you or take anything from it" (*Deut.* 4:2, 13:1). That is perfectly understandable when we remember that it is God, the Creator, who commands, but that does make the Covenant a very peculiar covenant indeed: all other covenants are subject to continual embellishment and emendation.

Upon closer examination, however, it becomes clear that the Covenant is also subject to change because by its own terms human beings are given interpretive powers in *Deut.* 17. The Rabbis expanded this judicial mandate significantly - so much so that they took it to include asserting human judicial authority despite a new, conflicting revelation (*B.M.* 59b), narrowing Biblical institutions like capital punishment to virtual non-existence (*cf. Makk.* 1:10), instituting a long list of new rules to the extent that they themselves recognized the Sabbath legislation to be like a mountain of Rabbinic rules hanging on a hair of Biblical law (*Hag.* 1:8), and actually legislating emendations in the law on occasion (*takanot*, e.g., *R.H.* 4:1,3; *R.H.* 31b). They clearly did all of this to make Jewish law viable in new historical circumstances and not to undermine or annul it, but it is important to realize that this was done: despite the special character of Jewish law as divine legislation, many of the normal legal techniques used to apply non-religious law have also been extensively used in Jewish law. Outright legislation is still uncommon in Jewish law, but rabbis use interpretation to produce judge-made law to fill the legislative vacuum. Consequently, the Covenant is methodologically a covenant in the full sense of the word.

9. *Do human beings have the power and/or the right to revoke the Covenant unilaterally?*

This question arises in a variety of different contexts, and it has a different meaning in each one of them. We shall consider three:

(a)   Since human beings can change provisions of the law, does not that ultimately amount to the power and/or right to revoke the Covenant entirely? When the question is put that way, the answer is definitely no. The interpretive mandate was always to be used to further the observance and objectives of the law, not to abrogate it. A man might even be permitted to violate all the laws of the Sabbath in order to save his life, but the purpose of setting aside the law in this way was explicitly so that he might observe many future Sabbaths (*Mekhilta Ki Tissa* on *Exod.* 31:12). Interpretation of the law for the purpose of abolishing it would be a gross abuse of the legal methodology of the system. It also would be a highly questionable exercise in the first place: if one wants to abandon Jewish law, why bother to try to justify that through exegesis of its provisions? There comes a point at which one simply has to decide whether one takes Jewish law seriously or not, and those who do not would best leave it in place. This brings us to the second formulation of Question 9:

(b)   Since no country in the world requires Jews to live by Jewish law (except Israel in matters of personal status), what prevents Jews from abandoning it completely? A traditional believer would answer that God does, and observance of Jewish law is thus mandatory regardless of what governments do and do not require. Those who do not believe that God enforces Jewish law certainly do have the power in the post-Enlightenment world to invalidate the Covenant for themselves, and many in fact do. Whether they have a *right* to do so depends upon one's understanding of the authority of the Covenant in the first place. The situation is thus directly parallel to civil legal systems: a citizen of Israel, for example, has the power to avoid army service if he lives outside of Israel, beyond the power of Israel to enforce its law; whether he has a right to evade the law in that way depends upon how one construes the basis of authority of Israeli law on him in the first place. Is it only a matter of enforcement? Are there moral obligations to abide by the law? If so, to what extent, and why? The exact same questions apply to Jewish law for those who have doubts about its divine enforcement.

(c) After the Holocaust do Jews have the right to abandon the Covenant since God seems to have reneged on His part of the bargain? The answer to that troubling question depends, in the first place, upon how one construes the relationship of God to the Holocaust. Was it only a man-made atrocity for which God shares no blame? Was God actively involved in creating it as the "Creator of good and evil" (*Isa.* 45:7)? Was He at least passively implicated for not stopping it sooner? Can we know? Even if God is to blame, does that free us of the Covenantal obligations? There are those that claim that it does. Rabbi Yitshak (Irving) Greenberg,[23] for example, argues that after the Holocaust Jews must voluntarily choose to obey the Covenant if they are to obey at all. In part this is because, for Greenberg, no divine punishment could be worse than the Holocaust was, and so *Lev.* 26 and *Deut.* 28 have lost their punch, as it were. In part, though, it is not a matter of power but of right: did not God lose the right to demand obedience when He let so many innocent people suffer so?

There are no clearcut answers to these questions. Some will in fact construe the Holocaust as a justification to abandon Jewish law. Those who continue to obey it, however, may well find the Covenant to be a good expression of their commitment for all of the reasons listed in Section A above. They may admit that the Holocaust is a major problem for their faith, but in that they are in no worse position than those who understand Jewish law through other analogies. On the contrary: the degree to which the Holocaust is problematic for a continued dedication to Jewish law is best understood when we see the law as the product of a Covenant between a benevolent, loving God and Israel; if the law is simply the practice of the people (realists), or the specific legislation of a sovereign power (positivists), or even natural law, the problem that the Holocaust poses is not nearly as poignant as it in fact is and as the Covenant theory portrays it.

---

23 Irving Greenberg, *Guide to Shavuot* (New York: National Jewish Resource Center, 1976).

This brings us to the second part of the claim of Section B: whatever the weaknesses in the above arguments in defense of the Covenant model, I would claim that the alternatives are no better and, often, are worse. We cannot reasonably expect an absolutely adequate analogy, but we can rank-order the ones available, and when we do, we find the Covenant to be the best of the lot.

A complete analysis to prove this point would take us well beyond the confines of a paper such as this, for it would require a full critique of each of the alternatives in addition to a comparison of their relative strengths and weaknesses. In addition to Professor Jackson's criticisms of each of the other positions in his introductory essay to this symposium and the comparative comments that I have made up to this point, two more observations should provide sufficient proof of the point. Both of them call attention to the transcendent thrust of Jewish law which is at the root of many of the strengths of the Covenant model discussed in Section A as well as the comparative evaluations that follow.

The fact that the authority of the law is derivative from, and dependent upon, God's antecedent authority is central to Jewish law. The fact is clearly expressed by the Covenant, modeled as it is after the suzerainty compacts of Biblical times, but other theories have difficulty with this feature of Jewish law. The two ways in which Professor Jackson criticizes the application of positivism to Jewish law are at bottom corollaries of this point: the subjects may not overturn Jewish law as they may annul the constitution in positivist theory precisely because of God's antecedent authority; and the legal and judicial discretion built into Jewish law is based upon the fact that God has granted those powers, and He could do that because of His dominion prior to, and independent of, the law. The Covenant also more clearly captures the element of revelation which is so crucial to Jewish law and which is absent in natural law theories: God establishes the Covenant in a direct, public act just as monarchs did in the ancient world, not just indirectly through His reign over nature. The historical school cannot explain why we ought to obey the law that developed from before Sinai to our own day, but the Covenant does: God commanded obedience to both the form of the law at Sinai and new forms that it would take in succeeding generations. It is for that reason that the Rabbis were so careful to establish the authority of the judges of each generation (e.g., *R.H.* 25a-25b) and to claim even that the process of judicial

interpretation represented a new and continuing revelation of God
(*B.B.* 12a; *Num. Rabb.* 19:6; *Tanḥuma*, ed. Buber, *Devarim*, 1a):[24]
only under those circumstances would the later developments of
Jewish law have juridical authority. A similar point can be made in
preference of the Covenant over realist interpretations of Jewish
law: the Covenant establishes the transcendent authority and
context of Jewish law, in contrast to the ethical relativism inherent
in legal realism.

But it is not just a matter of authority. Probably the most
important advantage of the Covenant theory over the alternatives
is that it clearly expresses the *relationship* between God and the
Jewish People on which Jewish law is built. The ultimate attraction
of Judaism in general and Jewish law in particular is that it enables
the Jewish People to relate to God as they understand Him. Through
Judaism they aspire to incorporate holiness in their lives, to capture
the divine element which gives direction to life and makes it worth
living. Judaism has historically claimed that the relationship
with God is best expressed through observance of the terms of the
Covenant as detailed in Jewish law, but even non-halakhic
approaches to Judaism like those of Buber[25] and Borowitz[26] have
used the Covenant model because of its powerful affirmation of the
bond between God and Israel. People vary widely in their
understanding of how and what God communicates to us, but some
link to God is necessary if many of the phenomena mentioned in
Section (A) are going to make sense. It is that transcendent thrust

---

24 For a presentation and discussion of the sources on this point, *cf.* my
    Conservative Judaism: Our Ancestors to our Descendants, *supra* note 5, at
    Chapter 3, Sec. C.

25 Martin Buber, *On Judaism*, trld. Eva Jospe (New York: Schocken Books,
    1937, 1967), 112-113; *Israel and the World* (New York: Schocken Books,
    1948), 170-171. Buber is not a complete antinomian: every I-Thou
    experience with God involves a demand upon the individual having the
    experience, but those demands are specific to the individual and not
    necessarily the requirements of Jewish law; *cf. Israel and the World*, 209,
    and Rosenzweig's response to him in "The Builders", in N. Glatzer, *On
    Jewish Learning* (New York: Schocken, 1965), 72-92.

26 Eugene Borowitz, *How Can a Jew Speak of Faith Today?* (Philadelphia:
    The Westminster Press, 1969), esp. at 68.

which the Covenant conveys: it is that relationship with God which provides much of the *raison d'être* of Jewish law.[27]

---

27 I would like to thank Professors Arnold Band, Stanley Gewirtz, Henry Fisher, Steven Lowenstein, and Joel Rembaum for their helpful comments on a previous draft of this paper presented to the Los Angeles members of the Association of Jewish Studies.

SOME TENSIONS IN THE JEWISH ATTITUDE TOWARD THE TAKING OF HUMAN LIFE

A Philosophical Analysis of Justified Homicide in Jewish Legal and Aggadic Literature.

by

MOSHE SOKOL[*]

I. Some Preliminary Comments About the Application of Philosophy to Jewish Texts

The intellectual enterprise we call Jewish philosophy can serve either a Jewish or a general philosophical end. That is, Jewish philosophy sometimes functions as a discipline which brings the light of Jewish sources and traditions to bear on an understanding of philosophical or religious problems which throughout history have animated general philosophical or religious thinking. Jewish medieval discussions of the nature of faith or the creation of the world are fine examples of this sort of intellectual labor. Here the explanatory arrow travels from the Jewish to the universal.

On other occasions (and sometimes on the very same occasion) Jewish philosophy travels from the universal to the Jewish. Here, the methodology and categories of thought characteristic of general philosophical or religious thinking are applied to Jewish sources. Thus, *Rambam* applied Aristotelian methodology and thought categories to specifically Jewish concerns such as *ṭa'ame hamitsvot*. When the arrow travels in this direction, the Jewish sources are sometimes merely explicated, and in a fashion not inconsistent with a traditional understanding of those sources. Sometimes, however, a radical reinterpretation of the tradition results.

Since in this paper the explanatory arrow will travel from the universal to the Jewish, I should like to say a few more preliminary methodological words about the kind of inquiry I shall engage in.

The methodology I employ in this paper may be best understood as analogous to the inquiry of a natural scientist. The scientist first

* Department of Philosophy, Touro College, 30 West 44th Street, New York, N.Y. 10036.

discovers a wide array of empirical data concerning some natural phenomenon, and then seeks to account for the data by constructing an explanatory scientific theory. Thus, Newton observed apples falling and celestial bodies moving and, through mathematical techniques, constructed a single theory which accounted for falling apples and celestial movement. I, too, shall first examine certain data contained in the Jewish traditions, in Jewish legal and non-legal texts, and through the techniques and categories of moral theory, seek to account for those sources by proposing an explanatory theory. The methodology I use is analytic in that it makes no claim to revealing the intent of the author who wrote the text in question. It is non-historical in that it does not propose to account for the data by recourse to explanatory categories normally employed by the historian, i.e. changing economic, social or political conditions. The methodology is philosophic rather than legal in that it seeks to explain non-chronologically the data of the tradition by recourse to *philosophic* rather than *legal* categories, in this case moral theory. Because my subject matter is partly legal, however, it might be said that my methodology is in the strictest sense that of a philosophy of Jewish law: the application of analytic, non-historical categories of philosophy to explain various positions in the Jewish legal tradition.

I shall have more to say about this methodology and its utility during the course of the paper. Indeed, this essay is intended to serve a dual substantive and methodological purpose. I trust, however, that the success of one is independent of the success of the other.

II. The Taking of Life in Jewish Law: An Introduction

The illegality of homicide in Jewish law is biblical in origin.[1] Very early on in Genesis, the Torah speaks of the reprehensibility of bloodshed, and the repetition of this attitude throughout the Torah, and its formulation as one of the Ten Commandments, bespeaks the cardinality of the crime.[2]

---

1   *Exod.* 20:13; *Deut.* 5:17. For a fuller discussion of biblical laws of homicide see, e.g., M. Sulzberger, *Ancient Hebrew Laws of Homicide* (Philadelphia: J.H. Greenstone, 1915).

2   *Gen.* 4:10; 9:5; *Num.* 35-36; *Deut.* 19:10,13; 21:28; 27:25.

Despite the illegality of homicide, Jewish law recognizes that under certain exceptional circumstances it is indeed permissible to take human life. In fact, a survey of the literature suggests that homicide is justified under at least three broad conditions: (a) execution, (b) rescue, and (c) war.[3] Execution includes court-enforced capital punishment and the participation in public executions,[4] as well as the killing in public of persistent heretics and apostates.[5] Rescue includes self defence[6] as well as preventing a murder or rape.[7] War includes wars of self defence, which really belong in the second category, as well as wars against Amalek,[8] and wars against the seven nations whom the Israelites were commanded to exterminate in order to inhabit the land of Israel.[9] This category also includes wars whose purpose is to expand Israel's borders, which while not obligatory are nevertheless permissible.[10]

Despite the perfectly clear status of homicide as justified by the tradition under these conditions, Jewish literature, nevertheless, reflects a very real ambivalence. In fact the sources reveal either implicit tension or quite explicit conflict concerning the morality of killing in *each* of these classes. I shall argue here that the underlying currents of moral worry which the sources reveal reflect a kind of underground Jewish morality, a morality which manages to surface halakhically only in the Jewish legal discussion concerning capital punishment. Moreover, I shall suggest that these tensions are best characterized as tensions between two fundamentally different versions of moral theory, which in themselves reflect two fundamentally different philosophical and moral stances towards the world.

3   See M. Elon, ed., *The Principles of Jewish Law* (Jerusalem: Keter, 1975), 476. It has been suggested to me that there may be additional categories beyond these three. Nevertheless, it seems fairly clear that these are the most inclusive.

4   *Lev.* 20:2; 24:14; *Deut.* 17:7; 27:22; 22:21.

5   *Maim. Yad, Rotseah, 4:10; Tur H.M.* 425.

6   *Sanh.* 72a.

7   *Sanh.* 8:7.

8   *Deut.* 25:17-19.

9   *Deut.* 20:16-18.

10   *Sot.* 44b.

III. Tensions in the System

With these words of introduction we may turn to an analysis of each of the three classes of justifiable homicide. Let us begin with war.

From the historian's point of view, if not that of the moralist, war has been a part of the human condition for a very long time. Apparently recognizing its occasional utility, Jewish law sanctioned aggressive war under certain limited conditions. One form of such sanctioned war, as noted above, is war to expand Israel's boundaries. Despite its clear sanction, however, no less than the Torah itself appears ambivalent about it, an ambivalence expressed in relation to the Davidic wars. While King David's stature in the tradition is unimpeachable, he did not, in the end, build the Temple. This omission must have troubled his contemporaries deeply; biblical explanation for it is found in *II Chron.* 22:8. Nathan the Prophet[11] tells David that he may not build the Temple because

"dam larov shafakhta"
"you have spilled much blood"

This appears to be an allusion, as most commentators point out,[12] to David's extensive warring. If homicide in the context of sanctioned war were completely without moral blemish, these words would have no force. It appears then that homicide, even in the context of sanctioned war, is in at least some respect morally blemished.

Of course, Nathan's critique of David can be taken as a moral critique of war whose justification is not morally derived but religiously derived. That is, wars of expansion may indeed be unjustifiable on purely moral grounds; their justification may derive only from special divine sanction, and while God may *sanction* such wars He might in fact *prefer* that we not engage in them. It could be argued, then, that it is to this dimension of David's warfare which Nathan objected.

11 See the commentary of David Kimhi, *loc. cit.;* as he points out, an alternative explanation of the verse, and one which may be most consistent with a straightforward reading of the test, has David accusing himself of excessive killing.

12 See, e.g., *Metsudot.* Kimhi includes war in a longer list of killings for which David was responsible.

Nevertheless, elsewhere we find similar ambivalence expressed in the case of wars sanctioned on clearly *moral* grounds: wars of rescue. I refer here to the comments of several *midrashim* on Abraham's participation in the War of the Kings, cited by Everett Gendler in his "War and the Jewish Tradition".[13]

First, the *Midrash Tanḥuma:*

> Still another reason for Abraham's fear after killing the kings in battle was his sudden realization: 'Perhaps I violated the divine commandment that God commanded all men, 'Thou shalt not shed human blood' *(Gen. 9:6).* Yet how many people I killed in battle!' *(Lekh Lekha 19, ed. Buber)*

Rabbi Levi in the *Midrash Rabbah* claims that:

> Abraham was filled with misgiving thinking to himself, 'maybe there was a righteous or God-fearing man among the troops which I killed'... *(Gen. 44:4)*

Abraham participated in the wars to rescue Lot, his "brother", which the Torah apparently presumed to be a morally legitimate reason for waging war. Nevertheless, the Rabbis had Abraham expressing clearly moral misgivings over what amounts to morally justified homicide. If the homicide is justifiable - and perhaps even obligatory - then why express moral misgivings? One does what one needs to, and that should be the end of it.

Ambivalence also appears in regard to the second class of justifiable homicide, that of rescue, no less than in regard to war. I refer here to midrashic comments on the Jacob-Esau cycles in Genesis. Upon his return from the house of Laban, Jacob hears that Esau is approaching with 400 men. Commenting on the verses: "And Jacob was greatly afraid and was distressed ..." *(Gen. 32)* the *Midrash Tanḥuma* notes:

> "And Jacob was greatly afraid and was distressed." One might think that Jacob was literally afraid of Esau ...but this was not the case. Why then was Jacob afraid? Because Jacob took seriously the prohibition

---

13 This essay originally appeared in *A Conflict of Loyalties*, ed. James Finn (Boston: Bobbs Merrill Co. Inc., 1968), 78-102. The essay is reprinted in *Contemporary Jewish Ethics*, ed. M.M. Kellner, New York, Sanhedrin Press, 1978, 189-211.

against murder *(shefikhat damim)*. And so Jacob reasoned as follows: If I succeed and kill him, behold, I have trespassed against the commandment "Thou shalt not murder". And if he kills me, woe is my lot!..

Thus in a clearcut instance of self-defense, the second of our classes of justifiable homicide, the Rabbis have Jacob saying that he would be committing the transgression against murder. While this is probably not to be taken literally, Jacob still seems to be saying that there is at least *some* dimension of wrong or blameworthiness even when homicide is justifiable. While this blameworthiness would not entail legal culpability, it nevertheless obtains, at least for Jacob. Ambivalence revisited.

The most explicit instance of moral tension concerning the taking of life, and the only one with legal consequences, arises in connection with the final class of justifiable homicide: execution. Here, my remarks grow out of the extremely fine essay by Gerald Blidstein, "Capital Punishment - The Classic Jewish Discussion".[14] Blidstein first approaches the problem of capital punishment from the semantic point of view. He notes that in English the word "kill" designates any taking of human life, while "murder" designates only unauthorized killing. Nevertheless, in both biblical and rabbinic Hebrew, Blidstein argues, the same root *r-ts-h* ranges over both killing and murder. Blidstein cites a variety of texts which seem to show that the term *ratsah* or *retsiah ah* can apply to both justifiable and non-justifiable homicide: there is no universally applied semantic distinction in Hebrew between "murder" and "kill". This suggests for Blidstein that there is some deeply rooted moral vision in the tradition which refuses to splinter homicide into the unjustifiable and the justifiable. He applies this insight to the famous clash between Rabbi Akiva and Rabbi Tarfon with Rabbi Simeon ben Gamliel.

> Rabbi Tarfon and Rabbi Akiva say: 'were we in the Sanhedrin (during that period when it possessed capital jurisdiction), no man would ever have been killed.' Rabbi Simeon ben Gamliel says: 'They, too, would multiply spillers of blood in Israel.' *(Makk.* 7a).

On the basis of a careful analysis of the text, Blidstein demonstrates, quite conclusively I believe, that Rabbi Akiva and Rabbi

14 *Judaism* 14/2 (1965), 159-171, at 164, reprinted in Kellner, *ibid.*

Tarfon's opposition to capital punishment is rooted not in fear of killing the innocent, but rather in a reluctance to kill even those who are guilty. If Rabbis Akiva and Tarfon were concerned about the possibility of executing an *innocent* person, then Rabbi Simeon ben Gamliel's public safety argument would not be to the point. As Blidstein says, "once the possible innocence of the men in the docket is admitted, one cannot have his head merely to insure public safety."[15] Therefore, the concern of Rabbis Akiva and Tarfon must have been over executing the guilty. In further support of this analysis, Blidstein cites Rabbi Akiva's claim in Tosefta that "Whoever spills blood destroys the image of God" (*T. Yeb.* 8:4). Similarly, Rabbi Meir, a student of Rabbi Akiva, claims that the sight of an executed criminal hanging from a tree provokes the thought that the king (God) himself is hanging.[16]

Now Rabbis Akiva and Tarfon nowhere dispute Rabbi Simeon ben Gamliel's *empirical* claim that the public good might be harmed if the person who deserves execution is not executed. It would therefore turn out that on their view killing is a wrong despite the admitted ill consequences for the public good of not killing the murderer.

In any case, we have here a quite explicit conflict concerning the morality of what the Torah itself clearly regards as justifiable homicide: capital punishment, the third and last of our categories. The recurrent ambivalence we have pointed to thus extends to each of the three classes of justifiable homicide.

IV. The Absolutist/Consequentialist Debate

Let us reflect a bit further about the Akiva, Tarfon and Ben Gamliel debate. The former appear to hold that the moral character of capital punishment is such as to be inherently wrong, irrespective of the consequences of not executing the murderer for the public good. The latter holds that since more public good will come of capital punishment than harm, capital punishment is justified. According to this formulation of the argument, it would appear that what is at issue here is exactly what is at issue in one of the funda-

15 Blidstein in Kellner, *supra* n. 13, at 316.
16 See A.J. Heschel, *Torah Min Ha-Shamayim*, (New York: Shunzin Press, 1962), 220-223.

mental "partings of way" in moral theory. I am referring to the great chasm in moral theory between Deontological or Absolutist ethics and Teleological or Consequentialist ethics. (In the course of this essay I shall take Deontological theory to be the equivalent of Absolutist Theory and I shall use the terms interchangeably. The same will hold for Teleological Theory and Consequentialist theory.)[17]

Consequentialism (in its strict form) holds that the moral rightness or wrongness of an action is determined exclusively by the consequences of the action, i.e., by the *non*-moral good or evil it produces. For example, Utilitarianism, the most popular form of Consequentialism, holds that it is happiness which is the non-moral good by which we measure the morality of the action. If an action maximizes the sum total of happiness in the world over its alternative, then it is moral; if it reduces the sum total of happiness in the world relative to its alternatives, then it is immoral. The action in question, say paying back a loan, has no moral features in itself; its morality derives from what it does in the world. To put it in other words, actions are not moral ends in themselves; they are only means to producing some moral (or immoral) end.

Absolutism, on the other hand, maintains that actions themselves are moral ends; that certain features of the act itself make it right or wrong; i.e., that it is just, keeps a promise or is truthful. Acting justly is good not because it has wonderful consequences for society; acting justly is good because the act has the property of being just, or of conformity to the moral law "Act justly!"

Perhaps, the best way to see the difference between these two theories is to consider an example where they conflict, and where the conflict is especially painful. H.J. McCloskey[18] considers the case of a sheriff in a small town who can prevent a serious riot in which hundreds of people will certainly be killed only by framing and executing an innocent man, a scapegoat. The case can be drawn up in such a fashion that the sheriff is faced with two options: kill the scapegoat and save hundreds of lives, or refrain from killing the scapegoat and watch helplessly as hundreds of lives are lost.[19]

17 The formulations which follow owe a great deal to William Frankena's fine work, *Ethics* (Englewood, N.J.: Prentice Hall, 1973), chapter 2.

18 "A Note on Utilitarian Punishment", *Mind* 72 (1963), 599.

19 Note the similarity of this case to *T.Ter.* 7:23. We shall return to this

The Absolutist would say that framing and executing an innocent man is simply wrong, irrespective of the consequences of not executing him. The Consequentialist would say that the net lives saved by framing the scapegoat morally justifies his execution by the sheriff. I might add here that the painfulness attached to the consequentialist imperative of framing the scapegoat in this case in part contributed to the abandonment of pure forms of Utilitarianism or Conseqentialism by most contemporary ethicists.

In any case the parallels between the sheriff case and the capital punishment debate in the Talmud should by now be apparent. It would appear that the position taken by Rabbis Akiva and Tarfon against capital punishment can be accounted for by the Absolutist position, and that the position taken by Rabbi Simeon Ben Gamiel, and especially the argument he himself proposes, is a Consequentialist one. Before addressing this account of the debate more fully, however, I should like to make a number of additional comments about the positions themselves.

In a very perceptive article,[20] Thomas Nagel suggests that the difference between the two positions may be far more than abstract philosophical theory. Rather, the differences may be grounded in fundamentally differing conceptions of what is to be a moral being operating in human society. Specifically, he suggests that:

> Absolutism is associated with a view of oneself as a small being interacting with others in a large world. The justifications it requires are primarily interpersonal. Utilitarianism is associated with a view of oneself as a benevolent bureaucrat distributing such benefits as one can control to countless other beings, with whom one may have various relations or none. The justifications it requires are primarily administrative. The argument between the two moral attitudes may depend upon the priority of these two conceptions.

According to Nagel, then, what is at stake in the Absolutist/ Consequentialist debate is no less than our conception of the very essence of moral behaviour.

Of special importance to our discussion here is an additional ob-

---

point later.
20 "War and Massacre", *Philosophy and Public Affairs* 1/2 (1972), 123-144. For the following quotation, see 137f.

servation which might be made about the Absolutist/
Consequentialist debate. A general feature which distinguishes the
two schools in all their variety appears to be the possibility of
morally ambiguous action, by which I mean ambiguity which grows
out of ignorance of matters of *value*. Let me explain. According to
the Consequentialist, say a Utilitarian, ignorance of matters of
value is theoretically impossible. Once committed to the principle
"Maximize happiness!", all the Utilitarian can and must do in as-
certaining the morality of some action is to calculate its happiness-
related consequences. While this is often extremely difficult to do in
practice, the difficulty is only an empirical one, not a moral one.
Will action *a* have consequence *b* for person *c* under complex set of
circumstances *d*? Even where action *a* will in fact make some people
unhappy, if the sum total of happiness is maximized by doing *a* over
doing (or not doing) the alternatives, then the action is unambiguously good, for it clearly and unambiguously satisfies the fundamental moral principle "Maximize happiness!"

Such clarity, while characteristic of the Consequentialist point
of view, is not characteristic of the Absolutist point of view. Indeed,
on the Absolutist position, an action may simultaneously have both
moral and immoral properties. This is because an action may be simultaneously deceitful but expressive of gratitude or, to take it an
instance closer to home, just but destructive of human life, as in
killing for self-defense. Here it is unjust for me to allow myself to be
killed, but I nevertheless destroy human life when I kill the aggressor. Indeed, one of the challenges faced by the Absolutist and not the
Consequentialist is the need to establish a hierarchy of rules or values in order to determine what course of action to take where moral
rights or obligations come into conflict, as in the above-mentioned
examples. Absolutists have long sought to do this, either by appeal
to some higher rule or set of rules, by appeal to moral intuition, or
even by appeal to divine revelation. But by-and-large, any attempts at prioritization still leave a set of a least *prima facie* conflicting obligations, conflicts which point to the deep ambiguities of
the moral life. Thus, even where I am justified in protecting my own
life against an aggressor by killing him, there is still an element of
evil - unavoidable evil, but evil nonetheless, which accrues to my
action. Of course, we are not blamed for doing such actions; indeed,
sometimes we are even *obligated* to kill. This is because, in the
morally imperfect world which we inhabit, we are often unable to

avoid morally ambiguous situations.   And when we are in such situations, we have no recourse but to choose a course of action; even refraining from acting has moral valence.   When we choose a course of action we cannot but choose according to our hierarchy of value, even where one legitimate value in effect rides over another legitimate value.   We may therefore be doing *exactly* the right thing in our morally imperfect world, where value conflicts are unavoidable, by killing the aggressor.   But killing is no less murder for its being justified.

Perhaps the best analogy to this kind of ambiguity is in the all-too-common instance of medication with undesirable side effects. Many forms of chemotherapy for cancer cause nausea, temporary baldness and other side-effects.   The remission or cure which may result from undergoing chemotherapy does not erase the undesirable side effects, or void the value of not feeling nauseous or losing one's hair.   Nevertheless, in this clash of values, the value of gaining a cure for cancer clearly takes priority over the value of avoiding ill side-effects.   According to the Absolutist, moral life is similarly full of essentially conflicting values, and our choices may be equally painful.

V. *Additional Comments on Methodology*

Before applying these comments to justified homicide, I should like to raise the specter of methodology once again, if only briefly. It is exceedingly difficult, if not downright impossible, to know what the Rabbis had in their minds when taking one position or another with regard to capital punishment, or when they expressed reservations concerning justified homicide.   The only evidence we have are the texts in front of us, and all too often they are not conclusive.   Even when the historian brings cultural, political, economic, or even personal and family data to bear in explicating, say, the position of Talmudic rabbis, he is doing no more than proposing a theory which he believes accounts well for the position taken in the text.   Interesting enough, we would generally regard some adequate historical analysis with favour, even where the historian does not claim that the rabbi was consciously aware of the influences of political or personal forces in the determination of his position.   This is because historical forces may operate outside the pale of human awareness.

Similar considerations pertain where the explanation is not historical (in the broad sense mentioned above), but analytic. When the jurist or philosopher analyzes a particular text he need not claim that the author intended the theory he proposes. First, such claims are exceedingly difficult to justify, no matter what the form of explanation. Second, and most important, positions are often taken on purely intuitive or textual grounds alone. The analytic approach of the philosopher or jurist seeks to provide a theoretical formulation which accounts for those underlying convictions. For example, I may believe that (a) capital punishment is wrong, and (b) justified homicide is morally blemished, and cite verses in the Torah to prove my position. The ethicist might then propose a theory which accounts for my strong intuitions concerning a and b. The ethicist does not claim that I knew of his theory when I took the positions I did. That may or may not be the case. He does claim, however, that his theory provides an excellent explanation for why one *would want* to take those positions. To put it differently and more precisely, the theory should seek to establish the *scope* and *grounds* for the position taken: by *scope* I mean the attempt to establish the connection between a and b, and to show that they are not randomly held positions but that there is some explanatory framework which encompasses them both. Similarly, Newton's theory of gravity succeeds in showing that falling apples and planetary motions are both expressions of a single law and are both accounted for by that law. The more data (or positions) which can be explained or connected by a single theory, the broader is the theory's scope and the better confirmed it is. Second, the ethicist's theory should provide adequate *grounds* for the position I took. It is meant to explain what kind of underlying reason(s) there might be for taking the position I did. By showing that (a) and (b) are expressions of a larger and reasonable theoretical framework, a justification is provided for affirming them.

As formulated, both these explanations make no claims whatsoever about authorial intent, yet they are no less valuable in not doing so.

We have, then, an explicit formulation of the explanatory aims of a philosophical (or legal) analysis of Jewish texts: it seeks to provide both *scope* and *grounds*, where each of these aims is understood as formulated above.[21]

VI. A Return to the Sources

The position taken by Rabbi Akiva and Tarfon concerning capital punishment seems best accounted for by an Absolutist position, which would hold that there is always wrong in the taking of life. In the case of punishment, this wrong would not be overridden by concerns for the public good. While Rabbis Akiva and Tarfon concede Rabbi Simeon ben Gamliel's empirical argument that not executing murderers results in future murders, they nevertheless claim that capital punishment should be banned. This is good Absolutist ethics. Absolutism would also account for other statements quoted above by Akiva and his students, and explicate the theoretical connection between them.

Absolutism also appears to be behind the expressions of pain attributed to Jacob and Abraham by the Midrash. Because the Midrash formulates that pain in religious and moral categories, rather than in purely emotional terms (note the quotation from the Ten Commandments) it seems likely that the pain was religious and moral rather than purely emotional; and for the pain to have such moral force the Midrash must take an Absolutist moral position. Indeed, only Absolutism can capture the moral ambivalence of the dilemma Abraham and Jacob faced. As argued above, Consequentialism admits of no moral ambivalence; the greater pub-

---

21 I hope to treat this methodological issue more fully in a separate essay. For a treatment of similar (but not identical) issues in Jewish law, see *Modern Research in Jewish Law*, ed. B. Jackson (Leiden: E.J. Brill, 1980, The Jewish Law Annual Supplement One).

An interesting parallel to this concept of formulating a theory to account for human intuitions about some aspect or other may be found in moral epistemology, where the moral epistemologist seeks to account for moral intuitions through ethical theory, and conversely seeks to justify the theory by appeal to intuitions. For a brief summary and explanation of this process, which probably started with Aristotle's *Nicomachean Ethics*, see, e.g., J. Rawls, *A Theory of Justice* (Cambridge MA: Harvard University Press, 1971), Chapter 9, and especially footnote 26 (p.51). Rawls, as well as Jackson and Albeck (In *Modern Research in Jewish Law*, above), all draw a parallel to the rules of grammar as an interpretation of the linguistic intuitions of speakers. Jackson and Rawls refer also to "deep structure" as a linguistic phenomenon.

lic good is clearly served by self-defense, and so if Jacob were a Consequentialist, he would feel no ambivalence.[22] Consequentialism therefore would be unable to account for an action which is morally obligatory yet morally blemished as well.

Similarly, Nathan's critique of David may be accounted for by an Absolutist position, although it is not as clear an expression of Absolutism as the others because it may represent, as noted above, a moral critique of wars not sanctioned on moral grounds.

Where then is a Consequentialist position entailed by the tradition? After all, the ambivalence reflected in those is consistent with the right to defend myself, my family, or others, a right which is embodied in *halakhah* and which the Absolutists themselves affirm.

First, there is the position of Rabbi Simeon ben Gamliel concerning capital punishment. As suggested above, the debate there seems to be no more nor less than the debate between the Absolutist and the Consequentialist. Second, Jewish laws governing war generally seem cast in a Consequentialist frame. It should not be forgotten that wars of self-defense make up only one limited slice of a much wider range of wars which are justified in the tradition. For example, there is the category of permissible wars, which Maimonides (based upon *Sotah* 44b) says are "... (wars) to expand Israelite borders and increase its fame and greatness."[23] Such wars are justified not on account of some moral property attaching to the war itself, but on account of the consequences of waging war - the expansion of Israel's boundaries - which the tradition regards as desirable. Even obligatory wars involving the conquering of Canaan for Jewish settlement (*milḥamot zayin am'mamin*) are regarded as good only because of their consequences - vacating the land for Israelite occupation. The element of punishment seems to be secondary.

A third instance of Consequentialist ethics is the second part of the *Tosefta* in *Terumot* 7:23, which bears a striking resemblance to the story of the sheriff mentioned above. The first part of that

22 An analogue to this clash of values in the religious sphere, where the religious value overrides another, but where the religious force of the overriden value is still binding, may be found in *Tosafot Ta'anit* 11a (beginning word *amar*). There, *Tosafot* claim that the value of fasting overrides the value of not fasting, but that when one fasts, one is still regarded as a sinner.

23 *Yad, Melakhim*, 5:1.

Tosefta reads as follows:

> If heathen said to a company of men: 'give us one of you so that we might kill him or else we will kill all of you', they should let themselves be killed rather than deliver a single soul in Israel.[24]

This is good Absolutist ethics. Nevertheless, even the Consequentialist might justify this point, on the grounds that delivering one person to the heathen, particularly in the trying political circumstances of those times, might promote further lawlessness on the part of heathens who would see and act upon the ease with which one can terrorize a group of Jews. In modern times, this consideration appears to lie behind the refusal of the government of Israel to make significant concessions to gain the release of Israeli hostages held by terrorists, on the grounds that making such concessions would promote further acts of terrorism.

The second part of the *Tosefta*, however, seems to be consistent only with a Consequentialist position:

> But if they specified a certain person, as they specified Sheba ben Bichri (*II Samuel* 20:1-22), they should not allow themselves to be killed and they should hand him over.

Since the *Tosefta* speaks of heathens, it seems highly unlikely that the Jew *deserved* death (unlike Sheba). Under these circumstances, the Absolutist could never justify unjustly delivering the specified innocent Jew, even where so doing would save many lives. Therefore, it seems fairly clear that this *Tosefta* takes a Consequentialist position.

In sum, then, classical Jewish literature ranges over two fundamentally conflicting positions concerning the taking of life, a conflict which appears to be well accounted for as the conflict between Absolutist and Consequentialist ethics. To use Thomas Nagel's felicitous formulation, each of these positions may in turn reflect two

24   This text has been discussed extensively by David Daube in his *Collaboration with Tyranny in Rabbinic Law* (Oxford: Oxford University Press, 1965), and more recently be Aaron Enker, *Hekhreh vetsorekh bedine onshin* (Ramat Gan: Bar-Ilan University Press, 1977). It is worth noting that the argument between R. Yohanan and Resh Lakish in *Y.Terumot* 3:26 may well revolve around the Absolutist/Consequentialist debate.

fundamentally different moral outlooks, the outlook of the individual person interacting with other persons, and the outlook of the bureaucrat seeking how best distribute the goods at his disposal.

VII. Some Closing Observations

Several observations are in order before our analysis is complete. First, with the notable exception of Akiva and Tarfon on capital punishment, the Absolutist position within Judaism appears far more extensively in aggadic than in halakhic literature. Second, because the Absolutist position takes individual human rights more seriously than does the Consequentialist position, it is generally regarded by most contemporary ethicists as in some sense a "higher" ethic. Utilitarian ethics, because it is more open to objective decision making, because it is less obstinate about individual rights when the safe and efficient functioning of society is at stake, is generally regarded as more practical and reality-centered.

Taking these two observations together, the following claim emerges naturally: our aggadic materials concerning the taking of life advocate the higher, Absolutist ethic; halakhic materials, on the other hand, with their generally Consequentialist ethic, take on a more practical, realistic orientation towards morality. Thus the *halakhah* sanctions certain forms of war, for example, for the greater good of society. The tensions in the tradition might then be described as tensions between practical *halakhah*, which seek to govern the minutiae of daily living and can do so only when sensitive to its practical demands, and the aggadah, which projects an ideal moral standard towards which all Jews ought to aspire.

While attractive, this formulation is too facile. Capital punishment is surely a halakhic issue, yet the tension between Absolutism and Consequentialism stands explicit in Talmudic debate. The counterexample is too striking.

Perhaps a better formulation might look to the *halakhah* itself as stretching between the ideal and the real. It has been argued by some theologians of *halakhah* that (1) the halakhic system is a compromised one in that it embodies a compromise between the practical demands of daily life and the highest spiritual and moral ideals; and (2) that through its "stretch" between the practical and the ideal, *halakhah* seeks to nudge reality ever closer to the ideal. In taking-of-life issues, the aggadic materials cited above express an ideal ethic which, in the capital punishment issue, *halakhah* itself sought progressively to embrace as it developed through Rabbis Akiva and Tarfon.   Capital punishment would thus reflect *halakhah* as it questioned the practical, utilitarian argument of Rabbi Simeon ben Gamliel and edged toward an absolute respect for human life in the context of punishment.

If this analysis is correct, then the capital punishment debate snaps a picture of *halakhah,* and the Jewish people, as they undergo a fundamental moral stretch in relation to the taking of a human life.

THE INTERACTION OF MORALITY AND JEWISH LAW[*]

by

IZHAK ENGLARD[**]

A meaningful and productive discussion of law and morality has always proven itself an extremely difficult enterprise, given the variety of meanings in which these terms have been employed. It is not only a problem of semantics, which probably could be solved with relative ease, but unfortunately one of basic philosophical and methodological assumptions. The definitional differences are founded upon divergent ideologies which often cannot be bridged. Furthermore, similar problems beset the notion of Judaism and to some degree even the term "interaction" is ambiguous. I shall try to overcome these indeed formidable obstacles to fruitful discussion by stating some of my assumptions.

First the notions of law and morality in general, their relationship and interaction will be treated. Only then shall I proceed to the specific problem concerning Jewish law.

I

Both *law* and *morality* are concerned with establishing rules of human behavior. They actually constitute sets of such rules, normative orders.

The essential difference between a legal and a moral norm resides in the nature of the respective sanction imposed for a violation. Whereas behind a legal rule stands the threat of a predetermined and organized societal sanction (generally physically executed by a State organ), moral sanctions are of a different kind. The notion of *morality*, however, is used in different meanings: in one sense, it denotes what can be called *positive morality*, a set of rules of behavior generally accepted by society. It comprises rules of etiquette, and

---

[*] This paper is based on a lecture given in 1976 in the framework of a theological conference in California, U.S.A. A completely revised, updated and fully referenced version is to be published by the Princeton University Press.

[**] Professor of Law, Hebrew University, Jerusalem.

general standards of human behavior. Very often it is used in relation to sexual behavior. Society enforces its rules of positive morality by imposing a variety of sanctions (ranging from derision to ostracism) but none of them by way of predetermined organized physical force.

In another sense, morality means what can be called personal ethics, a normative order created by the individual for his own behavior. It is the individual's decision on the ideal conduct sanctioned by internal feelings of remorse or gratification.

Formally, every normative system is by its very nature self-sufficient. It possesses all the necessary criteria for evaluating the human behavior with which it is concerned. In other words, a normative order is unitary and exclusive. According to Kelsen's school, the unitary test of validity of the single norm is to be found in the so-called *basic norm*, the fundamental hypothesis of any given normative order.[1] In the United States the basic norm of the legal system would accordingly be the hypothesis that one ought to abide by the provisions of the U.S. Constitution. Thus, no legal norm is valid in the United States which cannot be shown to derive its validity from the same Constitution.

Hence, from a purely normative and formal point of view no interaction is possible between law and morality, both constituting separate and exclusive normative systems.[2] The validity of a specific legal system is completely independent from morality or ethics, and *vice-versa*. In more concrete terms: a law may be considered immoral, but remain valid under its own legal criteria; an act judged moral may nevertheless constitute a violation of the law.

A relationship between law and morality can be created on the normative level only by formal incorporation. A law may refer explicitly to moral rules and standards, but normatively this would signify the transformation of these rules and standards into legal norms by providing them with legal sanctions. Conversely, positive morality or personal ethics may stipulate obedience to a law, not only because of its specific content but merely because of its being law

---

1   H. Kelsen, *Pure Theory of Law* (Berkeley: University of California Press, 1967).

2   On this problem in general see I. Englard, *Religious Law in the Israel Legal System* (Jerusalem: Harry Sacher Institute for Legislative Research and Comparative Law, 1975).

enacted by society. Thus, in the famous trial of Socrates, the latter considered himself morally bound to submit to judicial decision.[3]

The normative aspect of law and morality is of course not the only possible one. Psychology, sociology, history and other sciences will provide a different vantage point. But all these other outlooks are what can be called *"external"* to the system, whereas the normative one is *internal*, i.e. the system is seen from within. The "validity" and "legitimacy" of the norms must be based on the internal rules of the system itself.

II

Besides the formal distinction between law and morality, there exists another important difference concerning their substance. Morality and Ethics tend to base themselves on the content of normative principles considered "just", "good", "right", "moral", an expression of absolute values. The desirable human behavior in a given concrete situation is the application of these principles. Hence, moral behavior is the one in conformity to the substantive principle. In Kelsen's terminology[4] a moral system in this sense is a *static* normative order, since the validity of every moral rule can be traced back to a permanent substantive principle. For example, from the general principle "love your neighbor as yourself" one could derive rules such as: "do not harm him" or "help him in need", etc. The validity of these specific rules would be tested against the static content of the general principle. Moreover, from the general rule an indefinite number of concrete rules could be deduced.

Systems of positive law on the other hand are essentially of a *dynamic* character, in the sense that the presupposed basic norm does not supply any specific content to the norms constituting the system.

The basic norm determines only the authorization of a norm-creating authority. It is a formal test devoid of substance: one ought to behave according to the commands of the highest norm-creating authority or according to the norms created by custom. In the context of

---

3   See recently A. D'Amato, "Obligation to Obey the Law: A Study of the Death of Socrates", *Southern California Law Review* 49 (1976), 1079-1108.

4   *Pure Theory of Law, supra* n. 1, at 195-198.

the United States it states as above mentioned: one ought to behave as the Constitution prescribes, i.e., whatever the Constitution prescribes is legally binding. But once given this supreme dynamic principle, the Constitution by its concrete substantive content imposes upon the lower norms, including the laws of Congress, a static principle. Laws which contradict the *tenor* of the Constitution are (declared) void. Thus a supreme dynamic principle can be combined with static principles.

The substance of moral rules raises the fundamental problem of values. We limit ourselves to a simple and simplistic statement of our personal assumptions. There is no way to determine objectively *absolute* values. Neither reason nor nature can establish absolute human values. We do not deny the existence of values, but we consider them of an inherent relative nature.

We prefer therefore to define the problem of morality as one of *moral decision* which is the required value judgment in a given situation.[5] Moral problems are the result of conflicting values, the choice between which is a moral decision. These problems and their resolution demonstrate the relative nature of the values involved. In other words there is no human value which will prevail in all situations. For instance, human life itself, certainly a most important value in any moral system, has to yield in all societies before the country's survival (war) and in most of them before the aims of punishment (death penalty). The act of preferring one value over another, the essence of the moral decision, is therefore a *subjective* value judgment. It is precisely the basic legitimacy of all relevant values that renders in practice the moral decision so difficult. Indeed, very often each of the values involved in the conflict is, when separately considered, legitimate. It is their mutual inconsistency which requires a choice, a rejection of some of them in the given circumstances.

If we consider now the problem of morality and ethics as one of value judgment, of moral decision, the relationship between them and the law receives a further dimension, beyond the formal normative one.

Any specific law is the result of a moral decision made by the legislator. By imposing a certain behavior it necessarily restricts

5   See the excellent discussion in E. Goldman, "Religion, Morality, and Halakha", *De'ot* 20 (1962), 47-61; 21 (1962), 59-72; 22 (1963), 65-76.

the individual's freedom of action, preferring a collective aim over personal autonomy. By requiring obedience to the legislator's will, the law constitutes an institutionalized normative context (value) with a highly standardized solution of a moral problem.[6] In other words, the individual, faced with the problem of how to behave in the situation envisaged by the law, is required to forgo a renewed and independent weighing of the relevant values involved. He is asked to accept the law's solution of the moral problem.

But in reality most legal norms cannot provide a clear-cut solution. The reasons for this uncertainty of the law are manifold and we will mention some of them in discussing the application of Jewish law. It suffices to mention here that as a result, the judge, when applying the rules of law, has to make new moral decisions. This flow of value judgments during the judicial process is the well-known phenomenon of judicial creativity.

In conclusion, the interaction of law and morality, excluded on the pure normative level, is most significant in the legal and judicial process which determines the specific content of a legal norm.

Any actual conflict between legal and moral norms takes place only in the mind of the individual who considers himself initially bound by the two sets of norms. The resolution of this conflict requires individual moral decision, implying preference of one norm over the other and endurance of the rejected norm's sanction.

III

To what extent is our general discussion on the relationship between law and morality relevant to the specific problem of interaction between morality and Jewish Law? The concept of Jewish Law introduces the element of religion. Jewish Law, the *Halakhah*, is a religious law, which means that it assumes a supra-human lawgiver. Furthermore, it threatens the violator of its norms with additional transcendent sanctions which are beyond human control.

From a pure formal normative point of view, Jewish Law is an exclusive and unitary set of rules, exactly like any other normative order. Hence, its normative validity cannot logically be subordinated contemporaneously to another test besides its own basic norm, namely that one has to abide by the precepts of the divine legisla-

---

6   In Goldman's terminology, *ibid.*, a "closed moral context".

tor.

But this formal answer does not solve the actually experienced problem of the relationship and interaction between Jewish law and morality.

There is the primary and indisputable fact that we often experience a real conflict between positive morality and personal ethics on the one hand and specific religious rules on the other. Even if the norms of social or personal morality cannot claim to be of an absolute nature, we conceive them psychologically as binding or at least desirable in ordering human life.

In the context of Jewish Law this conflict is actually quite common in relation to the discriminatory rules against Gentiles, women, bastards (*mamzerim*) and in connection with the ideas of religious coercion implying a basically intolerant attitude towards non-believers and members of other religions.

This situation creates a deeply felt theological problem. The issue is by no means novel, witness the medieval discussions between rationalists and voluntarists. But it seems that these ancient speculations were of a more theoretical nature. In the modern context the fundamental question of the significance of religious experience and of the aims and functions of religious law is raised. This question is of crucial importance when the individual stands before the dilemma of a religious precept which contradicts his deeply felt own convictions, both norms being conceived as essentially binding. The easy intellectual escape of denying the very possibility of such a conflict does not exist. Hence the solution which presupposes the necessary rationality (morality) of *true* religion - as Kant assumed - is of no avail to the believer who accepts the authentic nature of the specific religious command.[7] In these cases there is a genuine conflict between the moral and religious experience of a person.

Morality as a normative order is necessarily anthropocentric, directed at the fulfillment of human interests. The human being is the end object of all moral rules. In traditional halakhic Judaism, however, the problem clearly requires a theocentric answer. Religion transcends human interest, its ultimate end is not human happiness but service of the Creator. This is probably true in many religions, but the specific Jewish idea is its implementation by

---

7   See for a criticism of Kant's position towards the religious experience, P. Haezrahi, *The Price of Morality* (London: Allen & Unwin, 1961), ch. 8.

means of detailed rules of behavior of a predominantly legal nature
(*Halakhah*). Service of the Creator is the absolute value in face of
which no contrary human value system can be considered legitimate.
An extreme formulation of this idea would be that the greater the
sacrifice of human values (morality, ethics), the greater the religious significance of obedience to the law. The sacrifice of human
values is an act of faith.

An illustration of the idea can be found in the Talmud in relation
to King Saul's conduct towards the Amalekites: "When the Holy
One, blessed be He, said to Saul: Now go and smite Amalek, he said:
If on account of one person the Torah said: Perform the ceremony of
the heifer whose neck is to be broken, how much more ought consideration to be given to all these persons. And if human beings sinned,
what has the cattle committed; and if the adults have sinned, what
have the little ones done? A divine voice came forth and said: Be
not righteous overmuch."[8]

The parallel passage in *Midrash Rabbah* adds: "Don't be more
just than your Creator."[9]

The basic attitude of modern orthodox Judaism has found its extreme formulation in the influential writings of Y. Leibovitch:
"Ethics has only one of two meanings: (1) Ethics is the direction of
man's volition according to his perception of the truth of reality -
this is the ethic of Socrates, Plato and Aristotle, of the Epicureans
and Stoics, especially of the latter, and in modern philosophy - of
Spinoza. (2) Ethics is the direction of human volition according to
his perception of duty - this is the ethics of Kant and German
Idealism. But in the *Shema* prayer it reads (*Num.* 1.39): '... and that
ye seek not after your own heart and your own eyes': 'seek not after
your own heart' - this is the rejection of Kant; 'seek not after your
own eyes' - this is the rejection of Socrates. Hence, there are no
moral precepts based on perception of reality or perception of duty:
there is only the command of the Creator."[10]

In the same line of reasoning Leibovitch rejects every attempt to
base religious precepts on purely utilitarian grounds. In his customary incisive language he stigmatizes the moral approach: "Only one
who considers the human being the ultimate end and supreme value,

8   *Yoma* 22b.
9   *Midrash Ḳohelet*, 7.33.
10   *De'ot* 9 (1959),15-22, at 20.

i.e., man in the place of God, can be a moral person."[11]

IV

Even if this direct opposition between the moral and the religious experience may be unexceptionable in principle under the neo-orthodox conception, the inevitable pre-legal and meta-legal dimensions of Jewish religion create a further level of interaction between morality and Jewish law. This relationship does not concern head-on conflicts between personal convictions and *halakhic* precepts, where the latter take absolute precedence. A possible positive interaction relates first to personal motivation in the fulfillment of religious precept. Judaism attaches considerable importance to the mental attitude of the individual abiding by the rule of behavior. He is required to act under the conscious acceptance of the obligatory nature of the precept *qua* religious command. A few Talmudic and rabbinic sources will illustrate this central point. First, the fundamental principle mentioned in the name of R. Hanina: "He who is commanded and does fulfill the law, stands higher than he who is not commanded and fulfills it."[12]

The required motivation is therefore not one of personal conviction but the conscious acceptance of the external character of God's command.

The same idea is articulated in the Midrash in relation to the prohibition of pork: "Don't say: 'I have no desire for it,' but 'I want it, but what can I do, God has ordered it to be prohibited.'[13]

We encounter this idea throughout rabbinic literature. Maimonides denies gentiles who abide by the seven Noahide laws, by virtue of their own reasoned conviction, the status of the "pious"; they have to acknowledge the obligatory character of the rules as *religious laws given on Sinai.* [14]

Further examples can be found in connection with universally accepted rules of behavior, which men tend to base on reason or "natural law." Many Rabbis underline the importance of bestowing on these acts a religious dimension, by accepting the obligatory

---

11 *Ibid.*

12 *Avoda Zara*, 3a and elsewhere.

13 *Kohelet, Kedoshim*, 11, 22, in the name of R. Elazar b. Azaria.

14 Maimonides, *Hilkhot Melakhim*, 8:11.

character of the divine command.

The idea is further developed in the classic problem, who is greater, the man who in order to behave well has to overcome his evil inclinations, or the one who by nature is good. It is of no surprise that in principle the former is considered greater in Judaism.[15]

It is true that an identical approach can be found in Kant's concept of moral *duty*. In his view, a man acting "good" out of natural inclination, does not perform a "moral act". But Kant's moral duty relates to an imperative based on human reason, not to a supra-human law.

Finally, the Talmudic distinction of serving God out of fear or out of pure love[16] stresses again the importance of the motivational aspect of human behavior in relation to religious law.

A second area of interaction between religious law and morality is to be found where the strict legal standards established by religious law are considered too permissive. In practice this situation does not constitute a very serious problem, since the possibility of forbearance is a satisfactory solution.

Interestingly, the *Halakhah* itself recognizes various grades of behavior - the requirements of a *Ḥaṣid* (just) are stricter than that of an ordinary man. A series of concepts introduces norms of a moral character (in the sense of being non legally-enforceable, but recommended to the pious). Mention should be made of such Talmudic notions as: "And you shall do what is upright and good (in the sight of the Lord)" (*Deut.* 6:18); "Beyond the strict law";[17] "Standard of Saintliness".[18]

One further, and possibly the most important aspect of interaction relates to the legal and judicial process of religious law.

Given the open texture of the *halakhic* system, a characteristic of all legal systems, moral decisions, in the sense of value judgments,

---

15 Compare Maimonides, *Shemone Pera ḳim*, ch. 6, and see Yaabez, *ad loc.*, who rejects the distinction made by Maimonides between two kinds of prohibitions.

16 On Fear of Heaven, Awe and Love in relation to human conduct, see generally, E.E. Urbach, *The Sages, their Concepts and Beliefs* (Jerusalem: Magnes Press, 1969), ch. 14.

17 *Baba Mezia* 24b, 30b; *Baba Kamma* 99b.

18 *Baba Mezia* 51b-52b, *Shabbat* 120a, *Ḥullin* 130b. See Silberg, *Talmudic Law and Modern State* (New York: Burning Bush Press, 1973), 93-130.

must be made during the judicial and legislative process.

Beyond the inherent flexibility of legal language-- which is partly the result of the ambiguity of language in general - the *Halakhah* has evolved principles which can serve as a vehicle for the infusion of human values. A few examples will illustrate the point.

Thus, the talmudic principle of "avoidance of hostility"[19] has been employed *inter alia* to implement norms of positive morality in relation to Gentiles. A similar role is played by the maxim: "Her [Tora's] ways are ways of pleasantness and all her paths are peace" *(Prov.* 3:17)[20] - the notions of pleasantness and peace having clear moral and utilitarian undertones.

Moreover, even if it is assumed that the ultimate and overriding aim of Judaism is "service of the Creator", the welfare of the individual and of society are important - albeit mediate - goal of religious law. They are not conceived as ends in themselves, but their realization is often a prerequisite for the achievement of the ultimate calling.

There can be no doubt that Jewish law has adapted to historical circumstances in order to maintain a proper social framework.

Any external historical assessment of the development of Jewish law will stress the reality of a multitude of moral decisions reflecting then current views and beliefs. But contrary to widespread belief, no normative conclusions can be drawn from the historical fact of legal changes. Historic reality by itself cannot determine or create a rule of behavior. It is the underlying ideology which is able to provide rules of conduct. From an internal halakhic point of view, the problem is one of legitimacy, namely, what are the legitimate considerations which may be taken into account when creating a new norm?

There exists, no doubt, a considerable freedom of choice in legislation and adjudication. The ubiquity of dissent in Rabbinic literature bears witness to the "leeways" of decision. Halakhic Judaism was always well aware of the central place personal value judgments occupy in the judicial process. As a result it has always required the personal commitment of the scholar and judge to the basic

19   *Avoda Zara,* 26a.
20   *Yebamot* 87b.

tenets of religion: the fear of God precedes wisdom.[21]

The legitimating factor of all norm-creating activity is to be found in the ideological assumptions of the individual decider. In *halakhic* Judaism they center around the theocentricity of all human concerns. The decisive element in the human condition is man's position before his Creator.

In conclusion: the basic question cannot be how do moral considerations affect the shaping of Jewish law, nor how does Jewish law respond to new moral problems.

The fundamental issue is normative: *should* current moral considerations affect the shaping of Jewish Law? *Should* Jewish law respond in an affirmative sense to new moral attitudes?

Any attempt to answer these crucial questions puts the believing Jew to his ultimate test. It requires from him to determine his position before the Creator in the light of a binding tradition. He will have to ask himself if his striving for the adaptation of religious law to his personal convictions and feelings of morality is not an act of human conceit and insubordination, manifesting an oblivion to his real position before God. No measure of intellectual knowledge and sophistication can relieve him from seeking an honest and humble answer.

---

21 *Psalms* 111:10; *E Avot* 3:9. Compare I. Englard, "The Problem of Jewish Law in a Jewish State", *Israel Law Review* 3 (1968), 254-278, at 270.

FACT SKEPTICISM IN JEWISH LAW

by

ABRAHAM M. FUSS[*]

Professor Lon Fuller begins his book on Legal Fiction with the statement: "Probably no lawyer would deny that judges and writers on legal topics frequently make statements they know to be false. These statements are called 'fictions'".[1] Similarly, in my view, the facts as stated by the judge in a case are not always intended as an objective recital of data. It is my thesis that not infrequently the conclusions regarding the operative facts in a case or with respect to precedent are made in light of the law affecting the facts. In this way a Rabbinic Court can reach substantially different conclusions in a given case without modifying or altering the established and hallowed principles of law.

This is not to say that distinctions based on facts not in evidence, but presumed, are in any way lies. On the contrary, Rabbis in attempting to reconcile seemingly conflicting rulings must presume facts that will uphold both custom, law, and perceived reality. This indeed is the foundation of any legal reasoning.

The late Judge Jerome Frank of the U.S. Federal Court wrote a number of books and articles on this subject wherein he reacted to the discerned process of the court applying legal rules to the facts of law suits. The classic view of the law (and Jewish law as well) assumes that the difficulty is to discover the rules while the facts appear before the court as cold objective data merely to be assembled and put into the legal computer. Finding the facts is considered a mechanical process.[2] The reality is quite different. Facts are not data of past

---

*   Attorney, Jerusalem and New York.

1   L. Fuller, *Legal Fictions* (Stanford: Stanford University Press, 1967), 1.

2   See J. Frank, *Courts On Trial: Myth and Reality In American Justice* (Princeton, N.J.: Princeton University Press, 1949), 14ff.; W. Friedman, *Legal Theory*, 5th edition (N.Y.: Carswell, 1967), 292-311; *Salmond on Jurisprudence*, 12 edition (London, Sweet & Maxwell, 1966), 35-43; E. Cohn, "Fact skepticism and Fundamental Law", *New York University Law Review* 33/1 (1958); J.M. Rosenberg, *Jerome Frank Jurist and Philosopher* (N.Y., Philosophical Library, 1970), 1ff.

events. Rather, they are the court's statements about events based on testimony, evidence and the Court's subjective attitude to these, which may or may not be influenced by the consequences of the decision. Frank illustrated this with the simple example of a jury having to decide whether Mr. Jones passed a red light or not. In the U.S. and England, of course, the lay jury are the triers of the facts while the Judge is the arbiter of the law. Suppose, now, that the fine for passing a red light is a ten year jail sentence as opposed to a $10 fine. Is it not likely that a jury would find far fewer cases where in fact the driver passed a red light? In other words the legal consequences affect the process of establishing the facts. This approach and analysis would fit under the heading of legal realism. Indeed I suggest that many of the great Posekim and Rabbinic Arbitors of the law in each generation were legal realists.

In Jewish law there are many examples where the finding of the facts is influenced by the conclusions of law. One is reminded, of course, of the views of R. Akiva and R. Tarfon who stated that had they been members of the Sanhedrin, no one would ever have been found guilty of the death penalty.[3] R. Tarfon and R. Akiva would reach this result by so cross examining the witnesses that their answers would be found deficient to impose the death penalty. Hence, the Tannaim would reach a desired result without disturbing the principles of law.

Before proceeding to give a variety of examples of what might be called fact skepticism or fact selection, it is useful to list various classes of facts which should be considered.

1. Facts of the case
    (a) events
    (b) intent of the parties
    (c) general socio-economic, geographic, political background of the case.
2. Ancient facts - of controlling precedent divided into the same subcategories
    (a) events including intent of parties as previously determined
    (b) intent of the Rabbis

3   *Mishnah Makkot* 1:10. See *Otsar Mefarshei Hatalmud* (Jerusalem, Makhon Yerushalayim, 5735).

(c) general background
3. Views of History - e.g. changes after the destruction of Temple.
4. Legislative intent.

Generally speaking the statement of facts as found in the Responsa literature is that which the enquirer has abstracted and submitted to the responding rabbi. We do not have a raw record to compare to the facts as stated in the responsum. Therefore we will have to look elsewhere for illustrations of our proposition.

An area of law which transverses both religious and civil law is that concerning an illegitimate child born of a union proscribed in the Torah *(mamzer).*

"A bastard shall not enter in the assembly of the L-rd; even to the tenth generation shall none of his enter into the assembly of the L-rd" *(Deuteronomy* 23:3). There is an interesting exchange in the Talmud.[4] A question was put to R. Eliezer: what is the rule with respect to the eleventh generation *mamzer?* He answered: bring me the third generation and I will purify him. What is the reason of R. Eliezer? Because he doesn't survive. R. Eliezer maintains, with R. Hanina, that once in 60 or 70 years G-d brings a plague in the world and wipes out all *mamzerim* and takes with him *kesherim* (not *mamzerim*) in order not to publicize the sinners [not to single out mamzerim...]. R. Eliezer doesn't challenge the Biblical rule proscribing *mamzerim* from entering the Jewish community. He merely states a fact that they are killed every 60 or 70 years and therefore those people who are alive are not *mamzerim.*

R. Huna says: a *mamzer* does not live more than 30 days. The Talmud explains that this refers to unknown *mamzerim;* known *mamzerim* live. On this basis people who are alive and are not known as *mamzerim* are not *mamzerim.* The above illustrates the efforts made to use supposed events to fortify halakhic presumptions.

R. Shlomo Luria (16th century) concludes as follows: We are prohibited from marrying both male and female *mamzerim.* This refers to those that we know definitely are *mamzerim.* Those we don't know about don't live. Thus where there is a question and there are rumors concerning a person's family purity we know that if his

4   *Y.Yev.* 41a, *Kidd.*43b, *Yev.* 78b. See also *Sdei Hemed* , vol.2, 878, No.34.

progeny survive for three generations there was no truth to the accusation.[5]

R. Josi in the name of R. Meir said: *mamzerim* will be purified in the days to come,[6] as it states in *Ezekiel* 36:25: "and I will sprinkle clean water upon you and ye shall be clean from all your uncleanliness and from all your idols I will cleanse you".[7]

Ran (d. 1380) concludes from this statement that the law will be according to R. Josi. Moreover even now those families who have become contaminated by having *mamzerim* will remain pure on the basis that any witness who could testify as to their impurity will not do so.[8] As we assume that when Elijah the prophet will return he will know the complete truth and yet he will not reveal it so too we are charged not to reveal which family has *mamzerim* in it.

We may then conclude from the above that at least R. Josi and his followers were interested in restricting the embarrassment of having a family declared impure. He therefore made some factual conclusion as to the state of events in the future from which Ran chose to conclude that the revelation of the truth for its own sake at this time was not necessary.

Indeed we do not usually fix the law which will be when the Messiah comes (*hilkhitah demeshih ah*). Nevertheless an exception is made when it has practical applications.[9]

This rather abstract discussion has halakhic implications. The following case decided by R. Ovadia Joseph, the former Sephardic Chief Rabbi of Israel, reported in the *Journal Moriah*, is of great interest, even though the case relies on principles of exclusionary evidence to reach a desired result.[10]

A girl from the United States testified that her mother was married to her first husband in 1953. According to the mother she was married in a religious ceremony performed by a Rabbi. The

5   *Yam Shel Shlomo, Yev.* ch.8, n.26.
6   *Y. Kidd.* 35a, *Kidd.* 72b.
7   The end of the passage in the printed Jerushalmi reads: R. Huna in the name of R. Joseph states that the halakhah is not according to R. Josi in the days to come. However, Lieberman based on *Midrash Vayi ḳra Rabba* concludes that the text should be that the law is with R. Josi, as it is in the Bavli (*Tosefta Ki-Fishutah, Kiddushin* 971-2).
8   On *Kidd.* 72b printed with Rif.
9   See *Encyclopedia Talmudit*, vol. 9, 388-390.
10 *Moriah* 14 (Shevat 5746), 47ff.

rabbi said that his usual practice was that he, together with the sexton, both being Sabbath observant, were the witnesses at the marriages he performed. The Rabbi, however, did not remember this particular marriage ceremony. Apparently there was a *Ketubah* but it has not been found. The mother lived with the first husband three months. At the request of the mother, the marriage was annulled by the civil court. The mother never went to the *mikvah* prior to or during the marriage. Two years later, the mother married the girl's father in a ceremony performed by a reform Rabbi. There was no *Get* from the first marriage. The question is whether the daughter is a *mamzeret* and prohibited from marrying a non-*mamzer*.

R. Ovadya Joseph invalidates the mother's testimony, based on a well known rule that a mother is not believed to invalidate her child.[11] Further he does not see a duty on the court to initiate an inquiry of the first husband to obtain the true facts. Moreover the first husband may have an interest in testifying that there was a valid first marriage in order to take revenge on the former wife.

As a result, the girl is eligible to marry any Jew. The opinion considers other problems and resolves them. This is a case where the rigid application of laws of evidence results in solving a heart-rending human problem. The subjective supposed knowledge of "the truth" has nothing to do with the court's decision. The decision is not unique. A similar case was reported in another Torah journal, *No'am*, some twenty years ago.[12]

R. Josi and R. Huna thus reach their conclusions by describing events which do not have historical validity. One must be careful however to distinguish cases where statements of historical fact are made without evidence and those cases which are based on either scriptural passages or historical information. An example of this kind of legal conclusion would be the following.

There is a prohibition of accepting proselytes from Ammonites or Moabites. The Mishnah[13] relates a debate between Rabbi Gamliel and R. Yehoshua. R. Gamliel prohibits accepting proselytes from among them, based on the explicit Biblical statement. R. Yehoshua,

---

11 *Mishneh Torah, Isure Biyah* 15:19, *Shulhan Arukh Even Ha'ezer* 4:29.
12 Vol. 14 (1971), 22-27, Responsum of R. Hayyim David Regensberg.
13 *Yadayim* 4:4. See S. Baron, *History and Jewish Historians* (Philadelphia, Jewish Publication Society, 1964), 136 and notes.

however, permits their entry based on a change of circumstances. To wit, Sannecherib, king of Assyria, came up and intermingled all the nations, as it is written (*Isaiah* 10:13) "I have removed the bounds of the peoples etc.", to which R. Gamliel answered from *Jeremiah* 49:6, "But afterward I will bring again the captivity of the children of Ammon." The halakhah is in accordance with R. Yehoshua. In fact Maimonides goes a step further. He rules that not only were Ammon and Moab intermingled with the other people, but Edom and Egypt also were intermingled.[14]

Hence there is no prohibition of accepting any proselytes. The Egyptians are not pure Egyptians, but a different people. This conclusion with respect to the historical events is what determines the legal decision. Rosh, R. Asher b. Yehiel (1250-1327), the thirteenth century rabbinic authority who came from Ashkenaz to Spain, concludes that Egyptians may not be accepted as proselytes to intermarry with an Israelite until after the third generation. Until then they can only marry another proselyte.[15] Although both Maimonides and Rosh each cite proof-texts to support their historical point of view, these are not determinative. In the 18th century R. Jacob Emden (1698-1776) ruled that a proselyte from Rome should not marry an Israelite, only another proselyte, on the grounds that Rosh denied accepting Egyptians because they never suffered complete uprooting and banishment. Intermingling is not enough to remove the basic character of the people. Similarly Rome which is Edom never suffered such an uprooting and therefore the name remains with the prohibition.[16]

In this connection we should mention the prohibition of Jews returning to live Egypt, which is mentioned three times in the Torah. Maimonides cites this prohibition and states explicitly that one may not return to Egypt to settle there. One may travel there on business or to conquer.[17] This prohibition still applied despite Sannecherib's intermixing of people. The Rabbis in reaching legal conclusions were in each case dealing with historical data which they thought to be correct probably without forcing the issue.

---

14 *Mishna Torah: Is̱ure Biyah* 12:25 based on *Tosefta Kiddushin*   5:6; see S. Lieberman, *supra* n.8, at 972.
15 *Ṭur, Even Ha'ezer* 4.
16 *She'elot Yavets*, no. 46.
17 *Hilkhot Melakhim* 5:7 and 8.

Having expressed this caveat we may proceed to illustrate our general thesis. It was thought that the Gentiles in ancient times were idol worshippers - as opposed to some Gentiles in the Talmudic period and most Gentiles in the post Talmudic period, who are considered as not being idol worshippers. R. Johanan (3rd century) ruled that Gentiles living outside of Palestine are not considered as idol worshippers, they only continue the usage of their forefathers.[18] There is no historical basis for such a statement, although there may be a basis for concluding, as do the later Rabbis, that the later generations were less pious in their idol worship than the earlier ones. Similarly Samuel ruled that the prohibition of dealing with Gentiles three days before their holidays is limited to the one day only. R. Menahem Meiri (1249-1316) went even further.[19] We are interested in the technique that distinguished the law in the Mishnah from that applied in the Middle Ages. The method used was one of distinguishing the facts as they pertain to Gentiles today from the ones defined in the Mishnah. Rashi bases the distinction on his conclusion that Gentiles in our days are not expert in idolatry.[20]

Various halakhot governing Jewish-Gentile relationships were based in good part on the fact that the ancient gentiles were idolators. Many of these halakhot were either abrogated or were less strictly observed once it was established that the gentiles in our days, and outside of the land of Israel, are no longer idol-worshippers. Therefore, we are now permitted to partake of their bread and beer. We may do business with them on their holidays, have our hair cut by them, and are permitted certain types of food cooked by gentiles, all of which was originally prohibited.[21]

Prof. Faur in an article on "The Legal Thinking of the Tosafists"[22] gives some examples where the Tosafists give explanations of Christian practice which are factually incorrect but which result in relieving Jewish business men in the Middle Ages from unwanted

18 *Hullin* 13b; see also H.J. Zimmels, *Ashkenazim and Sephardim* (London, Oxford University Press, 1958), 208.

19 *Beth Hab ehirah, Avodah Zarah,* 28; see also J. Katz, *Between Jews and Gentiles* (Jerusalem, Mosad Bialik, 1960) (Hebrew), 116ff., *Halakhah and Kabbalah* (Jerusalem, Magnes Press, 1984) (Hebrew), 291-310.

20 Resp Rashi No. 327

21 Reb Z.H. Chajes, *Darkhe Hora'ah* (Heb.), in *Kol Kitve Maharats Chajes,* Vol.1, 230.

22 *Diné Israel* 6 (1975), XLIII-LXXII, at LXVIII.

restrictions. Thus Jews were permitted to purchase bread offered in the Mass. The Tosafist explained that it was brought as a present to the priest, not as a sacrifice.[23] Also Jews were permitted to purchase candles which were offered in the Church on the grounds that they were brought as ornaments, not as votive offerings. It is a mute question whether these incorrect statements regarding the Christian religion were the result of ignorance or were intended to be the justification for permissive practice.

A different category of knowledge about the past relates to legislative intent. The judge deciding a case in 12th century France, for example, must decide what the intent of a rule of law is. In this respect, since he is generally dealing with case law he must determine what precisely were the facts in the case before the Ancient Court and what would that Court decide in the present circumstances. For example, Rabenu Tam, the leading authority in 12th century France, considered the question whether in a civil case it is acceptable to obtain testimony of a witness in writing rather than orally before the Court.[24] *Deuteronomy* 19:15 refers to the mouths of witnesses as the source for establishing facts. The interpretation that this applies to civil cases and to oral testimony seems to be clear from the Tannaitic sources (through 2nd century). Yet R. Tam found that the practice in France was to allow the witnesses to send their testimony by letter to the Court when they reside at a distance from the place of trial. He reconciled the literary legal source with the customary law by stating that the Biblical verse prohibited written testimony only in a case where the witness is physically incapable of giving oral testimony. However when one could give oral testimony the actual testimony may be in writing. This then is an example of an interpretation of the intent of the Law giver.

Change of Nature

In a paper on the idea of Progress and Decline which I delivered several years ago, I referred to the concept of *Shinui Hat̞ eva* (change of nature).

---

23 *Tos. A.Z.* 50b *Boenan.*
24 See A.M. Fuss, "Edut Bekhtav Bedinei Mamanot" in *Shenaton Hamishpat Ha'ivri* 3-4 (1976-7), 327-339 at 332.

This term is first found in Rabbinic literature in the Tosafot.[25] The concept involves ascribing a change in the law as it applies in a later period, to a change in the physical condition of people, animals, geography or climate. Thus the change of facts is the basis of change in the law. The concept is a device pregnant with possibilities for changes in the law. The advantage of this concept is that it allows changes in law to come about without upsetting tradition and the norms of Rabbinic jurisprudence.[26]

The rule in the Talmud is that one must wash one's hands before serving food to a child.[27] The reason given, is that we fear *"Shibbetha"* - which, the commentaries explain, is an evil spirit, but which may be identified with a specific illness.[28] The Tosafists explain that this law no longer applies, as the danger no longer exists. Similar regulations, prohibiting the eating of food that was left standing uncovered overnight, because of the danger that snakes will get to the food, were also abolished because the danger no longer exists. The same consequence affected the Talmudic prohibition against "eating pairs" (two of a kind, such as eggs or olives). Here it had involved the evil spirit, which no longer exists.[29]

Another regulation in the Talmud provides that one must eat salt with every meal and drink water after imbibing any other beverage, because of the danger of an illness.[30] The rule is recorded in the *Shulḥan Arukh*.[31] R. Moses Isserles states, however, that we are not particular about keeping it, because all our food and drinks contain salt and water. Other commentators simply give as the reason for the discontinuance of this rule the fact that the danger posed by

25 Tosafot to *A.Zarah* 24a *Parah;* see also H.J. Zimmels. *Magicians, Theologians, and Doctors* (London, Edward Goldston & Sons Ltd., 1952), 8; I. Jacobovits, *Jewish Medical Ethics* (N.Y.: Bloch Publishing House, 1959), XLff.; I. Low, "Haiddana", *Hebrew Union College Annual* XI (1936), 205.

26 It is similar to the fact analyses which distinguish cases based on facts which are found to be changed.

27 *Yoma* 77b. See the Tosafot there *"Meshum"*.

28 R. Hananel and Rashi take *shivate* to mean an evil spirit which chokes a baby. However, R. Eliezer ben Nathan in Sefer hara'avan (d.1170) identifies it with a specific disease. See also Arukh Completum, supplementary volume edited by S. Krauss. 391.

29 See Chajes, *Darkhe Hora'ah, supra* n.20, at 299.

30 *Berakhot* 40a.

31 *Shulḥan Arukh, Orah Ḥayyim* 179, No.6 and 170 at the end.

the lack of salt no longer exists.[32]

A case involving a change of nature in the physical condition of animals is recorded in the Talmud. The Mishnah provides that where a Jew acquires a cow from a gentile not knowing whether the cow has previously given birth, so that he may comply with the law regarding the first-born, he may assume that if the animal is less than 3 years old, it had not given birth.[33] The Tosafists comment on this that in their day (in the 12th to 13th century), it was an every-day occurrence for cows to give birth at two years of age.[34] The cows evidently matured earlier in the Middle Ages than they did in the ancient period.

Similarly, a twentieth century authority was asked to explain the fact that women who marry after the age of twenty continue to have children after the age of forty - contrary to a statement in the Talmud which specifically says that this cannot happen.[35] The reply given was that, based on the opinion of gynaecologists, the nature of women has changed, and therefore they now can have children later.[36]

One may circumcise a child born after seven months who has to have his circumcision on the Sabbath, and thereby violate the Sabbath. However one may not violate the Sabbath for a child born after eight months nor for a child where we are in doubt whether it was born after seven or eight months.[37] The Tosafists remark: according to Ri nowadays we are not expert and all babies are in the category of doubtful born after eight or nine months, even when he is certainly born after eight months.[38]

German Rabbis in the Middle Ages prohibited non-Jews from making a fire for Jews on the Sabbath in conformity with Talmudic Halakhah. French Rabbis permitted it on the basis that "nowadays

---

32 See the super commentaries on *Shulḥan Arukh* ibid. No. 170. See gener- ally I. Low, "Das Salz", in *Jewish Studies Memory of George Kohut* , ed. S. Baron & A. Marx (New York, Alexander Kohut Memorial Foundation, 1935), 429-462.

33 *Bekhoroth* III, 1.

34 *A. Zarah* 24b *Parah*. See Israel Isserlein, *Terumat Hadeshen:* Resp 271.

35 *B.B.* 119a.

36 R. Isaac Herzog, *Responsa, Hekhal Yi tsḥa ḳ, Even Ha'ezer,* I N.6.

37 *Shab.* 135a, see parallel passages cited in Lieberman, *Tosefta Ki-fshuta,* Part III, *Order Moed,* 245ff.

38 *Shab.* 135a, Ben Shemona.

we are all considered as invalids with regard to cold."[39] An invalid is allowed to benefit from the work of a non-Jew on the Sabbath. The conclusion that nowadays we are considered as invalids with regard to cold distinguishes the case before the French Rabbis on the facts from the precedents.

Measurements

As is well-known, compliance with many of the ritual laws depends on the determination of the correct measure required. It is necessary, for example, to define the minimum quantity of wine for *kiddush, havdalah,* or the quantity of *matsah* or *maror* to be eaten on the first night of Passover. To reconcile different Talmudic texts with modern weights and measurements, R. Yehezkel Landau (1713-1791), one of the leading 18th century authorities, concluded that the size of eggs in his days had declined.[40] Similarly the size of human beings has declined according to a number of the great authorities of our generation. This conclusion of fact is based on reconciling different Talmudic texts and not on any scientific studies. The factual conclusion is dictated by the necessity for consistent logical legal ruling. Thus the presumption of fact that human beings today are smaller than were their ancestors is arrived at not because of independent evidence that this is so but because it is a useful explanation for a legal conclusion.[41]

Suicide

A person is forbidden to commit suicide. A person who does so violates a Biblical prohibition and according to *Masekhet Semahot:* "We do not occupy ourselves with him".[42] One might think this means we do not bury a suicide. However Rashba explains that the statement means only we do not mourn the suicide and not that we

---

39 Resp R. Ḥayyim Or Zarua, No. 119; Zimmels, *Ashkenazim and Sephardim, supra* n.17, at 195.
40 *Tsiyon Lenefesh ḥayah* [Zelach] on *Pesahim* 116b. R. Landau measured the size of the eggs in his day and compared the measurements to those recorded in the Talmud and to the results which R. Yom Tov Lippman Heller obtained.
41 R.J. Kanefski, *Sheurin Shel Torah* (B'nei B'rak, 1974), Ch. 1.
42 Chapter II, 1.

don't bury him.[43] Indeed this is in accordance with the practice as mentioned in Josephus.[44] Moreover the Talmud does permit some condolence for the mourners as an expression of consideration for the living survivors.

What interests us is the method of determining that one committed suicide. R. Moshe Sofer (1762-1840), the leading Hungarian rabbi in the 19th century, ruled that in a case where a person was found hanging in a room which was locked from the inside under circumstances which indicate that he closed the door himself, we may presume the decedent killed himself by his own hand.[45] However, we also presume that he did so unintentionally for we assume some evil spirit took control of him, or that he was afraid that Gentile enemies would kill him, or any other such reason, unless we heard from him a calm calculated statement that he is intentionally going to commit suicide.

Similarly, there is the statement of R. Yehiel Michael Epstein, the author of the authoritative *Arukh Hashulḥan*, as follows: To sum up with respect to one who commits suicide we hang on whatever peg possible such as fear, depression, insanity or that he thought it a *mitsvah* without having other sins or similar things because it is unlikely that a person would do such a terrible thing with a clear mind.[46] Hence we presume a state of facts which in effect restricts the applicability of the law regarding suicide to very few cases if any.

---

43 Resp Rashba, Vol. I, No. 763. See also F. Rosner, "Suicide in Biblical, Talmudic and Rabbinic Writings", *Tradition* II/2 (1970), 25-40; D. Frimer, "Masada in the Light of Halakha", *Tradition* 12/1 (1971), 27-43.

44 Wars III, 377; see also S. Lieberman, "After Life in Early Rabbinic Literature", in *H. A. Wolfson Jubilee Volume* , ed. S. Lieberman (Jerusalem: American Academy for Jewish Research, 1965).

45 Resp Hatam Sofer, *Yoreh De'ah*, No. 321; see also Greenwald, *Kolbo Shel Aveluth* (N.Y.: Feldheim Publishers, 1957), 318.

46 *Arukh Hashulḥan, Yoreh De'ah* 345:5. A responsum which is attributed to R. Asher b. Yehiel (Rosh) considers someone who commits suicide as a result of poverty and problems as not included in the suicides for whom we do not mourn, *Resp Besomin Rosh*. However many Rabbis and scholars consider the responsum not to be from Rosh. See the introduction to the Jerusalem, 1984 reprint. See also M. Samet, "R. Saul Berlin and his Works" (Heb.), *Kirjath Sepher* 43 (1968), 429-441 and M. Wunder, "An Unknown Letter Concerning 'Besomim Rosh'", *Kirjath Sepher* 44 (1969), 300-308.

We must of course realize that the assumption that the decedent did not commit suicide would not involve us in Biblical transgressions.

R. Barukh Epstein, the author of the commentary *Torah Temima* on the *Humash* , recites a story in his autobiographical collection *Mekor Barukh* about R. Hayyim of Volozhin, the disciple of the Gaon of Vilna and founder of the famous Volozhin Yeshiva.[47] There once came before R. Hayyim a woman with a *she'alah* (legal question). She explained that she had prepared a dish of radish and fat only to learn that the knife used to cut the radish was a dairy knife. R. Hayyim after a moment's thought asked the woman what was the exterior appearance of the radish, to which she replied that it was white. R. Hayyim then ruled that the food was permissible to be eaten. The students attending R. Hayyim could not understand his ruling. R. Hayyim explained to them that his teacher the Gaon of Vilna taught him that he should rule in legal matters as he sees the law, and should not defer to the opinion of other authorities. "When there comes before me a matter in which I differ with the ruling of the *Shulhan Arukh* I try to find some opening or excuse no matter how weak to say as follows: either the *Shulhan Arukh* did not refer to a case like this one or given the facts of this case the *Shulhan Arukh* would have ruled differently. As a result I preserve both the *Shulhan Arukh* and my opinion."

Indeed, added R. Hayyim, I am not of the opinion that radishes are not bitter and therefore I disagree with the *Shulhan Arukh*, [48] which rules that where a knife recently used for cutting meat was used to cut radishes, the radish may not be eaten with dairy products. Since I did not want to be differing with the *Shulhan Arukh* I found a distinction in that the radishes in Israel are sharper and black on the outside. The author of the *Shulhan Arukh*, R. Joseph Caro, had lived in Tsfat (16th cent.) and most likely referred to the radishes where he lived when he gave his ruling, while we have white radishes which are not as sharp. Interestingly enough R. Michael Epstein refers to this discussion in the *Arukh Hashulhan*.[49]

---

47 Vol. III, *Darkhe Hora'ah*, 1166.
48 *Yoreh De'ah* 96.
49 *Yoreh De'ah* 96.

This episode is then a clear cut case of seeking to distinguish cases on the facts. It is more than an illustration of a judicial method which advocates of a mechanistic view of judicial determination believe does not exist. The judge-rabbi reached a conclusion which he then tried to justify in such a way as to not disturb judicial precedent, by pointing to a different set of facts.

Jewish law has a whole panoply of devices to adjust the rigors of the law to specific cases where the general rule may inflict a hardship or injustice on an individual or group. Some of the devices are used to adjust the law to changing circumstances. Among these devices are legal fictions, or *ha'arama*, changes of fact, procedural devices including the application of different standards of evidence and fact skepticism or fact selection. The use of any of these devices is not open ended but is limited to special situations and circumstances. Moreover, since Jewish law recognizes the subjectivity involved in their application it demands very high standards of the rabbis and judges who can apply them. Only the great Poskim of a generation are entrusted with the latitude to use these devices, for they must be used sparingly and with great respect for Tradition.

RABBI JOSEPH B. SOLOVEITCHIK'S PHILOSOPHY OF HALAKHAH

by

LAWRENCE KAPLAN[*]

I

Rabbi Joseph B. Soloveitchik's writings on the nature of halakhah and the personality of halakhic man are endowed with a special, almost unique, authority, not shared by any other of the many works in the modern era on Jewish thought in general and Jewish law in particular. For Soloveitchik, alone among the leading Jewish thinkers in the modern era to have written on the philosophy of halakhah, is the only individual who is, at one and the same time, an outstanding rabbinic figure - indeed he is considered by many to be the outstanding traditional rabbinic scholar and jurist alive - as well as a major, serious Jewish philosopher who has mastered the entire Western philosophical tradition and is thus able to write about Jewish law in universal philosophical and phenomenological categories. Soloveitchik, thus, embodies the halakhic tradition and creatively contributes to its ongoing development in his role as rabbinic scholar and authority. But, together with this, the philosophical tools he has acquired, coupled with his drive to achieve profound understanding, which, for him, is profound self-understanding, enable him to step outside that tradition which he himself embodies and represents and to reflect upon it and analyze it in universal categories. Soloveitchik, as master rabbinic scholar, is at home with the entire range of rabbinic literature, with its most complex, technical and recondite categories. More, as a major rabbinic scholar endowed with profound conceptual and analytical ability, he is able to discuss halakhic texts, issues and problems in a rigorous, subtle and invariably illuminating fashion. Therefore when he speaks as philosopher of the halakhah he speaks as one who has a unique, inside mastery of the field and would seem to be uniquely qualified to speak about the philosophic significance of

[*]   McGill University, Montreal, Quebec.

those halakhic categories and relationships which he, as halakhic scholar, has so profoundly explored.

Of course this great, *prima facie*, authority with which Soloveitchik's writings is endowed, does not necessarily mean that his philosophic views as to the nature of halakhah are free from objection. Nor does it mean they necessarily should be preferred to the views of Jewish philosophers who may not be great rabbinic scholars and halakhic authorities. Certainly the views of an outstanding scientist or outstanding jurist (I use these two examples advisedly for reasons that will become clear soon), who at the same time is a major and thoughtful philosopher, on the philosophy of science or the philosophy of law carry great weight and must be taken with the utmost seriousness. But, in the final analysis, while no one should enter into the field of philosophy of law or philosophy of science without a good working knowledge of the particular field in question, we may choose to follow the views of the philosopher of science or of law, who, while having that good working knowledge, may himself or herself not be an outstanding scientist or jurist. And yet, even if we ultimately can not accept, in whole or in part, the philosophical views of the scientist-philosopher concerning his own field, his views still retain great interest, insofar as they show how a great practitioner in a field understands the significance of what he is doing, of what he is about. Similarly, even if we can not accept, in whole or in part, Soloveitchik's philosophical views as to the nature of the halakhah, his views are still of intrinsic importance in showing how a great rabbinic scholar who has both the ability and desire to engage in philosophic reflection understands the significance of what he is doing, of what he is about,of, ultimately, who he is.

In this dual role of rabbinic scholar-philosopher, Soloveitchik must be compared, and no doubt would want to be compared, to such great medieval figures as Saadia, Maimonides and Crescas, all of whom were outstanding rabbinic scholars of their day and, of course, examined the nature of the law, the Torah in universal philosophical categories. Nevertheless, there is an important difference between Soloveitchik and the medievals. And I do not have in mind the rather obvious - or perhaps not so obvious - distinction that the philosophical categories with which Soloveitchik, as a modern thinker, operates are naturally modern ones, while the philosophical categories with which the medieval thinkers operated were medieval ones. Of course the fact that Soloveitchik - unlike many, if not most, rabbinic scholars in the modern era who are, in essence, medievals operating with medieval categories - is a modern thinker operating with modern categories, precisely because he, unlike them, seriously studied, grappled with, and confronted modern thought and its implications for understanding Judaism, is of great importance. But what I have in mind, and this may not be unconnected with the distinction between medieval and modern, is that while the medieval philosophers were primarily concerned with explicating the purpose of the Torah as a whole on the one hand, and with the meaning of specific *mitsvot* on the other *(t a'ame hamitsvot)*, Soloveitchik's prime concern is explicating the nature of the halakhah as a unique legal *system*. Indeed Soloveitchik has only touched upon the general question of the teleology of the Torah as a whole[1] and has only engaged in the enterprise of *t a'ame hamitsvot* in scattered and cursory fashion. Rather he has devoted most of his energy and writing to delineating the various features the halakhah manifests as a coherent system, as a functioning and ideal whole. Moreover, if I might, in a preliminary fashion, briefly elaborate upon my earlier cryptic remark - we can only fully develop this point further on in our analysis - I would like to suggest that Soloveitchik's avoidance of the issue of teleology may not be wholly unconnected with his *modern* approach to the halakhah.

While Soloveitchik's writings on the nature of halakhah are, for the reasons stated above, of extreme importance, they do not easily lend themselves to authoritative interpretation. For, interestingly enough, none of Soloveitchik's major essays is devoted to an analysis of the nature of the halakhah *per se*. His first major essay, *Ish hahalakhah (Halakhic Man)*[2] focuses, as the title itself clearly indicates, not so much on the halakhah itself but on the halakhic personality. In that essay he does have many important and profound things to say about the halakhah as a system but the context of his discussion is the nature of the individual whose character is

1   Rabbi J.B. Soloveitchik, "The Lonely Man of Faith", *Tradition* 7/2 (Summer 1965), 50.

2   *Ish hahalakhah* [Henceforth *I. H.*], in *Ish hahalakhah: Galui Venistar* (Jerusalem: World Zionist Organization, 1979), [reprinted from *Talpiot*, Vol. 1, nos. 3-4 (1944), 651-735]; *Halakhic Man* [Henceforth *H.M.*] translated from the Hebrew by Lawrence Kaplan (Philadelphia: Jewish Publication Society, 1983).

fashioned by his commitment to and mastery of that system. Two of his other major essays, "The Lonely Man of Faith" and *"Ubiḳ ashtem misham"* ("But From Thence Ye Shall Seek")[3] focus on universal postures of faith (again the focus is anthropological) and discuss the halakhah only insofar as it fits into those categories.[4]

The one essay where Soloveitchik does focus upon the nature of the halakhah *per se,* or rather where he devotes a *part* of the essay to this subject, is - unexpectedly - a eulogy he delivered in memory of his uncle, R. Isaac Zeev (Velvele) Soloveitchik, *"Mah dodekh midod".*[5] In Part 3 of the essay, devoted to his uncle's method of halakhic study, R. Soloveitchik discusses with great subtlety and rigor the nature of the conceptual system created by the halakhist in the course of his study and analysis of halakhic texts. Even in this essay, however, R. Soloveitchik does not so much focus on the nature of the conceptual categories of the halakhist, although that certainly is crucial, but rather concentrates on the halakhist's relationship to the halakhah and the type of free, spontaneous, spiritual-intellectual creativity made possible as a result of, or better constituting the essence of that relationship. Rabbi Soloveitchik's main concern is again anthropological: not the halakhah *per se,* but the halakhist, qua jurist, who constructs an ideal coherent, rational system of law out of the welter of oftentimes conflicting, perplexing, obscure, individual texts, decisions, rules, cases, or rather who creates this coherent system and imposes it upon the welter of source material at hand, imparting to it unity and rationality, is what interests R. Soloveitchik. To put the matter

3   *"Ubiḳ as ht em Misham", Ha-Darom* 47 (1978), 1-83.

4   *Halakhic Man,* or to be more precise, its first major part, then is distinguished from the latter two essays insofar as it takes as its starting point for its anthropological-typological analysis the particularly Jewish category of commitment to the halakhah, and not any universal religious or cultural categories. In this respect the second and briefer part of *Halakhic Man,* in terms of its methodology, resembles more "The Lonely Man of Faith" and *"Ubiḳ ash te m Misham,"* than it does the first part of *Halakhic Man,* insofar as the starting point for the second part is not the fact of commitment to the halakhah, but rather the universal category of self-creation. Halakhic man, then, is seen in the second part, primarily as an exemplar, albeit the outstanding exemplar, of the self-creating individual.

5   *"Mah Dodekh Midod",* in *Bes od Haya ḥid Veha yaḥ ad* (Jerusalem: Orot, 1970), 191-253.

even more precisely, neither the halakhah nor the halakhist stands at the center of *"Mah dodekh midod"*. What *is* central is the nature of halakhic creativity.

For many years, students of Rabbi Soloveitchik's thought eagerly awaited a long promised essay of his, originally entitled, "Is a Philosophy of Halakhah Possible?" The title of the essay seemed to indicate, clearly and unequivocally, that the essay would directly address and treat the subject of the philosophy of halakhah. However, when the essay - written in 1944-45[6] and announced for publication in *Tradition,* 1966 - finally appeared in 1986(!), under the new title, *The Halakhic Mind: An Essay on Jewish Tradition and Modern Thought,*[7] it turned out, clearly and unequivocally, that the essay is not concerned with the subject of the philosophy of halakhah. Rather the essay - a highly technical and abstract philo-

6   In the "Author's Note" preceding the published essay, Rabbi Soloveitchik writes, "This essay was written in 1944." However, Rabbi Soloveitchik told me that he still remembers how while working on the essay one morning, the news broke of the dropping of the atomic bomb on Hiroshima. This would mean that the essay was not completed before August, 1945. Hence, my "1944-45".

7   *The Halakhic Mind: An Essay On Jewish Tradition and Modern Thought* (New York: Seth Press, 1986). I have been told that this title was not given to the essay by Rabbi Soloveitchik himself. Indeed, the title misrepresents the essay's nature in two ways. First, it suggests that the essay is a companion piece to *Halakhic Man,* which it is not. The true companion piece to *Halakhic Man* is, as Rabbi Soloveitchik has often stated, *"Ubiḳ a sht em Misham".* (I discuss the complementary nature of *Halakhic Man* and *"Ubiḳ ash te m Misham"* in an as yet unpublished essay, "From Freedom to Necessity and Back again: Man's Religious Odyssey in the Thought of R. Joseph Soloveitchik"). Second, it suggests that the essay's concern is with psychology, which is not the case. Rather the essay's focus, as will become clear from my brief description of it immediately below, is with methodology and epistemology. An accurate, if somewhat Germanic, title for the essay, one that would correctly characterize the essay's nature and content, might be: *A Prolegomenon to the Halakhah as a Source for a New World View: On the Method of Reconstruction in the Philosophy of Religion.* In this paper, however, I will refer to the essay by its current title, *The Halakhic Mind.* (*The Halakhic Mind* appeared after I had completed this article. Therefore, with the exception of the first part of this article which I have revised, I have not been able to draw upon it in my analysis, though I have sought to offer some references to it, where appropriate, here and there in my notes.)

sophic monograph - has a very different agenda.

In this essay Rabbi Soloveitchik, on the basis of an epistemolog-ical pluralism,[8] argues for the possibility of an autonomous religious cognition of the world.[9] He then proceeds to construct an appropriate methodology for discerning this unique religious approach to reali-ty.[10] This methodology, termed descriptive reconstruction by Rabbi Soloveitchik, moves "from objective religious symbols to subjective flux,"[11] i.e. one starts from the objective religious order and then pro-ceeds to *reconstruct* out of that order subjective aspects of the reli-gious consciousness,[12] without, however, claiming that those subjec-tive aspects in any way generated, caused or determined that objec-tive order.[13] In terms of developing a specifically Jewish weltan-schauung this would mean that one would have to start from the ob-jective order of Judaism, i.e. the halakhah, and then, "in passing onward from the halakhah and other objective constructs to a limit-less, subjective flux we might possibly penetrate the basic structures of our religious consciousness."[14] Rabbi Soloveitchik concludes his essay with a flourish: "Out of the sources of halakhah, a new world view awaits formulation."[15] It should be emphasized that this is the *last* sentence of the essay. The essay, itself, as is evident from my brief description, is essentially a methodological prolegomenon to constructing that new religious world-view; it does not articulate that world-view itself.

The crucial point, however, for our purposes is that, as is again evident from my description, the essay's focus is not concentrated on the nature of the halakhah *per se* - the halakhah as the objective order of Judaism is pretty much taken as a given - but rather on the type of methodology that would justify using the halakhah as the starting point for reconstructing and interpreting "the structure of the

8 *Halakhic Mind, supra* n.7, at 3-28.
9 *Ibid.*, at 39-46.
10 *Ibid.*, at 46-81.
11 *Ibid.*, at 90.
12 *Ibid.*, at 80-81, 90-91.
13 *Ibid.*, at 74-75, 85-88, 92-98.
14 *Ibid.*, at 101.
15 *Ibid.*, at 102. This last sentence is obviously an allusion to and a play on Hermann Cohen's *Religion of Reason Out of the Sources of Judaism*. (Rabbi Soloveitchik explicitly refers to Cohen three paragraphs earlier, on the previous page.)

most basic religious cognitive concepts",[16] or, again, as the source for a new world-view.

The fact that none of Rabbi Soloveitchik's major essays, directly and systematically, explore the nature of the halakhah is highly suggestive.[17] Perhaps this omission stems, at least in part, from the fact that - as we have already indicated in our previous paragraph - in the deepest sense, the halakhah, for Rabbi Soloveitchik, as a system of a revealed, divine law, is a *given*. The full significance of this *givenness* of the halakhah for Rabbi Soloveitchik can only be adequately and fully discussed at the end of our essay. But already here, at the beginning of our essay, we might suggest that precisely because the halakhah is a given for Rabbi Soloveitchik, his concern is not and need not be so much with the halakhah *per se*, as with the halakhist, with his modes of cognition of the world and cognition of the halakhah, and his modes of creativity, both self-creativity and halakhic creativity. For, while the *halakhah* may be a given, certainly the *halakhist* is not a given. On the contrary, halakhic man, in Rabbi Soloveitchik's view, "forges for himself a concrete, this worldly personality".[18] He is "a free man [who] creates an ideal world, renews his own being and transforms himself into a man of God..."[19] And, therefore, the personality of the halakhist, of halakhic man, a personality which he, himself, has created, requires careful and precise analysis and delineation.[20]

And, yet, despite the fact that Rabbi Soloveitchik has not devoted any of his major essays to a systematic exploration of the nature of halakhah, an image, a picture, or, perhaps better, a model of the halakhah *does* emerge from his writings. In this essay, then, I wish to undertake two distinct, but intimately interrelated tasks. Certainly the most striking and central feature of R. Soloveitchik's

16 *Ibid.*, at 99.
17 See Endnote A.
18 *I. H.*, 71/*H. M.* 78.
19 *Ibid.*, at 113/137.
20 We should also mention that, in general, Rabbi Soloveitchik's interests and concerns are not so much theoretical but, rather, personal, existential and anthropological. See "The Lonely Man of Faith", *supra* n.1, at 8-9, and my essay, "Models of the Ideal Religious Personality in the Thought of Rabbi Joseph Soloveitchik", *Jerusalem Studies in Jewish Thought* IV (1984/85), 327-329, in Hebrew.

approach to the halakhah is his adoption of a scientific model, specifically the model of mathematics and mathematical physics, rather than a juridical model for understanding the halakhah. I would like, first, to elucidate and examine the nature of this scientific model, how R. Soloveitchik uses it and some of the problems involved in that use. This will lead me to my second task: an attempt to account for the reason or rather reasons behind Soloveitchik's preference of a scientific model over a juridical one. In the course of my discussion I trust that I will also be able to shed some light on Rabbi Soloveitchik's portrait of the halakhist as cognizer and creator.

II

A[21]

While in his two essays regarding the nature of the halakhah, *Halakhic Man* and *"Mah dodekh midod"*, R. Soloveitchik uses a scientific model for understanding the halakhah there is a radical shift in the way R. Soloveitchik draws the science-halakhah analogy. For while R. Soloveitchik's understanding of science, the scientist and the scientific process remains the same in both essays, he focuses, as he moves from one essay to the other, on a different level of halakhah and, consequently, on a different activity of the halakhist.

In both essays R. Soloveitchik, reflecting the influence of Hermann Cohen and his disciples, adopts a Neo-Kantian model of science. We will discuss this model in detail later on. For the moment the following remarks of Samuel Hugo Bergman regarding Cohen's philosophy of science ought to suffice.

> For Cohen, thought produces everything out of itself... According to Cohen sensation merely describes the problem posed to thought. Sensation demands something, it signifies a claim but it can not satisfy this claim from its own resources. Pure thought must come to its aid.

21 In this section I have utilized, in a modified form, a number of passages in my essay "The Religious Philosophy of R. Joseph Soloveitchik," *Tradition* 14/2 (Fall 1973), 48-55.

"Sensation stammers; thought must first supply the word. Sensation evokes the dark impulse; but only thought can illuminate its direction."

Thus thought "constructs" the world of objects. The objects of thought, of course, are not identical with things in everyday life. The scientific object, the electron, for example, is constituted by the network of laws and internal-relations of science.[22]

Rabbi Soloveitchik, unquestionably, subscribes to this view but would qualify the universality of this Neo-Kantian description of scientific thought by claiming that it applies only to modern science, as shaped by Galileo and Newton, and not to medieval Aristotelian science. Aristotelian science tried to understand the world in its own terms, that is, in terms of qualities. Aristotelian science was not creative but rather classified and organized the sense-data that natural phenomena present. The Galilean-Newtonian revolution was set into motion by the construction of abstract-formal mathematical systems in terms of which natural-sense phenomena could be explained.

This revolution was a dual revolution, a revolution affecting the nature of the scientific perception of the world and a revolution affecting the nature of the scientific process, of scientific creativity itself. First the scientist no longer perceives and explains the world in its own qualitative terms, but, rather, in abstract, ideal, a priori, quantitative, mathematical categories. Second, insofar as these terms and modes of discourse and understanding have been constructed by the scientist himself, the *world* of science, as a world of mathematical equations, or better, of mathematical *constructs*, can be said to be the product of man's thought, of man's creative intellectual power.[23]

In *Halakhic Man* the focus of the science-halakhah analogy

22 S.H. Bergman, *Faith and Reason* (New York: Schocken, 1963), 34-35.
23 *"Mah Dodekh Midod"*, *supra* n.5, at 221-222. *Cf.*, however, A. Ravitsky, *"Kinyan Hada'at behaguto: Ben Harambam leNeoKantianim"*, in *S ef er Hayovel likebod Harav Yosef Soloveitchik Shlit"a*, ed. R. Shoul Yisraeli, et al (Jerusalem: Mosad Harav Kook, 1984), 135-136 [= "Rabbi J.B. Soloveitchik on Human Knowledge: Between Maimonides and Neo-Kantian Philosophy", *Modern Judaism* Vol. 6, no. 2 (May, 1986), 166-167]. Ravitsky approaches R. Soloveitchik's distinction between Aristotelian and modern science from a somewhat different, albeit non-conflicting, perspective than our own.

centers around the issue of perception, of orienting oneself to reality. In this essay the halakhah that is being compared to a scientific system is the revealed system of laws given to Moses on Mount Sinai and the halakhist is like the scientist as both halakhist and scientist use their systems as comprehensive modes of orienting themselves to and comprehending reality, of perceiving the natural-sense world. The mathematical physicist in order to understand the world of sense,

> constructs an ideal, ordered and fixed world... fashions an a priori, ideal creation... Whenever he wishes to orient himself to reality and super-impose his a priori, ideal system upon the realm of concrete empirical existence, he comes with his teaching in hand - his a priori teaching.[24]

Similarly, the halakhist in approaching and understanding the world also approaches it with his a priori system.

> The essence of halakhah, which was received from God, consists in creating an ideal world and cognizing the relationship between that ideal world and our concrete environment in all its visible manifestations.... There is no phenomenon, entity or object in this concrete world which the a priori halakhah does not approach with its ideal standard.[25]

The halakhah, in this view, is not merely a set of norms, not merely rules of conduct, but also a logical, conceptual structure possessing cognitive significance. Laws are converted into general epistemological and ontological principles. The halakhah, then, is not only normative in nature but speculative as well. It speaks to our understanding as well as our will. The various halakhic spatial categories, for example, such as the bent wall, the imaginary vertical extension, upwards or downwards, of a partition, the imaginary vertical extension of the edge of the roof downwards to the ground, the measurement of four cubits, ten handbreadths, etc., are not merely categories which are to be used in building a *sukkah* or an *erub* on *Shabbat*, but, are modes of perceiving and organizing space, similar to the various principles of Euclidean or Non-Euclidean geometry. The sunset on the conclusion of the Day of Atonement is objectively different from other sunsets, for with it forgiveness is bestowed upon us for our sins ("the end of the day atones"). Atonement, holiness and

24   *I.H.*, 27/*H.M.*, 18.
25   *Ibid.*, at 28/19-20.

all other halakhic categories are rooted in the natural-sense world. And the natural-sense world is only of interest to the halakhist insofar as it is possible to apply halakhic categories to it, just as the natural-sense world is only of interest to the scientist insofar as it is possible to apply scientific categories to it. But just as the scientist attempts to embrace all natural phenomena within his a priori system, so too does the halakhist. Both seek to understand, though, to be sure, we should not forget that the halakhist's categories are normative as well as speculative.[26]

In *"Mah dodekh midod"*,[27] however, the science-halakhah analogy centers about the issue of scientific and halakhic creativity. In this essay the halakhah that is being compared to the scientific system is the ideal system of halakhah fashioned by the halakhist himself, as he attempts to understand the revealed, Sinaitic system of law. It is the system of halakhic constructs as that system emerges out of the halakhist's confrontation with obscure, refractory, recalcitrant halakhic texts, i.e. it is the system of halakhah as the product of the halakhist's thought, of his intellectual creativity, which is the object of R. Soloveitchik's concern in this essay. But just as the Neo-Kantian model of scientific creativity, in R. Soloveitchik's view, does not work for all of scientific thought, so too, he argues, such a model of creativity does not work for all of halakhic thought. To state the matter in positive terms, just as the Neo-Kantian model works only for modern Galilean-Newtonian scientific thought, so too it works only for modern, "Galilean Newtonian"(!) halakhic thought.

R. Soloveitchik - to explain my deliberately obscure and provocative formulation - is of the opinion that his grandfather, R. Hayyim Soloveitchik introduced a revolution in the study of halakhah comparable to the Galilean-Newtonian revolution in science. Before R. Hayyim halakhists studied and explained the halakhah in its own terms: organizing, classifying, resolving difficulties and problems. Rabbi Hayyim, however, created a whole system of abstract concepts by means of which he explained and understood the halakhah. Before R. Hayyim halakhists merely dealt with the technical and external aspects of many areas of law, for example, the laws of prayer, *kashrut*, documents, among

26   *Ibid.*, at 28-42, 59-61/19-39, 63-66.
27   *"Mah Dodekh Midod"*, supra n.5, at 217-227.

150   LAWRENCE KAPLAN

others. It was R. Hayyim who created conceptual structures into which these laws could be integrated and in the light of which their inner logic would become clear. In the place of conglomerations of diverse, seemingly unconnected laws, R. Hayyim introduced unified logical structures. R. Soloveitchik, no doubt partially motivated by family pride, is quite emphatic on this point. He writes:

> Torah scholars used to denigrate those who studied the laws of *kashrut*: only those who were about to enter the rabbinate would study this area of law. Who could guess that the day would come [when R. Hayyim would arrive on the scene] and these laws would be freed from the bonds of facticity, external and common-sense explanations, and become transformed into abstract concepts, logically connected ideas that would link together to form a unified system.... Suddenly the pots and the pans, the eggs and the onions disappeared from the laws of meat and milk; the salt, the blood and the spit disappeared from the laws of salting. The laws of *kashrut* were taken out of the kitchen and removed to an ideal halakhic world... constructed out of complexes of abstract concepts.[28]

And, we emphasize, this "ideal halakhic world... constructed out of complexes of abstract concepts" is constructed by R. Hayyim himself. It is his own creation.

In sum, our preliminary analysis has brought to light two different science-halakhah analogies. In *Halakhic Man* the comparison is between the scientist-world relationship and the halakhist-world relationship, for both the halakhist and scientist approach the world in terms of their a priori systems. In *"Mah dodekh midod"* the comparison is between the scientist-world relationship and the halakhist-halakhah relationship. As the scientist creates mathematical equations out of his own autonomous reason to answer the problems posed by the difficult, intractable, qualitative sense world, so the halakhist creates abstract concepts out of his autonomous reason to answer the problems posed by the perhaps even more difficult and intractable revealed halakhah.

Given this radical shift between one essay and the other, both in R. Soloveitchik's portrait of the halakhah and perhaps even more significant, in his portrait of the halakhist, each essay, with its own particular treatment of the halakhah-science analogy, raises its own set of issues and each, consequently, requires and deserves a

28   *Ibid.*, at 227.

separate treatment. Before we turn to this treatment, however, we may note that the fact that R. Soloveitchik can use the scientist-world relationship as an analogy for both the halakhist-world relationship and for the halakhist-halakhah relationship already indicates that his approach is not without its problems.

B

Let us turn, then, to *Halakhic Man*. We have stated that in that essay the halakhah that is being compared to a scientific system is the revealed system of laws given to Moses on Mt. Sinai and the halakhist is like the scientist insofar as both halakhist and scientist use their systems as comprehensive models of orienting themselves to and comprehending reality.

Rabbi Soloveitchik writes:

> When halakhic man approaches reality he comes with his Torah, given to him from Sinai, in hand. He orients himself to the world by means of fixed statutes and firm principles. An entire corpus of precepts and laws guides him along the path leading to existence. Halakhic man, well furnished with rules, judgments, and fundamental principles, draws near the world with an a priori relation. His approach begins with an ideal creation and concludes with a real one.[29]

For R. Soloveitchik, then, the halakhah, like science, is an a priori, ideal system for perceiving reality. This formulation immediately raises three questions: (1) in what sense is the halakhah a system?; (2) in what sense is it a priori?; (3) in what sense is it ideal?

1 In what sense is the halakhah a system?

The primary characteristic of a system is that no object in the system is meaningful *per se* but only as part of the network of inter-relationships that constitutes the system as a whole. Indeed, for the Neo-Kantians, one of the major features in the development of science is the shift away from the Aristotelian approach focusing on substance and its qualities to the modern approach, manifested by Galileo and Newton, focusing on relations "in terms of which the

29 *I.H.*, 28/*H.M.*, 19.

variety of (actually or potentially) given objects may be ordered." In the course of science, then, "thing-concepts are gradually replaced by relation-concepts, and a hierarchy of laws, stating invariant relations in terms of mathematical functions, occupies the place formerly held by a hierarchy of intrinsic qualities".[30] Rabbi Soloveitchik expresses a similar view of modern science when he speaks of the "physicist who... engages in complex and difficult calculations, involving the manipulation of ideal, mathematical quantities... ideal numbers that cannot be grasped by one's senses... [but] only are meaningful from within the system itself, only meaningful as part of abstract mathematical functions...".[31]

In the light of this, how does the halakhah, for Rabbi Soloveitchik, form a system? Let us look at the following passage:

When halakhic man comes across a spring bubbling quietly, he already possesses a fixed, a priori relationship with this real phenomenon: the complex of laws regarding the halakhic construct of a spring. The spring is fit for the immersion of a zav (a man with a discharge); it may serve as mei ḥaṭat (waters of expiation); it purifies with flowing water; it does not require a fixed quantity of forty seahs, etc. When halakhic man approaches a real spring he gazes at it and carefully examines its nature. He possesses a priori, ideal principles and precepts which establish the character of the spring as an halakhic construct and he uses these statutes for the purpose of determining normative law; does the real spring correspond to the requirements of the ideal halakhah or not?...

When halakhic man looks to the western horizon and sees the fading rays of the setting sun or to the eastern horizon and sees the first light of dawn and the glowing rays of the rising sun, he knows that this sunset or sunrise imposes upon him anew obligations and commandments. Dawn and sunrise obligate him to fulfil those commandments that are performed during the day: the recitation of the morning Shema, Tsitsit, Tefillin, the morning prayer, etrog, Shofar, Hallel and the like. They make the time fit for the carrying out of certain halakhic practices: temple service, acceptance of testimony, conversion, ḥalitsah, etc., etc. Sunset imposes upon him those obligations and commandments that are performed during the night: the recitation of the evening Shema, matsah, the counting of the omer, etc. The sunset on Sabbath and holiday eves sanctifies the day: the profane and the holy are dependent upon a natural cosmic phenomenon - the sun sinking below the horizon. It is not

30 F. Kaufmann, "Cassirer's Theory of Scientific Knowledge", in The Philosophy of Ernst Cassirer, ed. P.A. Schilpp (Evanston, Illinois: Library of Living Philosophers Inc., 1949), 190.

31 I.H., 74/H.M., 83.

anything transcendent that creates holiness but rather the visible reality - the regular cycle of the natural order. Halakhic man examines the sunrise and sunset, the dawn and the appearance of the stars; he gazes into the horizon - Is the upper horizon pale and the same as the lower? - and looks at the sun's shadows - Has afternoon already arrived? When he goes out on a clear moon-lit night (until the deficiency of the moon is replenished) he makes a blessing upon it. He knows that it is the moon that determines the times of the months and thus of all the Jewish seasons and festivals, and this determination must rely upon astronomical calculations.[32]

What is clear is that these various halakhic categories, for Rabbi Soloveitchik, are only meaningful as part of a complex, interweaving network of relationships that constitute the system of halakhah as a whole. The halakhic construct of a spring (ma'ayan) is only meaningful inasmuch as the spring is fit for the immersion of a zav, may serve as mei hat at, etc.; sunset and sunrise are only meaningful halakhic categories inasmuch as sunrise and sunset impose an entire series of obligations upon man, etc., etc. As Rabbi Soloveitchik states:

> Halakhic man's relationship to existence is not only ontological but also normative in nature. In truth, the ontological approach serves as the vestibule whence he may enter the banquet hall of normative understanding. Halakhic man cognizes the world in order to subordinate it to religious performances. For instance, he cognizes space by means of religious, a priori, lawful categories in order to realize in it the halakhic norm of Sabbath, the commandment of sukkah and the idea of purity. He "engages in the same type of calculations as do the astronomers" in order to determine seasons and festivals. He studies the plant world for the purpose of classifying their species, as such classification relates to the laws of diverse seeds, and for the purpose of determining the standards of growth, since such determination affects the agricultural laws. Thus his normative doctrine has priority, from a teleological perspective, over his ontological approach. Cognition is for the purpose of doing. "Great is study, for study leads to action." (Kidd. 40b)[33]

Nor should the above be taken as a fancy and unnecessarily involved way of saying that the concern of halakhah is practical in nature. Thus Rachel Shihor asserts:

32 Ibid., at 28-29/20-21.
33 Ibid., at 59/63.

> When the encounter between halakhic man and reality is over, when the
> [zav] has already immersed himself in the spring, and the sound of
> prayer has already been heard in the light of the sunrise, the spring and
> the rising sun are again unbinding [non-halakhic] objects.[34]

But this misses the mark. What is significant for the halakhist, in
terms of the system of halakhah, is that the spring is fit for the
immersion of a zav. It makes no difference to the halakhist
whether or not there is a zav present, at that moment, to immerse in
the spring. Moreover, even if there is a zav present, there is no difference for the halakhist, in terms of his perception of the spring,
between the moment before the zav immersed himself and the moment after he immersed himself. Before the immersion, the spring is
fit for immersion and after the immersion the spring is fit for
immersion. What is crucial is not the actual practice but the normative *principle*. Thus R. Soloveitchik, in the passage we cited
above, goes on to state:

> However, even the norm is, at the outset, ideal, not real. Halakhic man
> is not particularly concerned about the possibility of actualizing the
> norm in the concrete world. He wishes to mint an ideal, normative coin.
> Even those laws that are not practiced in the present time are subjected
> to his normative viewpoint, this despite the fact that he is unable,
> nowadays, to fulfill these particular commandments. The maxim of the
> Sages "Great is study, for study leads to action", has a twofold meaning:
> 　　(1) action may mean determining the Halakhah or ideal norm;
> 　　(2) action may refer to implementing the ideal norm in the real
> 　　　　world.
> Halakhic man stresses action in its first meaning.[35]

The halakhah, for Rabbi Soloveitchik, as he expresses himself
in another passage is, then, a "theoretical-normative" system.[36]

2 *In what sense is the halakhah a priori?*

This is a difficult issue, made more difficult by the complexity of
the whole concept of the a priori in the sciences in general. Certain-

34 R. Shihor, "On the Problem of Halacha's Status in Judaism: A Study of
    the Attitude of Rabbi Josef Dov Halevi Soloveitchik", *Forum* 30-31
    (Spring and Summer 1978), 147.
35 *I.H.*, 59-60/*H.M.*, 63-64.
36 *Ibid.*, at 76/86.

ly, halakhic categories are not synthetic a priori categories in the Kantian sense, i.e. categories which constitute the very (psychological or logical) ground of possibility of experience. For, certainly, Rabbi Soloveitchik does not wish to suggest that the halakhist can only coherently experience springs, sunrises, space, etc., etc. via halakhic categories![37]

Perhaps the following interpretation of the concept of the a priori may offer us a clue to R. Soloveitchik's use of the term. Once again it is significant that this discussion takes place in a neo-Kantian context, specifically an interpretation of Ernst Cassirer's doctrine of the a priori:

> The a priori character of any concept or category of the mind is ... derived from the definitive attitude of the mind which gives rise to this conceptual order and determines the characteristics which the given *must* exhibit, *if* it is to be classified under the category or the concept determined by that definitive attitude. The only certainty the mind can have with respect to any sensory datum yet to be given rests upon the mind's certainty with respect to the meaning of its own concepts and categories. This meaning is established and determined by the mind itself, by virtue of the definitive attitudes which it takes, and can be strictly and consistently adhered to regardless of what may be given in experience. This definitive attitude determines the criteria which any given datum must satisfy if it is to be interpreted under the concept or under the category which embodies and expresses these criteria. Failing to satisfy these criteria, the given datum is excluded from such classification and interpretation. For every classification which the mind makes is an implicit interpretation. But every interpretation is an implicit prediction with respect to some subsequent datum of experience. The interpretation of any set of sensory data under any definite concept or category implicitly asserts that such a set of data will be followed by certain other definitely specifiable data, namely, those which are implicitly demanded by the definitive criteria which constitute the essential meaning of the concept or the category under which the original data were classified. The only necessity which the mind can impose on the given, therefore, is the necessity which the given is under of conforming to certain definitive criteria of the mind or else being excluded from classification and interpretation under the specific concept or category which those definitive criteria establish. The mind can know, then, prior to the experiencing of any particular datum of experience, the character which

37 Cf. the criticism of R. Soloveitchik's contention that halakhic concepts are a priori in nature by Jacob Agus, *Guideposts in Modern Judaism* (New York: Block Publishing Co., 1954), 39 and Shihor, "On the Problem of Halacha's Status in Judaism", *supra* n.34, at 149.

that particular datum *must* exhibit if it is to be classified under any definite concept or category. The mind knows this because the mind itself, by its own definitive attitudes, determines those criteria to which the datum must conform, *or else,* and can make them hold regardless of what the given datum may or may not do. Thus all the necessity which the mind is capable of imposing on the given, through the use of its "conceptual order", is derived (i) from the character of its own legislative acts which determine the essential meaning of its conceptual devices and, (ii) from the alternative which the mind has of excluding from classification under any concept or category any given element of experience which does not conform to the criteria which are established by those legislative acts for the concept or the category in question.[38]

With this interpretation in mind let us return to the concrete spring as the halakhist approaches it with his halakhic construct of a spring in mind. Rabbi Soloveitchik states:

Halakhic man is not overly curious, and he is not particularly concerned with cognizing the spring as it is in itself. Rather, he desires to coordinate the a priori concept with the a posteriori phenomenon.[39]

Here, in brief, we have an exact parallel to Cassirer's doctrine of the a priori. The definitive attitude of the halakhist determines the criteria which the given datum, here the concrete spring, must satisfy if it is to be interpreted under the concept or under the category which embodies these criteria, here the halakhic construct of a spring. To be sure, there is a crucial difference between the scientific a priori and halakhic a priori. The a priori categories of the scientist, derive from "the mind [of the scientist] which gives rise to the [scientific] conceptual order"; the a priori categories of the halakhah as a revealed system. derive from the "mind of God", if we may be so bold to use such a phrase, which gives rise to the halakhic conceptual order. Granting this distinction, and it is no small distinction, we conclude that R. Soloveitchik's use of the term "a priori" to describe the system of halakhah does reflect an es-

38 I.K. Stephens, "Cassirer's Doctrine of the A Priori", *The Philosophy of Ernst Cassirer, supra* n.30, at 172-173.
39 *I.H.,* 28-29/*H.M.,* 20.

sential truth regarding the halakhist's approach to reality.[40]

3 In what sense is the halakhic system ideal?

In what sense, indeed?! Here I confess I find it difficult to attribute any meaning to this contention of R. Soloveitchik. In what sense is the scientific system ideal? Rabbi Soloveitchik is very clear on this point.

> To know means to construct a lawful, unified system whose necessity flows from its very nature, a system that does not require, as far as its validity and truth are concerned, precise parallelism with the correlative realm of concrete, qualitative phenomena. On the contrary, all that we have is an approximate accord. The concrete empirical triangle is not exactly identical with the ideal triangle of geometry and the same holds true for all other mathematical constructs. There exists an ideal world and a concrete one and between the two only an approximate parallelism prevails.[41]

Soloveitchik's analysis is strikingly similar to that of Ernst Cassirer:

> The structures of geometry, whether Euclidean or non-Euclidean, possess no immediate correlate in the world of *existence*. They exist as little physically in things as they do psychically in our "presentations" but all their "being", i.e., their validity and truth, consists in their ideal *meaning*. The existence that belongs to them by virtue of their definition, by virtue of a pure logical act of assumption is, in principle, not to be interchanged with any sort of empirical "reality". Thus also the applicability, which we grant to any propositions of pure geometry, can never rest on any direct coinciding between the elements of the ideal geometrical manifold and those of the empirical manifold. In place of such a sensuous congruence we must substitute a more complex and more thoroughly mediate relational system. There can be no copy or correlate in the world of sensation and presentation for what the points, the straight lines and the planes of pure geometry signify. Indeed, we cannot in

---

40   Cf. Z. Zohar, "Al H aya h*as* ben Sefat Hahalakhah leben Hasafah Hat*ivit*", in Sef*er* Hayovel likebod Harav Yosef Soloveitchik Shlit"a,, *supra* n.23, at 61-66, for a different analysis of the concept of the halakhah as an a priori system. Zohar combines his analysis with a penetrating critique of Rabbi Soloveitchik's position. (Zohar's article appeared too late to be used in this essay.)

41   I.H. 27/H. M. 19.

strictness speak of any degree of similarity, of greater or less difference of the "empirical" from the ideal, for the two belong to fundamentally different species. The theoretical relation, which science nevertheless establishes between the two, consists merely in the fact, that it, while granting and holding fast to the difference in content of the two series, seeks to establish a more exact and perfect correlation between them.[42]

Both Soloveitchik and Cassirer here speak of pure mathematics, specifically geometry, but the same is true of all scientific concepts; there is only an approximate accord, and necessarily so, between the ideal scientific concept of uniform motion or uniformly accelerated motion in a vacuum and concrete, empirical motion; there is only an approximate accord, and necessarily so, between the ideal scientific concept of "perfect" fluidity and concrete, empirical fluidity; etc., etc.[43]

Thus no empirical phenomenon can fully realize the ideal nature of the concept and this is necessarily so, inasmuch as the ideal concepts as ideal and the empirical phenomenon as empirical exist on two different levels.

But how, in terms of this view of what it means for a concept to be ideal, can it be claimed that halakhic constructs are ideal? On the contrary, in the halakhah we either have an exact accord or no accord between the concept and the reality. On the one hand, to return to our now overused spring, if the real spring, that the halakhist encounters, possesses defined characteristics that the halakhah prescribes, then it becomes the halakhic spring of which the halakhah speaks and it fills all of the halakhic functions that the halakhah has allotted to the halakhic spring. We are not dealing here with an approximate accord, with two different levels, but rather with an exact accord, with a concept that is completely exemplified and instantiated in reality. On the other hand, let us look at some other halakhic concepts that R. Soloveitchik terms ideal, the rebellious son and the idolatrous city, etc.[44] The Talmud states:

There never was an idolatrous city and never will be. For what purpose then was its law written? Expound it and receive a reward!... There

42   E. Cassirer, *Substance and Function* and *Einstein's theory of Relativity* (Chicago-London: Open Court, 1923), 433-434.-
43   *Ibid.*, at 112-130.
44   *I.H.* 31/*H.M.*, 23.

never was a rebellious son and never will be. For what purpose then was his law written? Expound it and receive a reward! (*Sanh.* 71a).

Here the halakhah sets down so many requirements for a city to be considered an "idolatrous city" or a son to be considered a "rebellious son" that, in point of fact, the Talmud concludes there never was and never will be either an idolatrous city or a rebellious son. For if a real idolatrous city or a real rebellious son lacks, even in the slightest, one of the rigorous requirements that the halakhah demands for a city to be considered an idolatrous city, halakhically, or for a son to be considered a rebellious son, halakhically, then the real idolatrous city, as far as the halakhah is concerned, is not an idolatrous city, and the same holds true for the real rebellious son. Here, unlike scientific concepts, an approximate accord is not enough; rather if the accord is not exact, it is the same as if no accord exists at all. A miss is as good as a mile.

Moreover, while ideal scientific concepts by their very nature are ideal and therefore, an exact accord between the ideal concept and the real entity is intrinsically impossible, the "ideal" halakhic idolatrous city and rebellious son are not intrinsically ideal and an exact accord between these ideal halakhic concepts and real cities or real sons is not intrinsically impossible; rather it is "just" that there are astronomical odds against a real city or a real son ever meeting all of the rigorous halakhic requirements necessary for the real city to be considered an idolatrous city, halakhically, or for the real son to be considered a rebellious son, halakhically. Indeed in response to the Talmudic statement "There never was a rebellious son and never will be," R. Jonathan retorted, "I saw such a one and sat on his grave!"

Finally, let us examine a third class of concepts that R. Soloveitchik terms ideal: those halakhic concepts which in order to be completely realized require a cultic, sacrificial element. Rabbi Soloveitchik writes:

> The concept of the Day of Atonement or the night of Passover, for example, is an ideal concept and halakhic man sees the Day of Atonement in the resplendent image of the glory of the sacrificial service of the day or the night of Passover in all its majesty, at the time when the Temple was still standing. Both the Day of Atonement and the Passover festival nowadays when we have no priest, nor sacrifices, nor altar and the whole temple service can not take place, are devoid of all that holiness and glory with which they were endowed at the time of the Temple.

Both are only a pale image of the ideal constructions that were given on Mount Sinai.[45]

But can we say that the halakhic concept of the Day of Atonement or of the night of Passover is an ideal concept, in the same manner as a scientific concept is ideal? We note that there is an approximate accord between every element of the real triangle and the ideal triangle. However, the real Passover night possesses all the non-sacrificial elements of the ideal Passover night while it completely lacks the sacrificial elements, i.e. in some respects there is an exact accord between the real and ideal, in other respects no accord. Finally, as we have already noted, while ideal scientific concepts are intrinsically ideal and therefore an exact accord between the ideal concept and real entity is intrinsically impossible, in the case of Passover night and the Day of Atonement the lack of an exact accord is a result of historical circumstances, i.e. the destruction of the Temple and the exile. Indeed, in contrast to the idolatrous city and the rebellious son, which, on account of the astronomical odds against their occurring, never were and never will be, the Ideal Day of Atonement and Passover night were and will be, and the present time in which these ideal concepts are not fully exemplified, "is only a historical anomaly... a temporary aberration."[46]

In a word, the "ideal" nature of halakhic concepts differs radically from the ideal nature of scientific concepts. Ideal scientific concepts, despite the fact that they are ideal, parallel the real world and precisely because of this parallelism are of practical import. As we have stated, between ideal scientific concepts and real entities, there always exist an approximate accord; between halakhic concepts and real entities there is either an exact accord or no accord.

We, therefore, can not accept Rabbi Soloveitchik's claim that the halakhah, like science, is an a priori, ideal, system for perceiving reality. And yet even if we must reject this claim in its strict sense, Rabbi Soloveitchik's view still contains a good deal of truth. Certainly, for the halakhist, the halakhah is not just a system of practical or even theoretical rules, but is above all a fundamental

45 Ibid., at 33/26.
46 Ibid., at 34/28.

mode of orienting oneself to reality, is a prism through which one sees, perceives the real world. As Jacob Neusner has stated in speaking of the Mishnah's rhetoric:

> To describe [the] transcendent purpose [of Mishnah] we return to Wittgenstein's saying "The limits of my language mean the limits of my world." Mishnah's formulaic rhetoric on the one side imposes limits, boundaries upon the world. What fits into that rhetoric, can be said by it, constitutes world, world given shape and boundary by Mishnah. Mishnah implicitly maintains, therefore, that a wide range of things falls within the territory mapped out by a limited number of linguistic conventions, grammatical sentences. What is grammatical can be said and therefore becomes part of the reality created by the Mishnaic world... Mishnaic reality consists in those things that can attain order, balance and principle... [In Mishnah] languages become ontology.[47]

Though Neusner here focuses on the Mishnah's rhetoric while Soloveitchik focuses on the halakhah's concepts, in the view of both Neusner and Soloveitchik the law for the halakhist is ultimately of profound cognitive significance, and its practical import is only secondary.

Indeed, the halakhah may serve as a cognitive system, as a mode of perceiving reality not only for the outstanding halakhist, be he a second century Mishnaic Sage or a nineteenth century Lithuanian Gaon, but also for the average, ordinary, twentieth century modern orthodox Jew. Samuel Heilman's recent monograph, *The People of the Book*, is a socio-cultural-ethnographic study of modern orthodox Jews who "regularly spend some of their free time in *lernen*, the eternal review and ritualized study of sacred texts".[48] In his chapter "The Religion of *Lernen*", Heilman discusses the cognitive significance of *lernen*. Speaking as a participant-observer, he writes:

> As orthodox Jews, as religious followers of the way of the Talmud, our concern lies not with the sensual world but with the cosmos as defined by our acceptance of the structures of the law.[49]

---

47 J. Neusner, "Form and Meaning: Mishnah's System and Mishnah's Language", in *Method and Meaning in Ancient Judaism* (Missoula, Montana: Scholar's Press, 1979), 175-176.

48 S. C. Heilman, *The People of the Book* (Chicago and London: University of Chicago Press, 1983), 1.

49 *Ibid.*, at 251.

162   LAWRENCE KAPLAN

Indeed, for Heilman, the participant-observer, and for the other
men of his study circle, the law possesses "the almost magical power... to transform reality, to shred sense perception and replace it
with a sense that is filtered through a faith in the divine origins of
that law."[50]

As the Rav of one of the study circles in which Heilman participated succinctly stated:

> What the law calls a wall [for the purposes of the commandment of
> Sukkah] is not identical with what is called a wall by a contractor. In
> the halakhah, however, this is a wall. And we believe in this wall
> more surely than in any real wall. This is the halakhah from Moses
> [who received it from God] on Sinai.[51]

The similarity between Heilman's discussion and R. Soloveitchik's
analysis is clear, indeed is striking in its similarity. Moreover, the
very example the Rav of the study circle used to demonstrate "the
ascendancy of halakhah and its divine power to transform reality",[52] viz. the wall of the Sukkah, was, as we have seen, also offered by R. Soloveitchik in Halakhic Man..

Once again, the power of the halakhah to serve as a cognitive
scheme comes to the fore.[53] R. Soloveitchik may draw upon the Neo-
Kantian categories of Cohen and Cassirer, Neusner upon the suggestive linguistic imagery of Wittgenstein, and Heilman upon the
cultural-anthropological terminology of Geerts and Turner, but the
underlying truth to which they point is one and the same.

Perhaps the best concrete example of this cognitive significance
of halakhah may be found in the collection of essays by the late
rabbinic scholar, Rabbi S.J. Zevin, Le'or hahalakhah, In the Light
of Halakhah.[54] This book treats an exceptionally wide range of

50 Ibid., at 251.
51 Ibid., at 256.
52 Ibid., at 255.
53 We may suggest, however, that the average modern orthodox Jew only
    senses the power of the halakhah to transform reality when he is actu-
    ally engaged in lernen. However, the outstanding halakhist, whose
    very personality and world-view is profoundly shaped and formed by
    the study and practice of the halakhah, utilizes the halakhah as a
    basic prism for viewing reality even when he is not, at the moment, en-
    gaged in formal halakhic study.
54 Tel-Aviv: A. Zioni, 1957.

subjects: war, heredity, old age, snow, the number 1000, etc., from an halakhic perspective. Similarly religious concepts, generally considered to be non-halakhic in nature such as the covenant between the pieces, the binding of Isaac, the Song of Songs, etc., are examined by R. Zevin in order to determine their *place* in halakhah. R. Zevin's work is a powerful illustration of R. Soloveitchik's contention, which we cited earlier, that "There is no phenomenon, entity, or object in this concrete world which the a priori halakhah does not approach with its ideal standard." Or, as R. Soloveitchik states in another context, "There is no real phenomenon to which halakhic man does not possess a fixed relationship from the outset and a clear, definitive, a priori orientation.... 'The measure thereof is longer than the earth and broader than the sea' *(Job 11:9)."*[55] Whatever technical criticisms we may have of Rabbi Soloveitchik's contention, and we do not wish in any way to minimize those criticisms, certainly his contention reveals a fundamental truth as to how halakhic man views and uses halakhah.

C

While it is true that the halakhist views the world through the prism of the halakhah, certainly the fundamental task of the halakhist is - to study the halakhah. The fundamental question, then, in defining the nature of the halakhist qua halakhist is not so much how he approaches, comprehends and orders the world through the medium of halakhah but how he approaches, comprehends and orders the halakhah itself. We therefore suggest that the central and ultimately more illuminating and challenging scientist-halakhist analogy drawn by R. Soloveitchik is not the scientist-empirical reality: halakhist-empirical reality analogy drawn in *Halakhic Man,* but, rather, the scientist-empirical reality: halakhist-halakhah analogy drawn in *"Mah dodekh midod".* In a word the world of the halakhist is the halakhah, with its texts, cases, rules, decisions, principles, etc. Moreover, it is precisely in confronting *this* world that the halakhist manifests his true creativity.

R. Soloveitchik, as we have already noted, argues that his grandfather, R. Hayyim Soloveitchik, introduced a revolution into

---

55 *I.H. 30/H.M.* 22-23.

the study of the halakhah comparable to the Galilean-Newtonian revolution in science. Just as the modern scientist, unlike the Aristotelian scientist, does not explain the world in its own terms, i.e. in qualitative categories, but rather constructs his own terms and modes of discourse and understanding, i.e. abstract-formal, mathematical equations and functions, so R. Hayyim was not simply content to explain the halakhah in its own terms but rather constructed an entire system of abstract concepts and definitions in order to explain and understand it. Both halakhic concepts and scientific concepts, then, are free constructions deriving from the powerful creative spirits of halakhist and scientist respectively.[56]

Our three questions which we posed previously: In what sense is the halakhah a system? In what sense is it a priori? In what sense is it ideal? are all easily answered if the halakhah in question is the abstract-conceptual halakhic system, *created by the halakhist himself*, in order to explain the halakhic texts and rulings, i.e. the *halakhic* data.

This halakhic system is a system in the strict sense for the halakhist introduces unified logical structures, complexes of abstract concepts on order to integrate conglomerations of diverse, seemingly unconnected laws. In this connection R. Soloveitchik offers a striking analogy to "illuminate" the function of halakhic explanation, as developed by the halakhists of the school of R. Hayyim.

> To what may the matter be compared? To a person who awakes in the middle of the night and can not figure out just where he is. It seems to him as if his bed is in a diagonal and he is sprawled out across it; he gropes hither and thither in the darkness and it is as if the door which was always found on one side of the bed is now on the other side. The whole picture of his room and its furniture is distorted and unreal. Suddenly he finds the lamp switch, flicks it on and a clear light shines on his surroundings. Everything is in order and he recovers his sense of place, his orientation. He can't understand himself, why wasn't he able to picture his room and its furniture, why did he have such a confused

56 For further discussion regarding the analytic method of the school of R. Ḥayyim Soloveitchik, see R. Shlomo Yosef Zevin, *Ishim Veshitot*, (Tel Aviv: A. Zioni, 1958), and the various studies of N. Solomon, "*Hilluq* and *Haqirah*: A Study in the Method of the Lithuanian Talmudists", *Diné Israel* IV (1973), LXIX-CVI; "Definition and Classification in the Works of the Lithuanian Halakhists", *Diné Israel* VI (1975), LXIII-CIIII; "Concepts of *Zeh Neheneh*.. in the Analytic School", *The Jewish Law Annual* III (1980), 49-62.

image? Wasn't everything so simple and clear?[57]

The concept, the definition, the abstract principle is, then, the light which orders, illuminates, clarifies, integrates and unifies the legal texts and rulings.

Similarly the halakhic system is a priori in the strict sense. For just as the scientist creates mathematical equations out of his own autonomous reason to answer the problems posed by the sense-data of empirical reality, so the halakhist creates abstract concepts out of his own autonomous reason to answer the problems posed by the halakhic data which confront him. Rabbi Soloveitchik writes:

> Kant, in his day, proclaimed the autonomy of pure reason, of scientific-mathematic cognition. R. Hayyim fought a war of independence on behalf of halakhic reason and demanded for it complete autonomy. Any psychologization or sociologization of the halakhah strangles its soul, as such an attempt must also destroy mathematical thinking... R. Hayyim provided for the halakhah specific methodological tools, created a complex of halakhic categories and an order of a priori premises through a process of pure postulatization.[58]

How does the halakhist create this system of rigorous, abstract concepts? R. Soloveitchik offers an intriguing two-tiered description. First, there is an intuitive, almost sensuous stage, and only then is there a conceptual, discursive stage. Rabbi Soloveitchik writes:

> On rare occasions the Torah can become wedded and united with an individual.... The Torah can become absorbed in the recesses of his being and fuses with him... When all barriers between the individual and the Torah are removed, not only do all the gates of halakhic and cognition become available to him but also the gates of halakhic sensation and inner sight. God endows him not only with a rational soul but also with a soul possessed of halakhic vision. Logical halakhic thought is nurtured from the pre-intellectual visions which storm forth from the depths of his personality, enveloped by an aura of holiness. This mysterious intuition is the origin of halakhic creativity.... The halakhic man, to whom

57 "Mah Dodekh Midod", supra n.5, at 231.
58 Ibid., at 224. Note the critique of the psychologization or sociologization of the halakhah expressed here. Rabbi Soloveitchik offered a similar critique, in his own name, in an address at the 1975 convention of the Rabbinical Council of America, cited in A.M. Schreiber, Jewish Law and Decision Making (Philadelphia: Temple University Press, 1979), 192. We will return to this point at the end of our essay.

the Torah is wedded, "sees" halakhic data, "senses" halakhic ideas as if they were data of tone, color, or smell. He dwells in the halakhah which constitutes his world, just as the natural world he dwells in is his world, with its profusion of colors, with its tones, its fragrances, its warmth.... The person to whom the Torah is wedded begins with a Torah of the heart and concludes with a Torah of the mind. The creative halakhic act does not begin with thought, but with vision; not with formulations, but with unrest; not by the clear light of logic, but in pre-logical opacity. The vision begins to glimmer like bewitching lights in infinite distances, which flare out and are extinguished, shimmer and fade, in a dark and rain-smudged night. These lights are intermittent and can not be used. However they direct the wanderer groping in the darkness and seeking the magical isle - the truth. Slowly, slowly, with the aid of these lights he penetrates the realm of intellectual darkness and reaches his destination - clear cognition. Bit by bit, he combines the light into a continuous chain of light that casts a refulgent brilliance. But how can the wanderer come to the domain of truth before he has wrestled in primordial, pre-cognitive realms, in the misty domain of obscure experience, lacking image and form and has triumphed with the help of the vision.

From this inspiration-laden vision one rises to limpid and pure discursive cognition. When the *gaon* raises his vision to the level of logical thought he begins with an act of spontaneous creation which does not explain the empirical given but gives rise to abstract constructions. The elevation of the vision to understanding, the intuition to conception is the act of a creator who builds an ideal, self-contained world that derives its value and its telos from within itself, from the midst of the complex of relationships between its abstract elements.[59]

This description is exceptionally suggestive, dramatic and powerful, but at the same time highly obscure. What is the need for this intuitive stage where the halakhist "senses", "sees", halakhic concepts? Is there a similar stage in the process of a priori scientific creativity?

The answer, as R. Soloveitchik has had the occasion to state explicitly,[60] is: yes. We have seen that, for R. Soloveitchik, the scientific concepts, the mathematical functions that are used in explaining the natural order are not derived from experimentation and observation via a process of induction but, rather, are free, a priori

59 *"Mah dodekh Midod"*, supra n.5, at 218-220.

60 Oral communication. I would like to thank R. Soloveitchik for discussing this entire matter at length with me in an interview on March 22, 1982. At that time he also related to me the two stories cited further on in the text.

constructions of the scientist, are the product of his autonomous, pure reason, constructions which "miraculously" parallel the empirical phenomena. But if this is so, what, then, is to guide the scientist in determining what mathematical-scientific principles will parallel and thereby illuminate the empirical phenomena? Certainly not the empirical phenomena themselves. Rabbi Soloveitchik answers: such guidance can only be provided by a powerful intuition which senses the direction in which pure thought can most profitably operate, which sees, feels, tastes the appropriate illuminating concepts even before such concepts are formulated in clear, precise, cognitive, mathematical, categories.[61] Indeed R. Soloveitchik has argued that those sciences which are essentially descriptive and not constructive in nature, e.g. zoology and botany, do not require for their progress the use of scientific imagination, intuition, vision, precisely because they are descriptive and not constructive.[62]

For the very same reason, then, the halakhic scholar requires a powerful, halakhic intuition, imagination, vision if his interpretations of the halakhic data are not to be simply descriptions of the halakhic data on their own terms, but rather free, abstract constructions that parallel and illuminate that data.

R. Soloveitchik has brought this likeness clearly to the fore, by relating two strikingly similar stories about the greatest halakhist and greatest scientist of our century: R. Hayyim Soloveitchik and Einstein.   R. Soloveitchik relates: I once asked R. Yeruham Levovits, the well-known Mashgiah of Yeshivat Mir, wherein lay the greatness of R. Hayyim. Rabbi Levovits answered: R. Hayyim was able to perceive the soul of the Torah, to sense its rhythm, to feel its pulse.   Similarly R. Soloveitchik relates - A scientific associate of Einstein once told me: Do you know wherein lay the greatness of Einstein? Other scientists were greater mathematicians than he; other scientists were more brilliant than he. But Einstein had a deep and profound intuition which could sense, even before he worked out the problems in clear, conceptual categories, the proper, most fruitful line of approach to take in applying pure thought to

61 See extended endnote B.
62 Oral communication. *Cf. Halakhic Mind, supra* n.7, at 122 note 68, where Rabbi Soloveitchik distinguishes between the "explanatory disciplines of physics and chemistry" and the "descriptive sciences such as general botany... and zoology".

empirical reality.[63]

In a word it is precisely the a priori, constructive character of the halakhah and the sciences that gives rise to the need for an intuitive stage in the process of halakhic and scientific discovery. Finally this halakhic system is ideal. The concepts, postulated by the halakhist, are always on a higher level of abstraction than the cases, or examples, or rules found in the texts themselves. We have already cited the example of the disappearance, underneath the magic wand of R. Hayyim's mode of conceptualization, of the pots and the pans, the eggs and the onions, the salt, the blood and the spit from the laws of *Kashrut*. Another wave of the wand and the candles, chairs, tables, vases, stove, etc., all of the daily domestic items of the household in the land of Israel in Mishnaic times, disappeared from the laws of purity and impurity. Perhaps the best example of this move away from concreteness is R. Hayyim's treatment of the halakhic "*sheṭar*", the document.

> Until R. Hayyim the matter of documents was based, on the one hand on the technical rules of writing and signing which are only the external form of the document, and on the other hand, presumptions rooted in responsive reactions and psychological behavior... R. Hayyim displaced the technical aspects from the center of the matter... The document was

---

63 Note, in this connection, what Cohen, *op. cit.*, 152-153, has to say about Einstein:

> Einstein boldly declared that reason and not empirical data is the basis of any 'scientific system". He stressed the 'free inventions of the human intellect' and said:

>> I am convinced that we can discover, by means of purely mathematical construction, those concepts and those lawful connections between them which furnish the key to the understanding of natural phenomena. Experience may suggest the appropriate mathematical concepts, but they most certainly cannot be deduced from it. Experience remains, of course, the sole criterion of the physical utility of a mathematical construction. But the creative principle resides in mathematics. In a certain sense, therefore, I hold it true that pure thought can grasp reality, as the ancients dreamed.

> Rabbi Soloveitchik cites Einstein on the nature of scientific concepts as "free creations of thought" and on man's ability to "grasp reality with our theoretical constructions" in *Halakhic Mind, supra* n.7, at 26, 111-112 note 29.

divested of its concrete sense reality....[64]

We have seen, then, that both the halakhist and scientist construct ideal, a priori systems. There is yet another striking and important point of resemblance, in R. Soloveitchik's view, between the construction of an halakhic system and the construction of a scientific system and this is the presence in both of the aesthetic dimension. All the great and enduring theories of modern science from the physical theories of Galileo and Newton to Einstein's special theory of relativity and Watson's and Crick's model of the double helix have been both profoundly intellectual and aesthetic constructs, exceptionally rigorous and, together with that, deeply imaginative. In a word, they possessed an almost irresistible intellectual elegance. As Watson stated about his double helix model, "It was too pretty not to be true."

Rabbi Soloveitchik is well aware of this aesthetic dimension of science. As he states in *Halakhic Man*:

Is not the physicist swept to heights of rapture in the act of cognizing the world?! Did not Newton delight in the beauty of the world when he discovered the law of gravity or, simultaneously with Leibnitz, the differential and integral calculus? "Precept to precept, precept to precept, line to line, line to line, here a little, there a little" (*Isaiah* 28:10,13), number to number, quantity to quantity, function to function, one physical law to another physical law, and as a result of scientific man's creativity there arises an ordered, illumined, determined world, imprinted with the stamp of the creative intellect, of pure reason and clear cognition. From the midst of the order and lawfulness we hear a new song, the song of the creature to the Creator, the song of the cosmos to its Maker. Not only the qualitative light, perceptible to the senses, with its wealth of hues and shades, its whirl of colors, sings to the Holy One, blessed be He; so do the quantitative light waves as well, the fruit of cognitive man's knowledge. Not only the qualitative world bursts forth in song, but so does the quantitative world. From the very midst of the laws there arises a cosmos more splendid and beautiful than all the works of Leonardo da Vinci and Michelangelo.[65]

64 "*Mah Dodekh Midod*", *supra* n.5, at 225. For further analysis of the shet.ar, as a pure halakhic concept, see Rabbi Soloveitchik's essay, "*Otiyot Ni k̲r̲o t beme ṣirah*" in *Shi'urim Lezekher Abba Mari Z"L*, *supra* n.17, at Vol.I, 260-279.

65 *I.H.*, 74-75/*H. M.*, 83-84.

And *mutatis mutandis* (or is it *mutatis mutandis?*) the same blend of intellectual and aesthetic appeal, of rigor and imagination is to be found in an halakhic discourse (*shi'ur*) or essay of a great creative halakhist, one example of whom is, of course, R. Soloveitchik himself. For, as R. Soloveitchik rightfully claims, the rigorous method of halakhic abstraction and conceptualization is characterized not only by its breadth and depth but also by its splendor and beauty.[66]

We have seen that R. Soloveitchik in developing his halakhist-halakhah: scientist-empirical reality, bases himself upon the philosophic understanding of the nature of modern science. Indeed, he is sharply critical of classical and medieval Aristotelian science.[67] This use of a philosophic model of *modern* science, I would suggest, is at the root of the radical difference between Soloveitchik's philosophic enterprise and that of the medieval Jewish philosophers. As we have already noted, while the medieval Jewish philosophers were primarily concerned with explicating the purpose of the Torah as a whole on the one hand, and with the meaning of specific *mitsvot* on the other (*ṭa'ame hamitsvot*), Soloveitchik's prime concern is explicating the nature of the halakhah as a unique legal *system*. And, indeed, he has only touched upon the general question of the teleology of the Torah as a whole and has only engaged in the enterprise of *ṭa'ame hamitsvot* in a scattered and cursory fashion. We suggest that, in truth, both Soloveitchik and the medievals are interested in explaining the commandments, but that drawing upon different scientific models they have divergent conceptions of the very nature and function of explanation in general and therefore of what it means to explain a

---

66 "*Mah Dodekh Midod*", *supra* n.5, at 235. Obviously the presence of this aesthetic dimension is intimately bound up with the role of scientific or halakhic intuition or imagination in the process of scientific or halakhic creativity, discussed previously.

67 *Ibid.*, at 221; "*Ubiḳ ash te m Misham*", *supra* n.3, at 5. In this connection, Rabbi Soloveitchik once commented to me:

There are times when nature refuses to cooperate with man, withdraws from the public scientific arena, displays an unfriendly face and wraps herself in mystery. In such eras all human scientific progress comes to a halt. The history of science in the middle ages [i.e. Aristotelian science] is the best example of how an inhospitable mother nature may precipitate scientifically disastrous results.

commandment in particular. Thus Maimonides in Part III of the *Guide* opens his discussion of the reasons of commandments with a chapter (III, 25) on the rationality and wisdom of the natural order and in the following chapters (III, 26, 32) explicitly compares the wisdom manifest in the commandments with the wisdom manifest in the natural order. However, for Maimonides, who subscribes to the Aristotelian conception of science, to offer a scientific explanation of a phenomenon is to explain it, at least partially, in terms of final causes, i.e. in teleological categories. Thus one understands the functioning of an organism as caused by the *telos* of the organism, by its drive to attain the highest level of perfection possible and proper for it.[68] Adopting this concept of explanation, for Maimonides to offer reasons for commandments, to explain commandments, means, first and foremost, to uncover the end and purpose of the commandment, or to show its utility. Thus Maimonides, very deliberately in our view, uses cause, reason, end, utility in his whole discussion of the commandments synonymously. Indeed he defines the causes of a commandment as its useful end *(Guide* III, 26). However, modern science, as founded by Galileo and Newton, does away with final causes. Rather, as R. Soloveitchik understands it, in modern science to explain a physical phenomenon means to understand it in the light of a general, abstract formal-mathematical equation that will account for the largest variety of physical phenomena possible and that will be integrated with other such abstract mathematical principles to form a unified, coherent system. Therefore, for R. Soloveitchik to explain commandments means first and foremost to subsume halakhic rulings under highly general, abstract halakhic concepts and principles, concepts and principles of which the specific rulings will be concrete particularizations. In this respect, for R. Soloveitchik, the rationality of the halakhah is immanent to it and the discovery of that rationality is part of the

68 Though Martha C. Nussbaum, "Aristotle on Teleological Explanation", in her edition of Aristotle's *De Motu Animalium* (Princeton, N.J.: Princeton University Press, 1978), 60-97, very cogently demonstrates that one ought not exaggerate the role of teleological causes in Aristotle's scientific thought and though S. Pines, in the Introduction to his edition of *The Guide of the Perplexed"* (Chicago: University of Chicago Press, 1963), LXX, LXXI note 29, advances a similar argument for the scientific views of Maimonides, one can still maintain that teleological explanations played a greater role in classical and medieval science than they do in modern science.

halakhic enterprise. On the other hand, while R. Soloveitchik will not deny that there may be "reasons" for the commandments in terms of the purposes and ends the commandments may serve, such a task of uncovering these ends and purposes is first, always tentative and speculative in nature and, second, extrinsic to the halakhic enterprise.[69]

R. Soloveitchik's model of the halakhist's approach to the halakhah is, then, a very powerful and coherent one. But is it true?

Perhaps the very question of truth is out of place. If a particular model is powerful, coherent and illuminating then it serves its purpose, though perhaps one might suggest alternate models. And certainly, if R. Soloveitchik who is a towering scholar, understands the halakhist's approach, i.e. *his own approach*, to the halakhah in this fashion then, perhaps, we ought ask no more of him. And yet we still feel driven to ask whether R. Soloveitchik's model, which ultimately, after all, is a description of how a halakhist reads and understands halakhic texts is the best model for illuminating that activity. Professor Jacob Taubes has argued:

> R. Soloveitchik's use of the model of mathematics or mathematical physics for explaining how the halakhist understands halakhah is unacceptable. For the fundamental task of the halakhist is to read and interpret texts and there are no two greater opposites than the hermeneutic required for textual interpretation and the construction of mathematical systems.

69 In this connection, see the rather sharp critique of Maimonides' rationalization of the commandments in the *Guide,* in *Halakhic Mind, supra* n.7, at 91-98. *Cf.* Rav Kook's equally sharp critique, albeit from a different perspective, of Maimonides' rationalizations in *"Talele Orot", Tahkemoni* 1 (1910), 12-24, reprinted in *Ma'amare Hareiyah* (Jerusalem:, 1984), 18-28, translated into English by Ben-Zion Bokser, "Fragments of Light", in *Abraham Isaac Kook* (New York: Paulist Press, 1978), 303-323. Both Rabbi Soloveitchik *(Halakhic Mind, supra* n.7, at 92) and Rav Kook ("Talelei Orot", 18/"Fragments of Light", 303-304), interestingly enough, claim that Maimonides' views on the reasons for the Commandments, as expressed in the *Guide,* have exerted less influence on the subsequent course of Jewish thought, than his views on any other religious subject, be it creation, prophecy, teleology, etc. For further bibliographical references to the modern criticism of Maimonides on "the assumption that Maimonides' philosophy of law is not adequate to the needs and claims of halakhah", see I. Twersky, *Introduction to the Code of Maimonides (Mishneh Torah)* (New Haven: Yale University Press, 1980), 432 note 190.

Unfortunately R. Soloveitchik when he studied in Berlin went "barking up the wrong tree". He came under the dominant influence of Hermann Cohen when he should have followed the path of Heidegger and later on of Gadamer and Ricoeur. R. Soloveitchik's philosophy of halakhah must, then, be pronounced a failure, albeit a magnificent failure.[70]

Taubes' objection is penetrating and fundamental. It aims at the very roots of R. Soloveitchik's philosophic enterprise. And yet, in another sense, it is beside the point. I do not wish to enter into the very lively and vigorous debate between the Gadamerians and the Hirschians regarding the possibility of objectivity in interpretation. But even if we grant that there is a need to develop a distinctive hermeneutic for reading Talmudic texts, and that that hermeneutic must necessarily incorporate within itself the historical, personal and existential horizon of the interpreter, R. Soloveitchik's enterprise is essentially unaffected.

For R. Soloveitchik is not concerned with a philosophy of the Talmud but with the philosophy of halakhah. He is not interested so much in the Talmud as a particular ancient text that needs to be interpreted (or should we say "deconstructed", if Gadamer is already passé and we wish to appear up to date) but with the Talmud as a corpus of law, as part of a larger, ongoing halakhic tradition. And as a jurist, his task, as he sees it, is analogous to that of the scientist: to create an abstract, self-contained, coherent system that will illuminate and order the multifarious and recalcitrant data that demand illumination and ordering. In a word, the task of both halakhist and scientist is to create an ordered world that will satisfy their intellectual and aesthetic needs for comprehension and coherence.

However, even if we reject Professor Taubes' thesis, there remains another objection to R. Soloveitchik's model, one that compels us, if not to reject it, at least to modify it. For even if we agree that the halakhah can, in many respects, be seen as a self-contained conceptual system, that halakhic categories can not be reduced to economic, social or "common-sense" ones, but must be judged on their own

70 Oral communication. This comment was made by Professor Taubes in the course of a conversation between him and me and I only wrote down his comments afterward. Therefore, while I believe that the comment, as I have reproduced it, represents the gist of Professor Taubes' remarks accurately, I must take final responsibility for its precise formulation.

terms, that though the halakhah has developed in response to external challenges, it has done so in accordance with its own inner, immanent logic, one still can not say that the halakhic system is wholly objective or wholly self-contained, as is mathematical physics. The halakhah is not wholly objective, for certain important halakhic categories are inherently subjective, e.g. "her ways are ways of pleasantness", "ways of peace", etc. Such categories can only be defined and applied on the basis of general, non-halakhic value judgements.[71] To put the matter another way, final causes are built *into* the halakhah in a way that they are not present in the natural realm. In the development and unfolding of the halakhic system we must take into account these categories which the halakhah itself posits as its end or rather ends, and the use of these categories then becomes *intrinsic* to the halakhic enterprise. Nor is the halakhah entirely self-contained, for many conceptual realms impinge upon it and affect major halakhic decisions, e.g. *aggadah*, *ḳabalah*, philosophy. science, etc. Surely Maimonides' philosophical convictions affected many of his halakhic decisions, as Professor Isadore Twersky,[72] among others, has convincingly shown. Professors Gershom Scholem[73] and Jacob Katz and others have des-

71 See E. Goldman, *"Hamu ṣar, Hadat Vehahalakhah*, Chapter Three", *De'ot* 22 (Winter, 1962-63), 65-84, and E. Berkovits, "Authentic Judaism and Halakhah", *Judaism* 19/1 (1970), 66-76. For an example, not cited in either Goldman or Berkovits, of a situation in which the principle of "ways of pleasantness" plays a role in influencing halakhic *pes aḳ*, see *Responsa of Haham Tsvi*, no.46 cited in *Sidre Ṭaharah* on *Shulḥan Arukh: Yoreh De'ah* 188:1. (I am indebted to Rabbi Moses Tendler for calling my attention to this reference.)

72 I. Twersky, "Some Non-Halakhic Aspects of the *Mishneh Torah"*, in *Jewish Medieval and Renaissance Studies*, ed. A. Altmann (Cambridge, Mass: Harvard University Press, 1967), 95-118; *Introduction to the Code of Maimonides (Mishneh Torah), supra* n.69, at 473-514.

73 Gershom Scholem, "Tradition and New Creation in the Ritual of the Kabbalists", in his *On the Kabbalah and Its Symbolism* (New York: Schocken, 1961), 118-157.

cribed in their clear and penetrating fashion the role of *Ḳabalah* in forming and influencing Halakhah.[74] Indeed, the question as to how wide or restricted a role philosophy or *ḳabalah* should have in halakhic decisions is a recurrent theme in the history of Halakhah.[75] The same considerations apply, equally well, to *aggadah* and science. This objection does not affect the essential validity and usefulness of R. Soloveitchik's analogy. Nevertheless, without pronouncing judgment on the ultimate validity of his model, we would argue that this objection would indicate that, at the very least, certain aspects of it require modification.[76]

D

In an earlier essay we had challenged R. Soloveitchik's science-halakhah analogy in view of the fact that the halakhah is, for the halakhist, a revealed system of law deriving from the divine will and wisdom, while science is a conceptual system created by the scientist himself. We attempted a preliminary approach to that problem in our previous essay and have already alluded to this issue in our present essay as well. This problem however is of such imp-

---

74 J. Katz, "Ya ḥase Halakhah veḳ aba la h bedorot shel'a ḥar Hitgalut Hazohar", Da'at IV (1980), 57-74; idem, "Tefillin be ḥolHamo'ed", Proceedings of the Seventh World Congress of Jewish Studies III (1981), 191-213 (reprinted in Halakhah veḳ ab al ah[Jerusalem: Magnes Press, 1984], 52-69, 102-124. Many of Katz's other essays in this volume also illustrate the interplay of halakhic and extra-halakhic factors in the formation and development of the halakhah).

75 See for example, the famous dispute between R. Solomon Luria (Responsa No. 98) and R. Menaḥem Azariah da Fano (Responsa No. 108) regarding the proper role of kabbalah in halakhic *peṣaḳ*. For a penetrating analysis of R. Menaḥem Azariah da Fano's views regarding the relationship between halakhah and kabbalah, see Robert Bonfil, "Halakhah, Kabbalah and Society: Some Insights Into Rabbi Menaḥem Azariah da Fano's Inner World", in *Jewish thought in the Seventeenth Century*, ed. I. Twersky and B. Septimus (Cambridge, Massachusetts: 1987), 39-61 (Harvard Judaic Monographs, IV). Bonfil's essay, indeed, sheds much light on the entire subject.

76 For recent discussion of the complex nature of rabbinic moral discourse, as reflected in the modern responsa literature, see Peter Hass, "Toward a Semiotic Study of Jewish Moral Discourse: The Case of Responsa", in *Biblical Hermeneutics in Jewish Moral Discourse*, Semeia 34 (1985), 59-83 and David Ellenson, "Jewish Legal Interpretation: Literary, Scriptural, Social and Ethical Perspectives", *ibid.*, at 93-114.

ortance that it requires a separate analysis.

Rabbi Soloveitchik in his essay, *"Ubiḳ ashtem misham,"* directly and forcefully addresses the problem the revealed status of
halakhah poses for the halakhah-science analogy. Since this essay has generally been neglected in the literature on Soloveitchik,[77] I
would like to cite his highly illuminating, albeit lengthy, analysis
of this issue in full.

> The unique significance which the halakhah bestows upon the intellect
> is so striking that it pervades, informs and colors the entire character of
> the halakhic outlook. The intellect is the final decisor in all matters of
> law and judgment. The content of halakhah which in its essence is rev-
> elational is subjected to the rule of intellectual cognition. The study of
> the Torah is a cognitive act like all intellectual activities. The sole
> authority is logic. The halakhah has banished all mystery and obs-
> curity from its domain. Both supernatural revelations and the mur-
> murings of supra-rational intuitions have been banished from the realm
> of halakhah. A prophet who delivers an opinion regarding a law of the
> Torah couched as a prophetic revelation - is deserving of death. The
> backdrop is revelational - visionary - the written Torah and the oral
> Torah revealed to Moses on Mount Sinai- but the whirl of colors painted
> on that background is cognitive - "natural". Human thought, bound by
> the fundamental rules of the logos, has "dared" to insinuate itself into an
> alien realm and seize hold of it. Freedom of inquiry and speculation in
> the field of halakhah is exceedingly great and broad. The sage is obl-
> igated to engage in original, creative interpretation *(ḥiddush)* to con-
> struct new, original concepts, and carefully delineated methods, and to
> plot distinct realms of thought. Profound and probing reflection and the
> discovery of new, enchanting cognitive horizons constitute the very
> essence of halakhah. There is no change or revision in the halakhah;
> however it is possessed of unbounded original, creative interpretation
> *(ḥiddush)*. Where such creative interpretation wanes, halakhah itself

77 Thus, for example, the recent discussions of Rabbi Soloveitchik's thought
    in D. Hartman, *A Living Covenant* (New York: Free Press, 1985), and D.
    Singer and M. Sokol, "Joseph Soloveitchik: Lonely Man of Faith", *Mod-
    ern Judaism* 2/3 (October, 1982), 227-272, focus on *Halakhic Man* and *The
    Lonely Man of Faith* and completely (Hartman) or almost completely
    (Singer and Sokol) ignore *"Ubiḳ ash te m Misham"*. Cf., however, the
    article of Aviezer Ravitsky referred to in note 23, which contains a
    penetrating analysis of certain central themes in *"Ubiḳ ash te m
    Misham"*. A thorough discussion of this essay will be found in an as yet
    unpublished paper of mine "From Freedom to Necessity and Back Again:
    Man's Religious Odyssey in the Thought of R. Joseph Soloveitchik",
    which I trust will see the light shortly.

is uprooted. Our enemies claim: The halakhah is frozen, fossilized, i.e. it is devoid of any creative activity. Such individuals have never studied a page of Talmud and have never enjoyed the radiance of creativity and original interpretation in halakhah. According to them: Rabbenu Tam never engaged in original, creative interpretation; Maimonides never engaged in original, creative interpretation; Nahmanides, R. Elijah, the Gaon of Vilna, R. Hayyim of Brisk never engaged in original, creative interpretation. What a grotesque accusation! These scholars, both earlier and more recent ones, constructed new worlds, dazzling in their beauty and sublimity. These sages were the greatest original, creative interpreters in halakhic thought. Anyone who is acquainted with the methodology of halakhah, as it has been transmitted to us through the generations by the *Rishonim* and the outstanding *aḥaronim*, the great commentators on the Talmud, in all of its varied epistemological aspects will acknowledge that in terms of the sweep of its ideal-deductive mode of creative thought, its subtlety, the acuteness of its analysis, the subtlety of its abstractions, the consistency of its system, it is not in the slightest whit inferior to any other of man's cognitive disciplines, no matter how abstract or precise. On the contrary it is superior to them. The principle of methodological unity and the synthesizing of free constructs into one conceptual whole - the most fundamental principle of intellectual cognition - are at the very core of halakhic cognition. Naturally the freedom of halakhic inquiry is bounded by categorical limits. The halakhah cannot free itself from its subjection to the complex of a priori postulates. This postulational complex constitutes the alpha and omega of halakhah. However any scientific inquiry is linked with a specific system of postulates and does not begin in a conceptual void. Freedom of cognitive creativity means free cognition within the framework of ideal postulates. Despite all of the transformations, both in terms of form and content, that have taken place in the contemporary era regarding the manner in which mathematical-physical reality is conceived and despite all of the fundamental changes that have occurred in the epistemological conception of the nature of axiomatics, which classical epistemology viewed as a fixed and unalterable postulational complex in which demonstrative science could find "absolute" anchorage and certainty, the fact of postulates remains as is. For example, the concepts of space and time and the concept of substance and causality have been thoroughly transformed by the theory of relativity and the theory of quantum physics; however scientific thought has still not freed itself from these postulates as the fundamental categories underlying the scientific conception of the cosmic drama which, in turn, impress their stamp on all acts of objectification of the chaos and void of the sense-data per se. Contemporary science has, indeed, dared to lay hold of the categorical complex and to adapt it to the needs of "strange" data that could not be satisfactorily explained by it [in its classical state], but it did not free itself from the yoke of the postulate. On the contrary, this development has only set forth the ideal, a priori character of postulates in bolder relief. It need not be said

that halakhic thought which is set firm in a revelational foundation
can not, unlike scientific thought, dominate its postulational complexes.
It must accept them as they are. Nevertheless halakhic thought also
enjoys a mighty and splendid freedom. We have here a blend of opposing
principles: a revelational principle and a rational principle.   The
halakhah opposes any changes in its axiomatics; it is subject to the tradition.   Despite this it pursues original, creative interpretation
(*hiddush*), the apple of its eye. In each and every generation an individual is obligated to speculate profoundly regarding the foundations of
the halakhah, the definition of its concepts, the principles of its epistemology, the classification of its achievements; his task is to hew out
new ideas and bold exciting concepts. The study of Torah means - creative interpretation. The postulational circle is fixed, but within the
circle itself halakhic understanding penetrates to the very depths and
ascends to the very heights. The halakhic method is free to examine, to
confirm, to refute, to engage in subtle, sharp analysis, in the careful
drawing of analogies, to create ideal concepts and to map a new world.
The postulates themselves, despite their fixed character, become imbued
with a content that is vibrant and alive. It is impossible to look at the
world of halakhah without seeing constant movement, continuous flow.
The study of the Torah is an act of independent, intellectual construction,
possessed of epistemological attributes and noetic values that derive
their life and vitality from the creative spirit and mastery of man the
knower who has penetrated into the revelational realm and seized hold
of it. The revelational consciousness is incorporated into the developing,
creative, cognitive consciousness. God gave the Torah to Israel and has
commanded us to engage in creative interpretation.[78]

Soloveitchik's thesis is powerfully and dramatically put. One
should note, however, that Soloveitchik here is speaking not of the
halakhist as he confronts empirical reality but rather of the
halakhist as he confronts the halakhah itself.   And here, par-
adoxically enough, I would argue that in terms of his own understanding of the nature of halakhic creativity, as developed in
"Mah dodekh midod", R. Soloveitchik concedes *too much*. For in the
light of that essay it is difficult to see how the copious halakhic
texts, rules, principles constitute fixed unalterable postulates.
Rather the welter of revealed texts, cases, rules, etc., constitute the
fundamental *sense-data* of the halakhist, similar to the natural-
empirical sense-data of the scientist.

The creative halakhist, like the creative scientist, then, constructs an abstract postulational system to order account for, ill-

78   *"Ubik ash te m Misham"*, supra n.3, at 49-50.

uminate and unify this data. Obviously, the halakhist does not and can not change his texts and they set his task for him. But similarly the sense-data of empirical reality set the scientist's task for him and they too are unalterable. A scientific wit once quipped: there is nothing so tragic as a recalcitrant fact destroying a beautiful theory.

Of course, the issue of fact and theory in science is a highly complex one. I do not wish to enter into the whole falsification debate raging between Kuhn, Popper, Putnam, Lakatos, etc. When, if ever, do facts finally and conclusively falsify a theory? When can they be perceived as simply a challenge to the theory's explanatory power? I would not presume to say. The case of the apparently irregular orbit of Uranus and the theory of universal gravitation is a famous example. I only want to note that the same problem of fact and theory, present in contemporary philosophy of science, is present in R. Soloveitchik's discussion of halakhah. For though R. Soloveitchik specifically states:

> The doctrine of the creation of pure constructions does not distinguish between that which is primary and that which is peripheral, between the general principle and the particular instance. Everything, from top to bottom, is important. Even if the scholar is convinced of the truth of the line of his thinking, its overall pattern, even if he feels that he is on the right path and that, indeed, he sees lights from afar, he will not rest if even a slight detail does not fit into his general conceptional complex. Just like the mathematician, he will not cease and desist until each and every detail finds its place in the system and he will not deceive himself with any vain comforts, and say to himself - aren't the principles ordered, worked out? why then worry about petty details?... If one i is not properly dotted it will invalidate everything. There is one law for the actual Torah scroll and the spiritual Torah discourse.[79]

in almost practically the same breath he can turn around and say:

> Halakhic man does not attempt to answer all questions. He is not overjoyed by an answer and is not overly distressed by a question. Man's task is to understand. If one understands the difficulty and the complexity which can not be explained - it is sufficient. Halakhic man does not fritter away his talents and efforts in order to answer questions which are unanswerable, and resolve problems that are unresolvable. Wherever the halakhic vision is present, there halakhic man feels the heartbeat of the halakhah and he distinguishes between those matters that can be explained and those conundrums which even the most skillful

79 *"Mah Dodekh Midod", supra* n.5, at 232.

workman cannot disentangle.[80]

Be this as it may, R. Soloveitchik unnecessarily diminishes the powerful, free, creative spirit of the halakhist as he describes that spirit in *"Mah Dodekh midod"*, if he takes halakhic texts, cases, rulings, as fixed postulates rather than simply as data posing the problems which the halakhist answers through creating out of his deepest inner resources an abstract, postulational system and imposing this system on the sense data, thereby depriving them of their sensual facticity and transposing them to the realm of pure ideality.

III

We now arrive at the second task of our essay. We wish to attempt to understand what consideration, or, rather, considerations, moved R. Soloveitchik to implicitly reject traditional juridical models for understanding the halakhah and to opt for his suggestive and stimulating, but certainly problematic, scientific model.

To a certain extent it seems reasonable to suggest that R. Soloveitchik's philosophic background and training played a part in his choice of models. R. Soloveitchik, while studying philosophy at the University of Berlin, came under the dominant influence of the Marburg school of Neo-Kantianism and wrote his thesis on the logic and ontology of Hermann Cohen under the supervision of the prominent Neo-Kantian, Heinrich Maier. The Marburg school viewed the physical sciences and mathematics as the highest form of cognitive knowledge. R. Soloveitchik, in accordance with this view, in addition to his strictly philosophical studies, pursued, and has continued to maintain an active interest in, mathematics and the natural sciences. It is not surprising, then, that R. Soloveitchik when attempting to understand the nature of the halakhah should draw upon the model of the sciences which were so near and dear to

80 *Ibid.*, at 234. In a lecture at Bar-Ilan University (Spring, 1983) on the halakhic methodology of R. Soloveitchik, R. Aharon Lichtenstein, the prominent rabbinic scholar, and son-in-law and leading disciple of R. Soloveitchik, also noted this tension between these two statements of R. Soloveitchik and argued that R. Soloveitchik's halakhic greatness consists precisely in his intuitive recognition of when a particular recalcitrant detail that does not fit into an halakhic theory is crucial and must be confronted and when it is simply a tangential difficulty that may be left for further analysis at some future time.

him.

Yet whenever we try to understand why a great thinker chooses particular options, simply to point to the thinker's background, noting external intellectual influences, is insufficient. For in dealing with any original thinker we have to ask what is it in the problems the thinker is grappling with, the task he sets for himself, the line of approach he develops to accomplish that task, that makes the thinker open to certain influences and closed to others. In a word, an original thinker does not merely passively absorb "influences", but selectively and creatively draws upon and transforms them in the course of his work.

Let us then examine some possible internal considerations which may have prompted R. Soloveitchik to prefer a scientific model to a juridical model.

Let us begin negatively. Why would R. Soloveitchik consider a juridical model inadequate for comprehending the nature of halakhah? In a recent article Professor Bernard Jackson suggests that there may be "a conflict between the ontological (and value) assumptions of halakhah and modern jurisprudence".[81] One prime example of these different assumptions is the differing attitudes to time on the part of halakhah and secular jurisprudence. Jackson writes:

> In jurisprudential theories, the concept of time is taken to be unproblematic. However that may be, Wacholder's recent study [on time and place in the early halakhah] suggests that it would be rash to assume that the conception of time of the Rabbis of the Mishnah was comparable. For them, past, present and future correspond to value-laden epochs in the history of Israel, with the result that the present was conceived as a somewhat unsatisfactory interim between an ideal past and its revival in an eschatological future. In other words, the present was downgraded. Wacholder suggests that this explains the character of much of the law of the Mishnah. Much of it would be regarded, in secular terms, as ineffective: because of the loss of the Solomonic temple and associated first commonwealth institutions, much of the law of the Mishnah could not be put into practice in the present. Yet the Rabbis themselves clearly regarded it as no less important (we might even use the terms "valid" or "binding") for that reason: the present was not the exclusive or even overriding time-reference of the *halakhah*.[82]

81 B. Jackson, "Secular Jurisprudence and the Philosophy of Jewish Law: A Commentary on Some Recent Literature", *The Jewish Law Annual* VI (1986), 3-39.

82 *Ibid.*

It should be noted that Wacholder's analysis of the time-consciousness of the Mishnah referred to by Jackson follows very closely
along the lines of Rabbi Soloveitchik's analysis of the time-consciousness of Maimonides, as it found expression in his *Mishneh
Torah*. In a dramatic and powerful passage, R. Soloveitchik writes:

When Maimonides describes the order of events on the fifteenth night of
Nisan he "forgets" temporarily that he is living approximately one
thousand years after the destruction of the Temple and paints the image
of the service of this holy festival night in a wealth of colors that daz-
zle the eye, that reflect the Passover service as it was celebrated
thousands of years ago in Ancient Jerusalem and as it once again will be
celebrated in the era of the Messiah. Thus writes Maimonides in *The
Laws of Hatmets and Matsah*, 8:1: "The order in which the
aforementioned commandments should be fulfilled on the night of the
fifteenth [of Nisan] is as follows: First a cup is mixed for each person and
he recites the blessing 'who has created the fruit of the vine' and he
recites over it the sanctification of the day and drinks." This
formulation is known to us from *Ora h Hayyim* , *Hayye Adam*, the
prayerbook of R. Jacob Emden, the prayerbook *Derekh Hayyim* of
R. Jacob Lissa, the abridged *Shulhan Arukh*, and similar works, and its
very ring recalls to mind the ditty *Kadesh u re hats*, so familiar to all
schoolchildren. It would seem that *The Laws of H atmets and Matsah*,
chapter 8, and an illustrated haggadah which one can buy for a few
pennies differ only in style and phraseology. However, as we continue to
read we suddenly come across a "peculiar" *Sed er* . "And afterward he
recites the blessing... and a table, ready laid, is brought in bearing a
bitter herb and another vegetable, unleavened bread, *haroset*, and the
body of the Paschal lamb and meat from the festival offering of the day
of the fourteenth.". Maimonides did not intend to set down the order of
the performance of the commandments on the night of the fifteenth for
the benefit of his generation, but rather for the pilgrims who went up to
Jerusalem, who roasted their paschal lambs and ate them with
thanksgiving and praise. Similarly when Maimonides continued his
description "And a second cup of wine is mixed and at that point the son
asks 'Why is this night different from all other nights?... For on all
other nights we eat meat roasted, stewed or boiled, but on this night it is
all roasted'," he had in mind not the innocent child of his own day who
would recline at his father's table in Cairo or Cordova, where there was
neither paschal offering nor a festival offering, but rather the son who
reclined at his father's table in ancient Jerusalem on the holy festival
night when the air would resound with the tones of the recited over the
eating of the paschal lamb. And Maimonides' text continues in this
fashion later on: "The table is then replaced in front of him and he says:
'The paschal offering that we eat is on account...' and afterwards he

recites the blessing 'Blessed are Thou O Lord, our God King of the Universe who has sanctified us with His commandments and commanded us concerning the eating of the festival offering'. And he eats first from the festival offering, then he recites the blessing 'Blessed... concerning the eating of the paschal offering' and he eats some of the body of the paschal offering, etc. Finally he eats some more of the meat of paschal offering even if only an olive's bulk and does not taste anything more." The *seder* with which Maimonides is dealing is an ideal conception of Passover night. Our great master pays no attention to the cruel and bitter present. The picture of a restored Jerusalem, the Temple in all its splendor, the priests at their service, and free Israelites performing the commandments of the night hovers before his eyes. However, from time to time he bestirs himself from his ideal dream and romantic vision and finds himself confronted with an exile filled with nightmares and terrors, with physical oppression and spiritual degeneration, and he states: "In the present time he does not say 'tonight it is all roasted' for we no longer have any paschal offering, etc. And in the present time he says 'The Passover offering which our fathers used to eat when the Temple was standing', etc., and in the present time one adds 'So O Lord our God.... bring us to other festivals... happy in the building of Thy city and joyous in Thy service. And there may we eat of the sacrifices and the paschal offerings', etc. In the present time when there is no offering, after he recites the blessing 'He who brings forth bread from the earth', etc. and in the present time he eats an olive's bulk of *matsah* and does not taste anything more after that.". In other words, the present time is only an historical anomaly in the ongoing process of the actualization of the ideal Halakhah in the real world, and there is no need to elaborate about a period which is but a temporary aberration that has seized hold of our historical existence. The Halakhah remains in full force, and we hope for and eagerly await the day of Israel's redemption when the ideal world will triumph over the profane reality.[83]

This conclusion of R. Soloveitchik finds a direct echo in the concluding statement of Wacholder's essay.

Between God's time in the past, brought to a halt by the sins of Israel and the endlessness of God's time to be resumed in the future, a less than ideal present - and with it a too-long endured pain - is reduced to "a yesterday that is past and a watch in the night."[84]

83 I. H., 33-34/H. M., 26-28.

84 Ben-Zion Wacholder, *Messianism and Mishnah: Time and Place in the Early Halakhah* (Cincinnati: Hebrew Union College Press, 1979), 47. It is worth noting that Professor Wacholder was, at one point, a student of R. Soloveitchik.

Certainly this type of time-consciousness for R. Soloveitchik does not only characterize Maimonides' *Mishneh Torah* but characterizes the time-consciousness of the halakhah generally. However, for R. Soloveitchik, the lack of present-mindedness derives from a more fundamental feature of the halakhah, a feature which again sets it apart from secular systems of law. This feature is the fundamentally theoretical nature of the halakhah. Indeed, R. Soloveitchik's passage about Maimonides is part of this larger point about the halakhah's theoretical-ideal nature. As R. Soloveitchik states:

> The foundation of foundations and the pillar of halakhic thought is not the practical ruling but the determination of the theoretical halakhah. Therefore, many of the greatest halakhic men avoided and still avoid serving in rabbinical posts. They rather join themselves to the group of those who are reluctant to render practical decisions. And if necessity - which is not to be decried - compels them to disregard their preference and to render practical decisions, this is only a small, insignificant responsibility which does not stand at the center of their concerns.
>
> The theoretical halakhah - not the practical decision, the ideal creation, not the empirical one represent the longing of halakhic man. Halakhic man engages in theoretical discussion and debate concerning the subjects of sacrifices and purity and plumbs the depths of those concepts, laws, and distinctions with the same seriousness that he investigates and searches out the laws of *agunah*, plaintiff and defendant, and forbidden fools.[85]

And as we saw earlier, R. Soloveitchik emphasizes that:

> Even the norm is, at the outset, ideal, not real. Halakhic man is not particularly concerned about the possibility of actualizing the norm in the concrete world. He wishes to mint an ideal, normative coin.[86]

This dovetails, once again, with Jackson's astute analysis of the problems modern jurisprudential theories face in accounting for fundamental features of the halakhah. Thus "jurisprudential positivism... leads to a conception of the law in terms of social control, in terms of order".[87] However, such positivism, with its utilitarian bias, can not account for the value inherent in legal scholarship - in

85   *I. H.*, 31/*H. M.*, 24.
86   *Ibid.*, at 59-60/63.
87   Jackson, *supra* n.81, at section 6.4.

Talmud Torah per se. Jackson, in place of "the utilitarian view of the function of law which today still dominates jurisprudential thought",[88] suggests a structuralist approach to Jewish law which would emphasize the communicative function of law. We might conclude, then, that many of the reasons which prompt Jackson to reject a secular jurisprudential model of the halakhah in favor of a structuralist model lead R. Soloveitchik, similarly, to reject any jurisprudential model in favor of, not a structuralist, but, rather, a scientific model.

This leads us directly to the positive side of our task: viz. the setting out of the internal considerations that prompted R. Soloveitchik to adopt the scientific model. For certainly those very characteristics of the halakhah for which a jurisprudential model can not account: the lack of present-mindedness, the emphasis on theoretical knowledge, etc., are also characteristics which belong to the world of science. For the scientist, science has, no doubt, a utilitarian function; but beyond that it provides one with a coherent, comprehensive system of knowledge, valuable in its own right. The scientist, like the halakhist, emphasizes the value of pure understanding, of knowledge for the sake of knowledge. Similarly the scientific model, unlike the jurisprudential model, is a timeless one. If the present is not devalued in the natural sciences, neither is it valued over the past and future. Indeed, for the natural sciences, historical time is, in a profound sense, irrelevant. The law of universal gravitation, nay Newtonian physics as a whole, is independent of historical time, Similarly, for R. Soloveitchik, the system of halakhah, rooted in revelation, is, in like fashion, also fundamentally independent of historical time.

Our observation about the revealed nature of halakhah leads to our next and very important point. We have seen that the revealed nature of the halakhah raises serious difficulties for the halakhah-science analogy of R. Soloveitchik, And yet we would argue that, in the final turn, the revealed nature of halakhah is a prime factor underlying R. Soloveitchik's adoption of this analogy.

R. Soloveitchik essentially accepts the distinction posited, most

88   *Ibid.*

prominently by Dilthey[89] but going at least as far back as Vico,[90] between the methods of the *geisteswissenschaften* and the *naturwissenschaften*. The method appropriate to the study of the *geisteswissenschaften*, a method Soloveitchik himself applies to the study of halakhic *man*, is Dilthey's *Verstehen*, a unique synthesis of personal empathy and critical rigor. The method appropriate to the study of the *naturwissenschaften* is the traditional scientific method, whether conceived of in empiricist, positivist, or critical idealist categories.

The dividing line between the *geisteswissenschaften* and the *naturwissenschaften* is this: the *geisteswissenschaften* deal with the human world, the world created by man, i.e. the realms of politics, economics, sociology, and above all, history; the *naturwissenschaften* deal with the external world given to man. If this is so then for R. Soloveitchik secular jurisprudence must belong to the *geisteswissenschaften*, since it is the science of human law, and the human law is the creation of man, of human cultures and societies. The science of halakhah, however, must belong to the *naturwissenschaften*, since the halakhah, insofar as it is a corpus of law revealed by God, is, like the natural world, external to man.[91]

However, while many proponents of the *geisteswissenschaft-naturwissenschaft* dichotomy, beginning with Vico, argued for the superiority of the *geisteswissenschaften* over the *naturwissenschaften*, claiming that man can only truly understand that which he himself has made - for R. Soloveitchik, perhaps as a result of the influence of the Neo-Kantians, the *naturwissenschaften* are superior to the *geisteswissenschaften*. "Mathematics and the mathematical natural sciences," states R. Soloveitchik, "[are] the

---

89   See M. Ermath, *Wilhelm Dilthey: The Critique of Historical Reason* (Chicago: and London: University of Chicago Press, 1978).

90   See I. Berlin, *Vico and Herder* (London: Hogarth Press, 1976); and L.Pompa, *Vico: A Study of the 'New Science'* (Cambridge: Cambridge University Press, 1975).

91   Rabbi Soloveitchik discusses at great length the methodological differences between the *geisteswissenschaften* and *naturwissenschaften*, throughout *Halakhic Mind*. Unfortunately, I was not able to revise my paper to take into account his very important and original thoughts on this matter. I believe, however, that my own comments, while requiring some refinement in the light of *Halakhic Mind*, do not need substantial modification.

crowning achievement of civilization."[92] This means, of course, that, for R. Soloveitchik, the science of halakhah which constitutes a *naturwissenschaft* is superior to the science of secular jurisprudence, which only constitutes a *geisteswissenschaft*. But it also means that the study of halakhah is superior to the study of halakhic man, which study, as R. Soloveitchik clearly states in the very first note of *Halakhic Man*, also belongs to the *geisteswissenschaften*. Thus, we would contend, for R. Soloveitchik, a strictly halakhic essay of his would be of more value than his essay *Halakhic Man*. Moreover, their very methodologies would and indeed do differ. While *Halakhic Man* is a very fine example of *Verstehen*, combining rigor and empathy, analysis and poetry, anecdote and generalization, introspection and historical description, R. Soloveitchik's halakhic essays consist of severely rigorous and highly abstract arguments presented in a spare, precise and rigorously conceptual style.[93]

Yet, if it is R. Soloveitchik's belief in the revealed status of the halakhah, in the halakhah as a given,[94] as the world of nature is a given, that is, in large part, responsible for R. Soloveitchik's cla-

---

92 *I. H.*, 27/*H. M.*, 18-19.

93 Indeed, the stylistic differences within *Halakhic Man* itself between the purely halakhic discussion contained in some the notes (see, e.g., notes 39, 40, 42, 120, and 122). and the rest of the essay, are striking. I briefly touch upon the different levels of style in *Halakhic Man* in my preface to my translation, at viii-ix.

It is also worth noting that there are stylistic differences between Rabbi Soloveitchik's halakhic essays themselves. Recently three collections of Rabbi Soloveitchik's halakhic essays have appeared: *Kovets Hiddushe Torah* (Jerusalem: Makhon Yerushalayim, n.d.), a collection of halakhic *novellae* of R. Soloveitchik that had appeared over the years in halakhic journals, and *Shi'urim Lezekher Abba Mari Z"L*, Vols. 1 and 2, *supra* n.17, a collection of Rabbi Soloveitchik's halakhic discourses delivered on the *yahrzeit* of his father, R. Moses Soloveitchik. The essays in *Kovets Hiddushe Torah* are written in the traditional, highly elliptic and telegraphic style of rabbinic Hebrew that characterizes most of the *novellae* of the *aharonim*. The essays in *Shi'urim Lezekher Abba Mari Z"L* are written in a highly lucid and elegant, modern, rabbinic Hebrew. If the articles in *Kovets Hiddushe Torah* then, belong to the genre of *hidushim*, the articles in *Shi'urim Lezekher Abba Mari Z"L* belong more to the genre of the modern rabbinic essay pioneered by Rabbi S. J. Zevin.

94 See my discussion of the *givenness* of halakhah in the first part of this article.

ssifying the study, the science of the halakhah together with the *naturwissenschaften*, as opposed to the *geisteswissenschaften*, this means that those who cannot accept this belief of R. Soloveitchik, but who rather view the halakhah as being primarily the creation of men in history (even if they do accept some notion of revelation) will, of necessity, find R. Soloveitchik's position at the least problematic, at the most wholly unacceptable. R. Soloveitchik's philosophy of the halakhah, then, would seem to be intimately bound up with his orthodox beliefs. And non-orthodox scholars, however much they might admire the power, ingenuity, insight and subtlety of R. Soloveitchik's analysis, would find it difficult, if not impossible, to accept its fundamental validity.

This issue just raised of the relationship of R. Soloveitchik's philosophy of the halakhah and his orthodoxy requires that we broaden our focus. And precisely in this broadened focus we may yet penetrate to the deepest roots of R. Soloveitchik's adoption of the scientific model for understanding the halakhah. For R. Soloveitchik, in developing the halakhah-science analogy, is, in truth, just the most recent, though perhaps the most outstanding, representative of a long line of orthodox thinkers in the modern era who have developed very similar models. Already Samson Raphael Hirsch, in a note to his *Nineteen Letters*, writes:

One word here concerning the proper method of Torah investigation. Two revelations are open before us: that is, nature and the Torah. In nature all phenomena stand before us as indisputable facts, and we can only endeavor *a posteriori* to ascertain the law of each and the connection of all. Abstract demonstration of the truth, or, rather, the probability of theoretic explanations of the facts of nature, is an unnatural proceeding. The right method is to verify our assumptions by the known facts, and the highest attainable degree of certainty is to be able to say, "The facts agree with our assumption" - that is, all the phenomena observed can be explained according to our theory. A single contradictory phenomenon will make our theory untenable. We must, therefore, acquire all the knowledge possible concerning the object of our investigation, and know it, if possible, in its totality. If, however, all efforts should fail in disclosing the inner law and connection of phenomena revealed to us as facts in nature, the facts remain, nevertheless, undeniable, and cannot be reasoned away. The same principles must be applied to the investigation of the Torah. In the Torah, even as in nature, God is the ultimate cause. In the Torah, even as in nature, no fact may be denied even though the reason and the connection may not be understood. What is true in nature is true also in the Torah: the traces of Divine wisdom must be sought for. Its ordinances must be accepted in their entirety as undeniable phenomena and must be studied in accordance with their connection to each other and the subject to which they relate. Our conjectures must be tested by their precepts, and our highest certainty here also can only be that everything stands in harmony with our theory. In nature, the phenomena are recognized as facts, though their cause and relationship to each other may not be understood and are independent of our investigation. So, too, the ordinances of the Torah must be law for us, even if we do not comprehend the reason and the purpose of a single one.[95]

Hirsch here is speaking of reasons for the Commandments. However, in the late nineteenth and early twentieth centuries a number of important rabbinic scholars, most prominently R. Isaac Reines[96] and R. Moshe Amiel,[97] argued that the traditional method of halakhic study is analogous to the method of the sciences. Indeed in their purely halakhic works they created new terminologies and methods of analysis in order to highlight the "scientific" character of halakhic study. Their ideological pronouncements along these lines have been justifiably criticized for lacking any real acquaintance with scientific method and for a general philosophical superficiality.[98] In this respect the work of R. Soloveitchik, whose philosophic learning is deep and broad, and who, while not a scientist, has engaged in a serious study of the sciences and the philosophy of science,[99] is richer, more challenging and stimulating than the work of his predecessors.

But this still raises the question: how is one to account for the appeal of the scientific model for this entire galaxy of orthodox rabbinic figures?

95 Rabbi S. R. Hirsch, *Nineteen Letters of Ben-Uziel*, translated by Jacob Breuer and Bernard Drachman (New York: Feldheim Inc., 1960), 143.

96 Rabbi Isaac Jacob Reines, *Ḥotam Tokhnit* (Jerusalem: R. H. Ha-Kohen Press, 1934).

97 R. Moshe Avigdor Amiel, *Hamidot leheḳer Hahalakhah* (Jerusalem and Tel-Aviv: Mosad Harav Kook, 1939-1945).

98 E. Schweid, *Ben Ortodoxiah lehumanism Dati* (Jerusalem: Van Leer Foundation, 1977), 34-38.

99 *Halakhic Mind, supra* n.7, in particular, is a philosophical *tour de force* that dazzlingly displays Rabbi Soloveitchik's exceptionally wide-ranging and detailed mastery of modern science and philosophy in all their depth, breadth and complexity. (Indeed a number of highly technical mathematical and scientific notes that appeared in the typescript of *Halakhic Mind* were dropped from the published version.)

Some scholars have argued[100] that all these rabbinic figures, including R. Soloveitchik, adopted the scientific model in order to lend the halakhah some of the modern prestige, the almost sacred aura attached to science. Indeed all of these rabbinic figures were, in some sense, modern figures, all sensitive to the challenges that modern, western, humanistic and scientific European civilization posed to traditional Judaism, all appreciative, in varying degrees, of the value or values to be found in that civilization, all consequently unwilling simply to reject that civilization out of hand in the name of preserving traditional Judaism. These orthodox rabbinic figures then, in reacting to the charge that the halakhah is backward, reactionary, primitive, etc., that the study of the halakhah is useless, deadening mummery, pedantry, logic-chopping, etc. in effect responded: No! There is nothing more modern, more up-to-date, more "scientific" than the halakhah and its study. In this view, then, R. Soloveitchik's whole enterprise would be an essentially apologetic one.

The claim that all these orthodox thinkers, including R. Soloveitchik, are motivated by apologetic considerations certainly contains a good deal of truth. Yet to leave matters thus is to remain on the surface. There is a deeper reason behind the general appeal of the scientific model for all of these rabbinic figures and, at least for R. Soloveitchik, this deeper reason is the essential reason. For the system of science provides the halakhah with a model of a system that has a strictly objective and autonomous character but at the same time allows for, indeed is the result of, profound and powerful human creativity. And the traditional halakhist seeks to maintain the strict objectivity and autonomy of the halakhah, rejecting all modern varieties of historical, sociological and psychological reductionism, but together with that, sees the halakhah as an unfolding conceptual system that allows for, nay demands, ongoing human creativity. This, indeed, is the central theme of R. Soloveitchik's portrait of the halakhic approach of his grandfather, R. Ḥayyim Soloveitchik. But, more, it is the central theme, the central dialectic pervading and coloring all of R. Soloveitchik's writings on the nature of the halakhah.

---

100 See Shihor, "On the Problem of Halacha's Status in Judaism", *supra* n.34, at 154; and *cf.* Schweid, *Ben Orthodoxiah lehumanism Dati, supra* n.98, at 38-42.

R. Soloveitchik's oeuvre should be seen as a bold and profound attempt, not only to maintain the two sides of the dialectic in fruitful tension with one another but to blend them together in a perfect unity.

One might be tempted to argue as follows. The emphasis on the objectivity and autonomy of halakhah has as its aim the defence of the tradition. The emphasis on creativity, though, is a peculiarly modern emphasis, in tune with the modern spirit that places such great stress on the powers of man, on man as creator.

Such a view of the matter again contains some truth. Yet, taken as the whole truth, it is overly simple and unfair.

First the emphasis on the autonomy and objectivity of the halakhah, as we have noted above, does point to an essential feature of its nature, even if, as we also sought to argue, we cannot claim for the halakhah the same degree of autonomy and objectivity possessed by the natural sciences. But, more important, R. Soloveitchik's emphasis on the creative spirit of the halakhist is not just intended as a portrait of the halakhist as modern man, but is true to the deepest experience of the halakhist. Nay, it is true to the deepest experience of R. Soloveitchik himself as halakhist, to his deepest sense of self-awareness, to his deepest self-perception. Certainly anyone who has attended the Talmudic lectures of R. Soloveitchik is overwhelmed by their sheer brilliance and profundity. However the most striking impression on the auditor or student is that of the almost boundless creative powers of R. Soloveitchik, the Rav par excellence. Out of the depths of his halakhic vision and intellect he constructs rigorous and abstract concepts that resolve and clarify opaque, complex, tortuous, problematic halakhic texts in a striking, yes, illuminating, fashion; he builds a self-contained, pure and logically coherent world that "miraculously" parallels that "empirical" world of the halakhic material he is studying; and he imposes this ideal, systematic order upon the recalcitrant data with which he struggles, thereby achieving the cognitive triumph of subject-knower over object-known.[101] R. Soloveitchik's halakhic lectures prove him to be a worthy recipient and self-conscious embodiment of those very accolades he has bestowed upon halakhic

101 Cf. Rabbi Soloveitchik's characterization in I.H., 67/H.M., 73, of knowledge as "the subjugation of the object and the domination of the subject".

man: intellectual strength of mind, autonomy, freedom, creativity.

We conclude: Even if the scientific model is not the best model for understanding the nature of halakhah, even if the scientist-world : halakhist-halakhah analogy is not free of serious problems, even if one argues that the objectivity and autonomy of science are of a different order than the objectivity and autonomy of the halakhah, nevertheless R. Soloveitchik, in focusing upon and fusing together these two different sides of the halakhah, objectivity and autonomy with creativity and freedom, has touched the very heart of the halakhist's complex dialectical, relationship with the halakhah: strict obedience, nay subservience, to the objective inner logic of the halakhah, combined with a sense of unbound intellectual freedom and profound creative power. Whatever criticisms, then, one may wish to put forward, of R. Soloveitchik's specific views, his portrait of halakhic man constitutes a valuable and enduring contribution to the philosophy of the halakhah.

R. Soloveitchik prefaces *Halakhic Man* with the Talmudic statement, "At that moment the image of his father came to him and appeared before him in the window" (*Sotah* 36b).[102] Indeed R. Soloveitchik once remarked[103] that he wrote *Halakhic Man* with the images of his father and grandfather constantly before his inner eye. Similarly, *"Mah dodekh midod"* is a portrait of his uncle, R. Velvele, another halakhic man par excellence. And yet we dare say that the lustre of R. Soloveitchik's philosophy of the halakhah and his portrait of halakhic man, a lustre that will not fade despite all of the criticisms, legitimate criticisms, that may be leveled against them, ultimately derives from the fact that in R. Soloveitchik's essays we see reflected not only the faces of his grandfather, his uncle, his father, but the face, the image, the personality, the creative spirit of R. Soloveitchik himself.

102 One should, incidentally, carefully note the context of this Talmudic statement.
103 Oral communication.

Extended Endnotes

A. It should be noted, however, that in a number of his halakhic essays, both in his collection of halakhic discourses on the topic of repentance, *Al Hateshuvah* (Jerusalem: Hahistadrut Hatsiyonit Ha'olamit, 1974), edited by P. Peli, and in the two volumes of his halakhic discourses delivered on the Yahrzeit of his father, R. Moses Soloveitchik, *Shi'urim Lezekher Abba Mari Z "L* (Jerusalem: Makhon Yerushalayim, 1983, 1985), Vols. 1 and 2, Rabbi Soloveitchik shows that many strictly halakhic commandments also have a more philosophical dimension. More precisely, in many of these halakhic essays Rabbi Soloveitchik focuses his attention on the special nature - the special halakhic nature - of an entire group of commandments: prayer, repentance, recitation of the *shema*, rejoicing on festivals, mourning, etc. What is special about these commandments?   Rabbi Soloveitchik has often pointed out that we may theoretically distinguish between the *ma'aseh Hamitsvah*, the indispensable deed whereby one performs a commandment, and the *Ḳiyyum Hamitsvah*, the actual fulfillment of that commandment. Normally, however, these two aspects coincide. Thus, for example, one performs the commandment of eating *matsah* through eating *matsah* and that act of eating simultaneously constitutes the fulfillment of the commandment. The act of eating is at one and the same time *ma'aseh* and *ḳiyyum*, performance and fulfillment. The same is true for most commandments. However, there are commandments where performance and fulfillment do not coincide, where the performance is an outward act but the fulfillment is an inward experience. Examples of such commandments are repentance, prayer, rejoicing on festivals and mourning, Thus with reference to the commandment to mourn for one's departed relatives, the indispensable deed whereby one performs the commandment is the whole set of fixed and defined rites of mourning; however, the fulfillment of this commandment resides in the inner experience of grief. The same is true for prayer and repentance. The indispensable deed whereby one performs the commandment of prayer is the verbal recitation of the words of prayer, the indispensable deed whereby one performs the act of repentance is the verbal confession of guilt and resolve. However, the fulfillment of these commands lies in the realm of inward experience, in the service of the heart in the case of prayer and in the difficult psychological process of recognition of guilt, contrition and turning away from sin in the case of repentance. We may say that in these commandments there is a dialectical relationship between inward and outward. The inner experience expresses itself in deeds, while the deeds help sustain and are the indispensable means to arriving at the true inner experience. Thus through this distinction the inner experience involved in such central commandments as prayer, repentance, rejoicing on festivals, mourning for one's departed relatives become an integral part of the commandments themselves. These inward, private experiences are integrated with the fixed, outward, public deeds. Normally this whole private, inner experiential aspect of the commandments is seen as belonging to the aggadah of Judaism. For Rabbi Soloveitchik, it is an essential part of its halakhah.

In this connection we should point to the radically differing views of R. Soloveitchik and the late Professor A.J. Heschel on this issue. For Professor Heschel, *God in Search of Man* (New York: Meridian, 1959), 281-347, Halakhah is the realm of deed, fixity, performance, outwardness, Ḳeva; Aggadah is the realm of meaning, spontaneity, experience, inwardness, Ḳavanah. If Judaism contains both poles it is because Judaism contains both halakhah and aggadah. However, halakhah, per se, for Professor Heschel, contains no realm of inwardness. For Rabbi Soloveitchik, by contrast, the halakhah itself, in at least some of its realms, contains an inward dimension as an integral part of itself. Certainly R. Soloveitchik would admit that there is a realm of inwardness, of experience, of meaning which is purely aggadic, but he would stoutly maintain that not all inwardness need be so, that there is a realm of inwardness, of experience which is strictly halakhic in nature.

It should be clear that Rabbi Soloveitchik in these halakhic essays, in working his way from *ma'aseh hamitsvah*, the outward, objective performance of the commandment to *ḳiyyum hamitsvah*, the inward, subjective fulfillment of the commandment, in moving from objective deed to subjective correlate is performing an act of reconstruction! We are thus confronted with a striking paradox. In many respects, *The*

Halakhic Mind is the most "non-Jewish", the most abstractly philosophical of Rabbi Soloveitchik's essays. Indeed, in the first seventy-five pages of this hundred-page essay there is barely a mention of Judaism. We have also already noted that The Halakhic Mind should be seen as a prolegomenon to the articulation of a new world-view. If we ask, however, where are we to find the continuation of this essay, if only a partial and limited continuation, where in fact does Rabbi Soloveitchik engage in the "reconstruction of subjective aspects within the objective halakhic order" (p.85), the answer would be: in his halakhic essays, or, to be more precise, in a fair number of them. But this entire matter requires a full scale treatment in a separate essay. (Our contention that Rabbi Soloveitchik in moving from outward, *ma'aseh hamitsvah* to inward, *ḳiyyum hamitsvah* is engaging in an act of reconstruction finds support in Rabbi J.B. Soloveitchik, "The 'Common-Sense' Rebellion Against Torah Authority", in A. Besdin, ed., *Reflections of the Rav* [Jerusalem: The Jewish Agency, 1979], 143-144, where Rabbi Soloveitchik almost explicitly links the process of reconstruction with the move from *ma'aseh*, outward deed, to *ḳiyyum*, inward fulfillment. Indeed, the similarities between this rather popular and homiletical essay and the forbiddingly technical *The Halakhic Mind* are striking and require further analysis).

B   I.B. Cohen, *The Newtonian Revolution* (Cambridge and New York: Cambridge University Press, 1980), has also argued for the crucial role of "imaginative reasoning", of "scientific imagination", of "disciplined creative imagination" in the work of Newton, for reasons similar to those offered by R. Soloveitchik. For Cohen (62-64) the Newtonian style is :

> A special blend of imaginative reasoning plus the use of mathematical techniques applied to empirical data. Its essential feature is to start out (phase one) with a set of assumed physical entities and physical conditions that are simpler than those of nature, and which can be transferred from the world of physical nature to the domain of mathematics. In [such a] construct Newton [would] not only simplify and idealize a system found in nature, but he... [would] imaginatively conceive a system in mathematics that is the parallel or analogue of the natural system. To the degree that the physical conditions of the system become mathematical rules or propositions, their consequences may be deduced by the application of mathematical techniques.

Because the mathematical system (to use an expression of Newton in another context) duplicates the idealized physical system, the rules of propositions derived mathematically in one may be transferred back to the other and then compared and contrasted with the data of experiment and observation (and with experiential laws, rules, and proportions drawn from those data). This is phase two.

The comparison and contrast with reality of experiential nature (that is, with the laws, rules, and systems based upon observations and experiments) usually require a modification of the original phase one. This leads to further deductions and yet a new comparison and contrast with nature, a new phase two. In this way there is an alternation of phases one and two leading to systems of greater and greater complexity and to an increased *vraisemblance* of nature. That is, Newton successively adds further entities, concepts, or conditions to the imaginatively constructed systems, so as to make either its mathematically deduced consequences or the set conditions conform more exactly to the world of experience.

For Newton there is a final stage in this process: when the system and its conditions no longer represent merely nature simplified and idealized or an imaginative mathematical construct, but seem to conform to (or at least to duplicate) the realities of the external world. Then it becomes possible to apply the aggregate of mathematical principles to natural philosophy, to elaborate the Newtonian system of the world. This is the final phase three of the Newtonian style, the crown of all.

As Cohen (64,101) notes:

It is a feature of the Newtonian style that mathematics and not a series of experiments leads to the most profound knowledge of the universe and its workings. Of course, the data of experiment and observation are used in determining the initial conditions of the inquiry, the features that yield the mathematical principles that are applied to natural philosophy, and Newton was also aware that the success of the eventual natural philosophy (or of the system of the world) must rest ultimately on the accuracy or validity of the empirical data out of which it was constructed.

As a pure mathematician, Newton had no need of placing any restrictions on the constructs or imagined systems whose properties he wishes to explore. But as a mathematical natural philosopher, he had as his goal to invent and elaborate the properties of only such constructs that seemed reasonable and that appeared to hold the possibility of being useful for natural philosophy, for explaining the world as revealed by experiment and observation.

Indeed Cohen (109) emphasizes:

The great advantage of the three-phase Newtonian procedure is that it separates the basic questions of science into separate categories. In phase one Newton could explore the consequences of any condition or conditions that he found mathematically interesting or stimulating - and he could do so just as his inspiration drove him, without being blocked or deflected by questions whether certain forces or conditions of resistance do or do not ever occur in nature (or might or might not do so).

One cannot overstress the importance of this lack of premature restriction for the creative effort of a scientific imagination such as Newton's.

One should not gloss over the differences between Cohen and R. Soloveitchik. For R. Soloveitchik, there are essentially two stages in the process of scientific discovery, the stage of formulating mathematical principles and the stage of comparing those principles to nature; Cohen speaks of three phases in the Newtonian style, each phase, itself, complex and multifaceted. In particular, the central role played by the idealized physical system, as described by Cohen, has no counterpart in R. Soloveitchik's description. In general, Cohen's description of the process of scientific discovery is both more subtle and more carefully elaborated than R. Soloveitchik's somewhat sketchy description, and certainly is truer to life. Nevertheless, what is common to both is their insistence on the central role of scientific imagination, precisely because it is not experimentation and induction that "leads to the most profound knowledge of the universe and its workings," but rather free constructs, be they physical or mathematical in nature.

LAW IN REFORM JUDAISM: A STUDY OF SOLOMON FREEHOF

by

DAN COHN-SHERBOK[*]

Introduction

According to traditional Judaism not only did God give Moses the law recorded in the Pentateuch, but He also revealed the oral law. Thus the ultimate authority for the legal system is God Himself. Very early in the 19th century, however, the Reform movement departed from this traditional view, taking an antinomian position. Subsequently various Reform rabbis and synods were concerned with the status of traditional law; yet only recently has there been an attempt to systematize Reform Jewish practice. In this regard Rabbi Solomon Freehof has been the leading figure and his writings have been of seminal importance. As W. Jacobs notes, "Solomon Freehof has been a leader in this area of Reform Jewish development. He has continued and broadened a tradition rooted in the beginnings of our movement."[1] The publication of Freehof's study of Reform Jewish observance in the light of its rabbinic background (Reform Jewish Practice, Vol. I and II) marked the beginning of a scholarly investigation into the sources of Jewish law which has resulted in the publication of six volumes of his responsa. The purpose of this article is to evaluate the procedure Freehof adopts in defending Reform Judaism's attitude to traditional law.

Solomon Freehof's Philosophy of Law in Reform Judaism

In various studies[2] Freehof discusses the role of law in the vari-

---

[*]   Rabbi; Lecturer in Theology, University of Kent at Canterbury, Canterbury, Kent.

[1]   W. Jacobs in an introduction to S. Freehof *Reform Responsa For Our Time* (Cincinnati: Hebrew Union College Press, 1977), xxvii.

[2]   In particular the introduction to *Reform Jewish Practice* (New York: Union of American Hebrew Congregations, 1963), and *Reform Responsa* (Cincinnati: Hebrew Union College Press, 1960), as well as *Reform*

ous branches of Judaism. Orthodox Judaism, he writes, is imposing. "Its self description appeals to all who have reverence for the past. It declares itself to be a system of law, going back consistently and without interruption for thousands of years to the beginning of our history. All the elaborations of the law found in the later Orthodox Codes are held to be not novelties at all but rediscoveries. Whatever the 'latest scholar' adduces from a comparison of texts and opinions is really not his own but "was already said on Mt. Sinai."[3]

Yet, according to Freehof, this picture of an eternal, onward-moving legal system breaks down when we face its astonishing shrinkages. Confronted by great areas in Jewish law that have disappeared, Orthodoxy is compelled to explain how such non-observance occurred. Some losses are attributed to the fact that certain laws can only be observed on sacred soil and are therefore temporarily suspended. Other laws, however, have practically vanished for no justifiable reason. People, for example, who consider themselves Orthodox have simply ceased to resort to rabbinical courts in a wide variety of areas of life. Thus there is a large gap between the total Orthodox doctrine and system and the limited observance of Jewish law. For Freehof this neglect of the law within Orthodoxy in the face of modern secularization illustrates the incompatibility of traditional Judaism with contemporary life.

The rapidly shrinking area of observance within Orthodoxy is, according to Freehof, the reason for the existence of Conservative Judaism. "The confidence of Conservatism that Judaism can be adjusted to modern life," he writes, "is rooted in the fact that Orthodoxy itself was never monolithic, that it has always changed. But whereas in the past the people changed and the law reluctantly followed, Conservatism would prefer to make the law itself more flexible so as to provide for change legally."[4] Yet, Freehof argues, there are two difficulties with this position. First, Conservative Judaism sets too great a task for Jewish law to accomplish nowadays: "There is no stretching of the law or liberating of it that can enable it to roof over the realities of modern Jewish life."[5] Second, the

---

Judaism and the Law (Cincinnati: Hebrew Union College Press, 1967).

3   S. Freehof, *Reform Responsa, supra* n.2, at 4.

4   *Ibid.,* 12-13.

5   *Ibid.*

Conservative approach is bound to intensify Orthodox bitterness: "Any liberal interpretation of the law emanating from Conservative circles is met with violent reactions, denunciations of the Conservative rabbis as being no true rabbis, whose evil aim is to lure Israel into sin."[6]

Given the problems that beset these two movements Freehof advocates a freer approach to Jewish law as embodied within Reform Judaism. Since Reform Jews do not consider the total rabbinic literature to be of Divine origin, it is not authoritative. Nonetheless Freehof believes that Reform Jews should respect traditional law and seek its guidance: "Some of its provisions have faded from our lives. We do not regret that fact. But as to those laws that we do follow, we wish them to be in harmony with tradition... Our concern is more with people than with the legal system. Wherever possible, such interpretations are developed which are feasible and conforming to the needs of life. Sometimes, indeed, a request must be answered in the negative when there is no way in the law for a permissive answer to be given. Generally the law is searched for such opinion as can conform with the realities of life."[7].

Despite this assertion, Freehof admits that there are considerable difficulties in declaring what role traditional law should play in Reform Judaism.[8] Nevertheless, he contends, it is urgent that Reform Judaism determine what are legitimate practices: "The lack of a sense of law in our movement," he writes, "gives us a feeling of frustration."[9] It is in response to this situation that Freehof attempts to establish an acceptable outline of Reform Jewish observance. These observances, however, ought not to be regarded as authoritative law; according to Freehof, they are guidelines whose purpose is to give shape to the religious life of the average Jew.

Criteria For Accepting Orthodox Law

Surveying present-day Reform Jewish practices in the light of traditional Judaism in Reform Jewish Practice, Vol.I and II, Freehof lays down explicitly the various criteria for deciding whether Or-

6   *Ibid.*, 14.
7   S. Freehof, *Reform Responsa, supra* n.2, at 22-23.
8   S. Freehof, *Reform Judaism and the Law, supra* n.2, at 19.
9   *Ibid.*, 20.

thodox laws should be retained. In accordance with his view that traditional Jewish practices should serve as the starting point for determining Reform observance, Freehof asserts that there are a number of traditional laws which should be rigorously followed. Concerning circumcision of Jewish babies, for example, he quotes as authoritative the provision in the Rabbi's Manual (Central Conference of American Rabbis, Cincinnati, 1928) which lays down that "the ancient practice of circumcising a male child at the age of eight days, the first commandment given to Abraham our father (Genesis 17.11) is strictly observed."[10] Similarly Freehof argues that Reform Judaism should adopt the same position as Orthodoxy regarding intermarriage: "The attitude of Reform Judaism... became exactly the same as that of all of Judaism, namely, that while marriage of a Jew and a converted gentile is considered a perfect marriage in every respect, marriage between a Jew and an unconverted gentile cannot be considered Jewish marriage and a rabbi cannot officiate."[11]

In these examples Freehof maintains that Reform practice should be in accord with Orthodoxy. In other cases, however, Freehof argues that traditional Jewish law, while providing general guidelines for Reform Judaism, should be extended. Concerning autopsy, for example, Freehof points that in general autopsy and dissection are forbidden by Jewish law, but there are some Orthodox authorities who permit autopsy when there is in the same locality a person suffering from the same disease. Thus autopsy is permitted if it could save a life (this accords with the Orthodox ruling that in order to save life all the laws of the Torah, except idolatry, incest and murder, may be violated). Extending this principle Freehof goes on to explain, quoting the Central Conference of American Rabbis Yearbook, Vol.35, that since "nowadays the discoveries made by one physician are broadcast all over the world and may result in the saving of innumerable lives",[12] it is in line with this Orthodox ruling to allow all autopsies to take place.

Yet it should be noted that Freehof is not always willing to extend Orthodox rulings. For example, in the case of the traditional ruling that marriages are not to be held during the first month of mourning except in certain circumstances, Freehof does not extend

10 S. Freehof, *Reform Jewish Practice, supra* n.2, at Vol.I, 113.

11 *Ibid.,* 65.

12 *Ibid.,* 116.

this leniency in the law to allow Reform rabbis to perform any marriages during that month.[13]

In other cases Freehof appeals to the spirit as opposed to the letter of the law. For example, concerning seating in the synagogue, the law requires each man to have a regular place. In Reform Judaism, however, this stipulation does not apply; each person can sit wherever he desires. Freehof argues that this free seating system fulfils the spirit of the law in practice "since people generally as a matter of habit occupy the same seats week after week."[14]

The preceding examples illustrate Freehof's dependence in one way or another on Orthodox law. Yet Freehof frequently argues that Reform Jewish practice should run counter to Orthodoxy where ordinances are based on custom rather than law. For example, he states that the popular custom to turn mirrors to the wall or to cover them in the room where a corpse lies has no basis in Jewish law and in fact is part of a general folklore.[15] Thus he contends there is no reason to observe it in Reform Judaism. Or again concerning the covering of the head in synagogue Freehof points out that this is an ancient practice, only the result of custom, and therefore it need not be continued.[16]

A legal argument of a different order is occasionally used by Freehof to justify a Reform departure from traditional practice. Freehof asserts that a particular observance should be adopted if it is grounded in Biblical Judaism even if it runs counter to present-day Orthodoxy. Reform Judaism, for example, celebrates one day of various festivals rather that two because "the Reform movement reverted to the Biblical observance of the length of the festivals."[17]

On other occasions Freehof recommends that traditional law should be abandoned for different reasons altogether. Concerning the equality of the sexes, for example, Freehof declares that "Reform Judaism... proclaimed from the very beginning the religious equality of men and women."[18] Thus Reform congregations abolished the seclusion of women in the synagogue and provided the family

13   *Ibid.*, 80.
14   *Ibid.*, Vol.II, 32.
15   *Ibid.*, Vol.I, 154.
16   *Ibid.*, 45.
17   *Ibid.*, 19.
18   *Ibid.*, 25.

pew in which the entire family sits together in worship.[19] The notion of equality also applies to the religious status of all Jews. In Orthodoxy there is a legal distinction between priests, Levites and Israelites, but this has been abolished in Reform Judaism. Therefore, Freehof notes, "the special prohibition of the law forbidding a priest to marry a divorced woman... seemed contrary to the modern spirit of equality of status."[20]

Traditional law should also be abandoned, Freehof asserts, if it is not well adapted to modern life. For example Freehof writes, "since in modern times it was difficult to obtain the close attention and the uninterrupted decorum of the service during the lengthy reading of the entire weekly portion, the custom arose in Reform congregations to shorten the reading."[21] Freehof also contends that certain laws should be eliminated on humane grounds. Where a husband has disappeared, for example, Freehof writes that "there is a tragic hardship involved in Jewish law of divorce which the best rabbinic minds have been unable to remove, namely, the case of the Agunah (the woman 'chained' to marriage even though her husband has disappeared)... in which countless women whose husbands have disappeared have no way of being freed from the bonds of matrimony." For reasons of humanity, he states, the Reform movement has abolished the traditional laws of divorce.[22]

Unseemly rituals, Freehof contends, should be abandoned as well. This applies to the Orthodox custom of avoiding stones in wedding rings based on the following law: "If he marries her with an object, with regard to the value of which it is easy to err, such as precious stones, it is necessary to make evaluations. Therefore it is the custom to marry with a ring that has no stones."[23] The idea of estimating the value of wedding rings, Freehof believes, is out of place in Reform marriages; thus any ring is used whether it is plain or is set with stones.[24]

Furthermore, Freehof states that Orthodox practices which are based on superstitions should be omitted. Freehof declares, for ex-

---

19 Ibid., 54-55.
20 Ibid., 105.
21 Ibid., 31.
22 Ibid., 105-106.
23 Shulḥan Aruk, Even Ha'ezer, 31,2.
24 S. Freehof, Reform Jewish Practice, supra n.2, at Vol.I,91.

ample, that the ritual of breaking a glass at wedding ceremonies is "of superstitious origin". Thus, "the breaking of the glass is entirely omitted from Reform marriage ceremonies."[25]

There are other instances in Reform Jewish Practice where, instead of offering a justification for overturning Orthodox law, Freehof simply asserts that this should be done. For example, concerning the Orthodox custom of leaving some blades of grass or a pebble on the tombstone after visiting the grave, Freehof decrees without explanation: "The custom of leaving pebbles on tombstones is not observed by Reform Jews."[26]

There are some instances, however, where Freehof advocates that Jewish law be observed out of respect for the Orthodox and Conservative community even though it goes against Reform convictions. For example, in the case of a Jewish couple (where one partner has been divorced civilly) who ask a Reform rabbi to marry them because they have been refused by their own Orthodox or Conservative rabbi, Freehof writes: "It would seem that consideration for the religious scruples of Orthodox and Conservative congregations should impel that the Reform rabbi to refuse to marry members of other congregations whose rabbi refuses to marry them (because they have not obtained a Jewish divorce)."[27]

From this brief survey we can see that Freehof has an ambiguous attitude to traditional Jewish law. Sometimes he advises following the letter of the law, and at other times the spirit, while in some instances he advocates observing traditional law merely out of respect for the Orthodox and Conservative community. Frequently, however, he recommends that Orthodox law be abandoned either because it is based on custom rather than law, because it is based on a rabbinic rather than Biblical precept, or because it is ill-adapted to modern life. Some laws he regards as discriminatory to women or to groups within Judaism (priests, levites and Israelites), and others as simply inhumane, unseemly or superstitious. In addition, as a final category there are some laws he recommends discarding without any explanation whatever.

---

25 *Ibid.*, 98-99.
26 *Ibid.*,
27 *Ibid.*, 109-110.

A Critique of Freehof's View

The central difficulty with Freehof's approach is that his rec-ommendations are internally inconsistent. On the one hand, Freehof stipulates without explanation that certain practices in Orthodox Judaism should be adopted by Reform Jews (such as forbidding mixed marriages), while, on the other hand, he regards other practices as unacceptable (such as leaving pebbles on tombstones). Yet there is no obvious criterion established to decide which laws should be aban-doned and which retained. Such seemingly arbitrary and contradic-tory judgments also apply to those cases where Freehof argues that Reform Jews should follow the spirit rather than the letter of the law. Regrettably he does not explain how to determine what the spirit of a particular law is. This is unfortunate since there is in-evitably an element of subjectivity involved in attempting to extract the spirit (his justification of the absence of fixed synagogue seats is an eloquent illustration of this), and it is by no means certain that one can preserve the essential point of a law if its provisions are eliminated.

It is equally mysterious why Freehof justifies extending the pre-scriptions of one law rather than another. For example it is not easy to understand why all autopsies are permitted in Reform Judaism whereas not all marriages during the first month of mourning are allowed. A similar criticism applies to the distinction he makes between rabbinically-based ordinances and Biblical practices (such as celebrating a festival for two days or one day). It is also not at all clear why Biblical laws should take precedence. Moreover, in stat-ing that one ought to observe traditional laws out of consideration for the Orthodox on some occasions (such as refusing to marry a cou-ple who had previously been refused by an Orthodox or Conserva-tive rabbi), Freehof offers no explanation why this principle should not apply universally.

Equally problematic is Freehof's stipulation that laws should be changed if they do not adapt to modern life. It is arguable that there are many traditional practices (such as circumcision of Jewish babies) which Freehof encourages Reform Jews to observe which ought to be eliminated on this basis.

Many of these criticisms apply to the several volumes of respon-sa literature in which, while attempting to answer specific questions concerning Jewish practices, he is similarly inconsistent. In some cases, for example, Freehof argues that Reform Jews should follow the spirit rather than the letter of the law, whereas in other cases he contends that the letter of the law is all-important. Thus in answer to the question whether there is any legal justification for the practice of some Reform groups of accepting adult converts without circumcision, Freehof points out that although the Talmud, Maimonides and the Code of Jewish Law have circumcision as a firmly established law, "it seems contrary to the spiritual and ethical spirit of Judaism to insist upon this ritual."[28] In other cases, however, he maintains that traditional law should be upheld. In the case of a married gentile couple where the man wishes to convert to Judaism, for example, Freehof argues that if we convert the husband he would become a Jew under the yoke of the law married to a gentile: "He was a righteous Christian before we converted him. Now, if he is the head of a gentile family, he becomes a sinful Jew... We have no right to convert him."[29]

Turning to the distinction Freehof draws between those practices based on custom as opposed to those based on law, there are similar difficulties. For example, in response to the question whether one ought to fast if the Torah is dropped, he writes: "fasting if the Torah is dropped is not a legal requirement... since this custom has no real legal status, nothing should be done by the entire congregation."[30] In other cases, however, he maintains that Jewish customs should be practised by Reform Jews. For example, concerning the question whether a marriage can take place without a rabbi and without Hebrew, Freehof contends that though these customs are not based on legal requirements they should be adhered to.[31]

There are also several occasions in his responsa where contrary to his approach in Reform Jewish Practice he advocates following rabbinically rather than Biblically based ordinances. Thus in answer to the question whether wearing costumes on Halloween is forbidden by Jewish law, he states, "There is a biblical basis upon which an objection could well be raised. The Bible, in Deuteronomy 22.5, clearly prohibits men from putting on women's garments and

28 S. Freehof, *Reform Responsa For Our Time, supra* n.1, at 77.

29 *Ibid.*, 69-70.

30 S. Freehof, *Contemporary Reform Responsa* (USA: Hebrew Union College Press, 1974), 119.

31 S. Freehof, *Reform Responsa For Our Time, supra* n.1, at 204-205.

women from putting on men's garments." Nevertheless Freehof believes that one should follow the ruling of the great Orthodox rabbi Judah Minz who decreed that it was permissible to wear masks and costumes on Purim. Though this decision relates specifically to a Jewish festival, Freehof argues that it should apply as well to Halloween since this holiday has no Christian associations.[32]

Questions concerning religious and sexual equality are also answered in a way inconsistent with the principles outlined in Reform Jewish Practice. For example, in reply to the query whether the children of a widow who are adopted by the second husband who is a cohen are to be considered cohenim, Freehof appeals to a number of distinctions made in the law about Jewish status. "If the woman's first husband was a cohen," he writes, "then the children remain cohenim. No matter how many times or whom she marries. If her first husband was not a cohen and her second husband is a cohen, this marriage does not affect the status of the children of a previous marriage."[33] In this instance he completely neglects to mention that the category of cohen has been abolished in Reform Judaism because of the Reform belief in religious equality. In another case Freehof declares that if a Jewish man is living together sexually with a non-Jewish woman who eventually converts to Judaism, he may never marry her. Yet he states that if a gentile man lives together sexually with a Jewish woman "perhaps it would be right to convert the gentile so that they may be able to marry in accordance with Jewish law and custom."[34] Here it is clear that Freehof undermines the view he repeatedly expresses that men and women should be treated equally.

There are also instances in the responsa where Freehof advocates following laws which are arguably ill-adapted to modern life. For example, in response to the question whether anaesthetics should be used for circumcision, Freehof states: "We should not institute the use of anaesthetics as a regular procedure, but should permit them when the surgeon or the parent asks that they be used."[35] Yet given that Jewish law does not insist that pain be expe-

---

32 S. Freehof, *Current Reform Responsa* (Cincinnati: Hebrew Union College Press, 1969), 93-96.

33 S. Freehof, *Contemporary Reform Responsa, supra* n.30, at 145-146.

34 S. Freehof, *Reform Responsa For Our Time, supra* n.1, at 69-70.

35 S. Freehof, *Current Reform Responsa, supra* n.32, at 105.

rienced in circumcision, there is every reason for Reform Judaism to adopt this modern scientific advance.

The same point applies to those laws which are arguably inhumane. For example, discussing the question whether it is in accord with the spirit of the Jewish tradition to encourage the establishment of a congregation of homosexuals, Freehof remarks: "Homosexuality runs counter to the sancta of Jewish life. There is no sidestepping the fact that from the point of view of Judaism, men who practice homosexuality are to be deemed sinners."[36] Here Freehof appeals to Orthodox law as a basis for the Reform attitude, but there are significant humane reasons for adopting a more accepting approach to homosexuals particularly since a more humane view is generally justified by modern medical and psychiatric opinion. Another example relates to the question whether a doctor should be permitted to inform a patient that he is dying. In this instance Freehof declares that "in the light of Jewish law and tradition, it is clearly wrong to tell a patient that his case is hopeless and that he is dying."[37] Yet there are patients who desire to know the truth about their illness so that they are better able to cope with death; to deny them such information, as Freehof recommends, could be a heartless act. Again, regarding the question whether euthanasia should be permitted in Reform Judaism Freehof declares that it is forbidden in Jewish law to take life; thus "the act of killing a patient for whatever motive is absolutely forbidden."[38] On humane grounds, however, it is possible that euthanasia could be a morally defensible act given the mental and physical agony of some patients in the face of a long, useless and incurable illness. Thus it is not clear why Freehof accepts that the law should be modified to be more in tune with modern life and general principles of humanity in some cases, but by no means in all.

Conclusion

In his lecture "Reform Judaism and the Law" Freehof emphasises that Reform Jews should engage in the study of traditional Jewish law. "We can begin", he writes, "by systematizing and indexing the

36 S. Freehof, *Contemporary Reform Responsa, supra* n.30, at 24.
37 S. Freehof, *Reform Responsa, supra* n.2, at 125.
38 *Ibid.*, 118.

great responsa literature, whose approximately three thousand tight-packed volumes are full of treasures of Jewish history, thought, feeling and experience."[39] This Freehof himself has admirably done in his writings, and in this respect he has made a major contribution to Jewish scholarship. However, as we have seen, when deciding which traditional laws should be retained in Reform Judaism, he frequently does not follow his own principles of selection. Sometimes his judgments seem to be based simply on modern expediency, while at other times they seem motivated by an unjustified prejudice for traditional ways. But whatever the reason, such inconsistency results in uncertainty and confusion about Reform Judaism's relation to traditional Jewish law.

What is clearly needed in Reform Judaism is a coherent and consistent philosophy of law where the criteria for accepting Orthodox practices are clearly delineated and rigorously followed. Indeed there are times when Freehof seems aware of the deficiencies of his approach. For example he states in the same lecture that Reform Judaism should now begin to "work out the entire philosophy of Jewish law and of our relationship with it. It will have to be a system that will find room for individuality and unity, for obedience and freedom, for recorded tradition and for operative originality. Such a philosophy of Jewish law will require much study, many articles by many thinkers and much debate. It may require a generation or two for its accomplishment."[40] What a study of Freehof's survey of Reform Jewish practice illustrates is the urgency of this task.[41]

39 S. Freehof, *Reform Judaism and the Law, supra* n.2, at 22.
40 *Ibid.,* 20.
41 See further my "Freedom and Law in Reform Judaism", *Journal of Reform Judaism* (Winter 1983), 88-97.

LEEWAYS OF CHOICE, NATURAL LAW AND JUSTICE IN JEWISH LEGAL ORDERING

by

JULIUS STONE[*] z'l

Among many rich issues stirred by this volume, no less than ten command the general jurisprudential concern to which this introduction is directed.

(1)   Is the "openness" of a legal order, manifest in the leeways of choice in application, consistent with the unchangeability of a divinely ordained legal order?

(2)   The significance (if any) of the susceptibility (or insusceptibility) of Jewish law to explanation within the jurisprudential frame of Kelsenite or other positivism.

(3)   What (if any) is the relevance of the time-dimension of human experience to the content of the divine covenant with the Jewish people? If we conceive this covenant as providing the context of the apex norm of Jewish law, does this preclude responsiveness of legal precepts to factual and value-changes in the particular society?

(4)   What is the legal standing of implicit "principles", standards, etc., drawn by study from the authoritative materials of the law, as against the precepts which are for the time being explicit in a positive legal order?

(5)   The problematics of natural law in a divine positive law.

(6)   "Natural law imperialism" and "justice" in the application of various frames of Greco-Roman or Thomist natural law to Jewish law.

---

[*]   A.O., O.B.E., S.J.D. (Harvard), D.C.L. (Oxford), LL.D. (Leeds and Sydney, honoris causa), Q.C.

(7)   Can "natural law" be overriding in a divine positive legal order?

(8)   Jewish law, natural law and the law of the state of Israel.

(9)   The Covenant model.

(10)   Divine Reason or Divine Will as content of the apex norm. An Unanswerable Question?

(11)   The role of a secularist natural law.

I shall conclude with some remarks on jurisprudential issues perhaps inadequately canvassed in this volume; but, of course, neither as to these nor as to the ten preceding matters do I seek to be exhaustive.

I. "Openness" in a Divinely Ordained Legal Order

Few would dispute Emanuel Rackman's observation that "In halakhic literature one can find support for virtually every theory of legal philosophy known to secular jurisprudence".[1] This would, indeed, probably be true of the literature of any developed legal order, but Dr. Rackman is also concerned to point out that this hospitality of the halakhic tradition to a diversity of legal theories is not inconsistent with the view of Jewish law as commanded by God. To theorise, for example, that the law, even if made by God, is still made for humans and is thus to be understood as serving human purposes, does not negate the divine command. Even the most devout traditionalist may still rest quiet in the faith that the law proceeds from the will and command of God. This faith is in the strictest sense not falsifiable, and in this sense is not a matter for either intellectual demonstration or refutation.

To point out this basis of faith is neither to reject nor even to diminish. It is rather to highlight the limits of intellectual demon-

1   Emanuel Rackman, "Secular Jurisprudence and Halakhah", *The Jewish Law Annual* 6 (1987), 45-63, at 45.

stration, and the fact that these limits are built into the tradition-alist assertion, which (for example) Norman Solomon's papers on the "analytic school" here restate, that human reason is unable "to provide exhaustive satisfying rational explanations for the com-mandments", so that learning is "ever necessary to discover more of the Divine Wisdom which permeates Torah".[2] In thus typifying and endorsing the conclusions of "analysts" such as Epstein and Leibovitch, Solomon also conceives himself as negating the adequa-cy of rationalist ethics to "tell the glory of God". This last negative assertion is, also, not "falsifiable", being beyond the ambit of juristic or other science; but the preceding endorsement of the method of "analysis" for revealing "correct" precepts of Jewish law is of con-siderable scientific interest.

The "analytical method" of discovering halakhic precepts as a way of providing "normal" rather than "revolutionary" intellectual movement, is explained as involving the reclassification of instances or notions having one or more of three effects. These are: (1) the removal of anomalies in existing precepts; (2) elimination of the need for *ad hoc* hypotheses to account for anomalies; and (3) creation of "an idea of more general application" than the one in use. The case discussions offered as examples by Solomon invite a number of reflections from contemporary jurisprudential thought.

What appears to be mostly involved is the raising of elements contained within a precept on to a higher level of generality. In the present author's now widely used example, the agent of harm pre-sent in the bottle of Stone's ginger beer from the drinking of which the plaintiff in *Donoghue* v. *Stevenson* allegedly suffered harm, could be stated as "a dead and deliquescent snail", or "a dead snail", or "organic matter", or "noxious physical matter", or "noxious alien entity". All of these levels of generality describe the situation of a deliquescent snail in a bottle of Stone's ginger beer. But a rule stated in terms of the presence of a "noxious alien entity" would obviously catch a great deal more than a rule centered on "a dead snail".[3]

---

2   Norman Solomon, "Anomaly and Theory in the Analytic School", *The Jewish Law Annual* 6 (1987), 126-147, at 145.

3   See J. Stone, *The Province and Function of Law* (here cited as *"The Province"*) (Sydney: Maitland Publications, 1946), 186-189; *idem, Legal System and Lawyers' Reasonings* (here cited as *"Legal System"*) (London: Stevens, 1964), 267-280, esp. 269-274. To assimilate the choice among such alternatives (as Norman Solomon does) to "scientific paradigm

Nor can we assume that movement from a more concrete to a more general level gives any warranty of better results, whether we measure these results by fidelity to Torah and halakhah, to the "glory" or "will" of God, or by aptness for social conditions, or conformity to human reason, natural law, or to justice simpliciter. As I have elsewhere stressed,[4] the more appropriate response in particular situations may be to "multiply categories". This means that it may be more appropriate to reduce a more general or abstract precept (for example, concerning all contracts) into a series of more concrete precepts (for example, differentiating out contracts containing standard clauses, or between husband and wife, or relating to money loans, or rental of dwellings, or hire purchase arrangements, or consumer good, or the like). The choices which face the interpreter, even of a divine code, therefore, include not merely a supposed "scientific" analysis of levels of generality of what is predicated in the precepts, but also acts of human will in choosing whether to move levels from the more concrete to the more general, from the more general to the more concrete, and at what level to rest in such direction, or to decline to do either or any of these operations in a particular instance.

All this is, perhaps, but to spell out what is implied in Professor Rackman's observation that what unites all who are committed to "the halakhah" is the belief that from the covenant between God and Israel there emerged the obligation to obey His law, a law subject to change and development only as that law - written and oral - made such change and development possible. What we have perhaps added is to make somewhat more explicit that - as a matter of

---

revision" is to ignore the most significant aspect of the lawyer's (including the judge's) situation. This is that no legal nor any other *necessity* compels the choice of any of these available ways of describing the agent of harm at different levels of generality or concreteness. This is an important (and omnipresent) source of leeways of choice for judges and all other actors in the law. Moreover, the presence of leeways of choice not only authorises such choice; it also compels it. And choice is always, as shown in the text, an act of more or less instructed human willing. The logical form which N. Solomon ("Anomaly and Theory in the Analytic School", *supra* n.2) thinks to be central to the analytical method, as a scientific process, does *not* determine such outcomes.

4   See, e.g., Stone, *The Province, supra* n.3, at 160-165, 626; *id., Legal System, supra* n.3, at 246-271, 306-311.

day-to-day operations (rather than epoch-making crises) - the interpreter - be his text narrow and concrete, or a most sweeping generality - still has choices to make within leeways left by the text. There is, indeed, no harm in saying, with Emanuel Rackman, that "change and development" are "made possible" by the written and oral law. Yet we should always remember that there are more-than-one "possibles", and this means that the interpreter has to make a human choice within the leeways of divine authority. So that, however deeply we agree with Yizhak Englard, that modesty and humility require us to interpret according to the transcendent principle of conformity to the divine will, the outcomes may still be determined by the rather immanent wills of each generation of human interpreters.

Conversely, the bold thesis of Hanina Ben Menahem is also here notable. This is that even according to the authorities of the talmudic system, that system sometimes tolerates or even imposes each of two conflicting solutions, thus implying "a pluralistic view", rather than the commonly accepted "monolithic" view that within the system there is always one and only one correct answer.[5] The

5   That thesis, cogent as it is, still needs placing within a more general jurisprudential frame, which would include the following elements. First, the "barrenness of logic" for warranting "correct" solutions within the leeways of choice. Second, "the fertility of language" in which all law - including Jewish - is "packaged", as a constant source of new leeways of choice. Third, the enhancement of the above factors by the impact on the society in question of changes in the environment or other social, economic and political facts. Fourth, the writer underestimates the competing levels of generality of statement of the facts predicated in an ostensibly "unequivocal" norm (see *supra* n.3 and text). The three conditions ("Is There Always One Uniquely Correct Answer to a Legal Question in the Talmud?", *The Jewish Law Annual* 6 (1987), 164-175, at 165) which Dr. Ben Menahem lays down for ensuring one and one only correct solution may thus be illusory, insofar as the facts predicated even in a "clear unequivocal norm" can almost always be stated on different and competing levels of generality. (See also *infra*, Section IV.) (Incidentally, Dr. Ben Menahem's formulation of these three conditions seems rather loose and overlapping.) Dr. Ben Menahem has established examples of "halakhic controversies that ended in the adopting of both opinions"; and his ambition is to show that these are but a part of a more general canon of halakhic interpretation, thus admitting the legitimacy of two or more conflicting solutions, so long as the present decision-maker is himself self-consistent (at 171). The understanding of this problem for Jewish law would be greatly increased by reference to the jurisprudential

strength of that thesis in bringing talmudic texts to witness that the decision maker may be required to choose between conflicting alternatives both available under the halakhah, also holds risks of obfuscating the operation in Jewish law of wider jurisprudential truths. For a whole range of reasons which this first section has introduced, and which will be further elaborated in Section IV, the decision makers of Jewish law would have been confronted by leeways of choice, the compulsion to choose within them, and the responsibility for justifying their choice. It may trivialise the significance of this area of choicemaking and responsibility to suggest that it arises only from some explicit ruling of earlier traditional authorities.[6]

II. The Supposed Positivist Frame of Jewish Law

One main question here debated by England, Jackson and others concerns the application to Jewish law of positivist models of law. Can the Kelsenite model of a body of norms dependent on the apex norm, or Hart's related notion of the "rules of recognition" observed by courts and law officers, serve to clarify any basic issues as to Jewish law? Can these models serve, in particular, to soften some of the apparent inconsistencies which jostle each other within the literature of Jewish law? Can we say, for example, that Jewish law is really within the subject-matter of jurisprudence, that is, of the systematic body of knowledge concerning the subject-matter "law"? If we think we can, can we nevertheless also say that Jewish law remains a unique legal order since its apex norm (and/or rules of recognition) rest on the bindingness of a unique covenant between God

----

frame of the present article, especially this Section IV. Moreover, this might present the case of *Kim Li* as cases of "competing legal categories", the plaintiff relying on one and the defendant on the other. This might also solve some other difficult questions about the *Kim Li* doctrine. How, for example, could the court decide on the basis of the defendant's competing legal rule without weighing it against the competing rule offered by the plaintiff? How could the court, in any case, do this without violating the principle *audi alteram partem* or its equivalent in Jewish law?

6   And see Section IV for further treatment of these points and citations to the literature.

and the Jewish people, expressed fully and exclusively in traditional materials of Torah and halakhah?

Both the Kelsenite model of a pyramid of norms flowing from the apex norm, and the Hartian model of a flow of primary rules from the rules of recognition, are so abstracted from any particular social or legal order that very few candidate bodies of precepts of any historical importance will fail their test. It should not therefore surprise us that we can fit some aspects of Jewish law into their frame. But both the Kelsenite and Hartian models also have a vice, born of their very virtues. This is that while each can certify, in its own sense, that a particular body of precepts has a "law-like" appearance, it cannot warrant either that the apex norm of a particular order has a particular content, or the content similarly of its rules of recognition, except after very elaborate inquiries which, in face of any controversy, will also be rather impractical and inconclusive. We should, perhaps, interpolate at this point, that any doubts affecting the contents of the apex norm (or "the rules of recognition") necessarily transmit themselves to all the norms dependent on the apex norm (or on "the rules of recognition").[7]

The most difficult part of these inquiries affecting the fashionable positivist models is as to the degree to which the norm-making power and any limitations on it, as described in the apex norm, or in the rules of recognition, correspond to or reflect the behaviour and attitudes of the particular community concerned. A certain high degree of such correspondence is what is referred to by Kelsen's clear (if thereafter neglected) requirement that the apex norm and its dependent norms designated as the legal order of a particular community, must be shown to have "efficaciousness on the whole" in that community. Without this showing it is not possible to specify with any assurance what is the content of the apex norm and its dependent norms (or what is the content of the rules of recognition and the "primary rules" warranted as law by those rules) of any concrete society.

Englard's brave effort to establish both the "lawness" of Jewish

7   Cf. on the too facile resorts to Kelsenite and Hartian models, B.S. Jackson, "Secular Jurisprudence and the Philosophy of Jewish Law: A Commentary on Some Recent Literature", *The Jewish Law Annual* 6 (1987), paras. 9.0, 9.4, *ibid.* at. 6.1.2. And *cf.* E. N. Dorff, "Judaism as a Legal Religious System", *Hastings Law Journal* 29 (1978), 1331-1360, cited by Jackson at para. 6.1.2.

law, and its uniqueness, by reference to what he calls "the ideological assumptions... centered around the theo-centricity of all human concerns", is thus not really assisted by restating them in terms of Kelsenite or Hartian positivism. No doubt the greater abstractness and "depersonalisation" of these theories relieve him of some of the difficulties which would have faced him had he resorted to *Austinian* positivism. He would then have had to designate the (sovereign) person or persons to whose commands the bulk of the community of Jews habitually pay obedience, to demonstrate the fact of that habitual obedience, and the like. While Austin himself provided an argument whereby Jewish law could be pronounced as divine positive law ("properly" though not perhaps "strictly" so-called), Austin did not venture on any empirical proof of habitual obedience to God. On the contrary, he rather evaded this issue by merging divine law - sometimes wholly, sometimes in part - into natural law. Even in Kelsenite theory, however, England would still have to show the required level of "efficaciousness on the whole" in Jewish society of the norms dependent on the apex norm expressing "the theocentricity of all human concerns". So also, in Hartian terms, he would still have to show that "the rules of recognition" represent an accurate factual description of the practice of courts and other officials and of the acceptance of these courts and officials as such in the particular social order. These specifications, though often forgotten, are (as just indicated) involved in any use of these positivist models in a specific society and its legal order. To be consistent in adopting these positivist models, Yizhak England would have to admit that the content of the apex norm of Jewish law could be transformed or displaced by evidence of changes in attitudes and levels of acceptance in the human community and its officials, by "unilateral action of the subject" as Bernard Jackson terms it.[8]

England's use of Hart's ideas does offer, perhaps inadvertently, a nice gloss on Hart's own exposition. It was not there clear whether "recognition" for Hart imported some kind of approval of the rules by the courts and officers concerned. So that the present writer found it necessary many years ago to raise the question whether, if it did not import approval, the theory would be formally inadequate, as not covering social orders in which the conduct described as "recognition" was based merely on fear or submission to naked pow-

8   *Supra* n.7, at paras. 1.1-1.2.

er.[9] In his bid to bring Jewish law within Hart's notions, Englard makes it interestingly clear that the "recognition" of Hart's theory does not import approval, and that conforming behaviour based on fear - at any rate on the fear of God *(yirat shamayim)* - is not only an adequate, but his own preferred, criterion of "recognition".

This mitigates very little, however, the difficulties of Englard's use of the Kelsenite and Hartian models. Both Kelsenite and Hartian theories implicitly, like Austinianism explicitly, presuppose that legal authority is manifest in a dimension of territorially based power. In the legal orders to which Hart's definition is primarily directed, the courts and other officials whose conduct gives content and force to the rules of recognition in the particular community, seem self-identified and not problematic. The accrediting of the courts and officials of Jewish law, when this is distinguished from the law of the State of Israel, is, however, rather problematic. Whether particular individuals have such judicial or official status as qualifies them to designate (or by conduct authenticate) rules of recognition, must depend on attitudes in the relevant community prerequiring the specification and delimitation of this community, and the authentication for it of the "rules of recognition" acted on by the putative courts and officials. While all this should not foreclose demonstration of the *legal* standing of such bodies of precepts, it does suggest caution in seeking shortcuts to such demonstration by simplistic applications of positivist models devised *alio intuitu.*[10]

Even if the difficulties of accrediting particular bodies of precepts as "law" by reference to such positivist models were overcome, the gains from such accreditation might still be somewhat illusory. For instance, they would leave untouched some central debates surrounding Jewish law, not only between secularist and religiously orthodox interpreters, but also between orthodox interpreters *inter se.* As against both secular interpreters and some orthodox colleagues, for example, Englard is much concerned to reject the possibility of emergence in history - that is in the time-dimension - of any precepts of normative binding force within the system of

9   Stone, *Legal System, supra* n.3, at 132-133.
10 These are part of the difficult problems facing the Canon Law of the Roman Catholic Church, of which Englard has discussed some aspects in his book, *Religious Law in the Israel Legal System* (Jerusalem: Harry Sacher Institute for Legislative Research and Comparative Law, 1975), Part 1.

toraitic and halakhic law. He is particularly concerned to deny that such precepts can be created by the application of human reason. Accreditation or not according to some positivist model of law could not settle such issues, to which I now turn.

III. The Covenant And The Time-Dimension Of Law

Yizhak Englard sternly resists recognition of the full role of history in legal change and development. He does, indeed, admit that Jewish law has in fact adapted itself to historical circumstances in order to maintain a proper "social framework". He even speaks, in terms I have myself used, about the creative aspects of the appellate judicial process, about leeways of rabbinic choice - making manifest "the ubiquity of dissent in Rabbinical literature". But he denies that "any normative conclusions can be drawn from the historical fact of legal changes".[11]

What creates legal changes is (he claims) not historical realities but the legitimacy of consideration relevant to the creation of new norms. For Jewish law this centres around "the theocentricity of all human concerns... man's position before his Creator". The fundamental issue, he thinks, is the normative one, whether Jewish law should respond in an affirmative sense to changing moral attitudes. The human decisionmaker is required to seek "an honest and humble answer" to the question whether his adaptation of the religious law to his own personal convictions is "not an act of human conceit and insubordination".

Yet, since the "honest and humble" answer may be (even then) that adaptation is required, and that no conceit or subordination is involved, Englard is constrained also to add that the answer must be given "in the light of a binding tradition". Respect for this "binding tradition", however, when ample leeways are ubiquitously enmeshed within it, can mean little more than that the human decisionmaker must attend conscientiously to the authoritative materials, as well as to the changing circumstances and moral ideas of the

11 Y. Englard, "Interaction of Morality and Law", *supra*, 114-124. On the juxtaposition of "law" and "history" in Englard, and of "law" and "history" in Albeck, see also B. S. Jackson, "Modern Research in Jewish Law, Some Theoretical Issues" in Jackson, *Modern Research in Jewish Law* (Leiden: E.J. Brill, 1980), 136, at 147-148 (Jewish Law Annual Supplementary Series, vol.I).

time. It is no doubt a part of this tradition that man is bidden not to be more just than his Creator.[12] It is also in this tradition, unmistakably expressed in the Torah text itself, that God made no such rebuke to Abraham when he pleaded that there might be some righteous people in Sodom and Gomorrah, and asked rhetorically, Shall not the judge of all the earth act justly? Shall he punish the righteous with the wicked?

Professor Rackman sees this divine exchange with Abraham as "biblical authority for the proposition that God respects natural law", so that accordingly natural law must be "part of the Covenant". This seems to come near to asserting that any elements of valuation in decisionmaking other than those already clearly expressed in the precepts of the divine positive law, must consist of "natural law". It receives a kind of support from Austin's usage, which either identified the divine law with natural law, or saw natural law as that part of the divine law discovered by human reason. This use of the term "natural law" also seems to be endorsing the imperialist claims of natural law (later to be discussed) to occupy the whole field of justice. But the more important meaning of Professor Rackman's assertion is that somehow the covenant basing Jewish law requires - or at least authorises - development and change in the content of the legal precepts necessary to maintain them as just amid the endlessly changing facts of social life.

This recognition of the temporal dimension of law and justice in Judaism, accords well not only with modern theories of justice, but with the insights for all legal systems from Maine's historical jurisprudence, and ensuing work of the anthropologists of law. It is the more important to observe that Professor Rackman takes this position from within the orthodox tradition, in which the precepts of Torah and halakhah, and perhaps also the continuing lines of dedicated interpretation into present day, are all divine and sacrosanct, all "words of the living God", all therefore equally binding as if revealed by God to Moses on Mount Sinai.[13]

---

12   Englard quotes the divine voice as enjoining King Saul, when he pleaded for the innocents of the Amalekites: "Be not righteous overmuch" or, according to the Midrashic version: "Do not be more just than your Creator" - supra, 120. The writer finds no hint of basis for this Midrash in 1 Samuel 15.

13   As contrasted of course with the Spinozist view of Jewish law as a secular system, and the Mosaic presentation of it as divine seen as an act of

Yet this acceptance - as it were - of a temporal dimension for the eternal law, has important (if too little noticed) limits.[14] Professor Rackman can see that the covenant incorporates by reference principles (which he thinks of as "natural law") permitting or even requiring change and development of precepts appropriate for changing social conditions and values. He also sees as significant the lack of differentiation manifest in Torah and halakhah between precepts of "law" in the modern secular sense, and precepts of morals and religion and other means of social control; and also the frequency of precepts governing external relations between persons, which, though still addressed to individuals, may involve neither duty to others, nor questions of enforcement.

He sees this notable contrast of ambitious range and modest implementation of Jewish law, as together resolving another great paradox. This is that while "halakhah affects almost everything that a person thinks, says or does", as a result of which "personal freedom is radically proscribed...", still "the diversity of rules and opinions that it contains... makes it the least monolithic system of law known to legal scholars in the West." He rejects the common view that this diversity of versions of so many precepts is a result of the "accident" of Jewish territorial dispersion, which prevented the consolidation of "ultimate authority" for determining disputed questions (p.12). Such an explanation, he observes, "is simply not true unless the ultimate authority is God himself." He should perhaps have added: "and unless God held himself always available to provide a prompt and final answer to every doubtful question at every point in the endless stream of time." For, carrying his position further, the source of the rich diversity of versions of which he speaks is not the fact that the human judges are dispersed, but the more elemental fact that they are human. Even within common law systems of precedent, where there is centralisation rather than dis-

----

statesmanship and legislative prudence, on which see H.H. Cohn, "The Methodology of Jewish Law" in *Modern Research in Jewish Law, supra* n.11, at 123-135, at 126, citing *Tractatus Theologico-Politicus* (1670) caps. IV and V.

14 On resistance to even limited recognition of the time-dimension in the traditional literature of Jewish law, *cf.* B.S. Jackson, "Secular Jurisprudence and the Philosophy of Jewish Law: A Commentary on Some Recent Literature", *supra* n.7, at para.8.1.

persion, and there are clear hierarchical as well as majority principles, and where there is clear and active corrective power by legis-
latures, competing precepts, competing versions of precepts, disputes
as to their ambit for governing concrete situations, the endemic problems of degree of generality or concreteness of formulation, the use of
indeterminate categories calling for value judgments, all tend to
increase rather than disappear.

The aspect of Professor Rackman's account which may merit reexamination, however, is his assumption that these characteristics
of traditional Jewish law - its undifferentiatedly wide coverage of
all affairs (including the merely moral and the religious), and its
related unenforceability over these wide areas - are themselves an
outcome of the uniqueness of this body of law. He does not apparently link these features of Jewish law with those jurisprudentially
found associated with bodies of law of other peoples at certain
stages of their social, cultural, economic and political development.
This linkage might raise the question whether Jewish law might in
some respects illustrate Maine's hypothesis about the characterisation of law in societies in which the power is not yet centralised in a
territorial sovereign, but is shared among comparatively small religious, territorial and kin groupings, and economic life is comparatively simple. Central among these characteristics is that what we
later recognise as law is not at that stage distinguished from other
means of social control, such as religion, morality and popular custom
or folkways.[15] Such a recognition of the relevance of time must no
doubt confront the orthodox claim of immutability and unchangeability of Jewish law; or face the equally unattractive alternative
of claiming that one uniqueness of Jewish society is that it must
remain, in this respect, at what many comparative legal studies
might term a "primitive" level of development. Yet, if the covenant
can be read as incorporating natural law (in Professor Rackman's
sense of the search for justice in each time and place), it is difficult
to see why the body of halakhah cannot also become more
differentiated in the course of development, so that its legal, moral,
religious and other sectors become analytically as well as
functionally distinguishable. This would certainly help to bring the

15 See for the vast literature and main lines of scholarship, J. Stone, *Social
    Dimensions of Law and Justice* (London: Stevens, 1966), 119-163, esp.126-
    141.

study of this law into the framework of current jurisprudential thought, including the structuralist outreachings which Bernard Jackson is struggling to express further.[16]

IV. *"Principles" and "Ideals" Implicit in Express Precepts*

As against his orthodox colleague Shalom Albeck, indeed, Englard seems to deny that human reason can discover principles underlying halakhic precepts. Even if they could be discovered, he also seems to say, they could not be invested with the timeless normative power associated with traditional law. Professor Albeck presents such principles as generalities which guide rather than command the decision-maker, so that a "principle" once discovered may stand even though particular halakhic decisions are found which do not obey it. Yet even in this mildly hortatory sense, Englard has been concerned to reject what he regards as a kind of dilution of the authentic precepts of Torah and halakhah. No less peremptory seems to be his rejection of the view of Justice Menachem Elon, also among the most learned of Jewish legal scholars, that specific legal ideals can be viewed as emerging in the perspective of history from the authoritative materials of Jewish law. Such emergent ideals, in Justice Elon's view, may have value both for particular halakhic determinations and for comparative law use, for instance in the enrichment of the law of the State of Israel.

Insofar as orthodox doctrine accepts as part of the law revealed to Moses on Sinai, whatever the learned in the law may yet contribute to its understanding, Englard seems to face formidable problems similar to those before which conservative common lawyers have finally (though after a long rearguard action) had to surren-

16 Related observations are called for by Justice Haim Cohn's account in H.H. Cohn, "The Methodology of Jewish Law" in *Modern Research in Jewish Law, supra* n.11, at 123-135. He seems (at 127ff.) to say that Jewish law, secularly viewed, is "a human creation for human ends and by human methods", and also that though subject to comparative study, it has nevertheless many (he lists 10) *"sui generis* features". We cannot understand this as asserting that each of these ten features were unique, for even the exposition shows many parallels with other systems. The uniqueness must be rather in the interplay of these elements in the particular history of Jewish law - a uniqueness only in the Bergsonian sense that all events in time are unique. One may hope for Justice Cohn's own further explication.

der. I refer to the problem of explaining how, when we can pinpoint the very judicial decisions which created (for example) a particular tort, it can ever be asserted as a matter of dogma that the list of torts is closed. It is no doubt in order to reduce these problems that Englard offers a distinction between mere scholarly commentation on halakhah, and halakhic *decisions* (decision-making *halakhot*).[17] For this at least may make it possible to discount at any rate some of the troublesome traditional material. The learned editor of this volume has already provided a balanced analysis of the various bases for Englard's rejection of the role of principles or other abstractions in aid of faithful application of the *halakhot*.[18]

Bernard Jackson detects no less than eight elements, controversy as to which is woven into the Englard-Elon-Albeck exchanges.[19] All of them deserve anxious jurisprudential attention. I am here only concerned, however, to support his general call for collective scholarly effort on these matters, rather than claims of individuals to

17 As B.S. Jackson here points out (*supra* n.7, at para.1.2), there may however be difficulties in basing even the prescriptive authority of the deciders. And see the balanced view of the distinction between mere scholars and *pe ṣak* in B.S. Jackson, "Modern Research in Jewish Law..." *supra* n.11, at 137-138. The reader may be intrigued to remember a rather similar attempted distinction offered by Kelsen, discussed in J. Stone, "Mystery and Mystique in the Basic Norm", *Modern Law Review* 26 (1963), 34-50, esp. 44-46.

18 B.S. Jackson, "Modern Research In Jewish Law...", *supra* n.11, at 151-156. And *cf.* his essay in the present symposium, *supra* n.7, at para.6.2. For a suggestive discussion of the relations between "motivations" of disputing pronouncements and "principles" underlying legal precepts, see H.H. Cohn, "The Methodology of Jewish Law" in *Modern Research in Jewish Law, supra* n.11, 123-135, at 123, 133. And *cf.* J. Stone, "From Principles to Principles", *The Law Quarterly Review* 97 (1981), 224-253, *passim*.

19 See his penetrating discussion of the arguments in "Modern Research in Jewish Law, Some Theoretical Issues", *supra* n.11, at 136-157, esp. 138-140, 151-156. Jackson's critique (*ibid.* 142-48 and 155, para.6) of Albeck's attempt to keep principles on a level which is not value-charged, would however be strengthened by reference to the main themes of J. Stone, "From Principles to Principles", *supra* n.18, at 224-253.

Cf. also the discussion of these controversies in Mr. Yuter's "Legal Positivism and Contemporary Halakhic Discourse", *The Jewish Law Annual* 6 (1987), 148-163, at 153-160, correctly criticising the reliance of the protagonists on positivist models. Yet, at 154, Mr. Yuter himself seems to accept at face value Kelsen's claim that his science has finally separated law from other objects of description.

speak the final words of the living God. I am led to this by jurisprudential concerns affecting any legal order, touching the accreditation
of norms as "legal" within the Kelsenite model, and touching the
application to particular facts of any precept which appears to be
predicated on those facts.

First, then, as to the accreditation of norms as "legal" by the
Kelsenite model. It is essential (I have already shown), in applying
the Kelsenite model to a particular society and its law, to ask first
whether the apex norm offered is empirically confirmable as being
by and large efficacious in the society concerned. Only after
"impure" resort to this preliminary empirical confirmation, can the
"pure science of law" do its work of testing whether subordinate
norms are indeed "legal" norms of that legal order. For even after we
have empirically confirmed that the contents of the apex norm we
are using have overall efficacity in the society, we can still not
"derive" from it any contents of the dependent norms of that legal
order without constant interpositions of socio-psychological facts of
human willing and human value-judgments. This was made clear
long ago.[20] Yet the Kelsenite theory as originally stated, and as still
too often discussed, proceeds in terms merely of criteria of
"derivability" of the dependent norms from the apex norm or of their
"consistency" with the apex norm. This means that testing for
"lawness" is solely by reference to the formal source of promulgation
authorised by the apex norm, and any restriction imposed on the
content by that apex norm.

A vital point is still too often ignored in all this. This is that
while "derivability" or "consistency" may be an adequate judicial
criterion for checking whether a norm tendered is a legal norm, they
offer very little guidance to the legislator - or to an appellate judge,
or a *bet din, acting in the leeways of choice* - as to what norm should
be laid down on a given matter. Yet such leeways of choice are, as
already observed, an inescapably central feature of any legal order
open to the future. They arise constantly where there is a lacuna in
the substantive law, or where an ostensibly applicable legal
category is illusory (consisting, for example, of competing rules, or
competing versions of a rule, or a circular rule, or a rule of concealed
multiple reference, or a rule of indeterminate content, or a rule of

20 See Stone, *Legal System, supra* n.3, at 123-130, and more fully in J. Stone,
    "Mystery and Mystique in the Basic Norm", *supra* n.17, *passim.*

self-contradictory, or otherwise meaningless content). And even in the absence of these specific "defects" in the authoritative materials, the decisionmaker must constantly choose between the different levels of generality at which the fact elements of legal precepts can equally be stated. To tell a decisionmaker faced with the need to fill a lacuna or apply an illusory legal category of this kind, or choose a level of generality of predicated facts, that he can and must apply a legal norm consistent with the apex norm, *is not to tell him what precept to apply.* At most, all it will tell him is which otherwise applicable norms the apex norm forbids him to apply; and it may perhaps limit somewhat in related ways the choices available in the leeways. It is better thus to specify the precise features of precepts and their application which compel the making of choices, than to continue to speak (as B.S. Jackson here[21] still does) in the rather mystical terms of "weak" and "strong" discretions associated with Dworkinian "principles".

If, therefore, what impels Professor Englard to reject the search for Albeck's principles and Elon's legal ideals historically perceived in the accumulation of halakhic decisions, is a resolve to set a kind of *cordon sanitaire* around the body of halakhic authoritative materials to protect them against dilution or neglect, his effort is necessarily vain. I take him at his word, and assume that it is possible to limit the halakhic decisionmaker to a specific body of preexisting precepts of past *halakhot*, and what is consistent with these. Even then, the decisionmaker would still often be free, and indeed be compelled, in applying *halakhah* to changing social, economic and psychological conditions, to choose which of a number of precepts, *all consistent with the halakhic precepts,* shall be chosen as applicable. "Consistency" with (or "derivability" from) the existing body of halakhic decisions, is like "consistency" with (or "derivability" from) the apex norm of a legal system on the Kelsenite model. By hypothesis a precept is being sought for a situation which is new in the sense that it is not yet governed by any decision, or is governed only by precepts which turn out to be "illusory" in application, in the sense of not compelling one clear solution. The test of "consistency" (or as Jackson sometimes prefers to term it, "conformity") will here lead the decisionmaker to more than one "consistent" precept. Among these the decisionmaker must choose;

21 *Supra* n.7, at para.5.3.

and his choice, imbued though it may be by "the fear of God", and a full sense of "man's position before his Creator", is still finally, his own.

It will not dispose of this analysis for Professor Englard to say that, despite the apparent reality of the development of Jewish law of "a multitude of moral decisions reflecting then current views and beliefs", nevertheless "no normative conclusions can be drawn from the historical fact of legal changes." Nor is it an answer for him to admit "the leeways" of legislative and judicial choice, and "the central place [that] personal value judgments occupy in the judicial process",[22] but to claim that this is still controlled by some halakhic apex norm (or rules of recognition) centered on "the theocentricity of all human concerns". For *ex hypothesi* it is this very body of materials already imbued with this very theocentricity which makes or leaves available a range of solutions among which human choice has to be made. Professor Englard admits that he can see "the central place of personal value judgments", at such points while he also passionately denies that such personal value judgments can base any "normative conclusions". But since *ex hypothesi* the body of precepts imbued as above left available alternative precepts equally consistent with halakhah, but offering different outcomes, it seems either a quibble or a self-deceiving fiction to deny that such value judgments can ever have normative outcomes.

In substance, then, the fitting of Jewish law into a positivist framework cannot exclude the normative effect of human choice-making within it. The positivist test of consistency with (or derivability from) the apex norm, for determining what are the contents of a legal precept to govern a situation not yet covered by existing precepts, necessarily involves choice by decisionmakers when two or more offered precepts both consistent with the apex norm offer different results.. *Ex hypothesi*, this situation is one in which the apex norm leaves the choice to be made by the human decisionmaker. This choice, and its consequences in terms of the induction of value judgments into the body of law, can only by a fiction be attributed to the preexisting precepts rather than the human decisionmaker. The authority and duty of the human decisionmaker under the apex norm

22 At 123. See Englard's concessional reference to "leeways" and adaptation to a "proper social framework", e.g. Section IV of his "The Interaction of Morality and Jewish Law" (*supra* , 121-124). And see text at nn.11 *supra* and 28 *infra*.

to choose between possibilities left open by the preexisting precepts clearly have normative effect. And such human choices cannot in fact be conscientiously made, in the cases *ex hypothesi* under consideration, without reference to the moral ideas with which each generation of human decisionmakers is imbued.[23]

This conclusion surely parallels what is perhaps the richest insight from the famous confrontation between Rabbi Eliezer, on the one hand, and his brethren led by Rabbi Yehoshua, on the other, which culminated in the intervention of the *Bat Ḳol* in support of Eliezer's view. To that divine intervention Rabbi Yehoshua is reported to have responded that the law is not in heaven; that "the law has been handed down to us on earth from Mount Sinai, and we no longer take notice of heavenly voices, for the law which we received provides that decisions shall be taken by a majority." No doubt it is warranted to infer from this, as is usually done, an important rule supporting majority against minority decision (of Rabbi Yehoshua and Company, as it were, against Rabbi Eliezer). Even more momentous, however, is the inference concerning the respective roles of the divine and the human. This is that the very fact of entrustment of a body of precepts to men for application in the dimension of time, vests in them both authority and responsibility for choice among precepts available to cover situations not clearly controlled by legal precepts up to then determined.[24] So it was - and so it was recognised by the traditional authorities that it must be. For we are also told that at that moment the Lord was walking with

23   B.S. Jackson's assertion in "The Concept of Religious Law in Judaism" in *Aufstieg und Niedergang des römischen Welt* ed. H. Temporini and W. Haase (Berlin and New York: Walter de Gruyter, 1979), 33-50, leaves this possibility open: "A structural principle - the difference between the human and divine - is reflected throughout Jewish law in all its periods," and it is the concern for this relation that makes "Jewish law a religious system" (at 38).

24   The leeways arising from the range of generality or concreteness with which elements of a precept can be stated are discussed above (at 226). They constitute extensions, therefore, of the authority to choose even for situations within the arguable ambit of legal precepts already determined. The choices to be made between "levels of generality" on which facts predicated in precepts may equally be stated are basic, endemic and inescapable. See J. Stone, "The *Ratio* of the *Ratio Decidendi*", *Modern Law Review* 22 (1959), 597-620, at 605-608, 613-614. And *cf.* Stone, *Legal System, supra* n.3, at 272-74.

Elijah the prophet; and that the Lord smiled and said: "My children have defeated me, my children have defeated me." Not only, in short, did the learned stand their ground even against the divine intervention. The divine assent was also forthcoming for the ground on which they chose to stand. This was the responsibility resting upon them to seek by study the reason and wisdom necessary for the doing of justice through law amid the ever changing circumstances of human life.[25]

Recognition of the unavoidable normative input arising thus in time from human choice-making, has great advantages, quite apart from its tribute to truth. As with choice-making by appellate judges,[26] there is the advantage of ensuring that the decisionmaker who exercises power is aware of his responsibility for the consequences of its exercise. There is also the advantage for the decision-maker's efficiency, of directing his mind to the real nature of the task before him.[27] Such recognition is, as I have shown, consistent with the decisionmaker's reverent awareness of "man's position before his Creator" to which all orthodox positions, including Professor Englard's, attach importance.

Looked at superficially, it is true, the learned rabbis of old stood their ground against the divine intervention. On a fuller view, however, they did so only in discharge of the responsibility arising from the original divine entrustment of law to them. It fell on them as rational creatures, questing after justice, to maintain the justice of its application, as best they could, in the changing patterns of social life. We could, indeed, restate this conclusion on the Elon-Englard issue as to whether there is normative effect of historic adaptations to changing conditions, in terms of the contents of a Kelsenite apex norm of Jewish law. Dr. Yuter, in exploring here some little-noticed distinctions within positivist models, has elegantly suggested that

25 Cf. E. Rackman's courageous effort (supra, n.1) to provide a balanced statement embracing attention to the traditional authorities, and the role of each generation of the learned as partners in the lawmaking process. God abdicated, as it were, in their favour when he bequeathed the law to them, and thereby restrained himself from any further revelations. These poles seem in great tension - "Yet both poles play their necessary roles."

26 See Stone, Legal System, supra n.3, at 281-298.

27 See also the fuller treatment of these matters in J. Stone, Social Dimensions of Law and Justice, supra n.15, at 656-695.

such an apex norm may embrace both *Torah min hashamayim*, and also *Lo bashamayim hi*. An apex norm combining such contents would take account of the contributions to just law both of the original words from heaven of the living God, and of human beings here on earth in their generations.

V. Problematics of Natural Law in a Divine Positive Legal Order

With the revival of positivist-*ius naturalist* confrontations after World War II, it is perhaps not surprising that natural law themes are prominent in no less than seven of the leading contributions to this symposium.[28] Even so, the range of meanings here variously attributed to "natural law" at this stage of history is rather surprising.

At one extreme, in Rivka Schatz's account of Rabbi Judah Loew ben Bezalel, the Maharal of Prague (1512-1609), the meaning of "natural" and "natural law" seems to fly off in a direction which identifies it with a divinely imposed order to which human beings must submit, but in which their reason does not participate. "If the ground of natural law was man and his nature," she thinks, "then the Maharal as well is interested in 'natural law' except that he defines man as essentially a metaphysical being who belongs to the Order... that is transnatural."[29] So that the authentic statement of that metaphysical nature of man is in the divinely given law, in the upholding of which the absolute (i.e. metaphysical, non-empirical) order of 'existence' is involved."

For Emanuel Rackman, on the other hand, natural law appears to include an input into the halakhah deriving from man's use of reason in the quest for justice in the course of changing social and personal needs.[30] David Novak comes close, at some points, to

28 Rackman, Bleich, Schatz, Dienstag, Novak, Leaman, Yuter.
29 "*Maharal's* Conception of Law - Antithesis to Natural Law Theory", *The Jewish Law Annual* 6 (1987), 109-125 at 116. With this diversion of the reference, Rivka Schatz spends much time exposing and rejecting the entanglements of Maimonidean thought with Greek and Christian versions of natural law. Oliver Leaman's article, "Maimonides and Natural Law", *The Jewish Law Annual* 6 (1987), 78-93, adds many cross-purposes to the debate on the Maharal's positions, mainly arising from the multiple references of the natural law symbols.
30 Emanuel Rackman in his "Secular Jurisprudence and Halakhah", *supra* n.1, sees the divine law as respecting natural law (at 45-49) and offers

resolving natural law simply into "the principle of the common good, namely, that which enhances the life of the human community".[31] He seems also generally to accord with the Thomist view that natural law is that part of divine law which is accessible to humans by dint of their participation in the divine reason, which (for him) it is part of the function of the covenant between God and man to express. For Rabbi J. David Bleich, natural law has similar classical attributes of moral precepts self-evident to the human reason (ṣevarah); precepts so obviously primary as to be "the epistemological equivalent of the propositions of logic" - for instance, Thou shalt not kill!.[32] But he also seeks to construct a bridge from this to divine positive law.[33] He presents as *a priori* the principles of "reason" which "demands both that men make an effort to discover God's divine will as expressed in revelation to man and that man obey the revealed will of God."[34]   In this somewhat inverted sense the divine law as an imposed ("positive") ordering arises from the prior subjection of the human reason to "the law of nature".

For Jacob Dienstag,[35] and a number of others, the natural law is-

---

the conflict of the schools of Shammai and Hillel as to the status of a person who is half slave, half free, as placing the former school squarely behind the natural rights of the slave: "You have taken care of the master, but have you taken care of the slave? He cannot marry a slave because he is half free, or a free woman because he is half slave."

This accords with Rackman's overall theme that the halakhah, whether based on covenant or revelation, "can be developed not only by the exercise of logic but also in response to man's sense of justice and man's social and personal needs" (at 59). As contemporary illustrations he offers a number of rulings of Rabbi Joseph B. Soloveitchik (at 55-59).

31 "Natural Law, *Halakhah* and the Covenant", *supra*, 43-67, at 65.

32 "Judaism and Natural Law", *supra*, 5-42, at 19, 23.

33 He also wishes to embrace within "ṣevarah", as a kind of natural law, its meaning as "the derivation of legal principles and even laws from dogmatically already accepted principles", as well as its meaning as "a direct and independent source of law". See Bleich, *op.cit.*, at 9-14, including the relation of this to Joseph Albo's natural law theses in Ṣefer Ha'ik ar im, bk.1, c.7.

34 *Op.cit.*, at 31.

35 "Natural Law in Maimonidean Thought and Scholarship...", *The Jewish Law Annual* 6 (1987), 64-77.

sue in Jewish law seems to be encapsulated in the well-known literary puzzle in Maimonides concerning the non-believer who by "reasoned conclusion", rather than in submission to the divine will, obeyed the seven commandments of Noachide law. Must such a non-believing but right-acting person be denied not only the title of a pious or righteous gentile (because of lack of belief in God), but also even the title of wisdom and reason (identified in the discussions with natural law)? Or, despite his denial of the former title, was Maimonides conceding that such a person still had merit in the Jewish tradition as an adherent of natural law? Part of the conflict turned on the absence or presence in the original Maimonides text of one single Hebrew letter which would change the word meaning "and not" into a word meaning "but"; part on whether the first printed version of the Mishneh Torah contained a misprint, and part on whether this misprint or the repetition of it was in good faith or by way of intended distortion, from whatever motives, of the original sense. Eventually, of course, these matters became heavily involved in the disastrous confrontation of the philosopher Spinoza with the Jewish religious authorities.

Oliver Leaman,[36] also regarding the natural law issue as central, refines (and perhaps somewhat defuses) it into an epistemological issue of the comparative standing of "knowledge" of moral precepts (prescriptive propositions) as compared with knowledge of observable existences (descriptive propositions). Yet, in another way, of course this identifies natural law with the whole range of the normative - yielding a natural law imperialism of the kind now requiring mention.

VI. "Natural Law Imperialism" and "Justice"

Space forbids any attempt to offer here a detailed critique of the many versions of positivism or iusnaturalism which intrude into this volume. Certain general fears may perhaps be expressed concerning the effect on Jewish legal scholarship of the intrusion of inadequately explained - sometimes, indeed, perhaps inadequately examined and inadequately understood - jurisprudential categories, including those especially of iusnaturalism. And it is to be observed by way of preliminary that whether "natural law" be regarded as

36 *Supra* n.29.

an elegy of folly, or as *philosophia iuris perennis*, no one is in a position to expound any particular version of it as authentic. It may be added that the historical instances are rare in which any simple versions of natural law have resolved rather than confused and exacerbated further any polemics into which they were introduced.

In these circumstances, one fear is that the difficulties of the jurisprudential problems associated with a "religious" or "divinely imposed" legal order, here under review, can only be compounded by superimposing on them the controversies concerning natural law as in some sense or other the product of human reason.

Again, one of the central *foci* of debate concerning natural law is whether this is to be regarded as a sub-order drawing its final authority from a divinely imposed order, or whether these two kinds of legal orders may not (indeed, must not) be mutually exclusive.[37] How far, for example, the "apex norm" (or "rules of recognition") of a divinely imposed legal order may authorise or require the incorporation of principles of "natural law" into that positive legal order depends on what content is attributed to the apex norm (or rules of recognition), on what the proponent means by natural law, and perhaps also on some unsettled questions about the nature of "apex norms" (and "rules of recognition"). Yet all this can be turned upside down as when Rabbi Bleich presents[38] Sa'adia's call of reason for gratitude to God for this goodness as a natural law enjoinder to all men to obey the divine will. Natural law ("reason") then prescribes (a) that God exists; (b) that he may issue and promulgate commands; (c) that men can and should discover God's will; and (d) that men must obey God's will. It in no way clarifies this chaos of natural law references to add, with Rabbi Bleich, that Jewish law thus proceeds on "a natural law" theory, but "of a very particular and limited kind". The potentiality for cross-purposes in controversy is therefore endless.[39]

I have the fear, second, whenever natural law enters the picture, of the imperialistic tendency of some natural law exponents to argue that (or at least as if) all who pursue justice can do so only by accep-

---

37 See also Section V *supra*, and Section VII *infra*.

38 See J.D. Bleich, "Judaism and Natural Law" *supra*, 26-31.

39 Rivka Schatz's study, *supra* n. 29, illustrates this potentiality at numerous points, including her account of the Maharal's rejection of the supposed natural law strain in Maimonides, and the rather bewildering variety of meanings which she seems to tie to the symbol, natural law.

tance of natural law positions. While this is commonest in theological contexts, where natural law is accredited as a branch of the divine law, it can also be found in secularist versions, such as that recently of John Wild.[40] As this last writer expresses it, only natural law makes possible "the very existence of ethics as a rational discipline."[41]

"Natural law" and other criteria of justice emerged side by side in history and mythology. Their common origins, and their overlapping concerns with criticism of law, necessarily entail many confusions and cross-purposes. Each term, for example, is sometimes taken to refer to the whole ambit of discussion of "good" or (in that sense) "desirable" law. In the competitive situations thus arising, "justice" is sometimes offered to provide the contents of "natural law", and (even more frequently) "natural law" to provide the contents of justice; but any reciprocity of impact is often obscured by claimed linkages of natural law with the divine law. Conversely, insofar as the criteria of each *may* fundamentally coincide, the choice whether these are stated in terms of "justice" *simpliciter*, or of "natural law" *simpliciter*, may depend entirely on accidents of the exponent's personal background and of the age in which he lives. The mere fashion of thought may even lead to the designation as "natural law" of bodies of thought in which what is involved is neither "natural law" nor "justice" in general, but rather what may be some other standard or symbol altogether, such as the love or fear of God.[42]

Does it increase our understanding of the enrichment of Jewish law in the course of application, rightly praised in this volume by Menachem Elon, Emanuel Rackman, and others, including at moments Yizhak Englard, to see it as an infusion of natural law, rather than in terms of justice *tout court*? My own view is that it is better to think in terms of justice *tout court*.

By whatever criteria we characterise justice,[43] it is important to

40 *Plato's Modern Enemies and the Theory of Natural Law* (Chicago: University of Chicago Press, 1953).

41 Quoted in Stone, *Human Law and Human Justice* (London: Stevens, 1965), 210-212.

42 On Duns Scotus as an example of the former, see Stone, *op.cit.*, 55-60. For an example of the latter, see the account of the Maharal in R. Schatz, *supra* n.29.

43 Stone, *Human Justice, supra* n.41, *passim,* provides a critical overview of

recognise two major levels of justice-entanglement with law and its problems.

On one level, each legal precept duly promulgated within the particular legal order is an embodiment of what the promulgating authority has determined to be a just solution for the facts predicated in it. At this level that legal precept duly imposed ("positive") within the legal order, cannot be *legally* challenged. It is at this level that the traditional language, here still endorsed by Professor Englard, denies that anything can be added or taken away from the perfection of toraitic and halakhic law. At this level, as it were, justice, as a measure of what law should be, already stands embodied by competent authority within the legal precept involved. Even here, however, and even on a positivist view, those concerned may still question the justice of the legal precept, as did Abraham with God concerning supposed innocents in Sodom and Gomorrah, and Socrates with the authorities of Athens concerning the laws for the education of the young. (I shall deal in the next section with the different natural law view of the position on this first level.)

On the second level, the entanglement of justice with even the most positivist-conceived legal order is far more pervasive and complex. It enlivens every point where the ambit of the facts predicated in existing legal precepts fails to prescribe or prescribes only ambiguously the legal consequence for the situation arising for judgment. Here, as already seen in Sections I and IV above, the positivist model provides the decisionmaker only with the rather dry criterion of "consistency" or "conformity" (with "the apex norm", etc.). Since (as already observed in those sections) the facts presented by new situations and the facts predicated in existing legal precepts can usually with equal consistency be stated at various levels of generality, two or more versions of each precept, with outcomes possibly conflicting with each other as applied to a particular situation, are usually available. While the competing precepts or versions of precepts are all available as "consistent" with the legal order in the above sense, decision cannot take place without a choice between them being made. It is the exercise of that choice left open within the legal order, and not the legal order itself, which decides the outcome. In these and other leeways of the legal order, the

---

the accumulation of criteria relevant to modern problems.

decisionmaker who chooses between the available precepts, decides what precept is to apply, as well as the outcome. The criteria by which he must choose (if he is to act rationally) between the available precepts, are the criteria of "justice", of "good law".

In human judgments of justice thus seen as made *tout court*, without aid of divine natural law, man himself develops the criteria of justice for the ongoing tasks of law.

The third fear I here express concerns our tendency as humans to shirk responsibility for our judgments of justice within these leeways, or at any rate to conceal these by invoking some form of iusnaturalist standard. This fear is not because I think the appeal to justice *tout court* is more correct than the appeal to natural law. The fear is rather of the additional complexities and confusions surrounding natural law notions. The word "natural" has at least nine diverse meanings, and the word "law" at least as many, yielding 81 possible meanings of "natural law", before we add many special references associated only with the combined symbol.

The effect most commonly sought when natural law is appealed to is to suggest that man does not create the criteria of justice, but rather discovers them already built into man's own "nature" as a rational social being. This "nature" of man is not what man wills, much less creates - it is what man is. Or rather, in Aristotle's formulation, it is potentiality - what he would become when fully developed. A creature cannot create its own nature, and its nature is in that sense transcendent of the creature. Insofar, however, as the human creature is endowed with reason, humans can *discover* (it is said) what human nature is. Reasoned contemplation of that "nature" as it embraces the creature's full potentiality of development, can also discover "principles of natural law", that is, the norms favouring that full development immanent in that nature.

I have tried in the above sentences to state an area of consensus concerning the meaning of "natural law", which Professor Rackman and some others here treat - in my view unnecessarily - as a body of principles supplementing the divine positive law of Judaism, in replacement of criteria of justice *tout court*.

The fourth fear which I now express is that whatever assistance may come from using the natural law symbol within the above simplified area of consensus, is likely to be overwhelmed by the torrent of conflicts, confusions, cross-purposes outside the area of consensus which will inevitably accompany use of the symbol.[44]

It is vital to observe, at this point, that the understandable impulse of the human decisionmaker to escape personal responsibility by invoking "natural law" cannot be taken at its face value. It is only because of the supposed transcendence and therefore objectivity and universality of natural law, that it seems to dispense him of responsibility. But when the surrounding areas of conflicts, confusions, and cross-purposes, as well as the abstractness, indeterminacy and countervailing principles of the core area of consensus, are squarely brought to mind, objectivity and universality of applications of natural law are both highly dubious.

So, conversely, the apparent subjectivity and arbitrariness of approaching the judgment of justice directly, involving the decisionmaker in the content of the criteria, so that "man is the measure", require a second glance. Even outside the matrix of some claimed transcendental natural law, the factors operating on the valuing individual to determine the contents of his criteria are of three very different clusters. Partly, it is true, they are peculiar to the valuing individual; partly, however, they are common to all men and women in a given time and place, even if still peculiar to the time and place; and partly they may be common to all mankind. A given theory which offers directly a criterion of justice may emphasise one or another of these clusters of factors. Insofar as the first or second are emphasised at the expense of the third, the result is obviously to detract from "objectivity" in the sense just specified. But conversely, so far as the third cluster comes to be stressed, the

44 As already observed, other reasons lie in the tangle of competing versions of natural law itself. A nice example here surrounds the thesis of Joseph Faur, that "the Sinaitic law" proceeds not from God's will as such but from the *berit* or covenant, i.e. acceptance as such by the entire people": "Understanding the Covenant", *Tradition* 9 (1968), 44 (cited in Yuter, *supra* n.19, at 149-50). Faur seems to offer this way of refuting iusnaturalist claims. In fact, insofar as he bases it on the freedom of God and man to negotiate terms, it may be thought rather to resemble iusnaturalist social contract models such as those of Locke or Rousseau. It should thus not surprise that, also in this volume, D. Novak, "Natural Law, Halakhah and the Covenant", *supra*, 43-67 at 61-67, challenges Faur's positivist version of the covenant, replacing it with a natural law version - in one of natural law's plethora of senses; or that Elliot N. Dorff, "The Covenant: the Transcendent Thrust in Jewish Law", *The Jewish Law Annual* 6 (1987), 68-96, here offers a suzerain-vassal version.

criteria might become *more* "objective" in the present limited sense.

VII. Can Natural Law be Overriding in a Divine Positive Legal Order?

The fears which I have expressed concerning the intrusion of *ius-naturalism* into Jewish legal scholarship, assume a specially harsh form in relation to the frequent claim that the principles of natural law override any positive laws which conflict with them. The importance of this aspect merits this separate section.[45]

If we accept a natural law approach in this aspect, the standing of both positive law and its positive justice are to be referred back (on the more critical matters) to natural law and its natural justice. These latter are then seen as basic concepts of all jurisprudence, for whose definition and analysis we are then referred forward to philosophy, including metaphysics, and possibly to theology also. This is perhaps an additional reason for what I have called "natural law imperialism" - the tendency of natural law adherents to accuse those who reject natural law doctrine, of indifference and even callousness towards justice. But the inference they thus draw would only be warranted where (if we may be rather Irish) the recusant was himself rejecting natural law *on the basis of a natural law credo*. For if (as is generally the case) the rejection is on the basis that justice consists of certain criteria or ideals to which men are personally committed, which they press for realisation through the positive law, and for the sake of which they may have to change or even defy and overturn the positive law, no such inference is warranted. And it has indeed been plausibly charged in reply that the natural law approach, by thrusting the problems of justice back into the abstract sphere of a supposedly objective "natural law" and "natural right", submerges and confuses the inescapably individual responsibility of men to resist and correct injustice.

At any rate, the present point is that when criteria of justice are put into the framework of a system of natural law, and used to test the justice of positive law, the duplication of the word "law" in both phrases may seem to have an additional effect rather independently of the criteria of justice themselves. This effect is that a theory

---

45 See on this aspect generally, Stone, *Human Justice, supra* n.41, at 247-262, 291-295.

of natural law tends not only to criticise positive law by reference to whether it realises justice, but also *to deny that its norms are valid law at all* unless they are in keeping with the principles of natural law.

This power of natural law to override human positive laws which violate its principles, is most commonly but not exclusively asserted since the Middle Ages, in theological versions of natural law, especially in the Thomist line, even though Aquinas himself was cautious about it. In such versions, since natural law is part of the divine law which man can discover by dint of his participation in the divine reason, the question of conflict of divine positive law with natural law is not a serious one.[46] On the contrary, the problem is preempted by insistence (for example) that "Justice and Reason, Nature and Law, are terms that must be held together", and that (theologically speaking) all these terms "rest upon an intuition... of the Transcendent God", as "Lord of Nature", and "as the divine Reason and Source of Justice".[47] That there is no right so to preempt is clear from the fact that we can find natural lawyers simultaneously lamenting the "obscurities", and the "static, abstract, *a priori* and unhistorical form" of natural law writings, from the classics to the present day, in the same breath as they insist that unless men accept natural law they are not concerned with justice.

The claim that natural law has the power to override or strike down positive law which violates it has been, of course, a main target of ridicule by leaders of modern positivism from Bentham and Austin through to Kelsen and Hart. No careful thinker since (and including) Aquinas has, to my knowledge, claimed that *every* principle of natural law overrides every precept of positive law which violates it. Yet it remains still a live issue, especially after the barbarisms of the Nazi period, whether at some level or other of outrageous violation of natural law principles, positive law may be held thus to be stricken down, even today.

When scholars now seek to present Jewish law as a divinely imposed system within a frame of jurisprudential positivism, and simultaneously seek to propose possible roles for natural law, the question about the claims for an overriding power of natural law

46 See Stone, *Human Justice, supra* n.41, at 44-45, 52-55, 615-619.
47 N. Micklem, *Law and the Laws* (Edinburgh: W.Green, 1952), 113ff.

receive a special dimension.[48]

It is not, indeed, a new dimension in general jurisprudence. Augustine (354-430 A.D.) had already offered a schema in which *lex naturalis* was the transcription of the *lex aeterna* in man's reason and heart, and in which the law of the State - the temporal law - must conform to the *lex aeterna* as transcribed in the *lex naturalis*. For Aquinas (1224-1274), the eternal law made known to man by divine revelation may, in that part of it called natural law, be apprehended by the reason in which God permits man to share. The law laid down by human authority - positive human law - is here again subject to the overriding authority of the eternal law as expressed for man through the natural law.

Now the *lex aeterna* of Augustine and Aquinas, like the Jewish law according to all its exponents, is itself, jurisprudentially speaking, a positive legal order - a divinely imposed order - but still an imposed one. It is, however, a kind of imposed order which the legal positivists have steadily set apart as not "positive law" within the concern of jurisprudence, even though it may be law "properly" and even "strictly" so-called (as Austin might say). Unless we similarly set aside the Jewish traditional law from jurisprudential concern, and if we now treat it as a system of divine positive law, the supposed power of natural law to override positive law might here raise rather grotesque problems. Whether the revealed law of Judaism is deemed to proceed - like Augustine's *lex aeterna* - from both the reason and will of God freed by love from arbitrariness;[49] or, like Aquinas's, only from God's reason (in which man participates) - or as a number of contributors here suggest - from one or other or some combination of these - the power of natural law to override the divine positive law could scarcely be acknowledged.

All this must be a rather basic reason why oversimple assertions about the role of natural law within traditional Jewish law are unlikely either to enlighten jurisprudence about Jewish law, or Jewish

48 *Cf.* on the conflict of divine positive law with "natural law", Englard, "The Interaction of Morality and Jewish Law", *supra*, and in terms of "morality" and "religious experience" see esp. 118-121. Englard seems to endorse Rabbi Leibovitch's assertion (obviously with disapproval) that according to natural law and utilitarian criteria "only one who considers the human being the ultimate end and supreme value, i.e. man in the place of God, can be a moral person".

49 Stone, *Human Justice, supra* n.41, at 44.

lawyers about jurisprudence.[50] Elliot N. Dorff's study of "The Covenant: The Transcendent Thrust in Jewish law" in this volume argues that efforts to apply general legal theories to Jewish law are enlightening both as to those theories, and as to Jewish law. Yet this must be subject to at least two caveats. One is that if legal theories (as here, natural law) are replete with competing and conflicting references and versions, such benefits are most unlikely without the clearest stipulation of meanings, and the sternest integrity and consistency in observing the stipulations. Another is that the notions both of "theory of Law" and of "Jewish Law" also require agreed stipulations of meaning, and respect for those stipulations.

VIII. Jewish Law, Natural Law and the Law of the State of Israel

If, despite the risks I have mentioned, the scholar of Jewish law still wishes to probe the possible roles of natural law within the *corpus iuris judaica,* the best arena would certainly lie in the relation between this last body and the law of the State of Israel, an area valiantly opened up in England, *Religious Law in the Israel Legal System.*[51] It is clear already that important principles and ideals of traditional Jewish law (for instance, as to master and servant) have been expressly incorporated into the Law of the State. Natural law notions may well prove useful in progressively identifying principles of traditional Jewish law so fundamental as to merit incorporation in the law of the State, and to serve as guidelines for law reform. Yet this does not seem very likely at the present stage of history; and the substance of these tasks has already, it seems to me, been entered on by Cohn, Elon and others[52] without much need for

50 *Cf.* on this and related points, B.S. Jackson, *supra* n.7, at para. 6.1.2, *initium.*

   Rabbi Bleich's questionings as to the self-evidence of the contents of Noachide law, apart from the prohibition of murder, *supra* 19-23, and as to its limited import for Jewish law *(id.* 23-26), are certainly welcome signs of more critical scholarly approaches.

51 *Supra,* n. 10.

52 See, e.g., besides Justice Elon's well-known work, H.H. Cohn, "The Methodology of Jewish Law" in *Modern Research in Jewish Law, supra* n. 11, at 123-135, esp. at 133-135. And see B.S. Jackson, "The Prospects for Codification or Restatement of Jewish Law..." *The Jewish Law Annual* 2 (1979), 180-184. The symposium in this latter volume includes valuable

natural law theorising.

IX. *The Covenant Model*

The covenantal form, which dominates the historical materials of Jewish law,[53] becomes deeply entangled in many of these contributions with versions of the apex norm of a positive legal order, as well as with iusnaturalist versions of a social contract. It deserves examination, however, in its own historical terms, and readers are indebted for the approach to this in Elliot Dorff's chapter just mentioned, whatever view they take of the General Editor's criticisms of the covenant model, to which Dr. Dorff is seeking to respond.

The historical covenant model itself, the author correctly points out, carries important insights even before it is suffused with later jurisprudential theorising.[54] First, it presents God as legislature, judge and emperor of law. Second, it presents the love of God as a motive of obedience. Third, it presents the plighted word, what later was termed *pacta sunt servanda*, as a source of obligation. Fourth, it presents these notions of legal bindingness within a national constituency. And yet, fifth, even within this limited ambit, Jewish law presents itself as reflecting "divine purpose" (and in this sense as reflecting "nature"). Sixth, this compact explains the wide scope of subject-matter of Jewish law. Seventh, it also explains the active and enduring role of human judgment and development in the movement of Jewish law, as well as the concurrence of this with, eighth, the Messianic thrust of Jewish law.

No less stimulating and fruitful are the perplexities which Dorff sees as consequential on this use of the covenant model *simpliciter*. How, if at all, can a supreme being be bound by, and even if bound, held to the terms of the covenant - issues well dramatised in the Book of Job?[55] On what basis can men change the terms of the covenant, unless (as Dorff finds to be the case) the covenant itself

----

comparative perspectives, e.g. on Roman and modern European codifications, and the American restatement of the law.

53 See the valuable collation of the biblical uses of the notion in Elliot N. Dorff, "The Covenant: The Transcendent Thrust in Jewish Law" *supra*, 68-96 at 68-70.

54 Dorff, *op. cit.*, at 71-82.

55 Dorff, *op. cit.*, at 87-89.

provides for its own development by human elaboration.[56] In what circumstances, if any, can either the divine or human parties withdraw unilaterally from the covenant, even without grounds given by the other side?[57] Regarding the Jewish people collectively as a party, how far may particular Jews choose to withdraw from participation? Do the obligations of individuals continue even though there is no enforcement?[58] Does the divine tolerance of undeserved catastrophes, such as the Holocaust in World War II, constitute a divine breach of the covenant, basing the freeing of the Jewish people from its terms?[59]

The questions thus raised by the covenant model are more interesting that Dorff's tentative answers to a number of them. His offered identification of "divine purpose" with the preservation of nature, and of the transcendence of divine purpose as a force for transforming both natural law and Jewish law,[60] is unhelpful to either natural law or Jewish law. After all, few serious exponents of natural law identify the "natural" with what is, as distinct from the full potentiality of what is. His view of the covenant as a pact not between equals, but between a divine suzerain and a vassal people,[61] may seem to explain why, but for God's goodness and compassion, God could revoke the covenant unilaterally; and why, even though human acceptance of the covenant was not necessary, God as "King" and "Father" sought this acceptance.[62] But the effect of this is to destroy much of the persuasiveness of the covenant as a matrix of *legal* thought.

In the last resort, indeed, Dorff has to admit that the covenant model is one of metaphor or analogy which cannot be followed through to all its implications. Indeed, as he at one point observes, the covenant merely covers over, for him, the reality of the divine command, of "God's antecedent authority". And insofar as this is so, his covenant model has no greater explicative power than positivist models such as the apex norm, or indeed the straight divine imposed

---

56 Dorff, *op. cit.*, at 91.
57 Dorff, *op. cit.*, at 89-90, 92-96.
58 Dorff, *op. cit.*, at 92-96.
59 *Ibid.*
60 Dorff, *op. cit.*, at 81-82.
61 Dorff, *op. cit.*, at 84, 85-87.
62 Dorff, *op. cit.*, at 89-91.

law of Austin. It in no way helps his main thesis to confront Professor Rackman's model of a covenant between God and men as equal parties, with his own suzerain-vassal covenant, nor to restate this confrontation in terms of whether the covenant is to be regarded as "the social contract" of the modern iusnaturalist tradition.[63] And while "the legal or judicial discretion exercised by the human subjects" is understandable in terms of the covenant model, it is (as has already been observed) understandable also in terms of these positivist models. The truth (in Dorff's words) that "God commanded obedience to both the form of the law at Sinai and the new form that it would take in succeeding generations",[64] has no absolute need of reference to the covenant model for its understanding.

Elliot Dorff's final point, that the covenant model conveys a transcendental thrust, representing "the relationship with God which provides much of the *raison d'être* of Jewish life and law", may be a way of restating whatever is meant by recognising Jewish law as a religious legal ordering, and the historic mission of those who administer it to keep it viable in a changing world. As a jurisprudential contribution, it repeats, rather than answers, the basic questions.

X. *Divine Reason or Divine Will as Content of the Basic Norm?*

It may seem tantalising, after what has preceded, for me to observe that certain rather special uses of natural law ideas could clarify important issues of traditional Jewish life, *if only circular argumentation could be avoided in exploring them.*

Thomas Aquinas gave a powerful prod to post-mediaeval thought by finally asserting the rationality of God, the participation of man in that rationality, and thence the mediatory role of natural law (as an expression of that rationality) between both God and humans and between the state and humans. This Thomist coup could not, even then, delete from theology the fact that Augustine saw the basis of the divine law in God's will as much or more than in His reason. Before the century was out, Duns Scotus had revived a voluntarist "natural law" reflecting not man's participation in the divine *reason*, but rather man's loving submission to the divine will.

63   Dorff, *op. cit.*, at 83-85.
64   Dorff, *op. cit.*, at 94.

In terms of "justice", "justice" is then what God wills, and human obedience to that will, rather than reasoned calculation of benefits, is what is called for. The attentive reader will find here some echoings of Professor Englard's earnest dissent from his orthodox colleagues.

As the will of God thus displaces His reason as the source of divine law, the precepts of divine law become a system of divine positive law. The human concern is to discover God's will and to follow it. The Maharal's conception of law, as presented here by Rivka Schatz, is as intelligible a Jewish reaction to Maimonides, as Duns Scotus' voluntarism was as a Christian reaction to Aquinas's rationalism. As between God's reason and God's will, Maimonides perhaps tried to choose both. He insisted that God's will was final and absolute, but also that good reasons always lie behind that Will, even when as to a specific command they are hidden from us by time or limited human understanding. This balancing of Maimonides' positions is probably best seen, as some interesting chapters here suggest, as part of the ongoing discussions of revived Greek philosophy transmitted to Aquinas, and to theology and jurisprudence generally, by earlier Arab and Jewish philosophers. These links are no doubt part of the essential background of the case of the gentile who observes the seven commandments of Noachide law, although for reasons other than their promulgation by God. The real issues are thus graver and more enduring than whether a printer changed a letter,[65] or whether this was innocent error, or calculated deceit. They are displayed in this volume by Rabbi J.D. Bleich's and Dr. Oliver Leaman's accounts of the literary and philosophical history, including the relation of these matters to Leibniz's philosophy, and by Rivka Schatz on their relations to the positions of the Maharal of Prague.[66]

---

65 Rabbi Bleich, indeed, argues that even if we accept *ela* (implying that such a gentile is one of "the wise"), this still says nothing about Maimonides and natural law, since "wisdom" may have reference to other matters than the "transcendental truths" referred to by this symbol. (See Bleich, *supra*, 7-10, esp. 9f.). Here again the intractability turns on our inability firmly to pin the various polemical positions to the precise particular meanings of natural law.

66 On Selden's *De Jure Naturali - Juxta Disciplinam Ebraeorum (floreat* 1584-1654), arguing that the Noachide code was pre-biblical natural law, and on Grotius' contemporaneous use of Old Testament narrative as a *posteriori* evidence of natural law, see Rabbi J.D. Bleich, "Judaism and

A final choice as between God's reason and His will for incorporation into the apex norm of the divine legal order would have great
consequences. There is, for good or ill, no convincing way of demonstrating either position.[67] At most there is the persuasive (rather
than conclusive) argument from the assumedly known rational capacities of man. It can be argued that since divine capacities can be
no less than human, God's reason (as well as man's reason) must play
its role in His law. Insofar as humans use reason in seeking what is
just, and they are made in God's image, and cannot be superior to God,
the divine precepts must also finally be supportable by reason. This
argument has hazardous phases, however, not least as to the role of
human reason. And insofar as it is not conclusive, the respective
protagonists of God's reason and of God's will take their positions by
faith; and only faith can move them.

We may, of course mislead ourselves and even others by treating
as self-evident some premise which we are not in a position to
demonstrate. Claims can be found in these pages, for example, that
the duty of obedience to the divine law rests on the human's reasoned recognition of God's loving concern for the human good. These
assume that there is a kind of natural law requiring unconditional
obedience to the precepts of divine law. Claims can also be found,
however, that the duty of obedience rests on the human reason's
recognition of the helplessness of humans before the will of God; the
precept prescribing this would similarly be requiring unconditional
obedience to the divine law, this time on the ground of fear - *yirat
shamayim*.[68] Such arguments appeal to those addressed to share the
speaker's faith. They may extend fellowship, and perhaps
compassion, but not knowledge.

Natural Law", *supra*, at 5, and Rivka Schatz, "The Maharal's
Conception of Law...", *supra* n.29.

On the inconsistency of such positions with *one interpretation* of
Maimonides' Mishneh Torah, *Hilkhot Melakhim* 8:11, see Bleich, *op.
cit.*, *supra*, at 7-8, 19-20.

67 On the inclusion of antithetical values within "the basic norm, the
Covenant itself", see Rackman, *supra* n.1, at 60-63.

68 See, e.g., the discussion of such claims by E. Rackman, *supra* n.1, at 59-60.

XI. The Role of a Secularist Natural Law

What, finally, it may be asked would be the bearing (if any) on Jewish law of a supposed merely secular natural law, a law which binds human beings quite independently of any divine precept or revelation?

Such a secularist natural law could probably be supportive of arguments that there is a natural law which itself guides or impels human creatures to recognise law issuing from the divine reason, in which mankind is deemed to participate. Insofar as there has been an entanglement of natural law with Christian theology, especially since Aquinas, a secular version of natural law might also serve to relax orthodox Jewish inhibitions against intellectual activity in this area. In any case, as several chapters of the present volume indicate, those aspects of the natural law tradition impinging on the literature of Jewish law, are mainly indebted (as of course was Thomism itself) to Greek and Roman versions of natural law. These, on balance, were secularist rather than theocentrist in basic mood and expression.

There are, of course, very serious questions as to how far, once origin in the divine reason is put aside, the arguments for the existence of natural law are sustainable. As I showed in *Human Law and Human Justice,* full success would require the discovery of principles immanent in the world of existence, based on human nature in its full potentialities.[69] It would require that the content of these principles be objectively found and recognised by people generally. And even when so discovered and so generally recognised, success would also require it to be shown that such principles become binding on people - that is, become prescriptive for their conduct, rather than merely descriptive of it. These conditions have not yet, so far as I know, been met, though John Finnis' recent work[70] comes perhaps nearest to it.

The durability (or is it the interminableness?) of the positivist-iusnaturalist debate arises, as has been seen, from the impossibility of proof when natural law is seen as part of the theocentric system. It has to be added that for a secularist natural law there seems to be a different but no less serious a stand off. However divergent men's

---

69 Stone, *Human Justice, supra* n.41, at 196-202.
70 *Natural Law and Natural Rights* (Oxford: The Clarendon Press, 1980).

observations of their actual and potential beings, and of what flows in obligation from these, the natural lawyers do not despair. For they know that reason can also be corrupt and that corruptness of reason blinds the vision. Many assertions of natural law may (they also admit) be erroneous; but this in no way shows (for them) that there is not an authentic natural law. And it is indeed true that - *Error multiplex veritas una!* Only, of course, that maxim cannot establish "the truth" of any version of natural law offered by even the sincerest and most ardent proponent.

When natural law is allowed to assert its imperium over the whole field of justice, many people have a choice only between divine revelation or natural law on the one hand, and utter moral scepticism on the other. And the need for a *tertium quid* may be a most compelling reason why justice should not be wholly surrendered to either. Another compelling reason is that the work of judges and others who apply law cannot wait indefinitely for either divine revelation or the discoveries of natural law. The difference, often enough, between the natural lawyer's attitude towards the *summum bonum*, and that of jurists who are not natural lawyers, is mainly that the former *claim* that its full content can be found while the others admit great areas of doubt. At this point, mere theologians and natural lawyers may rest; but decision-making jurists must, while still continuing the ultimate search, also provide solutions as just as they can make them for the problems raised here and now under the legal order.

The argument, moreover, that without "natural law" we cannot see justice as bound to men's most cherished values and therefore finally to God, through whom most men envisage these, is in my view rather misdirected to the Jewish legal tradition. It should have the reverent answer that the Hebrew prophets have inspired men's dedication to the highest ideals of justice without resort to a mediating "natural law". If the argument is that "Justice is not that which man ordains; it is that which he seeks to discover," the answer is also clear. Many theories of justice, besides natural law, are efforts at such discovery. Common dedication and exchanges of intelligence among all who search are more important than recrimination against those who refuse to join one's own particular expedition.

XII. Some Other Jurisprudential Concerns

It is no doubt a tribute to the infectious enthusiasm of many contributors that too much of this introduction has addressed itself to positivist-iusnaturalist issues in the context of Jewish law. I pause, finally, to recall how often I have wondered why many other philosophical aspects of law and justice have had so little concern. Has the debate between the metaphysicians of justice, like Kant and Stammler, and the empiricists like Duguit,[71] no bearing on *torah* and *halakhah*?   Has the contrast between absolutist and relativist positions no application to Jewish law except in the limited way in which it has become an issue between Yizhak Englard, Menachem Elon, Shalom Albeck and others, concerning the effects of historical applications, or logical conceptualisations on the supposed unchangeability of the precepts of divine law?[72]

A related major issue which has here barely been touched on in particular contexts is that of the functions of general formulae and concrete applications in law and justice - an important aspect of the relation between "principles" and "rules".[73] This is a central and a growing problem, not only in relation to criteria of justice, but in relation to the logistics of legal operations themselves.[74]

It is easy, on the other hand, to understand why a tradition as ancient as the Jewish, with a continuous and continuing literature preserved over two millennia or more, has little interest in the recently fashionable but waning faith that analysis of common linguistic usage can be a major source of basic jurisprudential knowledge.[75] Yet it is also strange that in a literary tradition which includes the intellectual refinements of rabbinic elaboration and *pilpul*, as well as the passionate vision and insights of the prophets,

---

71   Stone, *Human Justice, supra* n.41, at 297-299 and *passim*, among the criteria there examined.

72   See Stone, *op.cit.*, at 299-300 and *passim*, among the criteria there examined.

73   But see the sensitive probing of some of these issues of abstract v. concrete and implicit v. explicit, and the relation of these matters to empiricism, in B.S. Jackson, "The Concept of Religious Law in Judaism", *supra* n.23, at 33-50, esp.35ff.

74   See Stone, *Human Justice, supra* n.41, at 300-301 and *passim*, among the criteria there examined.

75   See Stone, *op.cit.*, at 303-313.

there has been so little explicit engagement with the understanding of law as an expression of the "sense of justice", or "the sense of injustice", as kinds of psychological facts empirically observable in human experience.[76]

Most striking of all seems the lack of serious scholarly engagement with the view of law as an expression of national character, of which Friedrich Karl von Savigny's notion of the *Volksgeist* was a pioneering modern form. The abusive *détournement* of such notions into the barbarisms of Nazi racism and other forms of totalitarianism may no doubt have deterred the interest of Jewish scholars, Jews being among the prime victims of the accompanying horrors and atrocities. Yet it remains difficult to neglect the central insights of Savigny's hypotheses, for instance, that legal change must respect the continuity of a people's shared experience and consciousness as embodied in its developing *Volksgeist,* and concerning the precise role of legal specialists in all this.[77] And it is made the more difficult by the emphasis given by Jewish traditions from earliest times to the bonds between Jewish peoplehood and commitment to the torah and halakhah.

Conclusion

Any sense of lack which readers may feel on these matters will, I think, be more than compensated by the steady focus in most of its pages on the dynamics of legal growth revealed by the history of the torah-halakhah of Jewish law. Many of my introductory comments have discussed the many acknowledgments - mostly proud acknowledgments - of the enriching transformations which have marked the three millennia or more of the history of Jewish law. The greatest need signalled by these accounts is the need for understanding how such transformations can (and indeed must) take place within a legal order without impairing its integrity and legitimacy.

I have ventured, especially in Sections I-IV, to relate these problems concerning Jewish law to the corresponding problems of other legal orders, and particularly those of the common law. I have suggested that the nature of the tasks of human interpretation of law may have common features, whether the initial body of pre-

76 See Stone, *op.cit.,* at 312-321.
77 See Stone, *Social Dimensions, supra* n.15, at 66-118, esp.101-118.

cepts be understood as of divine or of secular origin.

The processes of social, economic, technological and psychological change and development, to which a legal order must be continuously adjusted if it is to remain a living order for the successive generations of the society, are similar in either case. The question for the human interpreters in their generations is not whether they will stand inertly pat on the content of precepts delimited once and for all in a former age, or whether they will participate in a self-perpetuating self-renewal of the content. The reality, as Sections I-IV have recalled, is rather that the fertility of language in which the content of legal precepts is necessarily formulated, the limits of logic as a means of discovering and legitimising what content of precepts is appropriate, just or even *law*, for situations newly arising for legal governance[78] - that all of these do not merely *permit* choice-making by human interpreters - they *compel* such choice-making. It is on this very compulsion to choose, courageously exercised by infusions of contemporary insights, wisdom and factual knowledge from each generation of human interpreters within the very framework of the traditional law, that legal ordering is kept living and vibrant through the decades, the centuries - and in the case of the law to which this volume is devoted, through the millennia.

For all the participants in this volume, I permit myself to recall, as I did in 1965 on finishing *Social Dimensions of Law and Justice*, the role of the *Ḳaddish* in Jewish tradition. The *Ḳaddish* is a prayer of thankfulness, extoling and glorifying the Divine providence. It marks the consummation of an undertaking worthily completed, be it a phase of learning, or the ending of a cherished life. And it is, by the same token, a declaration of thanksgiving for what has gone before, and of faith in those who follow. May the high tasks to which my colleagues in this volume have set their hand, always command the dedication of successors.

---

78 The limits of logic embrace of course the choices left open by the ubiquitous categories of illusory reference within existing precepts at any particular time. See Stone, *Legal System, supra* n.3, at 209-335, esp.241-300. For a briefer account, see J. Stone, "Judicial Precedent and Common Law Growth", in *Law and Society: Culture Learning Through the Law*, ed. Richard R. Vuylsteke (Honolulu: East-West Culture Learning Institute, 1977), 143-154.

PART TWO

SURVEY OF RECENT LITERATURE

SURVEY OF RECENT LITERATURE

Contributors: H. Ben Menahem (Jerusalem), B.S. Jackson (Kent), L. Jacobs (London), R.A. Morgan (Oxford), K. Nielsen (Aarhus), D. Piattelli (Rome), D.H. Parker (Provo), M.J. Praver (Jerusalem), S.M. Passamaneck (Los Angeles).

Abbreviations:

BASOR	Bulletin of the American Schools of Oriental Research
BL	*Book List* of the Society for Old Testament Study
JBL	Journal of Biblical Literature
JJS	Journal of Jewish Studies
JLA	Jewish Law Annual
JNES	Journal of Near Eastern Studies
JRJ	Journal of Reform Judaism
JSOT	Journal for the Study of the Old Testament
KS	Kiryath Sefer
OTA	Old Testament Abstracts
PAOJS	Proceedings of the Association of Orthodox Jewish Scientists
RB	Revue Biblique
RQ	Revue de Qumran
VT	Vetus Testamentum
ZAW	Zeitschrift für alttestamentliche Wissenschaft

ABORTION

1080. Richard Alan Block, "The Right To Do Wrong: Reform Judaism and Abortion", *JRJ* 28/2 (1981), 3-15. - The author questions the presumed absolute nature of Reform Judaism's approval of therapeutic abortion and identifies several moral considerations that may modify an absolute acceptance of abortion as a valid position in liberal Jewish interpretation of traditional attitudes. S.M.P.

1081. Sandra B. Lubarsky, "Judaism and the Justification of Abortion for Non-Medical Reasons", *JRJ* 31/4 (1984), 1-13. - The author analyzes extra-halakhic assumptions which she contends undergird the rabbinic responsa on abortion and attempts to show that these assumptions are not required by tradition. On this basis it is argued that Judaism permits abortion for both medical and non-medical reasons. S.M.P.

1082. Mark Washofsky, "Abortion, Halacha and Reform Judaism" *JRJ* 28/4 (1981), 11-19, and the "Response" of Richard Alan Block, *ibid.*, 19-22. - Washofsky asserts that Reform Judaism can call upon traditional legal sources to support a broadly liberal position on therapeutic abortion. Block's response asserts that the liberal position which allows for abortion on demand is not really compatible with traditional legal views.   S.M.P.

AGENCY

1083.   Emmanuel Bulz, "The "Negotiorum Gestor" in Jewish Law" (Heb.), *Proceedings of the Eighth World Congress of Jewish Studies*, Division C (Jerusalem: World Union of Jewish Studies, 1982), 41-46.

1084.   S. Ettinger, "An Agent's Deviation from an Authorization in Jewish Law" (Heb.), *Shenaton Ha-Mishpat Ha-Ivri* 9-10 (1982-3), 29-51.

1085.   D. Frimer, "A Review of the Legal Character of Agency" (Heb.), *Shenaton Ha-Mishpat Ha-Ivri* 9-10 (1982-3), 113-127.

1086.   P. Segal, "No Agency for An Illegal Act" (Heb.), *Shenaton Ha-Mishpat Ha-Ivri* 9-10 (1982-3), 73-95.

1087.   Daniel Sinclair, "The Status of a Gentile as Agent under Jewish Law" (Heb), *Shenaton Ha-Mishpat Ha-Ivri* 9-10 (1982-83), 95-113. - An examination of the basis of incapacity of a non-Jew to serve as an agent for a Jew and non-Jew in Jewish Law, as developed in Talmudic and Post Talmudic literature. The source at the incapacity is grounded in the Agency of Biblical times being essentially an expression of tribal belonging generally used for ritual purposes, thus excluding those not of the tribe. Talmudic redaction reflects an extension of the prohibition of all facets of communal-economic life though S demonstrates a thread of opinion, developed substantially in modern Responsa, wherein a Gentile's incapacity is limited to ritual matters while in secular matters the non-Jew is fully competent to serve as agent under Jewish Law.   M.J.P.

See also 1172.

ARRANGEMENT

1088.   Zvi A. Steinfeld, "The Order of Halachot in Mishna and Tosefta Horayoth" (Heb.), *Proceedings of the Eighth World Congress of Jewish Studies*, Division C (Jerusalem: World Union of Jewish Studies, 1982), 9-12.

BAILMENT
See 1172.

BIBLICAL LAW

1089.   Calum M. Carmichael, *Law and Narrative in the Bible*, Ithaca and London, Cornell University Press, 1985, ISBN 0-8014-1792-9, Pp.356, Price: $38.50. - Sub-titled "The Evidence of the Deuteronomic Laws and the Decalogue", this book pursues further Carmichael's now-familiar thesis from *The Laws of Deuteronomy* (1974) and *Women, Law and the Genesis Traditions* (1979). He looks particular at the choices made in arranging and formulating the laws (some quite general, others extremely specific), and the reasons for their attribution to God in the case of the Decalogue, Moses in the case of Deuteronomy. "In order to preserve the prophetic impact of their material, the compilers closely studied existing biblical narrative, and selected laws which maintained the appropriate historical context. Using this perspective, Carmichael is able to detect strong logical continuity in both the structure and the content of the Decalogue and the Deuteronomic laws" (from the jacket).   B.S.J.

1090.   R. Clifford, *Deuteronomy, with an Excursus on Covenant and Law*, Wilmington: Michael Glazier Inc., 1982, Pp. x, 193, Price: $6.95 (New Testament Message, A Biblical-Theological Commentary, 4); see *BL* 1983 p. 46.

1091.   George W. Coats, "II Samuel 12:17a", *Interpretation* 40 (1986), 170-175; see *OTA* 9/3 (1986), no.790.

1092.   B.S. Jackson, "The Ceremonial and the Judicial: Biblical Law as Sign and Symbol", *JSOT* 30 (1984), 25-30. - The claim of A.J. Phillips that biblical law can be studied only as law is rejected. Starting from Aquinas's classification of biblical law in three categories of moral, ceremonial and judicial law, use is made here of legal semiotics, the study of the relation between sign and symbol and the thing signified. A semiotic approach has some similarities to literary structuralism but is distinct from hermeneutics. It is employed here to examine the function of the legal texts of the Old Testament. The work of a number of scholars who have made use of this method is examined. Jackson argues that a semiotic approach pays attention to what the texts have to say about the nature of the message, to the manner of use of biblical norms, to semiotic choices made by the text and the nature of the communities within which the biblical law was designed to be communicated. Such methods show that judicial and moral laws operated in wider groups than ceremonial laws.   R.A.M.

1093.   H. Lennard, "Die kultischen Anordnungen Gottes im Zusammenhang mit den übrigen Gesetzen des Alten Testaments", *ZAW* 97 (1985), 414-423. - The writer examines various investigations into categories of "Law" including those of Rendtorff, Koch, Preise, Reventlow, Schulz, Wagner and Halbe. General conclusions reached by such study has shown that casuistic law usually relates to the individual; law relating to death usually assumes the participial form and is often related to the cult; Divine commands relate both to everyday life and the cult, although the former often embrace ethical matters while cultic regulations do not, and "wisdom" exhortations are advice based on the commandments. Lennard examines the Prohibition and finds that some forms of it begin with a noun, others with a verb. Cultic regulations usually begin with a noun. The writer examines various forms of this kind, dividing them into a number of types which include the basic function of the cult related mostly to thanksgiving and expiation. Cult law is usually introduced by the word *torah* in the Tetrateuch which the LXX renders by *nomos* and this, in the New Testament, stands most often for "the cult".   R.A.M.

1094.   M. Lind, "Law in the Old Testament", *Christian Legal Society Quarterly* 4 (1983), 32-34. - In Lind's view, there is today "a revival of the church's interest in justice and law" and their proper foundation. He emphasizes that the Old Testament is itself a rich source of law, and is the original and still proper model, along with the New Testament, of law for all who seek to retain a covenantal relationship with God. Citing numerous passages from the Covenant code *(Exodus* 20:22-23:33), Deuteronomic code, and the Holiness code, Lind emphasizes the covenantal nature of Old Testament law and the continued recognition of covenantal law in the New Testament. Lind contrasts the direct teaching/preaching (parenesis) form employed by God in pentateuchal law, the numerous "motive clauses" which set forth God's reasons and purposes, and the second person singular, apodictic, form of Old Testament law with the secularity, human origin, and power orientation of law as set forth in other ancient Near Eastern codes. Contrast is also drawn with medieval legal theory based on the natural law theory of Augustine and Aquinas, which Lind characterizes as "paganizations" of law suited to administration through "the impersonal powers of the state".   D.H.P.

1095.   Rivka Nageh, *Ḥuḳe hatorah be ṣifre N'a ḥ,* Tel-Aviv: Or-Am, 1980, Pp. 86; see *KS* 57/3-4 no. 3029.

1096.   Dale Patrick, *Old Testament Law,* London: SCM Press, 1986, ISBN 0-334-02228-2, Pp.278, Price: £8.50. - Described as a basic introduction presupposing no prior knowledge, this book provides an introduction to biblical criticism. followed by chapters devoted to the Decalogue, The Covenant Code, the Deuteronomic Law and the Priestly Law, each one in the light of source criticism, form criticism and tradition history. There are commentaries on selected laws from each collection. Concluding chapters consider wider questions: the purposes of the collections, the relations between law and covenant, and the approach of the New Testament to Old Testament law.   B.S.J.

1097.   Anthony Phillips, "The Book of Ruth-Deception and Shame", *JJS* 37 (1986), 1-17; see *OTA* 9/3 (1986), no.788.

1098.   R. Rendtorff, "Esra und das "Gesetz"", *ZAW* 96 (1984), 165-184. - *Ezra* 7 and *Neh*.8 do not deal with the same law. In *Ezra* 7 the Aramaic *dat* has a much more restricted legal sense than the more general *torah* and anticipates later synagogue practice. When the books of Ezra and Nehemiah received their final form both *Ezra* 7 and *Neh*.8 were related to bring them into harmony by making it appear as though they reflect the same practice.
R.A.M.

1099.   Alexander Rofé, "Deuteronomy 5:28-6:1. Composition and Text in the Light of Deuteronomy Style and Three *Tefillin* from Qumran (4Q 128, 129, 137)", *Henoch* 6 (1984), 1-14; see *OTA* 9/2 (1986), no.626.

1100.   R. Westbrook, "Biblical and Cuneiform Law Codes", *RB* xcii (1985), 237-264. - The article examines nine so-called law codes of the Ancient Near East. The two in the Bible (*Exod*.21:1-22:16, *Deut*.12-25) show similarities in form and content with their extra-biblical parallels. The similarities argue for a common type of intellectual activity. This belongs primarily neither to the activity of royal apologists nor to scribal exercise but, just as omen series were designed to give guidance to diviners, so these law codes were designed to give guidance to royal judges as a practical guide in difficult cases.
R.A.M.

See also 1195, 1202.

CAPACITY
See also 1172.

CLASSIFICATION

1101.   David Altshuler, "On the Classification of Judaic Laws in the *Antiquities* of Josephus and the Temple Scroll of Qumran", *AJSReview* 7/8 (1982-3), 1-14.

COLLECTIONS OF ESSAYS

1102.   I. Israeli, N. Lamm and Y. Raphael, eds., *Sefer yovel likhvod morenu haga'on Rabbi Yosef Dov Soloveitchik*, Jerusalem: Mosad Harav Kook and New York: Yeshiva University, 1984, 2 vols.; see *KS* 60/1-2 no. 470.

1103.   E. Nielsen, *Law, History and Tradition, Selected Essays*, København: G.E.C. Gads Forlag, 1983, Pp.178; see *KS* 59/4 no. 5616.

1104.   M. Silberg, *Ba'in ke'e ḥad; a ṣufat devarim shebehagot uvehalakhah*, Jerusalem: Magnes Press, 1982, Pp. ii, 430; see *KS* 57/2 no. 1738.

1105.   Zorach Warhaftig, *Studies in Jewish Law* (Heb.), Ramat Gan: Bar-Ilan University, 1985, ISBN 965-226-054-1, Pp.296. - This is a collection of mainly previously published essays on central topics of Jewish law: the witness oath, arbitration, precedent, aspects of contract, family law (support of children, community of goods between spouses, coercion of *get*), the bases of tortious liability, and the plea of ignorance of the law in criminal cases *(dine nefashot)*.   B.S.J.

COMMERCIAL LAW

1106.   J. David Bleich, "Survey of Recent Halakhic Periodical Literature", *Tradition* 20 (1982), 358-367. - The author reviews halakhic opinions relevant to the sale of arms, Cholent, and the recitation of *ve-ten ṭal u'matar* by travellers.   S.M.P.

1107.   Israel Ta-Shma, "Judeo-Christian Commerce on Christian Holy Days in Medieval Germany and Provence", *Immanuel* 12 (1981), 110-122. - The author shows that in areas of Moslem dominance, Jewish authorities allowed unrestricted trade because there were no items in commerce that might violate the Jewish laws against idolatry. In the same areas, commerce with Christians was prohibited. Jewish authorities in Christian Europe, for obvious reasons of economic necessity, did not accept this stricture. Where there were both large Moslem and Christian groups, as in Provence, the employment of a Moslem "middle man" allowed retention of the prohibition in its main features.   S.M.P.

1108.   S. Warhaftig, "Restraint of Trade in Jewish Law" (Heb.), *Proceedings of the Eighth World Congress of Jewish Studies*, Division C (Jerusalem: World Union of Jewish Studies, 1982), 35-40.

See also 1270.

COMPARATIVE STUDIES

1109.   R. Borger, H. Lutzmann, W.H.P. Römer, and E. von Schüler, *Rechtsbücher*, Gütersloh: Gerd Mohn, 1982, Pp. 126, Price: DM 68.00 (Texte aus der Umwelt des alten Testaments, I/1). - A highly recommended German translation of the Sumerian, Babylonian, Assyrian, and Hittite law books; see *BL* 1983, p.98f.

1110.   H. Lazarus-Yafeh, "The Attitude to Legal Sources in Islam as Compared with Halacha" (Heb.), *Proceedings of the Eighth World Congress of Jewish Studies*, Division C (Jerusalem: World Union of Jewish Studies, 1982), 47-50.

See also 1158, 1317.

CONFIDENTIALITY

1111.   G. Tucker, "The Confidentiality Rule: A Philosophical Perspective with Reference to Jewish Law and Politics", *Fordham Urban Law Journal* 13 (1985), 99-112. - The Model Rules of Professional Conduct for lawyers, adopted in 1983 by the American Bar Association, permit (but do not require) a lawyer to disclose confidences when he reasonably believes his client will commit a future criminal act likely "to result in imminent death or substantial bodily harm" to another person. Tucker feels disclosure should be mandatory, and he would extend the requirement to cover prevention of serious harm of any kind, including harm to financial interests of property. Generalizing from examples in Jewish law, he argues that imminent specific harm to an individual should take precedence over general fears of potential harm to a client or society resulting from disclosure - and he sees just such fears as the traditional justifications for protecting confidentiality. Thus, in his view, Jewish law would agree with and support his proposal for reform of Model Rule 1.6.   D.H.P.

CONFLICT OF LAWS

See 1107.

CONTRACT

See 1105, 1172.

CONVERSION

1112.   Dan Cohn-Sherbok, "The Paradox of Reform Conversion", *JRJ* 27/1 (1980), 83-85. - The author suggests revision of the Reform Jewish conversion ceremony in order to eliminate the anomaly of a declaration of religious belief in situations where the perspective convert does not profess a belief in Deity.   S.M.P.

1113.   Steven E. Foster, "The Community Rabbinic Conversion Board - Denver Model", *JRJ* 31/3 (1984), 25-32. - A study of a Jewish inter-denominational conversion board which was an experiment in halakhic conversion procedures bringing toge ther rabbis from all Jewish denominations. The experiment has been discontinued and the reasons for its end are also studied in detail. S.M.P.

1114. Robert N. Levine and David H. Ellenson, "Jewish Tradition, Contemporary Sensibilities, and Halacha: A Responsum by Rabbi David Zvi Hoffman", *JRJ* 30/1 (1983), 49-56. - The authors analyze Hoffmann's responsum in respect to the Jewish status of a child born to a gentile mother and a Jewish father, specifically whether a twelve year old boy of such parentage, who had in fact been circumcised by a *mohel* at the age of eight days required *hatafat dam* before conversion. Hoffman decided it was unnecessary. S.M.P.

1115. Robert Levine and David Ellenson, "Rabbi Z. H. Kalischer and a Halachic Approach to Conversion", *JRJ* 28/3 (1981), 50-57. - An analysis of a responsum in which a strictly observant rabbi permits conversion to Judaism for the circumcised son of a Jewish father and a non-Jewish mother. S.M.P.

1116. A. Shaaki, "Fraud as a Ground for Nullification of Halachic Conversion", *Bar Ilan Law Studies* 3 (1984), 28-91.

See also 1238, 1243.

COPYRIGHT

See 1269, 1270.

COURTS

1117. Ya'akov Bazak, *Hashofet bedin ha'ivri*, Jerusalem: Ṣifriyat hamishpaṭ ha'ivri, 1985, Pp.52. - Judge Bazak here usefully collects classical Jewish sources on matters relating to the appointment, dignity and ethics of judges. B.S.J.

1118. H. Porat-Martin, *Rabbinical and civil courts in Israel*, Ann Arbor: University Microfilms, 1979, Pp. vi, 421; see *KS* 58/1 no. 753.

1119. Emanuel B. Quint and Neil S. Hecht, *Jewish Jurisprudence. Its Sources and Modern Applications*, Volume 2, Chur, London, Paris and New York: Harwood Academic Publishers, 1986, ISBN 3-7186 0064-1 (hard) 0293-8 (pbk), Pp. 237. - This is the second volume in a series designed to analyze and restate the substantive principles of Jewish law for the English speaking legal community. The authors have successfully achieved the objective stated in their Preface to the series: "Our objective is to present the Jewish legal system in an authentic and systematic manner. It is not a comparative study, not a literary criticism, nor an historical survey. We have striven to analyze Jewish law within its own unique framework as it was developed and formulated by the traditional halakhic authorities in the Talmud, compendiums, codes, commentaries, super-commentaries and Rabbinic responsa. Although writing in the English language, we have sought throughout to capture the spirit of halacha and its conceptual and linguistic nuances." The inclusion of the table of contents for Volume 1 is helpful in maintaining the continuity of the series and is a useful cross-reference. It also highlights the structure of the series which follows the order of *Shulḥan Arukh Ḥoshen haMishpaṭ*. In so doing, the authors follow a traditional and natural method of explicating substantive Jewish law topics by using the concise language of a code as the organizational point of departure for placing the normative law into a larger perspective. The authors trace the development of each concept from Talmudic through recent sources concluding each section with their view of the present status of Jewish law. The richness of this material is evident by the fact that Volume 2 covers the topics enumerated in Chapters 3-6 of Karo's *Ḥoshen haMishpaṭ*: The Numerical Composition of the Courts; The Manner in Which a Person May Engage in Self-Help; When Court Sessions May Be Held; and The Minimum Monetary Jurisdiction of the Court. The layman will experience an opportunity to taste the flavour of Jewish law. The scholar will find important issues reformulated in a novel way; and, on occasion, the authors develop relevant topics which have heretofore been neglected. One such example is the author's detailed analysis of the right of a community to engage in self-help where it is a party to litigation. H.B.M.

1120.   Y. Suzuki, "Juridical Administration of the Royal State in the Deuteronomic Reformation", *Seishogaku Ronshuu* 20 (1985), 50-94; see *OTA* 9/2 (1986), no.483.

See also 1155.

COVENANT - *BERIT*

1121.   P. Kalluveettil, *Declaration and covenant; a comprehensive review of covenant formulae from the Old Testament and the Ancient Near East*, Rome: Biblical Institute Press, 1982, Pp. xi, 284 (Analecta Biblica, 88); see *KS* 58/4 no. 5124.

1122.   J. W. Lee, "The New Covenant in Jeremiah", *Biblical Illustrator* 12 (1986), 24-29; see *OTA* 10/1 (1987), no.250.

1123.   Paolo Sacchi, "Legge e Patto nel'ebraismo. Una nuova prospettiva per lo studio delle fonti del Pentateuco", *Henoch* 7 (1985), 129-149; see *OTA* 9/2 (1986), no.602.

CRIMINAL LAW

1124.   Arnold D. Enker, *Duress and Necessity in the Criminal Law* (Heb.), Ramat-Gan: Bar-Ilan University, 1977, Pp.256. - While primarily devoted to the conceptual and dogmatic problems of modern criminal law, this book concludes with two chapters on Jewish law, one dealing with homicide committed under duress and necessity, the other (in collaboration with Dov Frimer) with the dividing line between necessity and self-defence in Jewish Law.   B.S.J.

1125.   Dennis H. Livingston, "The Crime of Leviticus xxiv 11", *VT* 36 (1986), 352-354; see *OTA* 10/1 (1987), no.191.

1126.   Ralph W. Scott, *A New Look at Biblical Crime*, Chicago: Nelson-Hall, 1979, Pp. xv, 211; see *KS* 57/3-4 no. 3178.

1127.   J. Weinroth, *The law of the rebellious wife* (Heb.), 1981, Pp. 566 (Tel-Aviv University thesis); see *KS* 57/3-4 no. 3357.

See also 1105, 1155, 1222.

DECALOGUE

1128.   C. Carmichael, *The Ten Commandments*, Oxford: Oxford Centre for Postgraduate Hebrew Studies, 1983, Pp. 27 (Sacks Lecture, 9).

1129.   F.-L. Hossfeld, *Der Dekalog: Seine späten Fassungen, die originale Komposition und seine Vorstufen*, Freiburg: Universitätsverlag and Göttingen, Vandenhoeck & Ruprecht, 1982, Pp. 308, Price: SF 62.00 (Orbis Biblicus et Orientalis, 45); see *BL* 1983, p.68.

1130.   R. Neudecker, *Die ersten beiden Gebote des Dekalogs in der Sicht der alten Rabbinen*, Augsburg: Katholische Akademie Augsburg, 1983, Pp. 21, (Akademie-Publikation, 22); see *KS* 58/3 no. 283.

1131.   K-D. Schunk, "Das 9 und 10 Gebot - jüngstes Glied des Dekalogs?", *ZAW* 96 (1984), 104-109. - The 9th and 10th commandments in the Decalogue consist of two prohibitions from an originally independent apodictic series. In the social conditions of the latter half of the 8th century, when injustice against the person and property was shown by the prophets to be so prevalent, these prohibitions were added and it was by this process that the Decalogue assumed its present number of commandments. A later expansion of the 10th commandment shows an altered understanding of the word "house" in its original sense of "family" or "household".   R.A.M.

DEEDS

1132.   Mordecai David Cohen, *Edut ushe ṭ arot*, Jerusalem: Makhon Yerushalayim, 1983, Pp. 420. - The question of evidence given in writing, as opposed to verbal testimony in the Court, is one of the most complicated in Jewish legal theory. The central problem is the apparent contradiction between the rejection of testimony sent in writing to the Court and the acceptance of written evidence in deeds of sale and the like. If the law refuses to recognise written evidence how are *sheṭ arot* validated? All the historical sources are surveyed, weighed and analysed in this very learned volume, though entirely on traditional lines. L.J.

DIVORCE

1133.   Ratson Arussi, "The Ethnic Factor in Rabbinical Decision-Making (Enforcement of Divorce on the Grounds of Revulsion in the Yemenite Community), *Diné Israel* 10/11 (1984), 125-177.

1134.   Judah Dick, "Is An Agreement to Deliver or Accept a *get*. in the Event of a Civil Divorce Halakhically Feasible?", *Tradition* 21/2 (1983), 91-106. - The author explores various halakhic problems attendant upon the preparation of a universal document to be executed at or prior to a marriage. This document would constitute an agreement of the parties to cooperate to achieve a halakhically valid dissolution of the marriage by the delivery and acceptance of a *get*. The author argues in favour of such an instrument and provides a sample text for it. S.M.P.

1135.   Harry B. Hunt, Jr., "Attitudes Toward Divorce in Post-Exilic Judaism", *Biblical Illustrator* 12 (1986), 62-65; see *OTA* 110/1 (1987), no.276.

1136.   L. Kahan, "Jewish Divorce and Secular Courts: The Promise of *Avitzur*", *Georget own Law Journal* 73 (1984), 193-224. - In 1983, New York's highest court upheld under contract principles a clause in a conservative *ketubah* which required a couple to appear before a rabbinical court after obtaining a civil divorce. This, of course, could help women whose ex-husbands refuse to deliver a *get*. This lengthy student casenote compares the court's decision with the New York "Jewish divorce law," a statute aimed at that same problem. The author finds constitutional defects in each approach, but argues that carefully-worded and carefully-explained clauses in a *ketubah* would be superior to the statutory approach, both in avoiding equal protection difficulties under the Fourteenth Amendment, and Establishment Clause and Free Exercise Clause obstacles under the First Amendment. Exhaustive footnotes provide citations to a number of articles on the New York statute, the *Avitzur* decision, and the agunah problem appearing in Jewish newspapers and magazines, as well as law review articles dealing with the judicial enforcement of religious marriage contracts.   D.H.P.

1137.   Bernard H. Mehlman and Rifat Sonsino, "A Reform *get*: A Proposal", *JRJ* 30/3 (1983), 31-36. - The authors present the rationale for a bill of divorce for the Reform Movement and present a proposed form for it, introduced by a discussion of its points of difference from the traditional bill of divorce.   S.M.P.

See also 1105, 1164, 1270.

EVIDENCE

1138.   D. Daube, *Witnesses in Bible and Talmud*, Oxford: Oxford Centre for Postgraduate Hebrew Studies, 1986, Pp. 39 (Oxford Centre Papers). - This booklet also contains Carmichael, no. 1295 *infra*.

1139.   Eryl W. Davies, "The Meaning of *pi senayim* in Deuteronomy xxi 17", *VT* 36 (1986), 341-347; see *OTA* 10/1 (1987), no.196.

1140.   Haim S. Hefetz, "The Place of Evidence in the Halakhah", *Diné Israel* 9 (1981-2), 51-85.

1141.   Paul G. Mosca, "Once Again the Heavenly Witness of Psalm 89:38", *JBL* 105 (1986), 27-37; see *OTA* 9/3 (1986), no.820.

1142.   N. Rakover, *Edut bishevu'ah*, Jerusalem: Ministry of Justice, 1980, Pp. 69 (Ṣ i dr at meḥ ḳar im u ṣeḳi ro t bamishpaṭ ha'ivri, 56); see *KS* 59/4 no. 6977.

1143.   Eliav Shochetman, "The Witness for the State in Jewish Law" (Heb), *Mishpaṭim* 11 (1981), 139-179. - Evidence proferred against accused by an accessory to crime in return for guaranteed immunity raises a problem of acceptability in substantive Jewish evidentiary Law for testimony proferred in return for immunity is potentially biased, thus invalid. S contends that since self incriminatory evidence is invalid insofar as it relates to the accused in Jewish Law, thus in cases where the accessory is only witness, the promise of immunity is unnecessary. It becomes necessary however either in cases where conviction of the witness is already secured by additional testimony and the witness refuses to supply the necessary testimony for conviction of the accused, or in cases where inherent judicial discretion allows self incrimination. The promise of immunity in these cases, though necessary as a means of procuring convicting evidence against the accused, also renders evidence invalid. S contends that in such cases, the Judge has inherent judicial discretion to relax formal evidential rules subject to basic considerations of reliability common to all systems. The preferred method however is that of an official ammendation *(Taḳa nah)* validating evidence rendered by the State witness in return for immunity.   M.J.P.

1144.   B. Susser, "Worthless Confessions: The Torah Approach", *New Law Journal* 130 (1980), 1056-57. - Under Jewish law, confessions are inadmissible as evidence of guilt. Susser prefers this to a system in which "voluntary" confessions are admissible. Where confessions may be used, he argues, police will try to obtain them - that is itself problematic. Where police have used or threatened harm, they may be able to persuade a jury otherwise. And even without such abuses, innocent people may incriminate themselves due to skilful interrogation, the intimidation inherent in the setting, or the power of suggestion. These dangers are even greater for those of lower intelligence. Susser indicates that "modern society" might profitably consider the Jewish approach.   D.H.P.

1145.   H. van Vliet, *Did Greek-Roman-Hellenistic law know the exclusion of the single witness?*, Franeker: T. Wever, 1980, Pp. 60; see *KS* 57/3-4 no. 3148.

See also 1105, 1155, 1207, 1287, 1288.

FAMILY LAW
See 1105.

GUARDIANSHIP

1146.   K. Reinitz, "Appointment of a Woman as a Guardian", *Bar Ilan Law Studies* 4 (1985), 167-203. - The Talmud imposes no restriction on the power of appointment of a guardian by a father, inheritor, or natural benefactor for an orphan. Women and slaves could not however be appointed as guardians, by the Judiciary. The former were restricted due to an assumption of the woman's basic domestic position rendering her unqualified to manage economic affairs of orphans put in her charge. R shows that this reasoning allowed the woman to be a guardian when specific reliance was placed upon her in financial matters by her spouse during life. Thus an assumption could be made as to a like intention of the spouse to rely upon her even after his death. R further points to a Modern Respondent, Chief Rabbi Uziel, according to whom the woman is fully capable of being appointed as a guardian by a Court, even without the express or implied agreement of her husband, this due to the changed position of women in modern society which sees women as equally capable of involvement in financial affairs, and thus of serving as guardian for the property and welfare of orphans.   M.J.P.

1147.   Y. Reinitz, "The Legal Standing of Orphans' Relatives in Jewish Law and in the Capacity and Guardian's Law (5722-1962)", *Bar Ilan Law Studies* 5 (1986), 151-180.

1148.   Y.K. Reinitz, *The Guardian of Orphans in Jewish Law* (Heb.), Jerusalem, 1984, Pp. 314 (Hebrew University Dissertation); see *KS* 59/4 no. 6010.

GIFT

See 1172.

HIRE

See 1172.

HISTORY OF JEWISH LAW

1149.   M. Elon, "The Legal System of Jewish Law", *New York University Journal of International Law and Politics* 17 (1985), 221-43. - To refute the notion that the growth of post-Talmudic halakhah was the result of mere sterile scholasticism, Elon traces the development of Jewish civil law (*mamona*), as distinct from ceremonial religious law (*isura*), from Babylon to the present. He argues that post-Talmudic judicial autonomy produced insightful and creative developments in the halakhic civil law to meet everyday problems. This post-Talmudic development over 1,300 years was chiefly facilitated by the enormous growth of Jewish case law represented by the responsa literature, embodying over 300,000 opinions. This civil law growth largely ceased with Emancipation. Post-Emancipation Jewish courts dealt mostly with ceremonial matters - matters with little room for innovation. Though Elon admits that making increased use of the halakhah as a growing supplemental source of Israeli law would be controversial and difficult, he posits that it is currently the only way to restore creativity and continued development in the Jewish civil law.   D.H.P.

1150.   Z.W. Falk, *Mavo ledine yisra'el biyeme habayit hasheni*, 2nd ed., Jerusalem: Mesharim, 1983, Pp. 388; see *KS* 58/4 no. 5297.

1151.   Z.W. Falk, *Religious Law between Eternity and Change* (Heb.), Jerusalem: Mesharim, 1986, ISBN 965-313-000-5, Pp. 146. - Sub-titled "On the Dynamism of Jewish Law in Jewish Thought and on Jewish, Christian and Muslim Attitudes towards Legal Change", this book first presents a series of rapid cameos of the views of Jewish thinkers from the Bible to Eliezer Berkovits, then looks at aspects of the phenomenon of legal change from a wide variety of interdisciplinary and comparative viewpoints: e.g. custom, public and opinion and royal edict in Jewish, Christian and Islamic sources.

B.S.J.

1152.   P. Grelot, "Elephantine. Araméens et Juifs en Egypte", *Le Monde de la Bible* 45 (1986), 32-35; see *OTA* 10/1 (1987), no.154.

1153.   Shnayer Z. Leiman, "Hazon Ish on Textual Criticism and Halakhah - A Rejoinder", *Tradition* 19/4 (1981), 301-310. - The author responds to Zvi A. Yehudah's article on Hazon Ish published in *Tradition* 18/2 (1980). He contends that Hazon Ish was not necessarily as antagonistic to textual emendation as Yehudah would have it appear. Hazon Ish was very cautious toward textual criticism, but Yehudah according to Leiman appears not to have done justice to the full scope of Hazon Ish's views.

S.M.P.

1154.   E.P. Sanders with A. I. Baumgarten and A. Mendelson, *Jewish and Christian Self-Definition, Volume Two, Aspects of Judaism in the Graeco-Roman Period*, London: SCM Press Ltd., 1981, Pp. xvi, 485, Price: £15.00 .- Part of an ambitious research project sponsored by the Canada Council, this volume considers the evidence from Jewish sources on the development towards a Jewish orthodoxy by the third century C.E., and the process by which this form of Judaism came to view itself as normative. Necessarily, considerable attention is paid to halakhic sources. Of particular interest to the historian of Jewish Law are the contributions by L.H. Schiffman, "At the Crossroads: Tannaitic Perspectives on the Jewish-Christian Schism", B.S. Jackson, "On the problem of Roman Influence on the Halakah and Normative Self-Definition in Judaism", D.W. Halivni, "The Reception Accorded to Rabbi Judah's Mishnah", and E.E. Urbach, "Self-Isolation or Self-Affirmation in Judaism in the First Three Centuries: Theory and Practice". The notes to all the articles are collected at the back and there is a single composite Bibliography, Index of Names and Index of Passages for the whole volume.

B.S.J.

1155.   Chaim Milikowski, "Law at Qumran. A Critical Reaction to Lawrence H. Schiffman, 'Sectarian Law in the Dead Sea Scroll: Courts, Testimony, and the Penal Code'", *RQ* 12 (1986), 237-249; see *OTA* 10/1 (1987), no.309.

1156.   E.E. Urbach, *Hahalakhah   mek̠ạrọteyha   vehitpat̠ḥutah*, Jerusalem: Yad LeTalmud and Givatayim: Masada, 1984, Pp. iv, 405; see *KS* 59/2-3 no. 2854.

HOMICIDE

1157.   A. Rofé, "The History of the Cities of Refuge in Biblical Law", *Beth Mikra* 31 (1985/86), 110-33 (Hebrew); see *OTA* 10/1 (1987), no.194.

1158.   Ulrich Sick, *Die Tötung eines Menschen ind ihre Ahndung in den keilschriftlichen Rechtssammlungen under Berücksichtigung rechtsvergleichender Aspekte,* Ostfildem: Copy Shop Kästl-Harmansa, 1984, 2 vols. (Inaugural-Dissertation). - This thesis is devoted primarily to homicide in the cuneiform laws, but with comparative reference to other ancient sources - Greek, Roman, Egyptian, Old German, and especially biblical. Separate treatment is accorded the various types of homicidal act and the range of legal consequences applied to them. A final major section considers the character and sources of the cuneiform legal collections. B.S.J.

HUMAN RIGHTS

1159.   Georg Braulik, "Das Deuteronomium und die Menschenrechte", *Theologische Quartalschrift* 166 (1986), 8-24; see *OTA* 10/1 (1987), no.268.

HUSBAND AND WIFE

1160.   A. Beeri, *The husband's obligation to support his wife in Israeli Law; the rebellious wife and her right to maintenance* (Heb.), Ramat-Gan, 1982, Pp. 484 (Bar-Ilan University Dissertation); see *KS* 58/4 no. 5802.

1161.   M. Chigier, *Ha'ish veha'ishah bedine yisra'el,* Jerusalem: Harry Fischel Institute, 1984, Pp. ii, 241; see *KS* 60/1-2 no. 1378.

1162.   M. Chigier, *Husband and Wife in Israeli Law,* Jerusalem: Harry Fischel Institute for Research in Talmud and Jurisprudence, 1985, Pp.281. - This is a useful summary of the legal regulation of marriage in the State of Israel. Commencing with a historical survey from the Pre-State period, the author deals successively with jurisdiction, matrimonial property, the rights of widows and divorcees, the positions of Muslim and Christian women, and the *Agunah* problem. B.S.J.

1163.   Y. Cohen, *Jewish Legislation (Talmudic Era) regarding the economic relations between spouses* (Heb.), 2 vols., Tel-Aviv University Thesis, 1980.

1164.   Hans-Aage Mink, "Indtil døden skiller jer ad. Ægteskab of skilsmisse i den antike jødedom of kristendommen", in *Tekster of Tolkninger. Ti studier i Det gamle Testamente,* ed.Kund Jeppesen & Frederick H. Cryer (Anis, 1986), 155-74. - In his article "Till death do you part" Hans-Aage Mink gives a survey of marriage and divorce in Old Testament law and storytelling. He concludes that polygamy does not seem to have been common in pre-exilic times, and argues that in post-exilic time polygamy as well as divorce has been limited as much as possible. In rabbinic literature discussions about divorce are frequent and show two main trends: a more conservative and a more liberal. The more restrictive trend can be found in the Qumran texts and in the New Testament. Monogamy is regarded as the will of God, all from creation. But in the teaching of Jesus divorce is regarded not only as something contrary to the original will of God, but as more or less belonging to the reality of human life. Monogamy is a blessed way of living, but other things than death are able to separate what God has brought toget her.   K.N.

1165.   S. Riskin, *The "moredet"; a study of the rebellious wife and her status in initiating divorce in Jewish law*, Ann Arbor: University Microfilms International, 1983, Pp. vii, 199; see *KS* 59/4 no. 6031.

1166.   B. Schereschewsky, *Dine mishp a h a h*, 3rd ed., Jerusalem: R. Mass, 1984, Pp. iv, 588; see *KS* 60/1-2 no. 1392.

1167.   Angelo Tosato, "Il transferimento dei beni nel matrimonio israelitico", *Bibbia e Oriente* 27 (1985), 129-148; see *OTA* 9/3 (1986), no.761.

1168.   Moshe Yismach, "Polygamy in Israel" (Heb), *Sinai* 92 (1983), 240-246. - An account of the development of the injunction against polygamy in Jewish Law. Y shows how the formal prohibitions against polygamy in the Middle Ages are rooted in Biblical and Talmudic tradition, both of which indicate that the practice while legally permissible was extremely rare and in fact discouraged by the authorities. Opposition to the practice was rooted in social and Halakhic considerations. In the Gaonic period the social censure was replaced by formal communal prohibitions or the introduction of a limiting clause in the marital contract, and later on by the famous injunction (*herem*) of Rabbenu Gershom. The author also examines similarities and differences in legal and social structures in polygamy.   M.J.P.

See also 1105, 1170, 1174, 1175.

INSURANCE

1169.   M. Slae, *Insurance in the Halacha*, Tel-Aviv: Israel Insurance Association, 1982, Pp. 318; see *KS* 58/4 no. 5302.

JEWISH LAW IN THE STATE OF ISRAEL

1170.   Z. Falk and D. Frimer, *Dine nisu'in*, Jerusalem: Mesharim, 1983, Pp. 178; see *KS* 59/2-3 no. 3896.

1171.   G. Leibson and P. Segal, eds., *Mishpat ivri bip şik at bet hamishpat ha'elyon*, Jerusalem: Akadmon, 1981, Pp. iv, 600; see *KS* 57/2 no. 2223.

1172.   Nahum Rakover, *HaRambam veha ḥoḳ bimedinat yisra'el*, Jerusalem: *S̱ifriy at hamishpaṭ ha'ivri*, 1985, Pp. 563. - The passing of the *Ḥoḳ Yesodot Hamishpaṭ* in 1980 has prompted an upsurge in research and educational activity in Jewish law which may come to be seen as at least as significant as any practical impact which the Law may have on the Israel legal system. Professor Rakover, Deputy Attorney-General and Adviser on Jewish Law in the Ministry of Justice, is at the very centre of this activity. This book adopts an ingenious approach to the problem of making the classical Jewish sources accessible to the Israeli legal public: Israeli civil law statutes are annotated, clause by clause, with comparable provisions taken from the Code of Maimonides. Such treatment is here accorded to statutes on the major areas of civil law: capacity, agency, contracts (general and special), security, sale, gift, hire, bailment, lost property, moveables and real property. A book like this cannot be reviewed in the normal manner: everything depends on how it will be used. And this admits of a multitude of levels, from the most superficial to the posing of the deepest conceptual and methodological problems concerning the character of Jewish law and the process of comparison itself.   B.S.J.

1173.   M. Shava, *Hadin ha'ishi beyisra'el*, Givatayim: Masada, 1983, 2nd ed., Pp. xvii, 665 (Publications of the Faculty of Law, Tel-Aviv University, 13); see *KS* 59/2-3 no. 3899.

1174.   P. Shifman, *Dine hamishpa ḥah beyisra'el*, Jerusalem: Harry Sacher Institute for Legislative Research and Comparative Law, 1984, Pp. iii, 335; see *KS* 59/2-3 no. 2458. - This book deals with family law as administered by the civil (as opposed to rabbinical) courts in Israel.

1175.   Peter Steensgaard, "Jødisk religion som faktor i israelisk indenrigspolitik", in *Religion och samhälle i Mellanöstern*, ed. J-O Blichfeldt & J. Hjärpe (Vänersborg: Plus Ultra, 1985), 161-83, ISBN 91-86668-06-4, Pp.311. - The article "Jewish religion as factor in Israeli domestic policy" has as its main aim to demonstrate the tension between orthodox religion and secular, public institutions in modern Israel. The author gives a survey of the political situation and underlines the problems of applying Halakhah in the twentieth century, e.g. in matters of marriage and divorce or matters of immigration.   K.N.

1176.   E. Tabory, "State and Religion: Religious Conflict Among Jews in Israel", *Journal of Church and State* 23 (1981), 275-83. - Tabory observes that in modern industrialized, Western nations, where "state and religion are structurally separate" and society is "not governed by religious adherence", different religions (or subgroups within a religion) can be very tolerant of each other. This is so in the United States where relations among Reform, Conservative, and Orthodox Judaism are fairly good. But when a government, such as that of Israel, links church and state, antagonism arises.

Israel has given some religions legal authority over even nonreligious members (whose membership is defined by the religion), has favoured some Jewish groups over others, and has given some Jewish symbols and observances a favoured status. In Tabory's view, a combination of political and cultural factors so far has kept protests from assuming major proportions. But further intertwining of church and state could upset that balance. To make of Israel a truly unified nation, Tabory feels a lessening of the tension is necessary.   D.H.P.

See also 1162, 1244.

JURISDICTION

1177.   R. Cover, "The Folktales of Justice: Tales of Jurisdiction", *Capital University Law Review* 14 (1985), 179-203. - In Cover's view, law is a bridge in normative space connecting the "world-that-is" with our projection of "alternative worlds that might be". As such, law along with sacred writ and myth proclaim the ideal. Courts normally charged with enforcing laws, are sometimes imperfect instruments in behalf of autonomous law when confronted with the king as the offender or as the obstacle to "Utopean reorderings of the world". To avoid their own destruction, courts sometimes decline to exercise jurisdiction over those who control armed might. Cover shows from examples drawn from the Talmud and from Josephus's Jewish Antiquities, that when, in practice, jurisdiction could not be used, religion may slant history to show a more courageous court; or a religious court may boldly claim. as a matter of doctrine only, the jurisdiction it would never dare use. Thus religion preserves the ideal as a goal when law fails to achieve it in reality.   D.H.P.

1178.   M. Shava, "The Rabbinical Courts in Israel: Jurisdiction Over Non-Jews?", *Journal of Church and State* 27 (1985), 99-112. - Israeli law currently gives rabbinical courts jurisdiction over matters of "personal status", broadly defined. The rabbis, of course, use Jewish law. Shava explores hypothetical situations in which this would subject non-Jews to the Law of Moses. Examples include estoppel (as, for example, when a person of questionable Jewish ancestry marries in a Jewish ceremony, then is sued for divorce), unilateral changes of religion (which, by law, do not defeat the jurisdiction of the court which otherwise would rule in marital matters); succession (where some heirs or legatees are non-Jewish); and referral to rabbinical courts by the president of the Israeli Supreme Court.   D.H.P.

1179.   Symposium, The Rabbinical Courts of the State of Israel, *Diné Israel* 10/11 (1984), 9-299.

See 1119.

KINGSHIP

1180. Gerald J. Blidstein, "Patrilineality and Presumption", *AJSReview* 7/8 (1982-3), 15-39.

1181. Gerald J. Blidstein, *Political Concepts in Maimonidean Halakha* (Heb.), Ramat Gan: Bar-Ilan University, 1983, ISBN 965-226-040-1, Pp.283. - There has been a resurgence of interest in recent years in Jewish political thought, not unnaturally emanating mainly from Israel. In this volume, Professor Blidstein analyses Maimonides' political concepts. He ranges over the appointment of the king, the purposes of kingship, the king and the administration of justice, legislation and the principle of 13 constitutional limitations on the king, treason, war and 'holy war' (Maimonides and Islam). B.S.J.

1182. Frank S. Frick, "Social Science Methods and Theories of Significance for the Study of the Israelite Monarchy: A Critical Review Essay", *Semeia* 37 (1986) 9-52; see *OTA* 10/1 (1987), no.151.

1183. M. Hengel, J. H. Charlesworth, and D. Mendels, "The Polemical Character of 'On Kingship' in the Temple Scroll: An Attempt at Dating 11QTemple", *JJS* 37 (1986), 28-38; see *OTA* 9/3 (1986), no.938.

1184. L. Kalugila, *The wise king; studies in royal wisdom as divine revelation in the Old Testament and its environment*, Lund: CWK Gleerup, 1980, Pp. 160 (Coniectanea Biblica, 15); see *KS* 57/3-4 no. 3082.

KINSHIP

1185. *Judaism*, No. 133, Vol. 34.1, Winter, 1985, is devoted to a symposium on Patrilineal Descent. The historian, Dr. Shaya J.D. Cohen, traces the development from an original patrilineal descent to the matrilineal as it has existed for well-nigh two thousand years. Cohen himself refuses to comment on whether, as some Reform Rabbis in the U.S.A. have advocated, patrilineal as well as matrilineal descent be now accepted, so that a child would have Jewish status if one of its parents were Jewish irrespective of whether it is the mother or the father. The participants in the symposium, drawn from all sections of the religious community, discuss Cohen's analysis and also consider whether the suggested change be adopted. Naturally, all the Orthodox and most of the Conservative participants are against the change. The symposium is valuable, too, in that it throws light on how scholars view the whole question of whether history should have a voice in determining *Halakhah*. L.J.

LAW OF WAR

1186.   J. David Bleich, "Preemptive War in Jewish Law", *Tradition* 21/1 (1983), 3-41. - The author analyses the Jewish law on warfare with regard to the Israeli operations in Lebanon in the summer of 1982. He argues that determination of the halakhic propriety of the Israeli incursion into Lebanon is contingent both upon accurate analysis of points of fact as well as resolution of questions of Jewish law. Nevertheless, he contends, it is beyond dispute, as a matter of fact and a matter of halakhah, that once hostilities have commenced Israel must prevail because it can not afford the luxury of military defeat. When the threat of such defeat looms military action assumes the guise of obligatory war "to deliver Israel from the enemy."

                                                                        S.M.P.

1187.   A. Rofé, "The Laws of Warfare in the book of Deuteronomy: Their Origins, Interest and Positivity", *JSOT* 32 (1985), 23-44. - A comparison of the Deuteronomic laws of warfare with practices which are recorded as obtaining before the monarchy shows that the Deuteronomic. laws are much later and date from the mid-monarchic period. For all that they are now scattered in the law code the war laws were once a unified corpus. They can be traced to three levels of redaction. The first comprised 24:5, 23:10-14, 20:14, 19-29, 21:10-14. This was redacted by Ds (*sōphetîm*) whose work appears in 20:5-7,1. Two further Deuteronomic additions occur, D2 (20:15-18) and Dp (priest) portraying the role of the priest in battle. These three redactional levels span the period of Josiah's reform. The Deuteronomic laws calling for humanity in war were addressed to the militia, not to professional soldiers. This accounts for their theoretical nature, one element of which was the call not to fear even before large armies. It was this quixotic understanding which led to Josiah's defeat and death.   R.A.M.

1188.   Aaron Soloveichik, "Waging War on Shabbat," *Tradition* 20/3 (1982), 179-187. The author considers warfare on Shabbat from three perspectives: legitimate war *per se;* the saving of human life; and the murderous pursuer. He asserts that war can be waged on Shabbat from all three perspectives provided the war is a *milḥemet mitsvah.*   S.M.P.

See 1106.

LEGAL PERSONALITY

1189.   H.W. Robinson, *Corporate Personality in Ancient Israel,* Edinburgh: T & T Clark, 1981, Pp. 64, Price: £1.95 - This edition has a different modern introduction to that noted at *Survey* no. 708 (*JLA* V); see BL 1983, p.94.

LEGAL PROFESSION

1190.   D. Frimer, "The Role of the Lawyer in Jewish Law", *Journal of Law and Religion* 1 (1983), 297-305. - The American adversary legal system treats the clash of lawyers as vital to the discovery of the truth by a nonparticipant fact finder. The Jewish legal system, however, needs no lawyers; the judge is an active participant in the search for truth, aided in past times by students, and the direct confrontation of the parties is thought more productive of truth and less of litigation than the meddling of lawyers. Lawyers have gradually obtained a limited role in Jewish law, and in the Israeli Rabbinical Courts, but not as indispensable participants - and it is preferred that they neither advise clients on litigable matters nor counsel them on how to legally arrange their affairs for maximum advantage.
D.H.P.

LEGAL REASONING

1191.   Michael L. Chernick, *Hermeneutical Studies in Talmudic and Midrashic Literatures* (Heb.), Lod: Makhon Haberman lemeḥḳe re siฅut, 1984, Pp. iv, 175; see *KS* 60/1-2 no. 471.

1192.   Shulamit Darans, "Formalism and Informalism in the Rabbinical Courts of Israel", *Diné Israel* 10/11 (1984), 27-124 .

1193.   David Ellenson, "Jewish Legal Interpretation: Literary, Scriptural, Social, and Ethical Perspectives", *Semeia* 34 (1985), 93-114; see *OTA* 9/3 (1986), no.934.

1194.   Michael Fishbane, *Biblical Interpretation in Ancient Israel*, Oxford: Clarendon Press, 1985, ISBN 0-19-826325-2, Pp.xi, 613, Price: £40.00. - This is a major work in biblical scholarship, developing a theory of "inner biblical exegesis" in which the interpretation of biblical documents by other biblical documents is traced. Of particular interest to readers of the Annual is the fact that a major section of the book (pp.91-277) is devoted to legal exegesis. In chapter 9 (231-77), the author offers his conclusions on the nature of the ancient Israelite legal tradition, as emerging from this analysis. This is an important contribution to the study of biblical law.   B.S.J.

1195.   Yitzhak D. Gilat, *R. Eliezer ben Hyrcanus, A Scholar Outcast*, Ramat-Gan, Bar-Ilan University Press, 1984, ISBN 965-226-043-6, Pp.536. - This is a welcome English translation of Gilat's 1968 book, which studies the legal methodology of R. Eliezer and his substantive halakhic teachings (mainly on ritual matters), concluding with an assessment of his place in the history of the halakhah.   B.S.J.

1196.   Tsvi Groner, *The Legal Methodology of Hai Gaon*, Chico Ca.: Scholars Press, 1985, ISBN 0-89130-748-6, Pp.xvii, 209, Price $24.95 (cloth),

$19.95 (pbk.) (Brown Judaic Studies 66). - Developed from a Hebrew University doctoral thesis, this is a study of the responsa of Hai Gaon, 11th century Gaon of Pumbeditha. As the author points out, legal methodology, especially for the process of adjudication, was not well-defined in this early period, and much depended upon the personal bent of the respondent. Nevertheless, Hai Gaon is much concerned with principles of adjudication derived from the Talmud - both formal (e.g. 'follow the majority') and substantive principles. The book is well documented, and includes a useful descriptive bibliography of gaonic responsa and their manuscript sources.

B.S.J.

1197.   Efraim Itzchaky, *The Halacha in Targum Jerushalmi I (Pseudo-Jonathan Ben-Uziel) and its exegetic methods* (Heb.), Ramat-Gan, 1982, Pp. 301 (Bar-Ilan University Dissertation); see *KS* 58/4 no. 5294.

1198.   C. Perelman, "Juridical Ontology and Sources of Law", *Northern Kentucky Law Review* 10 (1983), 387-97. - Perelman examines how the perception of the source of a nation's law influences its claim to authority and the proper way to work legal reform. Under our original system of common law, "law" already existed and judges merely discovered it. Change through legislation was then viewed with distrust as a departure from the normal manner in which laws were to be formulated. Therefore, common law judges construed statutes in a restrictive manner. In France, law flows from the people and only the people (through the legislature) can change it; judges are to apply without compunction whatever laws are provided. But Jewish law is postulated to come from God; man has not power to work any change. Faced with inequities in applying the biblical laws, the rabbis found a solution: the *interpretation* of law was left by God to man. Through free "interpretation", extraction of general rules of equity from the laws, and the use of fictions, flexibility is preserved.   D.H.P.

1199.   Kenneth J. Weiss, "Freehof's Methodology as A Reform Jewish Halachist", *JRJ* 32/3 (1985), 58-69. - The author analyzes the methods of responsa preparation used by Solomon B. Freehof, the pre-eminent responsa author in the Reform movement. The author concludes that Freehof's criteria are consistent, combining both traditional and Reform elements, and that he emphasizes the principle of looking beneath the letter of the law to its ethical basis. The criteria are in general harmony with tradition, yet go beyond what contemporary traditional correspondents use in framing replies to halakhic inquiries.   S.M.P.

1200.   D. Zafrany, *The Asheri's Methodology in Deciding the Law* (Heb.), 1980, Pp. xi, 275 (Tel-Aviv University thesis); see *KS* 57/3-4 no. 3358.

See also 1283.

LEVIRATE

1201.   H.F. Richter, "Zum Levirat im Buch Ruth", *ZAW* 95 (1983), 123-6. - The relation between Ruth and Boaz in Ruth c.4 fits more a case of Levirate marriage than that of a "Redeemer" (*gô'el*) marriage. The practice seems to reflect a situation earlier than that of *Deut*.25:5-10, *Ruth* 4:14f, represents an erroneous attempt to restore the text.   R.A.M.

LITERARY FORM

1202.   Pinchas Doron, "Motive Clauses in the Laws of Deuteronomy: Their Forms, Functions, and Contents", *Hebrew Annual Review* 2 (1978), 61-77; see *OTA* 9/2 (1986), no.507.

LOST PROPERTY
See 1172.

MARRIAGE

1203.   Norman E. Frimer and Dov I. Frimer, "Reform Marriages in Contemporary Halakhic Responsa", *Tradition* 21/3 (1984), 7-39. - The authors identify three positions on Reform Jewish marriages which traditionalist authorities have asserted. First is the position which renders Reform Marriages invalid *ab initio* and thus necessitates no need for Jewish divorce proceedings. Second is the position that does admit a measure of halakhic validity to Reform Marriages. Third is the position which would seek to determine the validity of the marriages on a case by case basis.
                                                                          S.M.P.

See also 1243.

MEDICO-LEGAL PROBLEMS

1204.   J. David Bleich, "Survey of Recent Halakhic Periodical Literature", *Tradition* 21 (1984), 80-90. - The author reviews material on physicians strikes, nuclear warfare, and Hanukkah lights for travellers.
                                                                          S.M.P.

1205.   J. David Bleich, "Survey of Recent Halakhic Periodical Literature", *Tradition* 20/3 (1982), 254-264. - The author discusses material on prostate surgery.   S.M.P.

1206.   Richard A. Block, "A Matter of Life and Death: Reform Judaism and the Defective Child", *JRJ* 31/4 (1984), 14-30. - The author argues that no single, standard, criterion or principle will be adequate for every situation. The best approach is seen as a combination of principles and tests presented by the author, which are to be applied as carefully and as narrowly as possible. Should the decision of whether or not to provide life-prolonging treatment to a defective child remain in doubt after the conscientious application of principles and tests, which are derived from tradition, the tradition demands a decision in favour of life.   S.M.P.

1207.   Paul Kahn, "Psychotherapy and the Commandment to Reprove", *PAOJS* 7 (1983), 37-49. - The purpose of the paper is to amplify the law of reproof and its application to psychotherapy, although the author's conclusions are explicitly not to be taken as a *peṣak din*. The author suggests that good psychotherapy might well provide an occasion for reproof if the therapist knows how to reprove.   S.M.P.

1208.   Fred Rosner, "Test Tube Babies, Host Mothers, and Genetic Engineering", *Tradition* 19/2 (1981), 141-148. - The author briefly reviews the matters of artificial insemination, test tube babies, host mothers, and genetic engineering, providing a brief statement of the halakhic view of each where such a view has been propounded. He concludes with a call to rabbis to examine these issues in a halakhic context so that they may offer Jewish legal guidance to both medical and lay communities.   S.M.P.

1209.   Fred Rosner, "Jewish Ethical Issues in Hazardous Medical Therapy", *Tradition* 19/1 (1981), 55-58. - The author argues that the basic tenet of Judaism is the supreme value of human life. Therefore when life is threatened, even when there is no hope for survival for a prolonged period but only for a very short time all commandments of the Bible are set aside. Any act which can prolong life supersedes all commandments except the three cardinal ones.   S.M.P.

1210.   S. Shilo, "Operations for the Terminally Ill" (Heb), *Mishpaṭim* 12 (1982), 565-574. - S argues that a recent High Court decision upholding a hospital's refusal to permit an experimental operation to a terminally ill patient, is at variance with Jewish Law. According to Jewish Law, in such cases the slight chance of long term survival is to be preferred against immediate short term survival. The variables are medical opinion regarding the risk factor and the patient's agreement. S argues that modern Responsa indicate that given the patient's agreement, even where the prevalence of medical opinion determines a high immediate risk factor, with minute chance of success, nonetheless the operation would be permitted assuming that the alternative is imminent death.   M.J.P.

1211.   Moshe Halevi Spero, "Halakhic Definitions of Confidentiality in the Psychotherapeutic Encounter: Theory and Practice," *Tradition* 20 (1982), 298-326. - The author compares general ethical perspectives with halakhic perspectives in respect to a patient's right to privacy and the professional's obligation to maintain (or to divulge) professional secrets. The matter of secrecy and confidence-bearing as a necessary good and right is explicated. There is also an examination of the value of confidentiality in regard to practical applications, including diagnostic conferences, situations involving danger to the patient or others, and professional testimony.   S.M.P.

1212.   Moshe Halevi Spero, "Further Examination of the Halakhic Status of Homosexuality: Female Homosexual Behavior as *Ones*", *PAOJS* 7 (1983), 99-122. - While the halakhically-observant mental health professional can not treat homosexuals who wish to be accepted as homosexuals or to have their sexual life style "improved" or even condoned, or even refer such persons to other mental health professionals, the halakhah does accept in principle the value of psychotheraputically modifying the homosexual toward heterosexuality or lessened homosexual behavior, notwithstanding some ethical objections to some current techniques used for this. The use of the concept of *ones*, compulsion, is of limited value in these matters and does not render acceptable or less sinful homosexual acts committed in a non-psychotic state and in full awareness of halakhic opinion on the matter.   The fact that the halakhically competent professional maintains specific moral beliefs about homosexual behavior does not preclude *professional* attitudes of empathy and sensitivity.   S.M.P.

1213.   Moshe Halevi Spero, "Toward a Halakhic Perspective on Radical forms of Psychological Manipulation and Behavior Control", *PAOJS* 7 (1983), 71-97. - The author demonstrates that current radical forms of psychotherapy may represent a potentially serious ethical challenge to our notion of freedom and to the idea of willful participation in the psycho-therapeutic process. A halakhic model for "radical intervention" is presented on the admittedly incomplete and problematic analog of *kofin oto ad sheyomar rotseh ani*. The halakhah is not able to accept the view that a person is not born free but rather subservient to genes and education.   S.M.P.

See also 1081, 1242, 1243, 1244, 1269, 1270.

NEW TESTAMENT

1214.   W.G. Boulton, *Is Legalism a Heresy?*, New York: Paulist Press, 1982, Pp. 130; see *KS* 59/2-3 no. 2458.

1215. J. Duncan M. Derrett, *Studies in the New Testament*, vol. IV: *Midrash, the Composition of Gospels, and Discipline*, Leiden: E.J. Brill, 1986, ISBN 90 04 07478 3, Pp. x, 244, Price: Gld. 112. - The first three volumes in this series were noted at *Survey* nos. 228 (*JLA* II) and 952 (*JLA* VI). Twelve further articles are here reprinted. Of particular interest to historians of Jewish law are those on "'Behuqey Hagoyim', Damascus Document IX,1 Again" (from *RQ* XI (1983), 409-15) and "Binding and Loosing" (from *JBL* CII (1983), 112-17). It is a pity that the opportunity has not been taken to include rabbinic sources in the indices sources in these volumes. B.S.J.

1216. E.P. Sanders, *Paul, the Law and the Jewish People,* Philadelphia: Fortress Press, 1983, ISBN 0-8006-0698-1, pp.xi, 227, Price $19.95; London: SCM Press, 1985, ISBN 334-01208-X, pp.xi, 227, Price: £8.50 (pbk.). - Sanders considers Paul's diverse statements on the law as responding to a variety of different questions (e.g. soteriology and ethics), and as not amounting to a coherent system. Paul struggled with these questions to the very end of his life. The author also discusses Paul's relations with his fellow Jews. He concludes that Paul's thought was largely Jewish, and that his work as apostle to the Gentiles is to be understood within the framework of Jewish eschatological speculation. B.S.J.

See also 1302.

OATH

1217. G. Giesen, *Die Wurzel sb' "schwören": Eine semasiologische Studie zum Eid im Alten Testament,* Bonn: P. Hanstein, 1981, Pp. xii, 445, Price: DM 98.00 (Bonner Biblische Beiträge, 56); see *BL* 1983, p.65.

OBLIGATIONS

1218. Berechyahu Lifschitz, *"Mattanah Le-hud* - Acquisition and Obligation in Contrast", *Diné Israel* 12 (1985), 125-155.

1219. Abraham Weingort, "Volonté et acte formel dans la structure juridique de l'obligation contractuelle en droit talmudique", *Revue historique de droit français et étranger* 64/2 (1986), 191-203. - Talmudic law occupies a middle position between consensualism, which dominates the concept of contractual obligation in Roman law, and the "real" character of the contract, as found in both Greek law and other legal systems of antiquity. Certainly, it attaches considerable importance to the formal act (*ķinyan*) as a constitutive element in the obligation. But such an act is not essential when the internal resolve of the contracting parties (*gemirat da'at*) can independently be made known in a sufficiently clear manner. In the last analysis, the formal act is only one form of expression of the will of the parties - which is itself the primary foundation of contractual obligation.

(A.W., trld B.S.J.)

PARENT AND CHILD

1220. J. Fleishman, *Legal aspects of parent-child relationships in the Bible and the Ancient Near East* (Heb.), Ramat-Gan: Bar-Ilan University, 1981, Pp. 263; see *KS* 57/3-4 no. 3030.

PENALTIES

1221. J. Bazak, *Ha'anishah hapelilit, darkeyha ve'i kronoteyha*, Jerusalem and Tel-Aviv: Dvir, 1981, Pp. 320; see *KS* 57/2 no. 2213.

1222. Richard A. Block, "'Death, Thou Shall Die': Reform Judaism and Capital Punishment", *JRJ* 30/2 (Spring 1983), 1-10 - The author argues that although Jewish sources show that one could not say Jewish tradition opposed capital punishment in practice, there is still ample basis in rejecting it.   S.M.P.

1223. Haim H. Cohn, "Is Hanging a Mode of Execution in Jewish Law?" (Heb.), *Proceedings of the Eighth World Congress of Jewish Studies*, Division C (Jerusalem: World Union of Jewish Studies, 1982), 19-28.

PRIVACY
See 1211.

PROCEDURES

1224. Eberhard Klingenberg, "Urteil, Schiedsspruch und Vergleich im römischen, griechischen und jüdischen Recht", in *"Wie gut sind Deine Zelte, Jaakow..."*, *Festschrift zum 60. Geburtstag von Reinhold Mayer*, ed. E.L. Ehrlich, B. Klappert and U. Ast, Gerlingen: Bleicher Verlag, 1986, pp.63-75.

See also 1105, 1190, 1243.

PROPERTY

1225. J.A. Dearman, *Property Rights in the Eighth-Century Prophets*, Ann Arbor: University Microfilms, 1981, Pp. 301; see *KS* 58/1 no. 100.

1226. Y. Grossman, *Sefer She'elot uteshuvot mashkenot yisra'el, al hilkhot batim meshutafim venizke shekeynim*, Jerusalem: Z. Grossman, 1984, Pp. xiii, 159; see *KS* 59/2-3 no. 2821.

1227.   Shmuel Shilo, "Split Ownership Rights in Property according to Jewish Law", *Diné Israel* 12 (1985), 173-193.

1228.   R. Westbrook, "The Price Factor in the Redemption of Land", *Revue Internationale des Droits de l'Antiquité* 32 (1985), 97-127.

See also 1172, 1218, 1328.

PUBLIC LAW

1229.   Shimon Bakon, "The Biblical Concept of Government", *Dor leDor* 14 (1985), 16-25; see *OTA* 9/2 (1986), no.320.

1230.   G. Blidstein, "Medieval Public Law - Sources & Concepts", *Diné Israel* 9 (1981-2), 127-165.

1231.   Mark R. Cohen, *Jewish Self-Government in Medieval Egypt; the Origins of the Office of Head of the Jews, ca. 1065-1126*, Princeton: Princeton University Press, 1982, ISBN 91-7728-194-2, Pp. 135; see further *KS* 57 no.372.

1232.   B. Halpern, *The Constitution of the Monarchy in Israel*, Chico CA: Scholars Press, 1981, Pp. xxviii, 410, Price: $18.00 (Harvard Semitic Monographs, 25); see *BL* 1983, p.86.

1233.   Walter Jacob, "The Right to Create a New Congregation", *JRJ* 32 (Spring 1985), 59-61. - A Responsum. The author holds that in a large Jewish Community nothing should stand in the way of attempting to establish a new congregation if that seems desirable to some members of the community. Tradition favours the establishment of synagogues that satisfy the needs of the worshippers.   S.M.P.

1234.   Ze'ev Safrai, "The Administrative Structure of Judea in the Roman and Byzantine Period", *Immanuel* 13 (1981), 30-38. - The author attempts to follow the administrative changes in the region of Judea and Idumea from the end of the Second Temple period until the Arab conquest. He assumes that all of Palestine was divided into administrative blocs, whose boundaries also reflected economic realities. The boundaries remained unchanged during the period considered, although the status of the district might have shifted, a new capital established, etc.   S.M.P.

RESPONSA

1235.   Robert Brody, *Halachic responsa of R. Natronai Bar Hilai Gaon (Heb.)*, Jerusalem, 1981, Pp. 442 (Hebrew University Dissertation); see *KS* 58/3 no. 3596.

1236.   M. Elon, ed., *Maf te a ḥ hashe'elot vehateshuvot shel ḥokhme ṣefarad utsefon afrika: Hamafteaḥ hahistori I*, Jerusalem: Magnes Press for Hamakhon leḥeker hamishpaṭ ha'ivri, 1981, Pp. xxxiii, 282; see *KS* 58/1 no. 266.

1237.   M. Elon, ed., *Maf te a ḥ hashe'elot vehateshuvot shel ḥokhme ṣefarad utsefon afrika: maft eaḥ hame ḳoṛo t I*, Jerusalem: Magnes Press for Hamakhon leḥeker hamishpaṭ ha'ivri, 1981, Pp. xxxiii, 328; see *KS* 58/1 no. 267.

1238.   Rabbi Moshe Feinstein, *Iggerot Moshe, Or a ḥ Ḥayyim*, Part 4; *Yoreh De'ah*, Part 3, Bene Berak: Yeshivat Ohel Moshe, 1981, Pp.556, Price £10.50. - This is the sixth volume of Responsa by the veteran *poseḳ* for the Orthodox world. Among the interesting Responsa are two which advocate censorship(!) of a work published from manuscript, allegedly by Judah the Saint of Regensburg, on the grounds that it denies the Mosaic authorship of parts of the Pentateuch. All the Responsa deal with religious law, among these: what are the religious grounds for outlawing drug-taking?; dialogue with Christians; the use of hypnotism for medicinal purposes, are teachers in a Yeshivah allowed to go on strike in protest at a delay in the payment of their salary?; may Sunday be a free day in a Yeshivah, being a Christian day of worship? There are a number of Responsa on conversion procedures and on charity distribution.   L.J.

1239.   Peter J. Haas, "Toward a Semiotic Study of Jewish Moral Discourse: The Case of Responsa", *Semeia* 34 (1985), 59-83; see *OTA* 9/3 (1986), no.902.

1240.   Peter J. Haas, "Responsa Reconsidered", *JRJ* 30/3 (1983), 37-42. - The author argues that there is indeed a place for the writing of responsa in Reform Judaism since it would be beneficial if one could show that the Jewish tradition, even in its classic sources, was more open to diversity than modern traditionalism would care to admit.   S.M.P.

1241.   Judah Herzl Henkin, *She'elot uteshuvot Bene Vanim*, Jerusalem, Weiss Mekor Barukh, 1981, Pp. 226. - These Responsa and other essays of the District Rabbi of Bet Shean deal with the contemporary situation in the State of Israel, discussing, for instance, the vexed question of how much separation between the sexes in the synagogue; the presence of the husband while his wife is in labour; artificial methods of contraception; artificial insemination; naming adopted children and their status in law; libelling others in order to prevent them doing harm; the rescue by force of hostages from terrorists and hijackers. The volume includes a tribute to the author's famous grandfather, Rabbi Elijah Henkin of New York.   L.J.

1242.   Rabbi Joel Teitelbaum, *Divre Yoel*, Brooklyn, New York: Jerusalem Book Store Publishing House, 1982, 2 Volumes, Pp. 95, Price:

£40.00. - Rabbi Teitelbaum, who died a year or two ago, was famed as a Hasidic Rebbe but achieved a reputation as an outstanding Halakhist when he was Rabbi of Sotmar in pre-war Hungary. This collection of Responsa covers both periods of the Rabbi's activity. Of especial interest are the series of Responsa in which Rabbi Teitelbaum debates the question of artificial insemination (AID) with Rabbi Moshe Feinstein, who has argued that in Jewish law it is the act of intercourse that constitutes adultery not the injection of semen. The debate has consequences over above this particular question since, on the basis of *Leviticus* (18:20) Rabbi Teitelbaum holds that it is the injection of semen that affects the status of the child (though, he agrees, the act of intercourse constitutes adultery even where there is no seminal emission). This leads to a wider discussion of how far present-day authorities are justified in applying Scriptural exegesis of their own in determining the law. The publishers have done no service to the late Rabbi by adding the vehement Responsa, written many years ago, in which he expresses in very intemperate terms his views on Rabbi Kook, "the notorious Chief Rabbi".   L.J.

1243.   Rabbi Issar Yehudah Unterman, *Shevet Yehudah*, First and Second Series, Jerusalem, Mosad Harav Kook, 1983, pp. 503 .- In these responsa and legal essays, the former Chief Rabbi of Israel applies in a novel way the methods he had learned in his youth in Lithuanian Yeshivot to the solution of contemporary problems. Most of the luminaries in these Yeshivot were theoreticians, only indirectly concerned with practical *Halakhah*. A prominent halakhic guide like Rabbi Unterman could not afford the luxury of pure theory, though this analysis of legal concepts falls in no way short of that of his teachers and, in fact, gains much from the need for definite application in concrete situations. Among the topics discussed are: the principles of *piķ uah   nefesh* (life saving); the reliability of the testimony of doctors for the purpose of the religious law (e.g. whether it is necessary to eat on Yom Kippur); marriage and divorce laws and questions of status; heart transplants; conversion procedures; and the differences of function between the clerks to the Court in Talmudic times in our own day.   L.J.

1244.   Rabbi Eliezer Waldinberg, *She'elot uteshuvot Tsits Eliezer*, Vol. 15, Jerusalem; Itah Publishing House, 1983, Pp. 200. - Rabbi Waldinberg's output is astonishing. This is the 15th volume of his Responsa, many of them dealing with medical questions, on which he is a world authority. In response to an appeal by a doctor, Waldinberg here comes out strongly against cigarette smoking because the evidence shows it can be damaging to health and argues further that non-smokers are entitled in Jewish law to stop others smoking in the same room. There is a lengthy essay on the status and authority of *Bate din* in the State of Israel and elsewhere in the Jewish world.   L.J.

See also 1196.

RITUAL LAW

1245.   Charles L. Arian and Clifford E. Librach, "The 'Second Day' of Rosh Hashanah: History, Law, and Practice", *JRJ* 32/3 (1985), 70-83. - The authors examine the history and reasoning behind the two-day observance of the New Year in terms of halakhah and aggadah, the codes, and other traditional literature. The examination is attempted from both traditional and liberal perspectives.   S.M.P.

1246.   W.A.M. Beuken, "Exod. 16.5,23: A Rule Regarding the Sabbath?", *JSOT* 32 (1985), 3-14. - A detailed examination of *Exod.* 16.5,23 shows that the former verse predicts a miracle in which the manna gathered on the 6th day will prove to be a double amount. Verse 23 says that the extra for the sabbath need not be cooked on the 6th day because it will miraculously keep fresh (unlike any manna left over on other days). Neither verse, therefore, anticipates later Jewish practice which forbade the cooking of food on the 7th day. They insist only that none must be gathered and are not, therefore, contradictory.   R.A.M.

1247.   Philip C. Hammond, David J. Johnson & Richard N. Jones, "A Religio-Legal Nabataean Inscription from the Atargatis/Al-Uzza Temple at Petra", *BASOR* 263 (1986), 77-80; see *OTA* 10/1 (1987), no.94.

See also 1195, 1285.

SALE

See 1172.

SECURITY

1248.   Y. Kaplan, "Elements of Tort in the Jewish Law of Surety" (Heb.), *Shenaton Ha-Mishpat Ha-Ivri* 9-10 (1982-3), 359-396.

1249.   Shalom Lerner, *Elements of the law of pledges in Jewish Law* (Heb.), 1980, Pp. 366 (Hebrew University thesis); see *KS* 57/3-4 no. 3359.

1250.   Chaim Povarsky, "The Lien on Property according to Jewish Law" (Heb), *Diné Israel* 12 (1984-85), 155-172. - Lien in Jewish Law differs from other systems wherein it is an inherent result of a debt, requiring no formal act. P examines the source of Lien, the normative distinctions between real or movable property, and examines possible explanations for its efficacy. Seen as an inherent result of a debt, its source may be found in the notion of a person's property (as opposed to movables) naturally guaranteeing the loan, due to their being in effect an extension of the person and the public knowledge of a person's real assets. An alternative explanation sees it as a separate acquisition, co-existing with the loan but not organically bound to it. Both concepts emphasize the element of personal liability attached to the Lien, thus the phenomena of limited liability for legally created bodies is problematic in Jewish Law. Modern Responsa offers tentative solutions, seeing "limited company" either as an extension of powers granted to public bodies, not limited by laws governing individuals or as the result of specific commitment by shareholders to limit their personal liability to specifically defined objects, thus creating a separate object of liability which in effect constitutes the "company". M.J.P.

1251. J. Shapiro, "The Shetar's Effect on English Law: A Law of the Jews Becomes the Law of the Land", *Georgetown Law Journal* 71 (1983), 1179-1200. - Shapiro explains in detail the development, in England, of contractual security interests in realty as derived from Jewish practice. The development covers the period 1066-1285 A.D. So long as Jews were the sole source of capital on interest, and profits derived from their transactions were susceptible to taxation to enrich the royal treasury, the English kings found it profitable to enforce their liens despite feudal traditions to the contrary. When Christians were later enabled to charge interest, the need for Jews as lenders diminished, but the law had become established. The forms of relief for non-payment of lien-accompanied debt formerly available only to Jews were now extended to Christian creditors. D.H.P.

See also 1172.

SELF-HELP

1252. E. Ben Zimra, "Use of Force for the Prevention of Crime", *Diné Israel* 9 (1981-2), 85-113.

1253. Shimshon Ettinger, *Self Help in Jewish Law* (Heb.), Jerusalem, 1982, Pp. 301 (Hebrew University Dissertation); see *KS* 58/3 no. 4115.

SEXUAL OFFENCES

1254. G.J. Wenham, "Why Does Sexual Intercourse Defile?", *ZAW* 95 (1983), 432-34. - The distinction of life and death is fundamental to Israel's concept of holiness. God who is perfect life is the ultimately holy. All the conditions described in *Lev.* 12 & 15 are polluting because they incur loss of "life liquids", for example blood (17:11,14), which is why a woman in menstruation is unclean. In the same way male semen must be seen as a "life-liquid" and so its loss, whether long-term (15:1-15) or temporarily (15:16-18) is polluting. R.A.M.

See also 1212.

SLAVERY

1255.   I. Cardellini, *Die biblischen "Sklaven"-Gesetze im Lichte des keilschriftlichen Sklavenrechts*, Bonn: P. Hanstein, 1981, Pp. xxvii, 441 (Bonner Biblische Beiträge, 55).

1256.   Carlos Alfonso Fontela, "Le esclavitud a través de la Biblia", *Estudios Bíblicos* 43 (1985), 89-124; see *OTA* 9/3 (1986), no.731.

1257.   Ayala Levy, *Aspects of Bondage and Release in the Bible* (Heb.), Ann Arbor: University Microfilms, 1981, Pp. 215; see *KS* 58/1 no. 85.

1258.   N. Naaman, "HABIRU and Hebrews: The Transfer of a Social Term to the Literary Sphere", *JNES* 45 (1986), 282-287; see *OTA* 10/1 (1987), no.166.

1259.   J.P.J. Olivier, *The Old-Babylonian mesarum-edict and the Old Testament*, Stellenbosch: University Library, 1981, Pp. viii, 362, 7 microfiches; see *KS* 58/1 no. 124.

1260.   A.J. Phillips, "The Law of Slavery: Exodus 21:2-11", *JSOT* 30 (1984), 51-66. - Parallels for the law of slavery in the Book of the Covenant should not be sought in comparisons with Ancient Near Eastern literature because it expresses "a statement of belief about the true nature of Israelite society". *Exod.* 21:2 refers not to the foreigner captured in war, but to the native Israelite who is forced into slavery for economic reasons. Since Israel is a society of freedom it is important that provision be made for restoring a member of that society to his true place. By removing the economic restraint against claiming freedom and extending the law to the female Israelite slave *Deut.*15:12-18 seeks to extend the promises of the law of slavery in B.

R.A.M.

See also 1303.

SOCIAL PROTECTION

1261.   Léon Epsztein, *Social Justice in the Ancient Near East and the People of the Bible*, London: SCM Press, 1986, ISBN 0-334-0233-4-3, Pp.xii, 178, Price: £7.95. - An English translation of *La Justice Sociale dans le Proche-Orient ancien et le Peuple de la Bible*, noted in *Survey* no. 1010 (*JLA* VI). B.S.J.

1262.   Leslie Hoppe, "Deuteronomy and the Poor", *The Bible Today* 24 (1986), 371-375; see *OTA* 10/1 (1987), no.193.

1263.   Rui De Menezes, "Social Justice in Israel's Law", *Bible Bhashyam* 11 (1985), 10-16; see *OTA* 9/2 (1986), no.598.

1264.   Jacques Pons, *L'Oppression dans l'Ancien Testament*, Paris: Letouzey et Ané, 1981, Pp. i, 250, FF 120.00; see *BL* 1983, p.75.

1265.   Carroll Stuhlmacher, "Justice toward the Poor", *The Bible Today* 24 (1986), 385-390; see *OTA* 10/1 (1987), no.293.

SOURCES (INTERTESTAMENTAL)

1266.   Torleif Elgvin, "Tempelrullen fra Qumran", *Tidsskrift for Teologi og Kirke* 1 (1985), 1-21. - The Temple Scroll from Qumran attests the great influence of Priests and Levites on the sect. The scroll is first of all concerned with matters of holiness and purity. It presents itself as a genuine Torah, with special interest in calendar, in the arrangement of the temple, and in the rules concerning the purity of the temple and the temple-city. The purpose of the scroll is not to replace the Pentateuch, but to clarify how the temple and the temple-cult should be, according to the Essenes. By this the scroll legitimates the sect and its dissociation from the unclean cult in Jerusalem.   K.N.

1267.   Emil Schürer, *The History of the Jewish people in the age of Jesus Christ*, revised and edited by Geza Vermes, Fergus Millar and Martin Goodman, Edinburgh, T. & T. Clark Ltd., Vol. III.1, 1986, ISBN 0-567-02244-7, Pp.xxi, 704, Price £27.50; Vol. III.2, 1987, ISBN 0-567-09373-5, Pp. xix, 705-1015, Price £.20.00. - These volumes complete the new version of Schürer noted in *JLA* IV, Survey no.497. Of particular interest to historians of Jewish law are the sections on the internal organization of the Diaspora Jewish communities, their constitutional position and civic rights (87-137), and on the Rules of the Qumran Community (380-419). However, Schürer's place as a classic of the scholarly literature rests primarily in its function as a handbook to the sources of the period. The main treatment of the rabbinic sources is found in Vol.I (as lying outside the main period of concern of the work), as is that of Josephus. Volume III contains extensive sections on the Jewish Apocryphal and Pseudepigraphical literature, the Qumran sources, and Philo. The editors can hardly be taken to task for the 14 years which have elapsed between publication of Vol.I and vol.III(2), the latter including an extensive Index to the entire work. Given the pace of scholarly output in these areas, one wonders whether the work should not be entered into a regularly up-dated electronic data-base, to which scholars could obtain on-line access.   B.S.J.

See also 1101.

SOURCES (RABBINIC)

1268.   Yair Ḥayyim Bacharach, *Mekor Ḥayyim*, ed. Rabbi Eliyahu
Dov Pines, Jerusalem: Makhon Yerushalayim, Vol. I, 1982, Pp. i, 356, Price
£12.50; Vol. II, 1984, Pp. ii, 541, Price, £14.50. - These beautifully produced
volumes contain the text of *Shulḥan Arukh, Or aḥ Ḥayyim* with the *Baer
Hetev* and the Commentary, together with editorial notes and Introduction,
by the famous 17th century German Halakhist, published from manuscript
for the first time. A bonus for students of Jewish law is the publication of the
various approbations by Bacharach's Rabbinic contemporaries. Bacharach
had the misfortune to be anticipated by the classical Commentaries of the
Taz and the *Magen Avraham* but both he and the editor call attention both to
where he agrees and where he takes issue with these and other
commentators.   L.J.

1269.   J. David Bleich, "Survey of Recent Halakhic Periodical
literature", *Tradition* 19 (1981), 348-360. - The author reviews halakhic
opinions on the matters of copyright, physicians' fees, the permissibility of
canned tuna fish, and maternal identity.   S.M.P.

1270.   J. David Bleich, "Survey of Recent Halakhic Periodical
Literature", *Tradition* 20 (1982), 155-166. - The author presents material on
indirect coercion in compelling a *get;* automatic banking machines; jaundice
and circumcision; and copyright of a tape recording.   S.M.P.

1271.   *Der tannaitische Midrasch-Sifre Deuteronomium, übersetzt und
erklärt von Hana Bietenhard mit einem Beitrag von Henrik Ljungman*, Bern:
P. Lang, 1984, Pp. viii, 943 (Judaica et Christiana, 8); see *KS* 60/1-2 no. 476.

1272.   Jacob Neusner, *Sifré to Numbers, An American Translation and
Explanation, Volume One, Sifré to Numbers 1-58*, Atlanta, Georgia: Scholars
Press, 1986, ISBN 1-55540 008-6, 009-4 (pbk.), Pp. xvi, 232 (Brown Judaic
Studies, 118.). - Neusner here embarks on the first complete English (dare one
say?) translation of *Sifre Bamidbar*, seeking a literalism which will bring
out the literary traits of the composition, and the philosophical positions
represented by those literary traits. In his Introduction, he subjects*Piska* 6 to
literary analysis, and concludes that through the literary structure the
authors make two complementary points: that reason unaided by scripture
produces uncertain propositions, while reason operating within the limits of
scripture produces truth.   B.S.J.

1273.   Jacob Neusner, *The Tosefta, Its Structure and Sources*, Atlanta Ga.:
Scholars Press, 1986, ISBN 1-55540-049-3, Pp.xi, 250 (Brown Judaic Studies
112). - Neusner here reprints the sections from his History of the Mishnaic
Law of Purities dealing with the literary and linguistic structures of the
Tosefta, and presenting the detailed lists supportive of his conclusions.
                                                                     B.S.J.

1274. Jacob Neusner, *The Tosefta, translated from the Hebrew. Fourth Division - Neziqin*, New York: Ktav Publishing House Inc., 1981, ISBN 0-87068-692-5, Pp.xxv, 374. - Earlier volumes in this series were noted in *Survey* no.404 (*JLA* III). This volume, of course, contains material of the greatest interest to the student of Jewish (civil, as against ritual) law. It will be widely consulted. B.S.J.

1275. Jacob Neusner, *A History of the Mishnaic Law of Damages*, Leiden: E.J. Brill, 1985: Part Four - *Shebuot, Eduyot, Abodah Zarah, Abot, Horayot*, ISBN 90 04 06853 8, pp. xxxi, 275; Part Five - *The Mishnaic System of Damages*, ISBN 90 04 07270 5, Pp. xxxi, 228, Price: Gld. 104 (Studies in Judaism in Late Antiquity, XXV). - These volumes conclude the series noted in *Survey* no. 1027 (*JLA* VI). The concluding volume, in particular, should be of the greatest interest to students of Jewish law, for the light it casts on the history of Mishnah *Nezikin*, and the law contained in it. However, Neusner's approach has been increasingly to separate the study of individual literary texts from the wider study (e.g. in tannaitic literature as a whole) of the themes they contain. Thus, historians of Jewish law will need to integrate into their own frame of reference the results of Neusner's purely literary history. For example, the main period of composition of the tractates on civil law, Neusner maintains, cannot be dated earlier than the mid-second century. The date of formation of each tractate is discussed individually, and Neusner then turns to "The Unfolding of the Law", arranging his restatement of the mishnaic rules in three chronological groups: pre-Yavneh, Yavneh and Usha. As for analysis of the content of the rules, Neusner restricts himself to the overall systemic message. The first three tractates (Baba Kamma - Baba Bathra) convey a systemic message of social stasis: no party in the end should have more than what he had at the outset, and none should be the victim of a sizable shift in fortune and circumstance. In combining within the Order substantive rules of civil law with the institutions of government, the Mishnah follows no scriptural model. While Scripture is a rich resource for Mishnah, at its foundation this division of Mishnah is essentially independent of Mishnah. "That is so even where Scripture plays a commanding role in what Mishnah will say about a given topic... The plan of Mishnah is prior, its principles of selection definitive... Scripture is a reference book, not a ground plan, or architect's design for the edifice built by Mishnah." He observes a "fundamental, systemic difference" between the Mishnah and the laws of the Qumran community. The latter takes no interest in the transactions of everyday life, but at least purports to regulate the lives only of its own members, whereas the Mishnah purport to legislate for all Israel on matters in which they clearly lacked competence. The sage or rabbi is not projected in Mishnah as a special caste: the message of the law is universalist - there is a single economy of Heaven and Earth, available to everyone. B.S.J.

1276.   Jakob J. Petuchowski, "Obscuring a Mishnah", *JRJ* 27/4 (1980), 72-74. - The author responds to the argument of Meir Ydit (*infra* no. 1279) and offers a rejection of it.   S.M.P.

1277.   G.G. Porton, *The Traditions of Rabbi Ishmael. Part IV: The Materials as a Whole*, Leiden: E.J. Brill, 1982, Pp. xiv, 261, Price: DF 96.00 (Studies in Judaism in Late Antiquity, XIX/4); see *BL* 1983, p.116f.

1278.   *Mishna Aboda Zara; a critical edition, with introduction by David Rosenthal*, 1980, Pp. viii, 267 (Hebrew University thesis); see *KS* 57/3-4 no. 3364.

1279.   Meir Ydit, "An Obscure Mishnah and Haggadah Text", *JRJ* 27/2 (1980), 76-80. - The author explores presumed hidden meanings of M. Berakhoth 1:5 and attempts to decode them in the light of the theological problems engendered by the destruction of the Second Temple.   S.M.P.

1280.   *Yerushalmi Neziqin, ed. from the Escorial manuscript with an introduction by E.S. Rosenthal, introduction and commentary by S. Lieberman* (Heb.), Jerusalem: *Ha'aka demiyah hale'umit hayisra'elit lemada'im*, 1983, Pp. xxxix, 225; see *KS* 60/1-2 no. 473.

1281.   Shmuel Safrai, *The Literature of the Sages*, Part One, Assen/Maastricht and Philadelphia: Van Gorcum and Fortress Press, 1987, ISBN 90-232-2282-2, Pp.xxi, 486, Price: Dfl.95.00 (Compendia Rerum Judaicarum ad Novum Testamentum, II.3a). - This is the long-awaited volume on rabbinic literature from the Compendia project (see *Survey* no.1019, *JLA* VI). The editor provides an Introduction and chapters on "Oral Tora" and "Halakha". Isayah M. Gafni describes The Historical Background. The main weight of the book resides in the analyses of the literary sources of talmudic halakhah by Abraham Goldberg, who contributes chapters on The Mishna (with an Appendix by Michael Krupp on Manuscripts of the Mishna), the Tosefta, The Palestinian Talmud and the Babylonian Talmud. M.B. Lerner adds chapters on Tractate Avot and the External Tractates (ARN, Derekh Erets, etc.). The volume well represents the contribution of Israeli scholarship to the study of the early rabbinic sources. Part Two will cover Midrash and Targumim.   B.S.J.

See also 1153.

SOURCES OF LAW

1282.   Chagi B. Artzi, "The Individual against the Establishment in Jewish Law" (Heb), *Sinai* 94 (1984), 79-81. - An examination of the function of minority opinions within a communal framework. The basic thesis is that divergent views are tolerated, indeed encouraged with a view to academic pluralism, only however to the extent that normative homogeneity of the community is maintained, and legal authority of the establishment not inveighed against. The author examines three Talmudic sections: the 'Rebellious Elder', the right of appeal on the basis of erroneous judicial decision, and the philosophical-legal function of rejected opinions appearing in Jewish Legal codes.   M.J.P.

1283.   Hanina Ben-Menachem, "Judicial Deviation from the Law in the Jerusalem and Babylonian Talmud" (Heb), *Shenaton Ha-Mishpat Ha-Ivri* 8 (1981), 113-135. - The author demonstrates conflicting attitudes adopted by the Jerusalem and Babylonian Talmuds with respect to judicial decisions and practices at variance with accepted Jewish Law suggesting a basically conservative tendency in the Jerusalem Talmud as opposed to a more liberal tendency in its Babylonian Counterpart. Three categories of judicial deviation are examined: the intentional decision at variance with accepted Law, the scope of discretionary powers in exceptional social conditions and generally divergent judicial practices. M posits that internal disunity in a Palestine confronted with a threat to traditional Pharisaic hegemony resulted in a more conservative constricting interpretation of the role of the Judge. The Babylonian communities, internally unified, were able to give a wider interpretation of the judge's role allowing greater deviance in the above categories.   M.J.P.

1284.   B.Z. Eliash, "The Limited Influence of Israel Rabbinical Enactments on the Israeli Rabbinical Courts", *Diné Israel* 10/11 (1984), 177-215.

1285.   Aaron Levine, *Zikhron Meir al Aveylut*, Toronto: Zikhron Meir Publications 1985, Vol. I, pp. xxxiv, 765. - This work is described on the English backpaper as : "A New Encyclopedic Compilation of the Laws, Customs, Prayers and Supplications Pertaining to Sickness, Death, and Mourning". The Volume takes any reader as far as he is likely to wish to go through to the burial. The actual laws of mourning will be treated in the second volume still to appear. The author, aware of how many of these laws are based on custom, first embarks on a very learned examination of the role of custom in the *Halakhah* but fails to note the distinction between legal and folk custom.   L.J.

See also 1105, 1110.

STATUS

1286.   Ernst Roth, "The Definition of Childhood and Adulthood in Talmudic Literature" (Heb.), *Proceedings of the Eighth World Congress of Jewish Studies*, Division C (Jerusalem: World Union of Jewish Studies, 1982), 29-34.

See also 1243, 1269.

STATUS (JEW)

1287.   Howard L. Apothaker and Mark Washofsky, "Patrilineality and Presumption", *JRJ* 31/3 (1984), 39-46. - A review of the difficulties posed by the concept of presumption in the Central Conference of American Rabbis resolution on patrilineality and the suggestion that conditional status be substituted for presumed status.   S.M.P.

1288.   Richard A. Block, "You're a Jew, I Presume? (Reflections on the Perils of Drafting Resolutions)", and Herman E. Schaalman, "Response", *JRJ* 30/4 (1983), 17-28. - Block points out logical difficulties presented by the use of the word presumption in the resolution in favour of patrilineality adopted by the Central Conference of American Rabbis and he offers an alternative phrasing to eliminate the problem. Schaalman defends the use of the word presumption in the resolution.   S.M.P.

1289.   Joseph A. Edelheit and Arthur Meth, "Accepting Non-Jews As Members of the Synagogue", *JRJ* 27 (1980), 87-92. - The authors discuss the particular needs of small town congregations, in which the synagogue serves as religious, social, and cultural center for all Jews since there is no alternative institution, and the modes of integrating non-Jewish spouses of members into community life. The authors assert that the non-Jewish spouse will pose a more and more significant problem for Jewish institutions as time goes on and this problem will have to be met satisfactorily in order to maintain harmony and unity in both families and communities.   S.M.P.

1290.   Warren Zev Harvey, "The Obligation of Talmud on Women According to Maimonides", *Tradition* 19/2 (1981), 122-130. - The author concludes that Maimonides manifestly obligates women with five commandments, in consequence of which they must study Talmud. This matter is significant for halakhists who must rule concerning education for women.   S.M.P.

1291.   Phillip Hiat and Bernard M. Zlotowitz, "Biblical and Rabbinic Sources on Patrilineal Descent", *JRJ* 30/1 (1983), 43-48. - The authors present various sources in support of patrilineality as a legitimate institution in Jewish life.   S.M.P.

See also 1114, 1115, 1175.

STATUS - WOMAN

1292.   *The status of the woman and the family according to Halakhah,*
Jerusalem: International Council of Jewish Women, 1979, Pp. 58; see *KS* 57/2
no. 1746.

1293.   D. Ben-Abo, *Ma'amadah shel ha'ishah beyisra'el uvemi ʒ̣a ḥ
Hak̦ a ḏu m,* Ramat-Gan: Bar-Ilan University, 1981, Pp. 245; see *KS* 58/2 no.
1693.

SUCCESSION

1294.   Sinai Deutsch, "The Validity of a Will Drawn up in a Foreign
Court" (Heb), *Diné Israel* 12 (1986), 206-239. - S analyses validity attributed
by Jewish Law to a will drawn up according to the Laws of the State. Such
validity must be granted both on the Jurisdictional level, i.e. recognition of
authorities empowered to give the will validity and uphold its execution,
and on the internal level of validating the testimonial capacity of witnesses
otherwise not recognized in Jewish Law *(Peṣuḳe Edut)*. S traces the
development of three parallel talmudic sources of recognition. The first is
the dictum of the Amora Samuel, the Law of the Land is Law, the second is
an extension of the talmudic recognition of documents drawn up by foreign
courts, and the third is a tendency in the Talmud to give recognition *de facto*
to prevalent customs of tradesmen, which, though at variance with
substantive Jewish Property Law, nonetheless are accepted norms, relied
upon for the transferral of property. S shows that according to some modern
Responsa, a grundnorm of *Gemirut Da'at* (subjective intention) may be inferred
from these categories, wherein the sufficient condition for recognition is the
intention and reliance of the Testator that his will, in its present form, will
be upheld, though the specific form, including the witnesses and the
appropriate jurisdiction, may be at variance with substantive Jewish Law. S
further posits that since intrinsic difficulties inhere in the extension of
Gemirut Da'at to all forms of property transfer, a preferable theory may be
found in drawing a basic distinction between substantive Jewish Law
applying to the will in Jewish Law, which is an immediate, *in rem* transfer of
property, as opposed to the will in other systems, which is only a
commitment or intention to transfer property, thus less stringent in its formal
requirements.   M.J.P.

TALION

1295.   C. Carmichael, "Biblical Laws of Talion", *Hebrew Annual
Review* 9 (1985), 107-126; also published in the booklet noted at no. 1138,
supra.

1296.   Richard Elliot Friedman, "Deception for Deception", *Bible Review* 2/1 (1986), 22-31, 68; see *OTA* 9/3 (1986), no.771.

1297.   R. Westbrook, "Lex talionis and Exodus 21,22-25", *RB* 93 (1986), 52-69; see *OTA* 9/3 (1986), no.780.

TAXATION

1298.   V. Hurowitz, "Another Fiscal Practice in the Ancient Near East: 2 Kings 12:5-17 and a Letter to Esarhadden (LA 5277)", *JNES* (1945), 289; see *OTA* 10/1 (1987), no.159.

TERMINOLOGY

1299.   Anneli Aejmelaeus, "Function and Interpretation of *kî* In Biblical Hebrew", *JBL* 105 (1986), 193-209; see *OTA* 10/1 (1987), no.103.

1300.   J.I. Bloomberg, *Arabic Legal Terms in Maimonides*, Ann Arbor: University Microfilms, 1980, Pp. v, 180; see *KS* 58/1 no. 274.

1301.   G.J. Botterweck and H. Ringgren, eds., *Theological Dictionary of the Old Testament*, trld. D.E. Green, Grant Rapids: W.B. Eerdmans Publishing Company, 1986, ISBN 0-8028-2338-6, Pp. xxi, 521. Price: £25.00. - The earlier volumes of this series were noted in *Survey* nos. 592 (*JLA* IV) and 1043 (*JLA* VI). The present volume extends from *ḥmr* to *YHWH*. Of particular interest to the student of Biblical law are the entries on *ḥeṣed, ḥaṣḥi, ḥaqaq, ḥaqar, ḥerem, ḥatam, ṭ.ame, yabam*.   B.S.J.

1302.   Bo Johnson, *Rättffärdigheten i Bibeln*, Göteborg: Förlagshuset Gothia, 1985, ISBN 91-7728-194-2, Pp. 135. - "Righteousness in the Bible" is an examination of the Hebrew concept of righteousness, primarily the root *sdq* The concept of righteousness is closely related to the covenant, but cannot be limited to be the content of the covenant. The fulfilment of the law is not the basis of righteousness, but rather an expression of it, and the same applies to the performance of offerings. The Old Testament concept of righteousness is almost exclusively a salvific one. It is the God-given relationship to Himself; the activity on man's side is merely response. In the New Testament, this righteousness is extended to all mankind through Christ.   K.N.

1303.   O. Loretz, *Habiru-Hebräer; eine sozio-linguistische Studie über des Gentiliziums 'ibri vom Appellativum habiru*, Berlin: W. de Gruyter, 1984, Pp. xv, 314 (Beiheft zur Zeitschrift für die alttestamentliche Wissenschaft, 160); see *KS* 59/4 no. 5611.

1304.   Daniel Sperber, *A Dictionary of Greek and Latin Legal Terms in Rabbinic Literature*, Ramat Gan: Bar-Ilan University Press, 1984, ISBN 965-226-050-9, Pp.226. - Upwards of 200 Greek and Roman legal loanwords found in rabbinic literature are here catalogued and discussed. The rabbinic occurrences of each are listed in chronological order, and translations given. Parallels, related references and variant readings are provided. The juristic value of the work has been enhanced by the collaboration of Prof. J. Mélèze-Modrzejewski, and there are plentiful citations of both comparative material from Hellenistic and Roman sources and of modern scholarly literature. There are indices to Greek and Latin terms. Conceived as a pilot project towards a complete Dictionary of Loan Words (to replace that of Krauss), this volume will prove an indispensable reference tool for students of the history of Jewish law.   B.S.J.

See also 1217, 1264, 1317.

THEORY OF LAW

1305.   J. David Bleich, "Judaism and Natural Law", *Proceedings of the Eighth World Congress of Jewish Studies*, Division C (Jerusalem: World Union of Jewish Studies, 1982), 7-11.

1306.   Antonio Bonora, "Amos difensore del diritto e della giustizia", *Testimonium Christi: Scritti in onore de Jacques Dupont* (1985), Brescia: Paideia, 69-90; see *OTA* 9/2 (1986), no.569.

1307.   Dan Cohn-Sherbok, "Law and Freedom in Reform Judaism", *JRJ* 30/1 (1983), 88-97; and Mark N. Staitman and Walter Jacob, "Response", *ibid.*, 98-104. - Cohn-Sherbok strongly criticizes Solomon Freehof, the author of numerous responsa in the Reform Movement, and claims he has an ambiguous and inconsistent attitude towards Jewish law. Staitman and Jacob undertake a point by point refutation of this thesis.   S.M.P.

1308.   Michel Desjardins, "Law in 2 Baruch and 4 Ezra", *Sciences Religieuses* 14 (1985), 25-37; see *OTA* 9/2 (1986), no.618.

1309.   I. Englard, "The Example of Medicine in Law and Equity: On a Methodological Analogy in Classical and Jewish Thought", *Oxford Journal of Legal Studies* 5 (1985), 238-47. - In both law and medicine, general rules or procedures designed for majority situations or general occurrences may produce undesirable results in individual cases. Medicine, however, more readily adjusts to individual needs inasmuch as concern for the particular patient does not yield to a "purpose beyond the patient", whereas legal results must be predictable and shielded against unbridled magisterial discretion even at the cost of some apparent injustice. Englard examines the importance of the medical analogy in Greek philosophy, and discusses how classical and Jewish authors such as Plato, Aristotle, and Maimonides would deal with deal with this problem, attempting to achieve equitable results without yielding to arbitrariness or (in Jewish law) tampering with the law of God. D.H.P.

1310.   H.B. Fassel, *Die mosaisch-rabbinische Tugend- und Rechtslehre*, Aalen: Scientia Verlag, 1981, Pp. 254, Price: DM 69.00. - Reprint of the 1862 edition; see *BL* 1983, p.107f.

1311.   Sidney Greidanus, "The universal dimensions of law in the Hebrew Scriptures", *Sciences Religieuses* 14 (1985), 39-51; see *OTA* 9/2 (1986), no.592.

1312.   E.E. Halevy, *Arkhe ha'agadah vehahalakhah le'or mek or ot yevaniyim velatiniyim*, Tel-Aviv: Dvir, 1979-82, 4 vols; see *KS* 57 no.1737, 58/1 no. 272.

1313.   John D. Levinson, "Covenant and Commandment", *Tradition* 21/1 (1983), 42-51. - The author develops the thesis that Jews live in awareness principally of two covenants, the Sinaitic and the Davidic. The former refers to personal obligations of the development of society and the world that must be built. It is predicated on choice between obedience and faithlessness, life or death. The Davidic covenant speaks of hope undeserved, an announced promise, and an all-embracing security.   S.M.P.

1314.   A. Lichtenstein, *The Seven Laws of Noah*, New York: Rabbi Jacob Joseph School Press, 1981, Pp. iii, 115; see *KS* 58/1 no. 282.

1315.   Aaron Lichtenstein, "Noahide Laws from Genesis to Genizah", *Dor leDor* 14 (1985/86), 88-93; see *OTA* 10/1 (1987), no.306.

1316.   Benedikt Otzen, *Den antike jodedom, Politisk udvikling og religiose stromninger fra Aleksander den Store til Kejser Hadrian*. Copenhagen: G.E.C. Gad, 1984, ISBN 87-12-67872-4, Pp. 202, Price: Dkr. 140,00. - The book is a general treatment of Judaism in the period between 300 B.C. and 130 A.D. The introductory chapter gives a survey of the historical development, and the final section concentrates upon Apocalyptic as a new movement in Judaism. In between the fundamental religious ideas of Judaism in antiquity are treated. A chapter is dedicated to the idea of the Law which is defined as "the Revelation" in a broad sense, and which is seen in the light of ideas of creation, election, and world-order. In another chapter the ethical ideas of Judaism are described, with references, mostly, to Sirach, The Testaments of the Twelve Patriarchs, and Pirqe Abot. In still another chapter the pharisaic movement is analysed, and the development of Law interpretation in early rabbinism is touched upon.   K.N.

1317.   W.H.Ph. Römer, "Einige Bemerkungen zum altmesopotamischen Recht, sonderlich nach Quellen in Sumerischer Sprache", *ZAW* 95 (1983),

319-336. - There is no parallel term in Mesopotamian literature to our term "law". The nearest is a Sumerian term meaning "rightness, that which is "fitting". Legal practices, therefore, have to be determined from context and the author examines examples from, among other sources, private contracts, judicial reports, commercial texts and legal codices.   R.A.M.

1318.   N. M. Samuelson, ed., *Reason and Revelation as Authority in Judaism*, Melrose Park, PA: The Academy for Jewish Philosophy, 1982, Pp. iv, 113, (Studies in Jewish Philosophy, 2); see *KS* 58/2 no. 1929.

1319.   Shmuel Shilo, "The Contrast Between Mishpaṭ Ivri and Halakhah", *Tradition* 20/2 (1982), 91-100. - The author advances the thesis that a scholar who wishes to work in the field of *Mishpaṭ Ivri* must have a secular, legal education; learning in halakhah is not sufficient. He further calls attention to the secular orientation of *Mishpaṭ Ivri*, which, he contends, does not negate nor contradict the religious dimension of Jewish law. The author also discusses the first three elements of the four-fold classification of method in legal studies (dogmatic/analytical; historical; comparative; ethical/philosophical) in regard to *Mishpaṭ Ivri* and shows how the halakhist and the scholar of *Mishpaṭ Ivri* differ in approach on the basis of those methods.   S.M.P.

1320.   Eckhard J. Schnabel, *"Law and Wisdom from Ben Sira to Paul"*, Tübingen: Mohr/Siebeck, (1985), Pp. xvi, 428, DM 84 (paper), ISBN 3-16-144896-0, ISSN 0340-9570 (WUNT, 2, 16).

1321.   S. Schneebalg, "The Philosophy of Jewish Law: A Reply to Professor Faur", *New York University Journal of International Law and Politics* 13 (1980), 381-92. - In 1979, Professor Jose Faur of the Jewish Theological Seminary published in this journal an article on Jewish jurisprudence. Schneebalg responds to clarify three major points. First, although the law is God's will and could command obedience on that basis alone, each law also has an independent purpose. Rabbis have power to act to effectuate that purpose. Second, although the law applies by covenant only to Jews, several fundamental laws (the Noachide laws) are applicable even to non-Jews, wherever they may live, and not just to non-Jews residing in Israel as Faur's article asserted. Third, he seeks to clarify a class of laws (neither strictly Mosaic nor strictly rabbinic in origin) called *Dinim Mufla'im*, which the author asserts are derived from the Torah through rules of interpretation.   D.H.P.

1322.   Yohanan Silman, "Halakhic Determinations of a Nominalistic and Realistic Nature: Legal and Philosophical Considerations", *Diné Israel* 12 (1985), 249-267.

1323.   Dixon Slingerland, "The Nature of *Nomos* (Law) Within the *Testaments of the Twelve Patriarchs*", *JBL* 105 (1986), 39-48; see *OTA* 9/3 (1986), no.946.

1324.   P. Sigal, "Reflections on Ethical Elements of Judaic Halakhah", *Duquesne Law Review* 23 (1985), 863-903. - Sigal's thesis is that Halakhah developed over time in response to ethical concerns, even in contravention of precedent in the Torah. He gives numerous illustrations including examples from the law of abortion, self-incrimination, and the punishment of the rebellious son. Sigal also argues that Jesus' teachings demonstrate this same process - reasoning from a basis in Jewish law and tradition to reach a just result. A lengthy introduction that precedes the development of the thesis examines the nature of halakhah as distinct from law, and stresses the variegated, diversified, non-monolithic, non-codified, multiple-option nature of halakhah. The introduction also identifies and examines the hermeneutic principles and the motivations and criteria by which the halakhah developed to serve the ends of social justice and human dignity in contrast to the politically oriented means by which the legislated laws of independent kingdoms and states are enacted.   D.H.P.

1325.   Leo Strauss, *Philosophy and Law, Essays Toward the Understanding of Maimonides and His Predecessors*, trans. Fred Baumann, Philadelphia, New York, Jerusalem: The Jewish Publication Society, 1987, ISBN 0-8276-027-1, Pp. xvi, 138. - Strauss is best known to students of political and legal philosophy for his *Natural Right and History*; to students of Jewish law for his Introduction to the Pines Translation of Maimonides' Guide. Here, in this translation of his *Philosophie und Gesetz*, published in 1935, he wrestles with the relationship between philosophy and *halakhah*. The argument is best summarised by quoting from the jacket: "If the law empowers the pursuit of philosophy, and the product of philosophical speculations conflicts with that of law, can the law then be reinterpreted in the context of these philosophical findings? To resolve this question, Strauss examines Maimonides' theory of prophecy and identifies in it a parallel of Plato's definition of the philosopher as one who is above - and yet bound by - the law. For Strauss, this Platonic distinction provides a possible reconciliation of the immutability of revelation with the rigor of philosophical inquiry." It can hardly be said that these issues have been laid to rest since Strauss's time; this book should be taken very seriously in the debates of contemporary theorists.   B.S.J.

1326.   E. Testa, *La Morale dell'Antico Testamento*, Brescia: Morcelliana, 1981, Pp. 378, Price: IL 18,000; see *BL* 1983, p.96f..

1327.   Walter S. Wurzburger, "Law as the Basis of a Moral Society", *Tradition* 19/1 (1981), 42-54. - The essay is a revised version of a paper presented at the Jewish-Anglican Consultation on "Law and Religion in Contemporary Society", held in Britain, Nov. 26-28, 1980. The author develops the thesis that in contrast to prevailing conceptions which divorce law from morality, Judaism links the two closely. The Jewish pattern is to ground morality in law rather than law in morality. Morality ultimately depends for its normative significance upon the transcendent authority of the law which in turn serves as the matrix for the development of moral conceptions.   S.M.P.

See also 1213, 1272, 1302.

TORTS

1328. Falk, "Unauthorized Use of Property", in *Studi in onore di Cesare Sanfilippo* (Milan: Giuffrè, 1983), III.201-210.

1329.   S. Friedell, "Some Observations on the Talmudic Law of Torts". *Rutgers Law Journal* 15 (1984), 897-925. - Friedell's thesis is that Talmudic tort law generally left losses on tort-victims to a greater extent than Anglo-American law. A plaintiff under Jewish law had a cause of action only upon the occurrence of events carefully specified in the texts, and even then many elements of injury were noncompensable or were measured in ways favourable to the defendant. For some specific occurrences, early systems of loss-sharing gave way in the Talmud to a tort system based on fault, including the fault doctrine of contributory negligence which, under Jewish law, totally denied recovery unless the plaintiff was less at fault than the defendant. Friedell's analysis is primarily based upon the Talmudic treatment of the various contexts in which damage is caused by the defendant's ox. These settings and their accompanying rules are compared with equivalent settings in Anglo-American law.   D.H.P.

1330.   Y. Liebermann, "The Coase Theorem in Jewish Law", *Journal of Legal Studies* 10 (1981), 293-303. - In 1960, economist R.H. Coase published a then-radical theory of regulation of noxious uses of property. Coase found not only the noxious use, but also its suppression and regulation, to be harmful; either way, someone loses maximal enjoyment of his rights. Coase also theorized that any legal right to conduct noxious activities should be freely marketable, and that economic incentives might lead protected parties to cede the rights they had won at law. Lieberman cites the *Mishnah*, the *Shulḥan Arukh* and several responsa for concurring examples of these principles, and identifies common factors which both English and Jewish judges have found important in reconciling conflicting uses of property.   D.H.P.

See also 1105, 1248.

UNJUST ENRICHMENT

1331.   I. Warhaftig, "Unjust Enrichment in Jewish Law" (Heb.), *Shenaton Ha-Mishpat Ha-Ivri* 9-10 (1982-3), 187-237.

USURY

1332.   J. David Bleich, "Survey of Recent Halakhic Periodical Literature", *Tradition* 19/2 (1981), 149-162. - The author presents a detailed review of the *heter is ka* in both commercial and non-commercial loans and then proceeds to examine the special problem of a mortgage loan in which the seller accepts a purchase mortgage representing all or part of the purchase price. This transaction does not lend itself to the usual *heter is ka*. The author then suggests modifications of the document so that it will apply to such purchase mortgages, and he further appends a sample *heter iska* and leasehold agreement reflecting his suggested procedures.   S.M.P.